Sectionalism, Politics, and American Diplomacy

by

EDWARD W. CHESTER

The Scarecrow Press, Inc.
Metuchen, N. J.   1975

Library of Congress Cataloging in Publication Data

Chester, Edward W
    Sectionalism, politics, and American diplomacy.

    Bibliography: p.
    Includes indexes.
    1. Sectionalism (United States)--History. 2. United States--Foreign relations--History. I. Title.
E179.C52   327.73   74-30418
ISBN 0-8108-0787-4

PREFACE

Among those great, all-encompassing themes that scholars have elaborated on in an attempt to interpret American history, none is perhaps more pregnant with implications than sectionalism. A survey of those key issues that have divided the American people over extended periods of time reveals that few, if any, have not been touched by this phenomenon, to at least a limited degree; many issues, in fact, have been tied to it to the extent that a proper understanding of them is not possible without extended references to sectionalism. It is therefore no surprise to learn that the literature dealing with this phenomenon generated by Frederick Jackson Turner and his followers is quite extensive, covering almost every phase of domestic activity.

Despite this extensive body of research, sectionally-minded scholars have been far less eager to cast their eyes outward, with the result that no full-scale synthesis has appeared in the area of foreign affairs. Writing in the Mississippi Valley Historical Review two decades ago, Richard Leopold observed that "... high on the list of topics worthy of future investigation is the role played by sectionalism in our thinking and our attitudes towards other countries." Fortunately, since that date additional progress has been made to fill in the gaps, with such pioneering studies as Alfred O. Hero, Jr.'s The Southerner and World Affairs leading the way.

Much, however, remains to be done, not only to fill in the gaps, but also to stake out the field as a whole. While it would have been possible to have written a computer-oriented, methodologically-strict treatise based upon primary materials, I felt that an open-ended approach selectively embracing the entire universe of pertinent data, secondary as well as primary, would be at least equally useful. Books and articles that examine at various lengths the impact of sectionalism on American diplomacy exhibit a bewildering variety of standards as well as approaches, and it is the basic objective of the present volume to synthesize these into a meaningful whole and hopefully to impose order upon chaos. While some of this information may be familiar, some is little-known except to specialists. There obviously remains room for, if not a dire need for, a computer-oriented, methodologically-strict treatise, but this study does not pretend to be it. I welcome constructive criticisms, but hope that my efforts will be judged on their own terms, not in terms of the book I did not intend to write.

Those primary materials that are available for a study of sectional attitudes towards American diplomacy include the debates and roll-call votes in the U. S. House of Representatives and Senate, the universe of newspaper editorials that have been preserved, and the opinion polls of the Gallup and other organizations. The present work employs numerous items from each of these categories, as well as from others, but there are inevitably problems in researching these materials. Senatorial debates and roll-calls have sometimes been held in executive session, newspaper editorials are frequently designed to shape public attitudes rather than to reflect them, and opinion polls conducted before the mid-1930's were often haphazard and inaccurate. With additional effort these obstacles may be by-passed or surmounted to a degree; still, it remains a most difficult task to ascertain sectional attitudes from the more distant past in the scientific, objective manner demanded by modern social scientists.

From the standpoint of originality, the greatest contribution of the present volume may be its systematic analysis of the key foreign policy votes in Congress, with special emphasis on the Senatorial reaction to various treaties. In determining both sectional and political trends the nay votes may be even more important than the ayes, since they may be more indicative of strong feelings. For purposes of convenience, this analysis has been gathered into brief introductions at the beginning of each chapter, although it is referred to throughout the text as well. Despite the mountain of writing that has accumulated over the years dealing with various facets of American diplomacy, there is not a single monograph in print which comprehensively measures these sectional and political trends, while the standard diplomatic histories frequently omit this type of data even in the case of some key diplomatic votes.

Perhaps the most important generalization that might be made on the basis of this data is that one-party domination of a section often leads to sustained bloc-voting on diplomatic questions in Congress, as has been the case both with New England Federalists and Southern Democrats. As for revisionism, the evidence assembled here indicates that Southern Democratic bloc voting emerged a generation before Dixie united in its support of President Woodrow Wilson's program of global idealism. This bloc voting, moreover, frequently took a negative rather than a positive form, as Southern Democrats on occasion voted against the diplomatic proposals of Republican Presidents during the 1880's and 1890's, and after the turn of the century were the leading critics of Theodore Roosevelt's Latin American policy. Few, if any, historians have emphasized the latter phenomenon.

It would be highly misleading, however, to stop at roll-call analysis in determining sectional attitudes, since an examination of supplementary data reveals that such factors as economics, race, ethnicity, and metropolitanism vs. ruralism have played a major role in the shaping of American foreign policy. As analysis of this supplementary data, which in certain instances is not as complete as one would hope, constitutes the basis for the chapters proper. Sometimes there have been diplomatic issues which generated bitter sectional divisions, but on which Congress never voted; sometimes there have been foreign policy questions which inspired pronounced sectional alignments in Congress, yet relative to which there does not appear to have been great interest outside of that body. This makes it difficult at times to tie all the pieces together into a neat package.

In addition, while decisive sectional trends are apparent with respect to some issues, in the case of others they may only be limited or ambiguous or even non-existent; their very absence, in fact, may be just as significant as their presence, and at various points throughout the narrative we have called attention to such sectionally non-divisive issues. While it would have been possible to have structured this monograph as an unbroken series of roll-calls, polls, tables, and graphs, it was deemed advisable for the sake of variety as well as enlightenment to interlace the narrative with references to the stands taken in newspaper editorials, the opinions of prominent sectional leaders, and the holding of mass meetings, etc.

The most obvious use for the present study is as a supplemental reading in a course on American diplomatic history, where it might be read in conjunction with other topical treatments, or in a course on American public opinion. Students of regional history, too frequently confined to domestic affairs, likewise should find it useful, in that it treats sectional attitudes towards foreign policy in a comprehensive, chronological manner. But this book is not meant only for classroom use or for perusal by those antiquarians solely interested in the past. Sectionalism remains as much a factor to be reckoned with today as ever, and any assessment of post-World War II America that fails to consider it, in the foreign relations area or elsewhere, is doomed to incompleteness if not to inaccuracy.

Dr. Edward W. Chester
Associate Professor of History
The University of Texas
at Arlington

ACKNOWLEDGMENTS

I would like to express my indebtedness to the following distinguished scholars who have read and commented on an earlier draft of this work: Chapter One, Bradford Perkins and Paul A. Varg; Chapter Two, Norman A. Graebner and Archie P. McDonald; Chapter Three, Robin W. Winks and John Hope Franklin; Chapter Four, H. Wayne Morgan and Walter LaFeber; Chapter Five, Warren I. Cohen and Ernest R. May; Chapter Six, Wayne S. Cole and Robert Farrell; Chapter Seven, John Spanier, Alfred O. Hero, Jr., and Samuel J. Astorino; Conclusion, Thomas A. Bailey and David De Boe. I strongly emphasize, though, that the final version presented here is entirely my responsibility. Portions of this manuscript have been presented as papers at annual meetings of the Missouri Valley History Conference, the Rocky Mountain Social Science Association, and the Southwestern Social Science Association, where they were discussed and commented upon. The Liberal Arts Organized Research Committee of the University of Texas at Arlington has also made available funds used in the preparation of this study.

INTRODUCTION

DEFINING THE SECTIONS

From a methodological point of view, the most difficult obstacle to be overcome in writing a book of this type
is the perpetual disagreement as to which states belong to
which sections. To complicate matters further, sectional
boundaries have shifted with the settling of the continent; following the Revolutionary War the West was that area to the
west of the Appalachian Mountains, while following the Civil
War it was that area to the west of the Mississippi River.
(As Frederick Jackson Turner pointed out, the frontier is a
moving section.) It is also possible that natural sectional
lines at any given moment in American history may shift
from issue to issue; although the Middle West is stereotyped
as an unusually isolationistic section, Ralph H. Smuckler has
pointed out that the "region of isolationism" is only partly
coterminous with that band of states traditionally labelled as
the Middle West. Consequently, any attempt strictly to de-
fine a section in terms of its component states, and to hold
to this definition over an extended period of time regardless
of the issue at stake, may in fact distort historical reality
rather than clarify it. This is a point often missed by meth-
odologists who are infatuated with systematic techniques and
rigid categories.

Surveying American history briefly from the sectional
standpoint, following our attainment of independence every one
of the original thirteen states was located to the east of the
Appalachian Mountains. The New England bloc of five states
included Vermont, New Hampshire, Massachusetts, Connecticut, and Rhode Island; Maine, then a part of Massachusetts,
did not attain statehood status until 1820. This New England
bloc was balanced off by a tier of four southern states (Virginia, North Carolina, South Carolina, and Georgia) which
were frequently in ideological disagreement with it, and the
four intervening Middle Atlantic States (New York, Pennsyl-

vania, Maryland, and Delaware) which often cast the deciding vote on key issues. In 1792, however, the first trans-Appalachian state, Kentucky, joined the Union; although we today characterize Kentucky as a border state, it was at one time regarded as the epitome of a western one. Next to become states were Tennessee, in 1796, at the time a part of the Old Southwest, and in 1803, Ohio, then a part of the Old Northwest. Today, of course, Tennessee is considered a southern state, Ohio a midwestern one. During 1803, too, the United States doubled its size with the Louisiana Purchase. In the generation between the War of 1812 and the Mexican War several states (Louisiana, 1812; Mississippi, 1817; Alabama, 1819; Arkansas, 1836; and once independent Texas, 1845) were added to the Union as members of the southwestern bloc, and several others (Indiana, 1816; Illinois, 1818; Michigan, 1837; Iowa, 1846; and Wisconsin, 1848) as members from the Northwest. Today we regard the first grouping as southern, the second as midwestern. The border state of Missouri also joined the Union in 1820, along with Maine, which had been carved out of Massachusetts. Florida, purchased from Spain in 1819, did not become a state until 1845.

Sectional perspectives were drastically altered with the annexation of Texas in 1845, the settling of the Oregon question in 1846, and the negotiation of the Treaty of Guadeloupe Hidalgo. When such Far Western states as California (1850), Oregon (1859), and Nevada (1864) were added to the Union, it became more and more difficult to refer to other newly admitted states such as Minnesota (1858) and Kansas (1861) as western; Minnesota is today generally placed in the midwestern camp, Kansas in the Great Plains one. A problem was also caused by the setting up of West Virginia in 1863, as many commentators remain unsatisfied with its categorization as a border state. Although it once had been a part of Virginia, in many ways it today resembles a midwestern or northeastern state instead. Following the Civil War the settlement of the Great Plains area pushed the trans-Mississippi frontier westward, and by the end of a generation the Bureau of the Census was pronouncing the frontier officially closed. Between 1867 and 1896 nine more states joined the Union, none of them to the east of the Great Plains: Nebraska, 1867; Colorado, 1876; South Dakota, 1889; North Dakota, 1889; Montana, 1889; Washington, 1889; Idaho, 1890; Wyoming, 1890; and Utah, 1896. When Oklahoma (1907), New Mexico (1912), and Arizona (1912) became states early in this century, their addition completed the continental forty-eight; these states are generally identified with the Southwest, a term at one time applied to such a state as Louisiana. Non-contiguous Alaska was admitted to the Union in 1959, non-contiguous Hawaii in the same year, both coming under the Pacific Coast or Far West heading.

For purposes of further analysis, let us set forth and comment upon the sectional breakdown offered by the Bureau of the Census in recent issues of the Statistical Abstract of the United States, this being perhaps as representative and as logical as any:

New England

Maine
New Hampshire
Vermont
Massachusetts
Rhode Island
Connecticut

Middle Atlantic

New York
New Jersey
Pennsylvania

East North Central

Ohio
Indiana
Illinois
Michigan
Wisconsin

West North Central

Minnesota
Iowa
Missouri
North Dakota
South Dakota
Nebraska
Kansas

South Atlantic

Delaware
Maryland
Virginia

West Virginia
North Carolina
South Carolina
Georgia
Florida

East South Central

Kentucky
Tennessee
Alabama
Mississippi

West South Central

Arkansas
Louisiana
Oklahoma
Texas

Mountain

Montana
Idaho
Wyoming
Colorado
New Mexico
Arizona
Utah
Nevada

Pacific

Washington
Oregon
California
Alaska
Hawaii

x

Were one to combine New England with the Middle Atlantic States, one would obtain a grouping identified generally as the Northeast; the further addition of the East North Central States would result in a bloc of states often described as the North: that area to the north of the Ohio River and to the east of the Mississippi. On the other hand, the combining of the South Atlantic States with the East South Central and the West South Central ones would produce a South considerably larger than the eleven-state Confederacy that seceded at the time of the Civil War. Delaware, Maryland, West Virginia, and Kentucky are usually regarded as border states (a category which the Bureau of the Census omits), and Oklahoma as a southwestern one. (After independence the first two states had functioned as a part of the Middle Atlantic bloc.) This division also ignores the possibility of dividing the South along Upper South-Lower South lines, while commentators sometimes treat the Gulf Coast tier of states stretching from Florida to Texas as a separate entity. Similarly, the grouping that results from the combination of the East North Central and West North Central States produces an area somewhat larger than the traditional Middle West, in that it includes the border state of Missouri and the four Great Plains states of North Dakota, South Dakota, Nebraska, and Kansas. The Bureau of the Census omits a Great Plains category as such, including Texas and Oklahoma in the West South Central one and New Mexico, Colorado, Wyoming, and Montana in the Mountain States bloc. (Such a state as Colorado admittedly is a problem, in that it is half-plains, half-mountains.) The Bureau also ignores the alternate Northwest/Southwest division in favor of its Pacific/Mountain formula, lumping non-contiguous Alaska and Hawaii with Washington, Oregon, and California.

The obvious conclusion to be reached from the above discussion is that even today there is little agreement as to what state belongs to what section, while some of the sectional categories actually overlap. Simply by transferring a single state from one group to another here and there, it is literally possible to produce dozens of arrangements, one of which is probably just as logical as any other. For those for whom precision is the ultimate virtue, such a plethora of possibilities may pose a problem, but the narrative that follows will hopefully demonstrate that one may detect significant sectional differences of opinion on assorted foreign policy issues and trace these over extended periods of time while yet employing fluid categories. History, let it not be forgotten, is acted out for the benefit of those actively participating in the historical process, not for some future analyst eager to reduce complex phenomena to simplistic groupings for the purpose of labelling.

TABLE OF CONTENTS

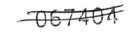

CHAPTER 1

FROM THE AMERICAN REVOLUTION
TO THE WAR OF 1812

Introduction

The first quarter-century of American history following the attainment of independence witnessed a bitter struggle between the Federalist Party entrenched in New England, and the Anti-Federalist Party or Democratic Republicans based in the South. Although the Federalists controlled the Senate during the Washington and Adams administrations, with the ".Jeffersonian revolution" of 1800 the Anti-Federalists or Democratic Republicans took over that body, maintaining a permanent two-thirds majority after the Congressional election of 1802. As for the House of Representatives, the Anti-Federalists or Democratic Republicans likewise dominated that body following the election of Jefferson; here they were able to establish an overwhelming majority two years before they were able to do so in the Senate. Discontent with the Madison Administration's handling of the prolonged crisis that culminated in the War of 1812 with Great Britain led to an increased Federalist representation in Congress, particularly in the House, but the ending of this conflict in conjunction with the disgrace of New England as a result of the holding there of the Hartford Convention plunged the Federalist Party into its final period of decline. A small Federalist minority remained in Congress for another decade, but Rufus King made the last Presidential run of any Federalist candidate in 1816.

During the first half of this quarter century, while the Federalists were generally in control of Congress, a number of important matters arose involving diplomacy. In 1795 the Senate ratified Jay's Treaty with Great Britain by a bare two-thirds majority of 20 to 10, with Anglophobic Anti-Federalists or Democratic Republicans accounting for all of the nay votes. Six Southerners and one Kentuckian cast their ballots against this treaty, thus leading the opposition, but Federalists from South Carolina, Georgia, Kentucky, and Maryland

1

voted for it.   The following year, in an almost evenly divided
House, the support of certain anti-Federalists or Democratic
Republicans from the pivotal Middle Atlantic states of New
York, Pennsylvania, and New Jersey made possible the enactment of an appropriation to implement Jay's Treaty. By way
of contrast, Pinckney's Treaty with Spain was ratified by the
Senate in 1796 by a unanimous vote.   As for relations with
France, that bête noire of the Federalists, Anti-Federalists
or Democratic Republicans, three of them from the South and
one from Kentucky, cast all five votes against the voiding of
the 1778 French alliance by the Adams Administration twenty
years afterwards. Conversely, Federalists led the opposition
to a new French commercial treaty signed in 1800, with the
Anti-Federalists or Democratic Republicans supporting this
agreement.   On the first ratification nine Federalists, eight
of them from New England or the Middle Atlantic States,
voted nay; on the second, four Federalists, three of them
from New England, followed suit.   Relations with Great Britain and France, it is apparent, invariably triggered sharp
partisan and sectional divisions during this period.

          After the Jeffersonian takeover the continuing hostility
of the Federalists towards France, now controlled by Napoleon, was reflected in seven Senators from that party representing New England and the Federalist stronghold of Delaware casting the only votes against the Louisiana Purchase
of 1803, with the Anti-Federalists or Democratic Republicans
from the South and West supporting it.   Two years later the
Senate ratified the peace treaty with Tripoli in a vote devoid
of partisan or sectional trends, but worsening relations with
Great Britain again evoked Federalist support for the former
mother country in the years that followed.   Thus the Embargo
of 1807 was generally opposed by members of Congress from
New England, the bastion of that party.   As for the War of
1812, historians have on more than one occasion challenged
the rather simplistic analysis of the vote on the declaration
of war which shows Federalists from New England in favor
and Anti-Federalists or Democratic Republicans from the
South and West opposed, but the fact remains that this was
the general trend, regardless of the various exceptions that
one might cite.   Three years later, however, the Senate was
unanimous in its consensus that the conflict be terminated
and the Treaty of Ghent be signed.

The American Revolution
and the Treaty of Paris

During the course of the American Revolution the newly-born United States became embroiled in a series of diplomatic controversies affecting the vital interests of several European nations and their colonial empires. Of these, those involving our various boundaries, the North Atlantic fisheries, and the navigation of the Mississippi River far outweighed others in importance, at least from the American point of view. In attempting to settle these questions the United States had to consider not only the interests of hostile England, but also those of friendly France and Spain, which despite their alliance under the secret Convention of Aranjuez did not always coincide. Under these circumstances, even a united nation would have experienced considerable difficulty in resolving these dilemmas acceptably, even with skilled diplomats working on its behalf.

But the United States was by no means a united nation while at war with its former mother country. Aside from the economic and social divisions traced by such distinguished historians of a later era as Charles A. Beard and Carl Becker, there existed from the dawn of American history a rivalry of sections. Exactly one century before the outbreak of the American Revolution--in 1676--Bacon's Rebellion erupted in Virginia; here the rival Tidewater and Piedmont sections had been unable to settle their differences amicably, and violence was the result. And when Carl Becker made the observation that the American Revolution was not only a question of home rule, but also of who was going to rule at home, he might well have broadened his generalization to include in addition to the warring social and economic classes the various sections whose foreign policy goals and objectives were so frequently in conflict: New England, the Middle Atlantic States, the South, the West.

On February 23, 1779 a special commission of five which had been set up by the Continental Congress to develop a foreign policy brought in its report. Composed of Samuel Adams of Massachusetts, Gouverneur Morris of New York, John Witherspoon of New Jersey, Meriwether Smith of Virginia, and Thomas Burke of North Carolina, it ran the entire range of Atlantic Seaboard attitudes and interests. Acceding to the wishes both of Northeastern imperialists desirous of a northern boundary cutting deep into Canada, the annexation of Nova Scotia, and fishing rights off Newfoundland, and of

their southwestern counterparts, who dreamed of the possession of the entire Mississippi Valley together with the freedom to navigate the full length of that mighty river, it established a series of goals and objectives that were to be
nibbled away rather than enlarged upon in the years ahead.
These imperialistic ambitions, of course, were by no means
new; since long before the American Revolution New England
had desired Acadia, New York the Iroquois lands up to the
lakes, Virginia the Ohio Valley, and the Carolinas and Georgia the Southwest.

Looking at this report in more detail, by proposing to
limit Canada to the boundaries sought by Great Britain in the
Seven Years War the commission opened the door to American
control of the Great Lakes, as well as American territorial
expansion westward to the Mississippi. Admittedly, the report did set the southern boundary of the United States to the
north of Florida, but it negated this self-denying gesture
through its proposal that the United States should conquer
Florida, and then sell it to Spain. The occupation of Nova
Scotia was likewise recommended, but with no provision for
its later sale. Also prominently set forth in the report were
rights to free navigation of the Mississippi and to the fisheries of Newfoundland. Considering the Drang nach Sud so
prominent in its pages, an uninformed reader might have concluded that the United States was at war with Spain as well
as with England; the shortly forthcoming convention between
Spain and our ally France, however, undercut American demands relative to Florida and the Mississippi, while the
difficulties we experienced in expelling England from the
Thirteen Colonies discouraged imperialistic designs on our
neighbor to the North.

One might best trace the subtle and not-so-subtle modifications of the foreign policy initially set forth in this 1779
document in the debates of the Continental Congress, and in
the intrigues of various foreign diplomats. The month of
March 1779 witnessed a spirited debate on the floor of Congress which focused on the key issues emphasized in the February 23rd report. In this connection the French Minister,
Conrad Gerard, played an important role; Gerard discouraged
a move on the part of certain members of the Western party
to negotiate directly with the British crown relative to the
navigation of the Mississippi by asserting that this might precipitate a war with Spain. Subsequently, on March 24, only
one state favored a resolution making the right to navigate
the Mississippi an ultimatum, all the others (except two that

were divided) voting in the negative.   As for the boundary,
the ultimatum formulated by Congress on March 19 provided
for one which "ran irregularly to the south end of Lake Nip-
issing, thence to the source of the Mississippi, down the
middle of that river to the thirty-first parallel, thence along
the northern boundary of Florida to the Atlantic." Thus New
England was denied Nova Scotia, and the South Florida, but
the entire Great Lakes region was brought within the confines
of the United States.

New England, however, was able on a close vote to
secure passage of a resolution asserting that American fishing rights off Newfoundland were not to be abandoned in any
peace treaty, even if the South and the West were unable to
obtain a guarantee of free navigation of the Mississippi.   An
attempt by New England on July 29 to strengthen the fisheries
resolution won adoption, thanks to the support of every state
from New Hampshire to Delaware; this provided that if after
the treaty of peace Great Britain were to molest the inhabitants in taking fish on the banks, Congress would deem it a
breach of the peace.   In August and September southern delegates again proposed the annexation of Florida and the free
navigation of the Mississippi as conditions of a proposed
alliance with Spain, but more moderate elements were able
to engineer the defeat of the first half of this platform.

Aside from the question of free navigation of the Mississippi, American claims to the Southwest were also an important question before Congress at this time.   Some states,
such as Virginia, laid claim to vast regions by virtue of their
ancient charters, while others, such as Maryland, possessed
or claimed no land at all there.   (The other landholding states
were New York, Massachusetts, Connecticut, North Carolina,
South Carolina, and Georgia; the other non-landholding ones,
New Hampshire, Rhode Island, New Jersey, Pennsylvania,
and Delaware.)   At the beginning of 1780, though, most of
the delegates from the South and the Middle Atlantic States
were firmly convinced that "the lands which extend from the
Atlantic to the Mississippi in parallel lines from the equator
belong to them, either in virtue of their charters or of divers
acts of possession."

On the other hand, some of the northern and eastern
delegates were more moderate; Gouverneur Morris, for example, feared the future growth of trans-Appalachian political
power, and thus was restrained in his support of western
imperialism.   In this connection the new French Minister,

the Chevalier de La Luzerne, attempted to enlist the support
of the delegates from New York, New Jersey, Pennsylvania,
and Delaware on behalf of Spanish demands, but with little
success. As one New York delegate observed, for him to
vote to abandon eastern Louisiana would open him to the
charge that he had sold out the interests of the states claiming land to the Mississippi.

More cooperative was Daniel St. Thomas Jenifer of
Maryland, who recognized the right of Spain to conquer as
much of the West as possible, even the part currently in
British hands; he eventually became the leader of the French
and Spanish party in Congress. Maryland, in fact, insisted
that all the states should surrender their western lands to
the new government as a condition of ratifying the Articles
of Confederation. It is not surprising that Virginia, with its
extensive western lands, would be violently opposed to Jenifer's program, but the opposition of New England, which
possessed or claimed no land in the Southwest, raises problems for the historian until he takes into consideration the
fact that New England was not sympathetic towards France
even before the French Revolution. In 1780-1 New York and
Virginia agreed to surrender their claims, and landless Maryland finally agreed to ratify the Articles of Confederation;
thus the United States could negotiate for peace agreed upon
a western boundary at the Mississippi.

In June 1781, several months before the successful
Yorktown campaign, Congress set up a five-man peace commission which represented all sections of the country, as
well as both commercial and agrarian interests. Representing the commercial interests of New England and the Middle
Atlantic states were John Jay of New York, Benjamin Franklin of Pennsylvania, and John Adams of Massachusetts. The
latter was instrumental in including those provisions in the
final draft of the peace settlement which protected fishing
rights. The southern agrarian interests were theoretically
safeguarded by the presence on the commission of Thomas
Jefferson of Virginia, who arrived in Europe too late to participate in the peace negotiations, and Henry Laurens of South
Carolina, who was captured and imprisoned by the British.
By this time, however, the formulators of the 1779 instructions, the Lee-Adams Junto, were out of power and their
political enemies in control; La Luzerne, in fact, bragged
that he had been responsible for the election of Robert R.
Livingston of New York as Secretary of Foreign Affairs. As
Merrill Jensen has pointed out, "Their new instructions re-

quired them to demand only independence. In all other matters they were to be subject to the guidance and control of
the French. They could even yield on the boundaries demanded in the instructions of 1779. "

The peace talks were conducted against a background
of constant intrigue, as well as of bickering within the delegations. On November 30, 1782 the American representative
signed the preliminary treaty of peace with England, and on
September 3, 1783 the final Anglo-American treaty. Despite
the terms of the French Alliance of 1778--"Neither of the two
Parties shall conclude either Truce or Peace with Great
Britain, without the formal consent of the other first obtained"--the American "go-it-alone" policy did not upset the
calculations of Vergennes, as he welcomed the opportunity to
get out of a bad hole vis-à-vis Spain.

As for the terms of the peace settlement, aside from
the British acknowledgment of American independence, the
Treaty of Paris of 1783 provided for a United States essentially corresponding to the present area east of the Mississippi,
minus Florida, which Spain obtained from Great Britain, and
also minus Nova Scotia, as well as other parts of Canada
which New England coveted. Thanks to John Adams, Americans were granted the "liberty" of fishing off Newfoundland
and Nova Scotia, and of drying and curing fish on any unsettled shore in Labrador, the Magdalen Islands, and Nova
Scotia. On the other hand, the peace settlement did not provide for the free navigation of the Mississippi, an omission
which disappointed most Westerners and led to further negotiations with Spain; other unresolved controversies led to the
formulation of Jay's Treaty with the former mother country
a dozen years later.

Under the circumstances the United States probably did
as well as could have been expected. British armies were
still present on the North American continent, and might well
have carried on the war had not the English been occupied
elsewhere by their European foes. Lord Shelburne, the
British Prime Minister, thus regarded as advantageous to
England a program of winning the Americans away from their
French ally, renewing commercial relations, and even perhaps loosely aligning the Thirteen Colonies with the British
Empire. As for public opinion in the United States, there
were complaints about the "soft" treatment of the Loyalists
(Americans supporting England) and the failure to reopen
trade with the British West Indies, but most Americans gen-

erally endorsed this settlement. In mid-January 1784 the
nine states present at Annapolis unanimously ratified the
Treaty of Paris.

Sectional Alignments in the Era
of the Constitutional Convention

        Now that it had won its independence, the United States
continued to operate under a form of government in which most
power resided with the states, there was no chief executive,
and each state had a single vote in the one-house national
legislature. This Articles of Confederation framework of
government proved distasteful to at least a vocal minority of
the populace, who preferred a stronger central authority.
When five states met at Annapolis in 1786 to discuss uniform
commercial regulations at the invitation of the Virginia legislature, the delegates assembled there agreed to a motion by
Alexander Hamilton that another convention be held at a later
date for the purpose of offering amendments to the Articles
of Confederation. The result was the Constitutional Convention that met at Philadelphia between May 25 and September
17, 1787--a gathering whose final achievements dwarfed its
original agenda.

        A number of interpretations of this key turning-point
in American history have been set forth by historians and
political scientists over the years. One popular theory holds
that the basic division there was that between the large and
small states, rather than a sectional one. On the other hand,
in his pathbreaking An Economic Interpretation of the Constitution Charles A. Beard postulated a split between such
coastal interests as "money, public securities, manufactures,
and trade and shipping, " and the small farming and debtor
interests of the interior. Still another hypothesis was that of
contemporary participant James Madison, frequently referred
to as "The Father of the Constitution, " who regarded the fun-
damental division as one between the free states of the North
and the slave states of the South. Other interpretations have
been set forth, but these are the most germane to our analysis.

        As for foreign policy issues at the Constitutional Con-
vention, that body did agree to a provision requiring a two-
thirds Senatorial majority on the ratification of a treaty,
thanks to a southern alliance with New England, which re-

mained perpetually anxious over the fishing rights question.
The South also joined forces with New England to effect a
compromise on the slave trade issue, with New Jersey,
Pennsylvania, and Delaware voting in the minority; this provided that the commerce in blacks was to become illegal
twenty years after the ratification of the Constitution. In
addition, the South agreed to jettison its original demands for
a two-thirds majority in Congress on navigation acts, most
southern delegates assuming that westward expansion would
eventually shift political power away from the "carrying
states" of the northern seaboard.

If compromises on such issues as the above represented a successful attempt to patch over old sectional differences, Secretary of the Treasury Alexander Hamilton soon
thereafter reopened these wounds with a series of proposals
that went through without significant compromise among the
various sections. These included paying off the domestic debt
of the Confederation at face value to the present holders of
the bonds, assuming the state debts incurred during the
American Revolution, setting up a Bank of the United States,
and imposing a tax on the distillation of whisky. The South
objected to the funding scheme on the grounds that it did not
distinguish between the original holders and the speculators;
following the American Revolution, too, the North held the
bulk of the national debt. As for the proposed assumption of
state debts, speculators also had been active in this area.
Many of the new owners lived in New York or Massachusetts,
while south of the Mason-Dixon Line only South Carolina benefitted to any considerable extent from assumption. Finally,
there was a general division along North-South lines on the
national bank and the whisky tax, with the North in favor aside
from Pennsylvania, whose embittered farmers rebelled against
the latter measure in the famous Whisky Insurrection of 1794.

Thanks to these and other polarizations, long before
John Adams ran for President against Thomas Jefferson in
1796, the Federalists had established themselves as the pre-
dominant party in the North (especially in New England), and
the Republicans in the South, with the Middle Atlantic States
the most hotly contested battleground. Thus Jefferson did
receive 14 electoral votes from Pennsylvania and four from
Maryland, but south of the Potomac Adams garnered only one
vote in Virginia and another one in North Carolina in winning
the Presidency. Down to the death of the Federalist Party in
its New England stronghold following the War of 1812, moreover, this geographical/political division continued to exert a

marked influence upon domestic as well as foreign policy. In
1794 the Republican South was that section most strongly
opposed to Jay's Treaty with Great Britain, while between
1798 and 1800 Federalist New England was that section most
in favor of escalating the "Quasi-War" with France. No examination of the diplomacy of this period is complete without
at least brief reference to the above background.

Spain and Pinckney's Treaty

        Hardly was the ink dry on the peace settlement than
the United States entered into negotiations with Spain concerning the unsettled question of American navigation of the Mississippi River. Here the leading dramatis personae were
John Jay for the Americans and Diego de Gardoqui for the
Spanish. Jay, a product of upper-class circles in New York
City, distrusted Westerners and was skeptical of the desir-
ability of westward expansion. His negotiating position in
Madrid was not improved by the fact that he was never officially received during the course of a two-and-one-half years'
stay; Jay was further humiliated by such Spanish government
actions as mail tampering. In addition, occasional American
military reverses hardly enhanced his bargaining position.

        During the American Revolution New England interests,
as well as southern ones, opposed concessions to the Spanish
in the Southwest, for reasons previously discussed. By the
mid-1780's, however, the coming of peace had wrought a
change in conditions. The northern ocean-carrying trade was
suffering under English orders in council, which forbade
American vessels to transport fish to the West Indies, or
any but English ships to transport American goods to Great
Britain, while Spanish-American ports were closed to all but
Spanish vessels. When the Spanish offered the United States
a treaty which would open Spain and the Canaries to such
American products as lumber, tar, fish, grain, and flour,
the North decided to sacrifice western interests if necessary
to obtain this privilege. Thus there arose the first great
North-South division of opinion on an important issue in
American history--a division of opinion on a diplomatic ques-
tion rather than a domestic one such as slavery.

        On May 29, 1786 John Jay proposed to Congress that
the United States, without abandoning in principle the right
of free navigation, might forbear the use of the Mississippi

within exclusively Spanish limits during the term of the
treaty, approximately twenty-five or thirty years.   This question was debated by Congress to the virtual exclusion of all
other issues throughout the whole summer of 1786; that body
eventually voted seven states to five (with Delaware abstain-
ing) to repeal Jay's original instructions, which stated that he
must obtain the free navigation of the Mississippi.   In contrast, the southern minority took the position that this move
was unconstitutional, threatening to block the ratification of
any treaty with Spain arising out of Jay's new instructions by
denying it the necessary two-thirds majority.   Fortunately for
the West, in 1788 the Spanish government did agree to let
Americans use the Mississippi River in return for the payment of duties.   In 1788, too, the Continental Congress voted
to transfer the Mississippi issue to the new government, also
adopting a resolution that the western settlers had a clear and
essential right to navigation on the Mississippi.

We have already noted how Gouverneur Morris of
Pennsylvania, among others, feared the future growth of
trans-Appalachian political power, and thus showed little enthusiasm for western imperialism.   In contrast, Charles C.
Pinckney of South Carolina bitterly lambasted Jay's proposal
in the Continental Congress.   Several leading Virginians,
such as James Madison and James Monroe, similarly took
the position in opposing Jay that Congress was under an obligation not to sacrifice the vital interest of one section for
that of another.

More flexible in his thinking was another Virginian,
George Washington.   Our first President originally had been
willing to forego the right of free navigation of the Mississippi
on the grounds that continued commerce down the Mississippi
would draw the West closer to Spain, while increased trade
with the East would unify this nation.   After supporting Jay
in his dealings with Gardoqui, though, Washington shifted his
position and backed the western settlers, having been converted by their great determination and the divisive nature of
the issue.   Washington, always a nationalist, favored joining
the Potomac and Ohio Rivers via a canal, hopefully tying the
western settlements to Virginia both economically and politically.   In 1785 the Potomac Navigation Company, of which
Washington was President, was established; the attempts by
this company to secure certain rights from Virginia led to
the Annapolis Convention of 1786, the forerunner of the Philadelphia Constitutional Convention of 1787.

Fortunately for national unity, the abovementioned congressional resolution of 1788 affirming that the western settler had a clear and essential right to free navigation on the Mississippi contributed to a disintegration of pro-Spanish sentiment in the West. The new constitution itself, despite Kentucky-led opposition at the Virginia ratifying convention, also drew West and East together by strengthening the Union. Even John Jay publicly began to doubt the wisdom of making the concession to Spain he had so strongly championed at the time of his negotiations with Gardoqui.

In November 1794 the United States signed a new treaty with England, which despite its controversial nature at least settled some of their major differences. Subsequently, in June 1795, Thomas Pinckney of South Carolina, then American minister in London, was sent to Madrid in a new attempt to negotiate a treaty with Spain. Fearful of a possible English alliance with the United States, as well as of a possible English attack on Spain, Manuel de Godoy, the Duke of Alcudia, quickly reached an agreement with Pinckney on October 27.

Pinckney's Treaty, or the Treaty of San Lorenzo as it is sometimes called, recognized the boundary claims of the United States under the Treaty of Paris of 1783 (the Mississippi on the West and the 31st Parallel on the South), granting to Americans free navigation of the Mississippi and the right of deposit for their goods at New Orleans for three years. A number of lesser concessions were also made. It was not the type of settlement that would have warmed the heart of Godoy's predecessor in negotiations, Gardoqui; unlike the Jay's Treaty of the previous year with England, moreover, Pinckney's Treaty received unanimous Senate approval on March 3, 1796. The West had won its battle.

Significantly, George Washington saw fit to include the following defense of his foreign policy in his "Farewell Address," a passage that posterity has chosen to neglect in its preoccupation with other aspects of this famous message:

> The inhabitants of our Western country have lately had a useful lesson.... They have seen in the ne-
> gotiation by the Executive and in the unanimous ratification by the Senate of the treaty with Spain, and in the universal satisfaction at that event throughout the United States, a decisive proof how unfounded were the suspicions propagated among them of a policy in the General Government and in the Atlantic

States unfriendly to their interests in regard to the Mississippi.

Within two decades, of course, New England was threatening secession during the War of 1812, while the South actually set up an independent Confederacy in 1861.   Such was the record of separatism in the United States during the Nineteenth Century, a movement in which the once discontented West did not play a leading role.

England and Jay's Treaty

By the early 1790's the French Revolution had begun to involve other countries, and France found itself at war with England.   As France had been our ally against Great Britain during the Revolutionary War, public opinion in most parts of the United States at first was pro-French and anti-British. New England, for example, had long been at odds with the former mother country about the Canadian boundary, the annexation of Nova Scotia, and fishing rights off Newfoundland. Paradoxically, however, that part of America which had been involved in the most controversies with Great Britain also became in the post-revolutionary era the section which was most sympathetic to her.   This love-hate relationship is in part explained by the fact that English influences in this country were strongest in the East, except for the Middle States, where the cosmopolitanism of parts of Pennsylvania and New York acted as a mitigating factor, and weakest in the West.   By this time, too, New England had become the mecca of the anti-Gallican, anti-French Party in the United States; during the 1790's France was no longer a highly conservative monarchy (as it had been in 1776-1783) but a hotbed of revolution, and was at war with Great Britain.   If New England Federalists experienced difficulty in swallowing Louis XVI, they would not even make the attempt with Robespierre.

As for the South, since the middle of the Eighteenth Century many leaders of this section had aspired to realize the ideal of the English country gentleman.   In this connection Daniel J. Boorstin has observed that: "The model in Virginians' heads was compounded of the actual features of a going community: the England, especially the rural England, of the 17th and 18th century." Nevertheless, many southern planters had long been in debt to England, and this led many New England Federalists to charge that the South was attempting to escape its financial obligations by precipitating a war with Great Britain. Thus Oliver Ellsworth maintained that the South was giving "a baleful ascendancy to French influence," while Fisher Ames lamented the violent treatment of the British in Norfolk and Baltimore.

By the time George Washington was sworn in for a second term as President the Virginia Republican, James Madison, had begun to view with foreboding the growing Federalist stranglehold over New England. Accordingly, in January 1794 Madison proposed discriminatory legislation against British commerce, hoping to capitalize on widespread resentment in his section (and elsewhere) against the various pieces of legislation known collectively as the English Navigation Acts. Although Madison's resolutions were sidetracked in favor of more immediate and drastic steps, they did attract considerable support in the Middle Atlantic States and New England. Threatened by this display of interest, Federalist leaders now decided to remove the question of commercial relations from consideration by the House of Representatives--where they faced defeat--by negotiating a new treaty with Great Britain which the Senate alone would ratify.

In May 1794 John Jay, then Chief Justice of the Supreme Court, arrived as our minister to the Court of St. James, while his predecessor in the latter position, Thomas Pinckney, shifted his base of operations to Madrid for the purpose of negotiating a treaty with Spain. Whereas Pinckney's Treaty of San Lorenzo won the unanimous support of the Senate, the companion treaty with England which Jay drew up was to prove nearly as controversial as the document which he had signed a decade earlier with the Spaniard, Gardoqui. Aside from the fact that Jay was serving in both a high judicial and a high diplomatic capacity at the same time, Southerners who recalled his willingness in 1786 to forbear the use of the Mississippi River for a quarter-century bitterly resented entrusting the difficult British negotiations to him. Jay's position was further undercut by Secretary of the Treasury and self-appointed Secretary of State Alexander Hamilton, an ardent Anglophile.

Jay's Treaty, which was signed on November 19, 1794, was most noted for its provision that the British were to withdraw from the Northwest posts on or before June 1, 1796. This stipulation quite naturally was most pleasing to the West. The treaty also provided for the admission of American vessels into British East Indian ports on a non-discriminatory

basis; the opening of the West Indian trade to American vessels not exceeding seventy tons burden; the placing of British
trade with the United States on a most favored nation basis;
and the referral to joint commissions of the payment of the
pre-Revolutionary debts, the northeast boundary question, and
compensation for illegal maritime seizures. Solutions to
three important controversies, though, were omitted from the
final draft of the treaty: impressment, the Indian question,
and the British-held American slaves. The first of these
omissions might be expected to offend the northern shipping
and commercial interests, the second the western settlers,
and the third the southern planters, who in fact were most
unhappy with the article that was included providing for the
settlement of the debt. The North, too, doubtless noticed
the failure of the treaty to deal with impressment, but this
was not a highly important issue there in 1796; thus the
merchants of that section were not alienated enough to oppose
its ratification. With regard to the West, the Battle of Fallen
Timbers of 1794 had at least reduced the Indian menace, and
there was no great agitation there over the omission of this
issue. In fact, Westerners generally supported Jay.

After an acrimonious debate on June 24, 1795, supporters of the document were able to muster on its behalf
the necessary two-thirds majority--20 votes for, 10 against--
with the South quarterbacking the opposition. One casualty of
the debates was article twelve, which permitted American
trade with the British West Indies on a highly restrictive
basis, New England being bitterly opposed to this particular
provision. This article also banned tropical products, including sugar and cotton, thus alienating the southern planters. The treaty's passage was achieved with the support of
the two Maryland Senators, plus that of Humphrey Marshall
of Kentucky, James Gunn of Georgia, and Jacob Reed of South
Carolina, all five of them Federalists. Marshall's national
career was ruined by his vote; the reputations of Gunn and
Reed were tarnished by charges that they had received bribes.
At this time the Federalist Party was still strong in parts of
the South, but the passage of this treaty permanently damaged
its position in Virginia, the Carolinas, and Georgia. Generally speaking, Northerners favored the treaty, although John
Langdon of New Hampshire and Moses Robinson of Vermont
were exceptions. It has been speculated that the delay in
transmitting the treaty from London to Washington was a
blessing in disguise for its supporters, as it enabled several
new pro-treaty Senators to take their seats who otherwise
might not have voted on the documents.

Southern opposition to the treaty following its passage took many forms. Norfolk, for example, abandoned the traditional Fourth of July celebration in favor of the French Bastille Day (July 14), while the Virginia legislature and the lower house of South Carolina passed resolutions attacking it. Among the southern cities holding protest meetings against the treaty were Richmond, Petersburg, Savannah (where Gunn was burned in effigy), Charleston, and Columbia. Occasionally a pro-treaty meeting did take place in the South, as in Norfolk, Savannah, or Westmoreland County, Virginia--George Washington's home; a grand jury in North Carolina condemned the anti-treaty meetings, while Governor Richard Henry Lee of Virginia issued a proclamation forbidding the circulation of anti-treaty petitions. Such occurrences, though, were the exception rather than the rule.

New England Republicans also attacked the treaty in public meetings in Boston, New York, and Philadelphia, where John Jay and his document were burned in effigy, but they were in a decided minority. One commentator went so far as to blame opposition to the treaty in Congress on the "foreign" members in the House of Representatives: "Take away the Representatives for the southern Negroes, which amount to ten or eleven, the anti-treaty majority in the House of Representatives of Congress, and probably every anti-government majority shrinks instantly into a minority--But when to these you add the Foreigner Representatives the minority is still more diminished." Here one encounters an unusual example of racial bigotry in supposedly enlightened New England.

Unfortunately for the Washington Administration, the ratification of the treaty did not end matters. An appropriation bill remained to be passed, and this was only adopted by the House of Representatives on April 30, 1796, after two months of debate, by a three-vote margin, 51 to 48. Its enactment, in fact, was made possible only by the support of certain Republicans from New York, New Jersey, and Pennsylvania, who apparently feared that the Senate might not ratify the Pinckney Treaty or that the Union might break up. They were joined by a grand total of four Southerners. Votes also may have been swung in the direction of approval by a speech of the great Federalist orator, Fisher Ames of Massachusetts, who predicted a recurrence of war should the bill be defeated: "I can fancy that I listen to the yells of savage vengeance and the shrieks of torture; already they seem to sigh in the western wind; already they mingle with every echo from the mountains."

Jefferson and the Louisiana Purchase

Unlike England and Spain, in the case of France it was
an event within that nation--the French Revolution of 1789--
which brought about a crisis in its relations with the United
States, rather than the persistence of some controversy involving its New World colonial empire, such as the free
navigation of the Mississippi or fishing rights off Newfoundland. Despite the prominent role that Lafayette had played
in the American Revolution, relatively few Frenchmen had
come to settle in the American colonies; in contrast, the Germans built up pockets of settlement in Pennsylvania and elsewhere, consequently influencing public opinion there. Nor
had France possessed a continental empire in North America
since 1763 which might have stood in the way of American
imperialistic ambitions. As for economic ties, an extensive
trade had never developed between France and the United
States, although the two nations did sign a commercial treaty
at the time of the consummation of the alliance of 1778; some
trade did grow up between New England and France but, as
we have already pointed out, the Napoleonic Wars had rendered precarious the economic ties between them. Whereas
Federalist New England long had been the mecca of the anti-
Gallican, anti-French party in the United States, one found
considerable sympathy for France among the Southern Anti-
Federalists and their leader Thomas Jefferson, who was influenced by such philosophes as Montesquieu and Rousseau and
whose brand of economic democracy was in part built upon
the teachings of the French Physiocrats. The fact that many
southern planters were in debt to England also tended to drive
that section into the arms of France.

A survey of American newspapers for the year 1789
reveals that there was a striking lack of regional differences
in their reporting on events in France, but it also demonstrates that the single papers available for Baltimore, Charleston, and Lexington, Kentucky were a little more aristocratic
in their point of view. When the National Assembly was established, most American newspapers, regardless of region,
generally looked upon its aims as moderate and desirable,
but when the Bastille was captured on July 14, northern
papers in this country tended slightly to emphasize the hero-
ism of the common people, while those of Baltimore and
Charleston stressed various acts of violence by the people
against individual nobles or officers. The latter newspapers
also paid less attention to the Declaration of the Rights of
Man than their northern counterparts. On the other hand,

when news arrived in this country in December that the allied
invaders were in retreat from France, it triggered off gigantic celebrations in such cities as Baltimore, New York, Boston, Charleston, Savannah, and Norfolk.

At home the French Revolution was to take many un-
expected and, in the minds of many Americans, unwanted
turns during the decade that followed, not the least of which
was the internationalizing of the event into a general European
war pitting France against England. On February 1, 1793
the Girondist regime declared war on Great Britain; on April
22 George Washington issued a proclamation of neutrality.
By this time the new minister of the French Republic to the
United States, Edmond Genêt (better known as Citizen Genêt)
had already sailed from France. Having been instructed by
his government to win the friendship of the United States and
to negotiate a new treaty of commerce, Genêt commissioned
privateers to prey upon British vessels, planned expeditions
against British and Spanish territories, and eventually appealed over the head of the President to the American people
when our government unsuccessfully attempted to block his
dispatch of a French privateer to sea. Ironically, by the time
that Washington had become provoked by Genêt to the point
where he demanded his recall, the Jacobins had replaced the
Girondins in power in France. When Genêt's Jacobin successor arrived the following year and attempted to have him
arrested, Genêt successfully sought asylum from the country
that he had caused so much trouble, eventually becoming an
American citizen and marrying a daughter of Governor George
Clinton of New York.

Upon his arrival in the United States in April 1793,
Genêt embarked upon a leisurely month's long journey to
Philadelphia, stopping along the way to sample public opinion.
Although various explanations were offered for his landing at
Charleston in the first place, the fact remains that he could
easily have proceeded from there to Philadelphia by sea instead of by land; much to the distress of his enemies, his
journey northwards has been described as one long ovation.
Nor did the latter die out at the Mason-Dixon Line, as Philadelphia itself had been preparing for nearly a month for his
arrival, and his reception there surpassed all previous efforts
elsewhere. After Genêt's confederates and agents had stirred
up the Philadelphia mob, in the words of John Adams, "ten
thousand people on the streets of Philadelphia, day after day,
threatened to drag Washington out of his house and effect a
revolution in the government, or compel it to declare war in

favor of the French Revolution and against England. " It is
not improbable that an insurrection would indeed have broken
out, had not the epidemic of yellow fever there hindered the
realization of this threat.

Shortly after Genêt's arrival in Philadelphia a Democratic Society was organized there, the first of its type in
this country. Other chapters were eventually set up in such
cities as Charleston, Baltimore, New York, Boston, and
Portland as well as in a number of smaller towns. Although
individual Democratic Societies took stands on a wide variety
of issues, all were united in their opposition to Washington's
policy of neutrality. The President quite naturally looked with
disfavor upon these organizations, going so far as to blame
them for having instigated the Whisky Insurrection of 1794 in
Pennsylvania. His opposition proved to be a heavy blow to
their cause, although a number did linger on.

By 1797 relations between the pro-English Federalist
government of the United States and the French Directory had
weakened to the point where they were hanging by a thread.
At this time there occurred an episode that almost plunged
the two nations into war: the famous XYZ Affair. X, Y, and
Z were code names for the three French agents sent out by
Talleyrand, the French foreign minister, to negotiate with a
three-man American commission composed of Charles Pinckney, John Marshall, and Elbridge Gerry upon the latter's
arrival in France in October 1797. On this occasion X, Y,
and Z not only requested an American loan to France, but
also demanded a bribe of $240, 000 for Talleyrand. The
commission's refusal led to the stirring slogan: "Millions for
defense, but not one cent for tribute, " and the anti-French
Federalist Party began to clamor for war. (This slogan has
been erroneously attributed to Pinckney.)

This time the Atlantic Coast of the United States, which
only four years previously had been so hospitable to Genêt,
exploded in wrath against the French. Many towns, and cities,
in fact, even began public subscriptions to build armed ships
for loan to the American government; among these were Boston, New York, Portland, Portsmouth, Charleston, Norfolk,
Philadelphia, and Baltimore. As for the Federal government, Congress voted to scrap the French alliance of 1778,
appropriated money for an expanded navy, and provided for
the issuance of letters of marque to privateers against French
armed vessels. Generally speaking, the New England Federalists led the agitation for war. Thanks to the efforts of

a New England Federalist, President John Adams, however, the so-called quasi-war with France of 1798-1800 remained only a quasi-war, and did not break into open conflict.

During the last decade of the Eighteenth Century the geographical focal point of Franco-American relations in the New World was the French island colony of Santo Domingo in the Caribbean. (Today the eastern half of this is the Dominican Republic, the western half Haiti.) Despite its proximity to the South, prior to 1790 Santo Domingo had been mainly of interest to New England, whose merchants had actively traded low-grade fish for cheap molasses. But in 1791 there was an uprising of the slaves there which apparently caused disaffection among their Louisiana counterparts; when the French Convention officially decreed the emancipation of slaves in Santo Domingo in 1794, a meeting was called in South Carolina for the purpose of adopting effective measures against the "diabolical decree of the national convention which emancipates all the slaves in the French colonies, a circumstance the most alarming that could happen to this country." When numerous French aristocrats began arriving in the United States as refugees following the sack of Cap Français in June 1793, the legislatures of the Carolinas and Virginia, as well as those of Maryland, Pennsylvania, and Massachusetts, made appropriations for their relief. With regard to the blacks, though, Virginia specifically prohibited Negro immigration from the West Indies at once, North Carolina following suit in 1795 and South Carolina in 1803. Southerners were further disturbed by the defeat of the French general Leclerc in Haiti at the hands of yellow fever and the black revolutionary Toussaint L'Ouverture, but Napoleon's dream of a New World empire embracing both Louisiana and the French West Indies was thereby punctured, thus opening the door to the sale of Louisiana to the United States in 1803. (Thanks to southern opposition, this nation did not recognize Haiti until after the Civil War had broken out.)

In October 1802 the Spanish intendant at New Orleans suspended our right of deposit there, thus infuriating the West and re-opening a controversy that the Pinckney Treaty, signed seven years earlier, had not permanently settled. Subsequently, President Thomas Jefferson commissioned James Monroe of Virginia and Robert Livingston of New York to approach the French concerning the purchase of New Orleans and West Florida; when the empire-weary French offered to cede all of Louisiana to the United States for $15,000,000,

Jefferson discovered that there was no provision in the Constitution authorizing such a transfer.   Confronted with a
choice between principle and expediency, Jefferson abandoned
his strict constructionism and by purchasing Louisiana won
the affection both of those western settlers who wanted the
American flag to fly on both sides of the Mississippi, and
those southern planters and farmers of whom he was the
spokesman and leader.   Less enthusiastic were the New England Federalists who, fearful of the political consequences of
the growth of an agrarian society in the West, opposed the
purchase despite the fact that they were loose constructionists.

Foes of the treaty in the Senate, though, were able to
muster only seven votes against a twenty-five vote majority,
and it easily passed.   The division was basically along party
lines, the Antifederalists or Republicans from the South and
the West in favor, the Federalists from New England and the
Middle Atlantic states in opposition.   Newly-elected Federalist
Senator John Quincy Adams of Massachusetts arrived too late
to cast his vote for the treaty; a dissenter against the section's foreign policy like his father, J. Q. Adams was later
a prominent advocate of continental expansion.   More representative of New England were the views of the other Senator
from Massachusetts, arch-Federalist Timothy Pickering, who
already was urging that his section should secede from the
United States and set up a confederacy of its own, if possible
with New York, rather than play a subordinate role in a nation dominated by the South and the West.   (The defeat of
Aaron Burr in the New York gubernatorial election of 1804
threw cold water on the dream of a northern confederacy.)
Those historians who interpret the Hartford Convention
strictly in terms of the frustrations arising out of the later
War of 1812 are merely examining the branches of the tree
without inspecting its trunk; New England had long before begun to simmer with ire at its alleged mistreatment by other
sections.

Jefferson and the Embargo

The growing alienation of New England from the remainder of the country was accompanied by an intensification
of the war between England and France.   When both nations
attempted to place restrictions on the neutral carrying trade,
American commerce began to suffer; Napoleon's Berlin Decree (November 1806) was answered by the British Orders in

Council (January and November 1807), which in turn were
countered by Napoleon's Milan Decree (December 1807). During the latter year, in August 1807, Aaron Burr was placed
on trial for treason in Richmond; Burr had been intriguing
with the Spanish, possibly in an attempt to set up an independent state in the West, although the complete details of
his intrigues have yet to come to light. Betrayed by one-
time separatist enthusiast James Wilkinson, Burr was nevertheless acquitted.

It was in the midst of this period of tension, in June
1807, that a confrontation occurred between the American
vessel Chesapeake and the British frigate Leopard ten miles
off Norfolk Roads. When the British commander demanded
the right to search the American vessel, the American commander refused; the British then opened fire on the Chesapeake, boarded the disabled American vessel, and removed
four sailors, hanging one at Halifax for desertion. Not surprisingly, this episode threw the entire country into an up-
roar, just as the XYZ Affair had done a decade previously.

In this connection the reaction of New England is edi-
fying. At first, resentment was as great there as anywhere.
The British were denounced in public meetings in such cities
as Portsmouth, Newport, and Providence, and in editorials
in such newspapers as the Massachusetts Spy, the Connecticut
Courant, and the Salem Gazette. Only in Boston was there
hesitation. But within a fortnight arch-Federalist Timothy
Pickering and his Essex Junto were at work soothing public
opinion. Thus the aforementioned Salem Gazette, so eager
for war on July 10, by July 24 was lamenting the fact that
the newspapers which "come to hand teem with the resolves
of meetings throughout the state." One editorialist, writing
shortly thereafter in the Boston Columbian Centinel, not only
denied the necessity or expediency of war with England, but
even defended the British impressment of American sailors;
the New England Palladium elaborated on the concept of economic self-interest, pointing out that war would ruin the
farmers and merchants. Pickering himself summed up the
pro-British position beautifully in his observation that "...
although England, with her thousand ships of war, could have
destroyed our commerce, she has really done it no essential
injury." By the end of the summer anti-British sentiment in
New England had cooled off considerably, as that section resumed its former ideological sympathies.

A Southerner, President Thomas Jefferson, likewise

was opposed to American involvement in a war with Great
Britain.   During 1807 he came to the conclusion that only
through the imposition of an embargo which would interdict
landborne and seaborne commerce with foreign nations could
he prevent the United States from being dragged into war with
the former mother country.   The embargo bill which he presented to Congress in December quickly passed the Senate
(22 to 6) and the House (82 to 44); opposed by New Englanders fearful of its impact upon the commerce of that section,
it gained passage thanks to the support of many southern and
western Representatives and Senators.   Aside from forbidding
all American vessels and goods to leave for foreign ports, it
placed severe restriction on the American coastal trade and
on importations by foreign vessels.

        Examining the impact of and the reaction to the Em-
bargo, section by section, let us first analyze that of the
South.   It has been pointed out by more than one observer
that the South's support of Jefferson's measure constitutes a
denial of the economic interpretation of history, where economic self-interest is the golden rule.   Of all the sections of
the country, the South economically suffered the most from
the Embargo.   Ports like New Orleans and Savannah were
crowded with ships lying idle at the docks; denied an overseas
market for such products as cotton and tobacco, the South had
to pay more for manufactured goods, and to support in idle-
ness a costly system based on Negro slavery.   Thomas Jefferson's Virginia was particularly hard hit.   As Francis P.
Beirne has observed, "No people ever suffered more for
party loyalty than did the Republicans of the South in the last
year of Jefferson's administration"; Louis Sears has written
that "... the embargo contributed the final blow to the old
tidewater prosperity, no substitute for which was ever found
in the region affected. " Ironically, by its apparent stimula-
tion of manufacturing in various parts of the country--to some
extent in New England, and even more so in the Middle Atlantic States--the Embargo may have moved the United States
a few degrees away from its then ascendant agrarianism.
The South, moreover, despite the severe economic dislocation
it suffered because of this measure, failed to turn to manufacturing, a development which, had it occurred, might have
acted as a deterrent to slavery and helped therefore to prevent the Civil War.

        A detailed analysis of southern opinion towards the
embargo does reveal some fluctuations from time to time
and from place to place.   In North Carolina, for example,

the planters favored the measure, while the merchants (apparently having been influenced by a Pickering pamphlet) opposed it.   As for Jefferson's native Virginia, sentiment there at one time was seemingly almost unanimous in support of his program, but public opinion eventually began veering in the direction of dissent.   Here one must consider the actions of the erratic John Randolph of Roanoke, leader of the Quids, who opposed the measure in Congress.   Surprisingly, South Carolina, which once had been a hotbed of Federalism, now gave its firm support to the President.   Even New Orleans, located deep in the heart of the separatist Southwest, reaffirmed its allegiance to the administration on this issue; generally speaking, therefore, one might conclude relative to the South that even where sentiment for the Embargo was not enthusiastic, it was at the very least submissive.

New England, of course, was an entirely different story.   As one contemporary journalist wrote of Boston: "What is the huge forest of dry trees that spreads itself before the town?   You behold the masts of ships thrown out of employment by the embargo. "   Exports, in fact, did decline; for the period from October 1807 to October 1808 they were some eighty-six million dollars less than they had been in the preceding years, and they did not again reach the levels set from 1806 to 1807 until after the War of 1812.   Yet New England, by virtue of its geographical position, was confronted with a golden opportunity to engage in illicit trade and smuggling, while capital formerly invested in commerce found a ready outlet in manufacturing.

Nevertheless, the campaign of abuse against Jefferson and the Embargo reached no loftier heights than it did in New England, with the hated President drawn, hung, and quartered innumerable times in print and in conversation.   Ironically, in attacking the chief executive Federalists there invoked that states' rights philosophy which long had been a favorite of Jefferson and his southern and western followers.   The Boston Gazette even went so far as to openly propose secession: "It is better to suffer the amputation of a limb than to lose the whole body. "   More common were suggestions that the Embargo be disregarded, a curious precurser of that arch-Southerner John C. Calhoun's nullification doctrine relative to the 1828 Tariff of Abominations.   Resolutions to this effect were passed by town meetings in Newburyport and Boston, and by the Massachusetts legislature.   Speaking in the United States Senate on November 30, 1808, Timothy Pickering reached the apex of Congressional rhetoric against Jefferson in an unprecedented harrangue in which he attributed sinister motives to the President.

Occasionally a voice was raised in New England on behalf of the President, generally from Republican quarters. Thus the New Hampshire legislature resolved in June 1808 that: "We will suffer any privations rather than submit to degradation, and will cooperate with the General Government in all its measures. " But in the fall elections of 1808 the Republicans went down to defeat in New Hampshire, despite the fact that the population of the state partially consisted of the backwoods type more in sympathy with Jefferson than with the merchant princes of Newport or Salem. Throughout all of New England, moreover, the Federalists ran well, as they did in the election for the New York state legislature. As a result, Republican James Madison garnered only 122 electoral votes in his successful bid for the Presidency, as compared with the 162 Thomas Jefferson had received in 1804 upon his re-election.

Perhaps the most prominent victim of this Federalist ground-swell in New England was Senator John Quincy Adams of Massachusetts, who conditionally supported the Embargo. Adams was described in the Northampton Hampshire Gazette on April 20 as "one of those amphibious politicians, who lives on both land and water, and occasionally resorts to each, but who finally settles down in the mud. " The following month the Massachusetts legislature, acting a half-year in advance, denied Adams re-election to his Senate seat. In 1825, however, Thomas Jefferson revealed that Adams had sought an interview with him during this period; at this meeting Adams had warned of the dissatisfaction of New England with the Embargo, and had convinced him of the necessity of abandoning this measure! At the time of this revelation Adams, far from suffering continued political ostractism, had become President of the United States.

As for the impact of the Embargo in the Middle Atlantic states, it is undeniable that it had an adverse effect on its commerce. In New York sailors were hired who were glad to work for rations only; throughout the whole region the price of wheat fell from two dollars to seventy-five cents a bushel. But whereas sentiment in New York tended to side with New England against the Embargo, as evidenced by the results of the fall election of 1808, the Republicans managed to hold Pennsylvania. Admittedly there was discontent among

the merchants of Philadelphia (as well as those of New York
City) as a result of the Embargo, but the fact remains that
this measure triggered a manufacturing boom in Pennsylvania
which more than offset the adverse effects that it had there.
What held true for Pennsylvania also held true for the region as a whole to a lesser degree.

Finally, turning to the West, one discovers that this
section backed the President on the Embargo as strongly as
any other, if not more so.   In an episode that stands as the
antithesis of that involving John Quincy Adams, Representative
Matthew Lyon of Kentucky, who opposed the measure, lost his
bid for re-election in 1810.   On February 6, 1809 the Carth-
age Gazette of Tennessee observed: "We never witnessed a
greater unanimity to prevail in any considerable district of
country, and relative to any important question, than now pre-
vails throughout the state of Tennessee respecting the measures of the General Government.   The voice of approbation
is universal. " At least in part, this general western support
of the Jefferson Administration's stand on the Embargo is
attributable to the section's Republican political orientation.
Nevertheless, as George Rogers Taylor has pointed out in
his pioneering article, "Agrarian Discontent in the Mississippi
Valley Preceding the War of 1812, " Westerners were confronted during this period with a decline in foreign trade, culminating in a depression, which economic setback they tended
to blame on the British rather than on the Embargo.   Taylor's hypothesis is one of several "western" interpretations
of the War of 1812 that stresses a factor other than that of
land hunger.

The War of 1812 and the Hartford Convention

No single theory of causation adequately explains the
War of 1812, as we have just noted.   The traditional, or
maritime, interpretation stresses the impressment of American
seamen, the violation of neutral rights by the British, and
that nation's Orders in Council.   Its appeal began to crumble
when a growing number of scholars came to realize that it
was the most commercial section of this country, New England, which was most opposed to war; in addition, impressment and the Orders in Council had become old grievances by
1812, having failed to trigger a war in such tension-filled
years as 1807 and 1808.   More recent attempts to develop a
southern and western interpretation, however, have merely

resulted in a muddying of the waters rather than a final
judgment.   Two of the founders of this school were Louis W.
Hacker and Howard T. Lewis, who stressed a "land hungry"
West intent on conquering Canada; Julius W. Pratt and Dice
R. Anderson later set forth a variant of this theory, holding
that the proposed American forays into Canada were a defensive measure designed to eliminate the Indian threat.

These land hunger and Indian threat interpretations in
turn were followed by an economic one, appropriately first
developed extensively in an article published by George R.
Taylor during the years of the Great Depression, which traced
western resentment against the British to the latter's inter-
ruption of their exports that ushered in an era of low prices
in the West.   In more recent years there has been a movement in the direction of less sectionalistic interpretations of
the war; Norman K. Risjord thus has pointed out that the
sense of humiliation was universal, while Reginald Horsman
has emphasized the almost national character of the drive for
Canada.   The easy way out, of course, is to take the position
that all of the above theories of causation have merit to a
greater or lesser degree.   Here we will attempt to point out
that, at least outside of New England, there was no unanimous
support for the war, although the South and the West did
generally back it.

During the Congressional elections of 1810 a number
of individuals were elected to the national legislature whose
aggressive stance towards Great Britain has caused them to
be categorized as "War Hawks. " (This interpretation has
been challenged by Bradford Perkins.) Among these were
John A. Harper of New Hampshire, Peter B. Porter from
western New York, Henry Clay and Richard M. Johnson of
Kentucky, Felix Grundy of Tennessee, John C. Calhoun,
William Lowndes, and Langdon Cheves of South Carolina,
and George M. Troup of Georgia.   Some had previously served
in the Eleventh Congress, so that the actual increase in numbers was not spectacular.   Most of them hailed from rural
constituencies in the South and West, although Harper and
Porter were exceptions to this rule.   Not all, though, were
elected on the basis of their foreign policy stands; many elections turned on personalities and state and local issues.
Still, when the new Congress assembled in December 1811,
there were no less than 63 new faces in a House of 142, a
circumstance which doubtless mitigated against that body following a conservative and traditional course.   Perhaps the
actual "War Hawks" were in a minority, but this minority

possessed a number of gifted leaders, and the average long-
term Republican seemed ripe for conversion.

Unlike World War II, there was no Pearl Harbor which
precipitated the War of 1812. Instead, the American declaration of war was basically the result of an accumulation of
grievances. President James Madison's war message to
Congress on June 1, 1812 thus listed four major grounds for
war: the British impressment of American seamen, the
British violation of American neutral rights and territorial
waters, the British blockade of American ports, and the
British refusal to revoke the Orders in Council. In the
closest war vote in American history, the House approved
the declaration of war on June 4 by a 79 to 49 vote; the Senate
followed suit two weeks later by a narrow 19 to 13 margin.
The formal proclamation of war by President Madison followed
on June 19.

That public opinion in New England would violently
oppose the war should be predictable on the basis of the material presented so far. In March 1812 James Madison paid
$50,000 to a British agent, John Henry, who had been in the
employ of the governor general of Canada; Henry had been
investigating pro-British sentiments in New England to dis-
cover whether the area was ripe for revolt against the federal government. Among his confidants had been a number
of prominent Federalists. Hoping to discredit the Federalists, Madison submitted Henry's report, from which the names
of his informants had been deleted, to Congress; unfortunately
for Madison, the expensive document contained little information that was not already public knowledge.

As for the remainder of the country, it is significant
that in both the South and West there was some sentiment at
this time for the declaration of a double war against both
England and France. Petitions to this effect were drawn up
in the Virginian cities of Richmond and Manchester, while a
mass meeting was held at Charleston, South Carolina, attended both by Federalists and Republicans, which resolved that
both France and Great Britain had given adequate cause for
war. The Kentucky legislature, moreover, specifically attacked both major belligerents, and four other legislatures
referred to France by implication.

Far from wanting a double war, there were those in
every section who were opposed to any war. Leaving aside
New England, one might cite as representative that group of

citizens in Philadelphia and Delaware counties in Pennsylvania who stated that "the United States are not impelled to war against Great Britain." Similar anti-war memorials were drawn up in New York (signed by John Jacob Astor) and in Arundel County, Maryland (signed by Charles Carroll). In the May elections in New York the Federalists recaptured the legislature, and immediately passed a resolution opposing "offensive war." Turning to the South, the orations on behalf of peace by John Randolph in Congress were among the highlights of the debates; in such parts of that state as Caroline, the Valley, and Norfolk there was considerable anti-war sentiment. According to Bradford Perkins, "Aside from the West (and even here Ohio was a notable exception) and perhaps Georgia, not a single state, even the traditionally Republican ones, failed to provide evidence of anti-war feeling." This may well be true, yet it is difficult to accept the statement by Perkins that the opponents of war outnumbered its supporters, or the contemporary assessment by Samuel Taggart that a majority in every state opposed war, as one must question whether Congress would dare to disregard such a groundswell of public opinion.

The traditional interpretation of the vote for war in Congress postulates a pro-war South and a pro-war West allied against an anti-war New England. This rather simplistic breakdown of the vote was modified by Julius W. Pratt in favor of a "frontier crescent" of "War Hawks" extending from New Hampshire to Kentucky and Tennessee, and ending in South Carolina and Georgia. A closer examination of the vote in both chambers, however, reveals many additional details worth citing. Ohio, for example, voted for war in the House, but opposed it in the Senate. In the House, moreover, Congressmen from north of the Delaware River actually provided the war resolution with its majority, including no less than six from Massachusetts! Admittedly, every Westerner did vote for war, but there were only nine members from beyond the mountains; in contrast, the three states of Pennsylvania, Maryland, and Virginia (despite the opposition of John Randolph) furnished no less than thirty-five of the pro-war votes. As for New York, it split eleven to three in favor of peace, having been alienated from the Madison Administration by the dissident Clintonian faction. When the war resolution came before the Senate, there was a somewhat similar division of opinion, but a closer vote, with New England exclusive of Vermont again opting for peace, the South and West for war. Only one Senator outside of New England and the Middle Atlantic States, in fact, opposed the resolution.

Once war had broken out, it is not surprising that the opposition to it would be bitterest in New England. The governor of Vermont threatened to use force if the federal government attempted to compel that state to assist in the prosecution of the war, while the governors of Massachusetts and Connecticut denied that the federal government had the power to make a draft upon their militias. The legislature of Massachusetts also sent a war memorial to Congress declaring the war improper, impolitic, and unjust; state officers and leading Federalists there even refused to attend the public funeral of Captain Lawrence of the <u>Chesapeake</u>. New England banks, too, lent more money to the British during the war than they did to the United States government, and the continuing New England trade with the former mother country led to the British not even blockading that section until 1814. It was the policy of the British commander-in-chief in Canada "to avoid committing any act which may even by a strained construction tend to unite the eastern and southern states." Conversely, such leading New England Federalists as Josiah Quincy opposed the capture of Quebec on the grounds that it might result in an American "dynasty by the sword," declaring that the United States had enough territory. The loyal minority, though, furnished the regular army with nineteen regiments, compared with fifteen from the Middle Atlantic States and ten from the South.

Southern enthusiasm and support for the annexation of Canada, too, perceptibly lessened following the blocking of the passage of a bill in the Senate in February 1813 which would have provided for the acquisition of East Florida. When Langdon Cheves of South Carolina won election over Felix Grundy of Tennessee as speaker of the House of Representatives in January 1814, it marked a victory for the Southeast and international trade over the Southwest and local manufacturing. Henry Clay, who had resigned as speaker when he was appointed a member of the peace commission, was of course from Kentucky and that state, like Clay, had along with its support of the war taken an increasing interest in industrialization.

In the Presidential election of 1812 James Madison managed to win re-election, 128 votes to 89 for the Federalist-anti-war Republican nominee, De Witt Clinton of New York, thanks largely to the support that he received in the South and the West. Clinton did carry all of New England and the Middle Atlantic States to the Potomac, exclusive of Vermont and Pennsylvania, whose industries had been stimu-

lated by the war.   Nevertheless, the Federalist representation in Congress was doubled in the new Thirteenth Congress,
there now being a total of eleven Federalist members from
such non-New England states as Maryland, Virginia, and
North Carolina.   (John Randolph, however, did lose his seat
in 1813.) One year later, in the Congressional elections
held in 1814, Vermont, Rhode Island, New Hampshire, and
Connecticut returned all Federalist Congressmen, Massachusetts eighteen out of twenty, in an impressive outpouring
of anti-war unanimity.

This strong display of pro-Federalist, anti-war, anti-
administration sentiment in New England was accompanied on
October 17 by a call by the Massachusetts legislature for a
convention that was to discuss "public grievances and con-
cerns, " as well as to consider possible amendments to the
federal Constitution.   Meeting in secret session beginning on
December 15, 1814, twenty-six delegates from Massachusetts,
Connecticut, and Rhode Island assembled at Hartford; although
New Hampshire and Vermont took no action as states, two
New Hampshire counties and one Vermont one sent delegates.
Significantly, the conservatives and moderates were in the
majority, with George Cabot being chosen as president of the
convention.   Among the more important Constitutional amendments proposed by the Hartford Convention were that Congress
was to declare no embargo of more than sixty days duration,
that no new state was to be admitted into the Union without
the consent of two-thirds of both houses of Congress, and that
Congress was not to suspend commerce or declare war without a similar two-thirds majority.   By moving in the direction
of a check by a single section upon acts of Congress, these
proposals anticipated arch-Southerner John C. Calhoun's doctrine of the concurrent majority.

One of the leading critics of the Hartford Convention
was John Quincy Adams, a one-time supporter of the Embargo, who authored an "Appeal to the Citizens of the United
States. " Yet many of the Essex Junto set--the extreme Fed-
eralists--were also dissatisfied with its report; John Lowell,
for example, was disappointed because the convention had not
opted for New England's neutrality for the remainder of the
war.   The legislatures of Massachusetts and Connecticut did
endorse its work, but by the time that a committee headed
by Harrison Gray Otis (which the Massachusetts legislature
had appointed to deal with the federal government) had reached
Washington, news of the signing of the Treaty of Ghent and of
Jackson's victory at New Orleans had arrived.   If not traitors,

the Hartford Convention members at least seemed fools to
most people outside of New England in the aftermath of these
two events.

   In the fall of 1814, when the British peace proposals
first became known in this country, New England took the
greatest exception to those touching on the fisheries question,
the Middle Atlantic States and the South to those touching on
the Indian territory and the boundary question. Fortunately
for the dissenting section, John Quincy Adams took a strong
stand on the fisheries question at the peace negotiations; in
contrast, the spokesman for the West, Henry Clay, was willing to yield on the "stinking codfish" if the British would
concede navigational rights on the Mississippi River to the
United States. Among the other American negotiators were
Albert Gallatin of Pennsylvania and James Bayard of Delaware.

   As finally agreed upon, the Treaty of Ghent constituted
little more than a reversion to the status quo ante bellum.
Impressment, according to one school of interpretation, was
one of the major causes of the war, but the final draft of the
treaty ignored this issue; such important questions as the
fisheries, commercial relations, and boundaries were left for
later conferences to resolve. Thus fifteen years later, in
1830, Andrew Jackson reached an agreement with England re-
opening the British West Indies to American trade in return
for the reopening of American ports to British ships, a delayed triumph for the New England molasses importers. In
the words of John Quincy Adams, the Treaty of Ghent was
"a truce rather than a peace ... an indefinite suspension of
hostilities. " A mere truce or not, the peace settlement won
the unanimous approval of the Senate on February 15, 1815,
as did the 1817 Rush-Bagot Great Lakes Disarmament Agreement and the 1818 Northeastern Fisheries Convention.

                    FOR FURTHER READING

   Pre-Revolutionary imperialistic ambitions are discussed
in Max Savelle, The Origins of American Diplomacy: The International History of Anglo-America 1492-1763. For emerging sectional divisions, see Paul C. Phillips, The West in the
Diplomacy of the American Revolution, and for its topic,
Thomas P. Abernethy, Western Lands and the American Revolution; for the events leading up to the peace treaty, consult
Richard Morris, The Peacemakers: The Great Powers and

American Independence. The latter is also useful for sectional attitudes towards foreign policy under the Articles, as
is Merrill Jensen, The New Nation: A History of the United
States during the Confederation. Works on the present fund-
amental law include Charles A. Beard, An Economic Interpretation of the United States; Robert E. Brown, Charles
Beard and the Constitution; and Clinton Rossiter, 1787; The
Grand Convention. Joseph Charles discusses Alexander Hamilton's fiscal policies and the resulting sectional divisions in
his provocative The Origins of the American Party System:
Three Essays.

     The standard work on Pinckney's Treaty is Samuel
Flagg Bemis' book with that title; Bemis' work also includes
considerable data on the Jay-Gardoqui Treaty. Aside from
Bemis and Cox, James Wilkinson and his separatist movement
in Kentucky are treated by Isaac J. Cox in his The West
Florida Controversy, 1798-1813, and by Herbert Bruce Fuller
in his The Purchase of Florida: Its History and Diplomacy.
For John Jay and the West, consult Cole; for George Wash-
ington, Burton Ira Kaufman, Washington's Farewell Address:
The View from the 20th Century.

     With regard to Jay's Treaty, the standard work for
many years was that by Samuel Flagg Bemis, at least prior
to the appearance of a recent study by Jerald Combs. Authors
aside from Bemis who deal with Ethan Allen and his separatist movement in Vermont include John Bartlett Brebner in
his North Atlantic Triangle: The Interplay of Canada, the
United States, and Great Britain, and A. L. Burt in his The
United States, Great Britain, and British North America.

     For sectional attitudes towards England following the
American Revolution, see H. C. Allen, Great Britain and the
United States; for ties between the New England Federalists
and the former mother country, James Truslow Adams, New
England in the Republic 1776-1850 and Alexander de Conde.
Entangling Alliance: Politics and Diplomacy under George
Washington. Studies other than that of Bemis which touch
upon public opinion and Jay's Treaty are Thomas P. Aber-
nethy, The South in the New Nation 1789-1819 and Bradford
Perkins, The First Rapprochement: England and the United
States 1795-1805.

     Much has been written about the reaction in this country
to the French Revolution. Three articles of particular interest are the two by Beatrice Hyslop, "The American Press

and the French Revolution of 1789" and "American Press Reports of the French Revolution, 1789-1794, " and the one by
Huntley Dupre, "The Kentucky Gazette Reports the French
Revolution. " For the reception given Citizen Genêt in this
country, consult Charles M. Thomas, American Neutrality in
1793: a Study in Cabinet Government; for attitudes in general,
see Charles D. Hazen, Contemporary American Opinion of
the French Revolution. Alexander de Conde's abovementioned
work discusses French attempts to stir up secession in the
West, while Doris A. Graber's Public Opinion, the President,
and Foreign Policy: Four Case Studies from the Formative
Years treats the East Coast reaction to the XYZ affair. Books
dealing with developments in Santo Domingo and Haiti during
this period relative to the United States include Rayford W.
Logan, The Diplomatic Relations of the United States with
Haiti 1776-1801, and Ludwell Lee Montague, Haiti and the
United States 1714-1938. One should examine the abovemen-
tioned book by Cole, as well as Samuel Flagg Bemis' John
Quincy Adams and the Foundations of American Foreign Pol-
icy, for material on the Louisiana Purchase.

      Shifting New England attitudes towards the Chesapeake
Affair are discussed in the abovementioned book by Adams.
The best treatment of sectional attitudes towards the Embargo
is Louis Martin Sears, Jefferson and the Embargo. For the
nation as a whole, also see the abovementioned work by Allen,
Francis F. Beirne's The War of 1812, and Patrick C. T.
White's A Nation on Trial: America and the War of 1812; for
New England specifically, consult Corinne Bacon's article
"New England Sectionalism, " as well as the abovementioned
works by Varg and by Bemis on John Quincy Adams. A
revisionist article essential to an understanding of western
attitudes towards the Embargo (as well as the War of 1812) is
the one by George Rogers Taylor entitled: "Agrarian Discon-
tent in the Mississippi Valley Preceding the War of 1812. "
As for West Florida, the abovementioned studies by Cox and
Varg touch on this topic, as does Charles Griffin in his The
United States and the Disruption of the Spanish Empire 1810-
1822.

      Rather than attempt to list all those books and articles
that touch upon the War of 1812, the author proposes instead
to limit himself to a listing of those items that have influenced the presentation offered here. He would like to single
out for special praise two books by Bradford Perkins: Prologue to War: England and the United States 1805-1812 and
Castlereagh and Adams: England and the United States 1812-

1823. Perkins is valuable for his treatment of opposition to
the war at the time of its inception, his analysis of the vote
on the declaration of war in Congress, and his discussion of
developments at the state level in the Election of 1812 and
thereafter. Julius Pratt's classic, Expansionists of 1812,
presents its Indian threat interpretation in a comprehensive
manner; Francis F. Beirne's abovementioned work contains
a stimulating treatment of the Hartford Convention; Thomas
P. Abernethy's, of developments in the South. As for articles, one must again cite the Bacon treatment of New England, that by Taylor on the Mississippi Valley, Reginald
Horsman's "Western War Aims, 1811-1812, " a rebuttal of the
Pratt thesis, and Norman K. Risjord's "1812: Conservatives,
War Hawks, and the Nation's Honor, " which includes a rather
original treatment of the "War Hawks. " Opposition to the
war is discussed by Samuel Eliot Morison in Dissent in Three
American Wars.

CHAPTER 2

FROM THE WAR OF 1812
TO THE MEXICAN WAR

Introduction

The years between 1815 and 1825 are frequently re-
ferred to by historians as the "Era of Good Feelings. " When
President James Monroe ran for re-election in 1820, only
one member of the Electoral College failed to vote for him.
Despite the fact that a handful of Federalists remained in
Congress, the Senate ratified a number of treaties by a unanimous or near-unanimous vote, including the abovementioned
Treat of Ghent.   Not a single vote was cast against the 1817
Rush-Bagot Great Lakes Agreement or the 1818 Northeastern
Fisheries Convention, both with Great Britain, or against the
1819 Adams-Onis Transcontinental Treaty with Spain providing for the acquisition of Florida.   (Four Westerners did
oppose the latter the second time around, in 1821.) As for
the 1824 treaty with Russia surrendering that nation's claim
to Oregon, it only incurred the displeasure of one Senator
from Rhode Island.

That same year the hotly contested Presidential election saw John Quincy Adams emerge victorious over Andrew
Jackson in the House of Representatives after Henry Clay
(whom Adams later made Secretary of State) threw his support to the New Englander.   Partisan and sectional hostility
towards Adams in the diplomatic sphere was most apparent
in the vote on American participation in the Panama Congress; all 19 votes against this bill in the Senate were cast
by Democrats, 10 of them from the South, while in the House
southern opposition to the appropriation bill was responsible
for a fatal delay.   Considering the bitter opposition of many
Jackson supporters to Adams, one might logically deduce that
the Adams backers would have returned the compliment once
Jackson became President.   Yet such was not the case relative to the treaties signed during this period, despite the furor
over such domestic issues as the rechartering of the Second

Bank of the United States. Even the French spoliation claims
treaty of 1831 passed the Senate unanimously, as did various
other agreements with Russia, Siam, and Muscat. It is also
significant in this connection that Jackson, whose majorities
in the House were decisive during the eight years that he
served as President, had less substantial backing in the
Senate, never enjoying a two-thirds majority there.

During the 1840's diplomatic activity reached more
feverish heights, as the United States entered the era of western expansion and the Mexican War. The Whigs captured the
Presidency for the first time in 1840 with the short-lived
William Henry Harrison, controlling the Senate (by narrow
margins) for the next four years and the House for the next
two. When the Senate ratified the Webster-Ashburton Treaty
of 1842 with John Tyler President, Democrats cast eight of
the nine nay votes; on the other hand, there were no pronounced sectional trends relative to this agreement, or to an
1844 treaty with China which won unanimous Senatorial approval. Sectional opposition was much more apparent in the
case of the Texas annexation treaty, which the Senate rejected
by a lopsided 16 to 35 vote on June 8, 1844, with Whigs
casting approximately two-thirds of the nay votes. Only one
New Englander--Democrat Levi Woodbury of New Hampshire
--voted aye, while the South divided more sharply, the Democrats favoring it and eight Whigs opposing it. The following
year, when Texas was annexed by a joint resolution, the
measure was approved by the House in a vote that saw the
Democrats generally in favor and the Whigs largely opposed.
The 27 to 25 vote in the Senate was even more partisan, with
only a handful of members bolting their parties; but on this
occasion sectional considerations played only a minor role,
geographical support and opposition manifesting no clear-cut
pattern.

When Democrat James K. Polk was elected President
in 1844, the Democrats won control of the Senate for the next
four years, the last two of them by a substantial 36 to 21
majority over the Whigs, despite the fact that the Whigs re-
gained control of the House in the Congressional election of
1846. Polk, who originally was a 54°40' extremist on Oregon, later agreed to compromise for half a loaf; the Middle
West, which had spearheaded the movement for "All Oregon,"
also cast seven of the fourteen votes against the 1846 treaty
with Great Britain dividing the Pacific Northwest with Canada.
Even with a Democrat sitting in the White House, not a single
Whig opposed this treaty. There was some sentiment in the

United States for annexing Mexico during this era, but there
were also a number of individuals (including Abraham Lincoln) who did not wish a military conflict with that nation.
Nevertheless, the vote on the declaration of war was far more
nearly unanimous than it had been a generation before, only
fourteen Representatives (most of them from Ohio and Massachusetts) and two Whig Senators from Delaware and Massachusetts opposing it. Unlike the Treaty of Ghent ending the
War of 1812, however, this time there were more than a
dozen Senators (14 to be precise) opposed to the peace settlement contained in the treaty of Guadeloupe Hidalgo. While
approximately two Democrats out of three favored it, the
Whigs split equally; yet an analysis of the roll-call manifests
no significant pattern of sectional voting. Summarizing the
reactions in this country to the key diplomatic happenings of
this decade, one must conclude on the basis of the votes in
Congress (and especially the Senate) that partisan alignments
were more pronounced than sectional ones, despite the interest of New England in the Canadian boundary, of the Middle
West in Oregon, and of New York City in Mexico.

The American Peace Movement

        One direct result of the War of 1812 in New England
was the organization of peace societies there and elsewhere
in the wake of this conflict. As early as August 1815, a
peace society was founded in New York City, and four months
later another was established in Massachusetts; by 1817 New
England had twelve auxiliary societies, three in New Hampshire, eight in Massachusetts, and one in Connecticut. In
addition, there were fourteen similar organizations scattered
throughout the country, one in Maine, one in Rhode Island,
four in New York, five in Ohio, two in Indiana, and one in
North Carolina. (Of all the New England states, only Vermont indicated a lack of enthusiasm.) An American Peace
Society was eventually founded in New York in 1828.

        The European counterpart of these American peace
societies, at least in the eyes of the latter, was Czar Alexander I of Russia's Holy Alliance, established in the aftermath of the Napoleonic Wars. Composed of Russia, Prussia,
and Austria (England had been invited to join, but failed to
do so), the Holy Alliance pledged the sovereigns of these three
nations to conduct their government according to Christian
principles and to "remain united by the bonds of a true and

indissoluble fraternity" in order "on all occasions and in all
places to lend each other aid and assistance. " On July 4,
1817 Alexander, who had been written by the corresponding
secretary of the Massachusetts Peace Society, replied to the
latter in approval of its objectives, promising that he would
perpetually strive to obtain for all nations the "blessings of
peace. "

Of all those names that one might associate with the
American peace movement, perhaps none merits mention more
than William Ladd, who was born in New Hampshire, but later
lived in Maine.   His Essay on a Congress of Nations first
appeared in 1840.   Among other schemes, Ladd developed the
concept of a world court, presenting his ideas at peace conferences held at Brussels in 1848, at Paris in 1849, at Frank-
furt in 1850, and at London in 1851.   Although Ladd did not
live to see it, his pet scheme eventually won realization as
the International Court of Justice at the Hague.   Unfortunately,
he has not received the acclaim that he deserves.

Outside of New England and New York, the peace movement initially enjoyed its greatest success in Ohio.   Although
that state had been far more enthusiastic about the War of 1812
than Massachusetts had been, a peace society was set up in
Warren County, apparently independent of any efforts elsewhere.
In this connection its corresponding secretary stated: "Having
seen the Solemn Review of the Custom of War and impressed
with the horrors, the devastations, the grief, misery and woe,
a number of citizens of Warren County, of different religious
denominations, formed themselves into a society without having
any knowledge at that time that any similar society existed on
earth. " The peace effort in Ohio, one might add, apparently
was led by the Shakers and the Quakers, who seemingly were
more active there than they were in such states as New York
and Massachusetts.

By 1850, though, attempts to establish a flourishing
peace movement outside of New England and New York had
ended in general failure, especially in the South.   A touring
minister discovered in 1854 that many from that section
seemed open to appeals, but were practically all unacquainted
with the subject of peace.   As for the West, it is noteworthy
that many of the peace movement leaders there were from the
East, especially from New England.   There were occasional
success: in 1854 the Methodist Conferences of Wisconsin and
Michigan adopted resolutions asking that its members support
the efforts of the American Peace Society.   Yet around this

time a Chicago periodical devoted to the cause of peace failed,
as did newly-founded peace societies in Ohio and Wisconsin,
and many ministers remained cold towards the movement's
objectives. Among the factors contributing to this apathy were
the slavery question in Kansas, the militant anti-British feeling throughout the West, and hostility towards the Mormons.
The West was not in the mood to back peace.

The Annexation of Florida

Before examining in depth American attitudes towards
the annexation of Florida and the independence of Latin
America, along with related topics, it is necessary to summarize briefly developments in Spain during this period, for
these had a profound impact on that nation's international
policies. Again the Napoleonic Wars emerge as an important
factor, as in 1808 France invaded Spain, driving King Ferdinand VII from the throne; the juntas set up at Buenos Aires,
Bogota, Caracas, and Santiago in the name of the deposed
Spanish monarch actually proved to be the initial stage of the
later independence movement. Following the fall of Napoleon,
Ferdinand again assumed power in Spain. That monarch
sought to maintain the Spanish colonial empire intact, but
with only limited success, the Latin American countries having irrevocably moved in the direction of independence.

As for developments in the United States during these
years, President James Madison, in October 1810, issued a
proclamation announcing the American possession of West
Florida and authorizing its military occupation, an event which
followed the revolt of a group of southern expansionists there.
In May 1812 Congress voted to incorporate West Florida into
the Mississippi Territory. During the War of 1812, too,
General James Wilkinson captured the Spanish fort at Mobile,
in the process occupying the district around this fort. This
marked the only territorial conquest which the United States
retained after the War of 1812; American annexationist efforts
to the North involving Canada proved fruitless.

In the case of East Florida, as early as January 1811
Congress passed a resolution which authorized the extension
of American rule there, provided that the consent of the local
authorities was obtained, or a foreign power made an attempt
to occupy it. Nothing came of this resolution at the time,
but following the war the Indians of East Florida began allying

themselves with runaway slaves.   In 1818 General Andrew
Jackson expanded his military campaign against the Seminoles
in that territory, where he captured two Spanish forts and
hanged two British citizens for aiding the Indians.   Jackson's
"Rhea Letter, " written to President Monroe on January 6,
affirmed that "the possession of the Floridas would be desirable to the United States and in sixty days it will be accom-
plished. " Such Southerners as William Crawford and John C.
Calhoun attacked Jackson in the Cabinet, while both House
and Senate committees brought in reports unfavorable to Jackson.   But "Old Hickory's" actions won public approval, and
Monroe refrained from disciplining him.

Examining sectional attitudes towards a possible war
with Spain over Florida, the West and the South in 1818 appear to have been more belligerent in their attitude than the
Monroe Administration.   Thus a Georgia newspaper declared
that if Spain was unable or unwilling to compel the Indians
within its jurisdiction to act peacefully, then the United States
should do so; equally concerned was the group which dominated the early years of Alabama's political life, the "Georgia
Machine. " Land hunger, it would seem, was only a secondary
consideration, the Indian threat being the ascendent issue.
Less enthusiastic were such prominent Federalists as Senator
Rufus King of New York, who echoed the sentiments of New
England in opposing action which might lead to war.   Unfortunately for the latter, the widely ridiculed actions of the
Hartford Convention and the decisive Federalist defeat in the
Presidential election of 1816 (the last in which they were to
field a candidate) mitigated against their swaying public opin-
ion nationally on the Florida question.

It was against this background that the negotiations
culminating in the so-called Transcontinental Treaty took place
between John Quincy Adams, representing the United States,
and Luis de Onis, representing Spain.   Spain renounced all
claims to West Florida and ceded East Florida to the United
States, but the latter also agreed to abandon its claims to
Texas; this provision was to engender much criticism in the
West, even though Spain accepted a boundary there which
barred her from Oregon.   Our government, moreover, agreed
to assume five million dollars in claims by American citizens
against Spain, a highly important consideration.   Except where
it was superseded by this Adams-Onis Treaty, the Pinckney
Treaty of 1795 remained in effect.

Editorial reaction to the Transcontinental Treaty in

this country was generally favorable, if the sentiments of the
Savannah Republican, the Boston Patriot, the New York National Advocate, and the Kentucky Reporter are to be taken
as representative. In the House, Henry Clay expressed his
dissatisfaction with the provision dealing with Texas, but the
Senate nevertheless quickly approved the treaty by a unanimous
vote in February 1819, two days after Adams and Onis had
signed it. Although Thomas Hart Benton of Missouri also
attacked the provisions concerning Texas in the St. Louis
press, western opposition to the treaty did not begin to cry-
stallize for several months. Even Andrew Jackson, who had
lusted so greedily for Florida, dismissed the loss of Texas
without a public display of concern.

    Back at Madrid, however, the welcome accorded the
treaty was less enthusiastic. When word was received in the
United States that Spain was hesitant to sign the Adams-Onis
Treaty, tempers flared across the land. Highly mercantile
New England, which was actively trading with Cuba and other
parts of the Spanish colonial empire, entertained thoughts of
war. When President James Monroe proposed a bill providing for the optional occupation of Florida, the House Committee on Foreign Affairs countered with a substitute measure making the occupation mandatory; even more important,
the latter did not provide for any method for satisfying the
claims of individual citizens. Essentially an expression of
southern and western attitudes, this committee substitute was
anathema to John Quincy Adams and the Northeast. Angered
by this committee report, Monroe, who was awaiting the
arrival of Vives, managed to stall the substitute measure.

    Thus was shattered the harmony of sectional interests
that existed prior to the signing of the Transcontinental Treaty.
Then the South and the West had desired to pressure Spain
into ceding territory, the North and the East to obtain reim-
bursement for the losses they had suffered at the hands of
Spain during the Napoleonic Wars. Of the two alliances, that
of the North and the East was more opposed to war as a
means of obtaining its objectives than that of the South and
the West, but all sections were willing to work for an acceptable peaceful settlement if it were obtainable. Now the sections were split asunder on foreign policy issues, with each
going its own way to the neglect of or at the expense of the
others; Georgia wanted Florida, the East wanted the claims
issue settled, and the Southwest wanted Texas. To complicate matters further, agitation of the Missouri controversy
had pitted the North against the South on the slavery issue,

a question directly related to territorial expansion.

Fortunately for the United States, there now occurred a liberal revolt in Spain, a take-over which resulted in that nation adopting a more conciliatory approach to the Adams-Onis Treaty. The new regime not only recognized that a danger existed that this nation might seize Florida, treaty or no treaty, but saw that it might grab Texas as well; in addition, liberal Spain now stood in isolation against a conservative Europe dominated by men like Metternich and Talleyrand. Thus the Spanish monarch finally agreed to sign the Transcontinental Treaty in October 1820. As the terms of the original treaty had provided that ratifications must be exchanged within six months, President Monroe was forced to place it before the Senate again, which body voted its endorsement a second time in February 1821, almost exactly two years after the original ratification had been obtained. This time, however, there were four dissenting votes, all from the West: James Brown of Louisiana, the brother-in-law of Henry Clay, Richard Johnson of Kentucky, William Trimble of Ohio, and John Williams of Tennessee.

To some Americans greedy for more territory the annexation of Florida was not enough; a number of ultra-imperialists began turning their eyes southward. Thus in March 1820 the St. Louis Enquirer published an article declaring that the acquisition of Cuba by the United States was essential to the preservation of the Union, while in August 1819 a Philadelphia editor suggested that this nation should seize the West Indies island. On the other hand, during the same month a southern newspaper observed that there was no widespread desire in the South for Cuba. Nevertheless, annexation or no annexation, the West Indies island remained of vital strategic and commercial significance to all sections; in the words of New Englander John Quincy Adams, the latter considerations "give [it] an importance in the sum of our national interests, with which that of no other foreign territory can be compared, and little inferior to that which binds the different members of the Union together." A similar interest in Cuba was expressed by Southerner John C. Calhoun, who viewed American trade from the standpoint of the procurement of specie. To others this commercial tie furnished one of the chief arguments against going to war against Spain.

Almost nowhere in evidence during this period was southern agitation for the annexation of the black republic of Haiti. In fact, southern commerce with Haiti, unlike with

Cuba, was quite limited; after the Denmark Vesey Plot had
erupted in Charleston, South Carolina in 1822, stories began
to circulate that Vesey had come from Santo Domingo. Consequently, expressions of interest in trade with the black republic are to be found mainly in the northern press. Two
senators from the new state of Maine did successfully sponsor
resolutions encouraging trade with Haiti, but Congress nevertheless refrained from acting positively on the recognition of
the latter, thanks largely to southern opposition. One may
find editorials in favor of recognition in such northern newspapers as the Boston Columbian Centinel, the New London
Advocate, and the United States Gazette (Philadelphia), but
even in Pennsylvania and in Maryland the press was sharply
divided on this issue. Fearful of a possible invasion by Haiti
of Puerto Rico or Cuba, not a single southern newspaper
opted for recognizing the black republic; in Calhoun's "Greek
democracy, " one must remember, whites did not associate
with blacks as equals.

Latin American Issues

       Even before the negotiations that resulted in the Adams-
Onis Treaty began, Spain had been confronted with an even
more difficult problem: stifling the independence movement
that had erupted throughout Latin America. While José de
San Martín was liberating the southern part of the South
American continent, Simón Bolívar was freeing the northern
part; the armies of both eventually converged on Peru. Even
Portugese Brazil broke with the mother country in 1822, with
the prince regent, Dom Pedro, becoming emperor. In Mexico, a revolt under Father Manuel Hidalgo in 1810 had failed,
but a decade later Agustín Iturbide defeated the Spanish forces
with the help of Vicente Guerrero, in the process setting up
a short-lived empire that included Central America.

       When Great Britain was unable to obtain a promise
from the French that the latter would not intervene in Latin
America, George Canning, the British foreign secretary, at-
tempted to reach an agreement with this nation barring further
European intervention in the New World. Under the Polignac
Agreement of October 1823 France eventually did bow to
British wishes, but on this side of the Atlantic Secretary of
State John Quincy Adams was able to persuade President
James Monroe to go it alone and to issue a statement regard-
ing Latin America independent of Great Britain. The Monroe

Doctrine, as set forth in the President's annual message to
Congress on December 2, 1823, featured two major points.
The first of these, the no-colonization or no-annexation prin-
ciple, prohibited further European territorial acquisitions in
the New World, while the second, the Doctrine of the Two
Spheres, emphasized the separateness of the New World and
Europe.

Yet even before the Monroe Doctrine there had been a
flowering of economic contacts between the United States and
Latin America. During the Napoleonic Wars (especially from
1797 on), an increasing commerce began to develop between
such American ports as Baltimore and Salem and the South
American cities of Montevideo, Buenos Aires, and Callao,
although admittedly this trade was of less consequence than
that with the Spanish West Indies. Unfortunately, Jefferson's
Embargo had an adverse effect on American commerce with
Latin America, as well as that with Europe. Thus by the
end of 1808 such northeastern members of the House of Rep-
resentatives as Timothy Pitken of Connecticut, James Lloyd
of Massachusetts, and Barent Gardenier of New York, who
feared an alliance between an independent Latin America and
Great Britain, were lamenting the decline in trade with the
Spanish colonial possessions. (In his dislike of England
Gardenier broke with the overwhelming majority of his fellow
Federalists.) Generally speaking, the Federalists of New
England and New York were prejudiced in favor of Spain by
Napoleon's invasion of the latter, hatred of France being one
of their main preoccupations. In retrospect Henry Adams
noted that:

> In the Eastern States, the Democratic and Southern
> indifference toward the terrible struggle raging in
> Spain helped to stimulate the anger against Jeffer-
> son. ... The New England conscience, which had
> never submitted to the authority of Jefferson, rose
> with an outburst of fervor toward the Spaniards, and
> clung more energetically than ever to the cause of
> England, --which seemed to last, beyond the possi-
> bility of doubt, to have the sanction of freedom.

Following the termination of the Embargo a grain trade
developed between this country and the Iberian Peninsula
(Spain and Portugal), benefitting every section of this country;
by 1817 this amounted to three times the total United States
commerce with Latin America. That most of these foodstuffs
were destined for the stomachs of Wellington's British soldiers

and their Spanish and Portugese allies in their battle against the French, moreover, was especially pleasing to maritime New England. Thus the New England Puritan and the Spanish Roman Catholic joined hands in an alliance in which mutual hatred of Napoleon took precedence over deep-rooted religious prejudices.

As for pro-Latin American independence sentiment in this country, as early as the time of the Burr Conspiracy there was some support for the Latin American revolutionary Francisco de Miranda in New York City and other Atlantic Seaboard ports, while in New Orleans and the West James Wilkinson and others championed the cause of Mexican liberation. Following the War of 1812, a number of unemployed army officers in Boston and Baltimore decided to join the revolutionary armies of Latin America; a group of merchants from Philadelphia, Baltimore, and New York also purchased 30,000 surplus army rifles from our government for resale to the insurgents. Such activities as these led Congress to pass additional neutrality legislation in 1817.

It was not until 1818 that Congress finally engaged in a full-scale debate on what position it should take towards Latin American independence. On this occasion Henry Clay of Kentucky emerged as the leading spokesman for the latter, while John Floyd of Virginia lent his support with the argument that once independent, Latin America would engage in a free and direct trade with the United States. Clay's attempt to obtain passage through the House of a pro-independence resolution failed by a vote of 115 to 45, despite western support, but in 1820 the House did adopt a resolution expressing sympathy with the Latin American republics, thanks in part to additional backing from such Middle Atlantic States as New York and Pennsylvania. (In both cases New England led the opposition.) As in 1818 the South again opposed ratification, perhaps in fear of undermining the negotiations with Spain over Florida, although it did support recognition in 1821 following the ratification of the Adams-Onis Treaty.

Examining public opinion in general towards Latin American independence between the end of the War of 1812 and the proclamation of the Monroe Doctrine, Baltimore seems to have been the center of the privateering business, as well as the rendezvous point for most of the Latin American agents in this country. With regard to newspapers, the Philadelphia Aurora and the Richmond Enquirer were among the first to support independence; on the other hand, the con-

servative newspapers of the large seaports of the Atlantic
Coast favored caution.   The businessmen of the Atlantic Seaboard, too, were lukewarm in their attitudes towards an independent Latin America, as they still enjoyed a lucrative
trade with Cuba, Spain, and the remaining remnants of the
Spanish colonial empire.

By 1823, on the eve of the pronouncement of the Monroe Doctrine, subtle sectional shifts in public opinion towards
Latin American independence had begun to occur.   Thus the
North American Review, which was still basically a New England organ, started taking a more sympathetic attitude; this
magazine was now under the editorship of Jared Sparks, who
had spent five years in independence-conscious Baltimore.
In contrast, a coolness towards Latin America by this time
was permeating the South, as the Haynes and Calhouns who
now spoke for the latter were expressing the sentiments of
an increasingly conservative and defensive section hostile to
liberalism and revolution.   Another factor contributing to this
coolness was the growing Southern fear of Latin American
economic competition, which we will examine more fully after
our discussion of the Monroe Doctrine.

The Monroe Doctrine itself received a widespread and
vigorous editorial greeting in tho newspapers of this country.
Thus Addington, the British chargé in Washington, observed
that: "It would indeed be difficult in a country composed of
elements so various, and liable on all subjects to opinions so
conflicting, to find more perfect unanimity than has been displayed on every side of this particular point. "   Even in New
England it won praise.   Most editors seemingly were of the
opinion, unlike historians writing a century and a half later,
that a real and present danger did exist necessitating such a
message.   Among the handful of editorialists who criticized
the Monroe Doctrine, one of the more eloquent condemnations
was that of the Boston Advertiser:

> Is there anything in the Constitution which makes
> our Government the Guarantors of the Liberties of
> the World?   of the Wahabees?   the Peruvians?   the
> Chinese?   the Mexicans or Colombians?....   In
> short, to reduce it to the actual case, though we
> acknowledged the disturbed and unsettled Govern-
> ments of South America as being de facto independ-
> ent, did we mean to make that act equivalent to
> treaties offfensive and defensive?   I hope not.

The almost universal endorsement of the Monroe Doctrine by American newspapers, one might add, was accompanied by expressions of friendship on the part of both the northern and southern press for England, that nation which originally had proposed the issuance of a joint Monroe Doctrine-like message with the United States. In fact, editorial sentiment in this country had become more pro-British than during any period since the beginning of the War of 1812; thus John Quincy Adams' Fourth of July address in 1821, with its challenge to Great Britain, was widely condemned everywhere, even in the South and the West. With regard to the Holy Alliance, however, editorial sentiment throughout this country had become decidedly negative, despite the enthusiasm of various peace societies centered in New England for Czar Alexander's brain child. In the words of the Eastern Argus,

> It is enough that despotism must reign on the other side of the Atlantic; let the nations on this side forbid its approach to our shores. If tyrants must possess the old world, free men shall possess the new; and we would admire and follow that spirit in our government which would say to the crowned heads of Europe, thus far ye shall come and no further.

Less enthusiastic in its reception of the Monroe Doctrine was Congress. When Henry Clay introduced a resolution into the House embodying its principles, it never even came to a vote. Among its critics were John Randolph of Virginia, who condemned Monroe's stand on Latin America as quixotic, and John Floyd, also of Virginia, who regarded the Monroe Doctrine both as unconstitutional and likely to lead to war with Europe. The Monroe Doctrine, moreover, was never mentioned once in the debate on a naval construction bill, which also did not come to a vote in the House. Two state legislatures eventually did pass resolutions endorsing the Monroe Doctrine.

Aside from the question of our diplomatic relations with newly independent Latin America, there was the matter of economic contacts. In 1824, to cite only one example, 73 American merchant vessels docked at the port of Buenos Aires and 51 at Montevideo, most of which came from Philadelphia, New York, Boston, and Baltimore. While at this time representatives of the Atlantic Seaboard States had expressed interest in Latin America as an outlet for American manufacture, such Southerners as Hayne of South Carolina were warning that economic competition from this region might pose a threat to the United States.   More complex was the position of the father of the "American System, " Henry Clay of Kentucky; this economic nationalist was of the opinion that with the end of the war for independence the demand for American foodstuffs throughout Latin America would lessen, but that a demand for manufactures would develop.   (In rebuttal to Clay, Hayne argued that this nation could not hope to compete with England abroad.)   The general northern pro-commerce, southern anti-commerce division of opinion on this issue of Latin American trade, as we shall see, was mirrored two years later in the sectional alignments on the Panama Congress.

On December 7, 1824 Simón Bolívar, the liberator of northern South America, penned a letter to Latin American heads of state requesting that an "Assembly of Plenipotentiaries" meet in Panama to discuss such matters as a code of international law, commercial treaties, and a defensive alliance.   The only Latin American states to send delegates were Mexico, Central America, Colombia, and Peru, none of which ratified all of the Assembly's discussions; Great Britain, the only non-American state invited, dispatched Edward J. Dawkins as its agent.   It was not until November 1825 that the United States received its invitation from Mexico and Colombia.   President John Quincy Adams, having been encouraged to do so by Secretary of State Henry Clay, recommended to Congress on December 26 that Richard C. Anderson of Kentucky and John Sargeant of Pennsylvania be sent to Panama as delegates.   Adams' request for funds, together with his justification of the mission, followed on March 15.

Unlike the Monroe Doctrine, which was never even voted on by Congress, the proposed American participation in the Panama Congress triggered off a bitter debate which ended in Senate endorsement of the mission on March 15 by a bare majority of 24 to 19, and House approval of the appropriations on April 22 by a more substantial 134 to 60 margin.   Opponents of the mission included Robert Hayne of South Carolina (the abovementioned critic of Latin American trade), John Berrien of Georgia, Hugh White of Tennessee, Thomas Hart Benton of Missouri, Martin Van Buren of New York (who had allied himself with John C. Calhoun), Mahlon Dickerson of New Jersey, Levi Woodbury of New Hampshire, and John Holmes of Maine, a roster that geographically represents every major section.   On the other hand, among the more prominent supporters of American participation were Daniel Webster, who was now representing Massachusetts in Con-

gress, Asher Robbins of Rhode Island, and J. S. Johnson of
Louisiana.

    Despite the widespread sprinkling of opponents cata-
logued above, however, the bulk of the votes against our involvement came from the South, most of those in favor from
the North. Thus the Senate Committee on Foreign Relations,
which was composed of four Southerners and one Northerner,
rejected the nominations, while in the House Congressmen
from Virginia, North Carolina, South Carolina, Alabama, and
Tennessee held up the appropriation bill so long that Sargeant
arrived at Panama late.   (Anderson had died enroute.) Apart
from commercial considerations, the major factor mitigating
against southern support of the mission was the widespread
belief that the Panama Congress represented a threat to the
institution of slavery; not only was the abolition of the slave
trade to be discussed, but also plans were being formulated
to liberate Cuba and Puerto Rico from Spain.   To Southerners
the existence of one "black republic" (Haiti) in the Caribbean
was one too many.   Thus south of the Mason-Dixon Line only
Maryland and Louisiana voted for the mission, leading the
Pittsburgh Mercury to observe that: "The Southern opposers
of the Panama Mission have practically formed a sectional
slave party."   Perhaps the most violent reaction to the Panama Congress came from the volatile John Randolph of Virginia, who referred to the Adams-Clay "team" as a "combination of the Puritan with the black-leg," a "coalition of
Blifil and Black George"; to Randolph "this Panama mission
(was) a Kentucky cuckoo's egg, laid in a Spanish-American
nest."   Angered by these remarks, Clay challenged him to a
duel, in which fortunately neither combatant suffered injury.

    In summary, the decade between the termination of the
Napoleonic Wars and the convening of the Panama Congress
witnessed a number of shifts in sectional attitudes towards
Latin America, the most complex evolution thus far examined.
Pro-independence sentiment seems to have first developed in
New York City and other Atlantic Seaboard ports, and in New
Orleans and the West.   When Henry Clay of Kentucky engi-
neered a pro-independence resolution through Congress in
1820, he received his greatest support from the West, assisted
by the Middle Atlantic States, with New England in opposition.
By 1823, though, sentiment in New England was becoming
more and more favorable towards Latin America, that in the
South less and less favorable; as for the Middle Atlantic
States, Baltimore had become the center of the privateering
business, as well as the rendezvous point for most of the

Latin American agents in this country.   Nevertheless, Congressional and editorial reactions to the Monroe Doctrine
were generally favorable, regardless of section, this marking
the point of greatest national unanimity on Latin American
questions.   Following 1823, as we have noted, a widening
split developed between the North and the South on the latter,
with the result that by the time that the Panama Congress
assembled in 1826 that part of the United States south of the
Mason-Dixon Line was generally hostile towards Latin America.
At this time southern imperialistic designs on the West Indies,
Mexico, and Central America, so prominent in the decade
prior to the Civil War, had yet to materialize on a large
scale, as that section pursued a policy of Latin American
isolationism.

The Aroostook War and the
Webster-Ashburton Treaty

Since the time of the American Revolution New England
had coveted Nova Scotia and that part of Canada to the north
of it.   During the War of 1812 plans were afoot to make this
dream a reality, but military setbacks and the peace treaty
returned the northern boundary to the status quo ante bellum.
American and Canadian migration into the St. John River
country, however, made eventual conflict between the two nations inevitable; when Maine split off from Massachusetts in
1820 as a separate state, it liberalized its land disposal laws
and encouraged settlers to move into the Aroostook region.
On the other hand, the fact that the only feasible line of com-
munication between the Maritime Provinces and Quebec when
the St. Lawrence was frozen over in the winter ran through
the disputed territory militated against Canada ceding it to the
United States.

As early as 1818 the Canadians had begun to complain
about American "squatters" who had moved onto the land in
dispute, and Secretary of State John Quincy Adams attempted
to obtain their names when the object of persuading the governor of Massachusetts to remove them peacefully.   Four
years later, in 1822, the governor of Maine complained that
Canadian "squatters" from New Brunswick also had been infiltrating the timber-rich Aroostook country.   In 1825 his successor as chief executive began seizing any timber found in
the possession of the interlopers, while the legislature passed
a measure authorizing deeds to lands in the St. John and

Madawaska River region. Thanks to such activities as these, the lieutenant governor of New Brunswick complained to the British minister in Washington.

In the autumn of 1827 British and American negotiators signed a convention providing for the arbitration of the disputed territory by some friendly sovereign, an agreement which the Senate ratified in 1828 by a vote of 35 to 4 (all Democrats, 3 from New England). When King William of the Netherlands rendered an award in January 1831, though, the Maine legislature objected, despite the fact that the monarch had granted this nation 7, 908 square miles of the 12, 027 square miles in dispute. As a result of this action of the Maine legislature and the opposition of such prominent statesmen as Henry Clay and Daniel Webster, on June 16, 1832 the Senate voted 35 to 8 (7 of them Democrats, 5 from the South) that the award was not binding and that new negotiations should commence. On June 21 the actual recommendations of King William were rejected by a narrower 23 to 22 vote which was devoid of sectional or partisan significance. This sabotaging of the arbitral award led to an increase in tensions along the border, and in March 1837 the Maine legislature requested a federal appropriation for defending the northern border.

At this stage in its history Canada was also being confronted with an occurrence far more serious than a boundary dispute: the Mackenzie-Papineau Rebellion of 1837-1838 was led by Louis Joseph Papineau in Quebec and William Lyon Mackenzie in Ontario. Both leaders eventually sought men and supplies across the American border. Theoretically the independence of Upper Canada and the Maritime Provinces might have facilitated the settlement of the northeastern boundary and led to free American navigation of the St. Lawrence, but newspapers in the cities along the North Atlantic Seaboard generally recommended neutrality rather than intervention. There were probably a number of reasons for this, but the most obvious was a feeling that the Mackenzie-Papineau Rebellion was a lost cause against overwhelming odds.

The strongest support for the Canadian insurgents in the United States came from those counties lying immediately to the south of the Canadian border. Among those cities where meetings were held were Buffalo, Oswego, Ogdensburg, and Troy in New York, Montpelier and Middlebury in Vermont, and Detroit. Yet even here moderation rather than extremism was the rule; those meetings did resolve to send

donations to the Canadian revolutionaries, but not to outfit
armed expeditions, which action would violate American neutrality laws.   Thus the governors of New York and Vermont
issued proclamations discouraging their citizens from illegal
activity.   Nevertheless, by the spring of 1838 a number of
more radical Hunters' Lodges were forming all over the
northern United States in support of Canadian independence.
The total membership of these has been estimated as high as
200, 000, but a figure somewhere in the 40, 000-50, 000 range
probably is more accurate.   Although the organization was
founded in Vermont, it held its first major convention in
Cleveland in September; among the sites of the more important lodges were the ones in that city, Rochester, Buffalo,
Lockport, Cincinnati, and Detroit.   None of these, it will be
noted, was in New England.

As conditions grew more and more tense, a number
of militants were arrested in this country, but at first it was
next to impossible for the government to secure convictions.
Beginning with 1839, though, their cause became increasingly
discredited in the East, and even William Lyon Mackenzie
himself was brought to trial, found guilty, and fined ten dollars and sentenced to eighteen months' imprisonment.   In this
connection the New York Evening Star observed that:

> The trial, conviction, and sentence of Wm. Lyon
> Mackenzie may be justly considered a triumph of
> the laws and civil government and will atone in a
> measure for that unjustifiable outbreak, that reck-
> lessness of law and public opinion, that illegal
> attack upon a neighboring and friendly power, which
> nearly drove us into a war with England, and caused
> a wanton sacrifice of human life and treasure.

Nevertheless, in Michigan and the West it was almost impossible to serve indictments against the revolutionaries, let
alone obtain convictions.   This situation was in part attributable to the influence of a large number of immigrants from
Upper Canada who had recently settled there.   In addition,
the West always had been more radical in orientation than
New England, as well as more sympathetic to revolution.

Returning to the boundary dispute, in 1838 the Maine
legislature made it known that it could not agree to the resumption of negotiations or the selection of an arbiter, while
its Massachusetts counterpart took the position that the national government lacked the authority to cede territory to a

foreign nation.   The following year the so-called Aroostook
War broke out after the Maine legislature passed an act providing for the arrest and imprisonment of trespassers; when
New Brunswick fought back, Maine retaliated by authorizing
the expenditure of eight hundred thousand dollars (a consider-
able sum then) for a military force.   Not only did President
Martin Van Buren back up Maine by sending General Winfield
Scott into the war zone, but Congress authorized an army of
50, 000 and set aside 10 million dollars for an emergency.
Congressional opinion having been united by the threat of attack, only six dissenters arose in the House, none in the
Senate.   By the end of March, though, an agreement was
reached between Maine and New Brunswick under which the
Aroostook region was to remain under the control of Maine
and the Madawaska River region under the control of New
Brunswick.

        One indication of the wide national support for Maine
in this confrontation, regardless of section, is the number of
resolutions passed by state legislatures in Maine's support:
Massachusetts, Pennsylvania, Maryland, Virginia, Alabama,
Kentucky, Ohio.   Only one of these was a New England state.
There was some criticism in the Whig journals of Boston and
New York and among commercial interests; the Boston Evening Mercantile Journal thus commented: "How like idiots or
madmen people will act in the middle of a war excitement!
What good will this mad movement do the state of Maine?"
But more prevalent was the war spirit.   In this connection
one might quote from the "Maine Battle Song, " a poem that
hardly ranks with Walt Whitman in genius of inspiration:

               We'll lick the red coats anyhow,
               And drive them from our border;
               The loggers are awake--and all
               Await the Gin'ral's order;
               Brittania shall not rule the Maine,
               Nor shall she rule the water;
               They've sung that song full long enough,
               Much longer than they oughter.

               The Aroostook's right slick stream,
               Has natural sights of woodland,
               And hang the feller that would lose
               His footing on such good lands.
               And all along the boundary line
               There's pasturing for cattle;
               But where that line of boundary is,
               We must decide by battle.

Stirred by lyrics such as these, Maine's ardent long-
ings for territory to the north were not cooled by the cessa-
tion of hostilities. In March 1840 the state legislature resolved that, unless the British government made an attempt
to settle the dispute immediately, the American government
should occupy the territory in dispute militarily; should the
latter refuse to take action, then Maine should seize the ini-
tiative. Congress itself, aware of the danger of war, passed
a fortification bill in September 1841. Here there was a
sectional division of opinion, with the northern and southern
members of the House and the Senate favoring coastal fortifi-
cations, their western counterparts a line of posts along the
northern frontier as protection against Indian attacks. As
finally executed, the measure provided for appropriations for
Fort Ontario at Oswego, Fort Niagara, Buffalo, a Lake
Champlain fort, and armed steamers on Lake Erie.

But war did not come again. A new British minister,
Alexander Baring (better known as Lord Ashburton) arrived at
Washington in the spring of 1842, while Secretary of State
Daniel Webster successfully persuaded Maine and Massachusetts not to block a compromise settlement should the Senate
approve it, even if it were not entirely to their liking. In
settling the Maine-New Brunswick boundary Webster and Ashburton formulated a division of territory that actually was less
favorable to the United States than the award which the King
of the Netherlands had made in 1831; a grant of $150,000
apiece to Maine and Massachusetts helped smooth their ruffled
feelings, as did the acquisition of navigational rights on the
St. John River. Not only were the boundaries of Vermont
and New York adjusted, but also that between Lake Superior
and the Lake of the Woods in the Mesabi Iron Range area.

Acceptable to everyone but fervent expansionists in
Maine and Massachusetts and ardent Democrats in the South
and the West, the Webster-Ashburton Treaty passed the Senate
39 to 9 on August 20, 1842. Among its critics were James
Buchanan of Pennsylvania, who complained that on three sides
Maine was now left "naked and exposed to the attacks of our
domineering and insatiable neighbor, " and Thomas Hart Benton
of Missouri, who categorized the treaty as a "solemn bam-
boozlement. " More enthusiastic was the New York Chamber
of Commerce, which personally thanked Webster; in New York,
Brooklyn, and Jersey City salvos of artillery celebrated the
news. Disappointing as the treaty was to extremists in Maine
and Massachusetts, it nevertheless marked one of the few diplomatic victories, or even semi-victories, that that perennial

loser, New England, was to enjoy during the ante-bellum
years.

The Annexation of Texas
and the Election of 1844

While New Englanders were infiltrating across the
border into Canada, Southwesterners were infiltrating across
the border into the Mexican state of Texas. In 1821, one
year after Maine became a state, Moses Austin secured a
charter from the Mexican government which set aside lands
for colonization sufficient for 200 American families. Moses
Austin died six months later, but his son Stephen F. Austin
carried on with this project. In 1824 Mexico passed a law
making Texas a state in the Mexican republic, and it also enacted legislation the following year opening Texas to colonization. The American government did make an attempt during
the Presidencies of both John Quincy Adams and Andrew Jackson to purchase Texas, but these efforts ended in failure.
Newspaper interest in Texas began to flourish around 1829,
with the Nashville Republican and Gazette publishing a long
essay on August 8 analyzing the advantages of the proposed
purchase. Among the members of Congress one of the most
prominent Texas enthusiasts was Senator Thomas Hart Benton
of Missouri, who was still smoldering in resentment at the
Adams-Onis Treaty of 1819.

Just as the United States was beginning to take an interest in Texas, the Mexican government began placing restrictions on the activities of Americans there. A law was
passed by the Mexican Congress in 1830, for example, which
both prohibited slavery and further settlement, while Stephen
F. Austin was arrested by Santa Anna on a visit to Mexico
City in 1834 and imprisoned until Christmas, remaining under
house arrest in Mexico City until July 1835. By the fall of
1835 Texas was ready to fight; the ensuing conflict witnessed
the famous Siege of the Alamo, at which David Crockett,
William Travis, James Bowie, and the entire American gar-
rison fell, and the Battle of San Jacinto, at which Sam Houston triumphed over Santa Anna. Texas now became an independent republic, with Sam Houston as President, and in July
1836 the U.S. Congress adopted a resolution calling for
American recognition. President Andrew Jackson, however,
procrastinated, and did not nominate a chargé d'affaires until
March 3, 1837, one day before leaving office; Texas sought

annexation by the United States in August of that year, but
the American government rejected her request.

   In this country the focal point of pro-Texas activity
during the mid-1830's was New Orleans, where there were
public meetings in July and October 1835. A military company also was organized in Kentucky in November. Early in
1836 Austin and a number of other Texans made a tour of
such cities as New Orleans, Nashville, Louisville, Washington, and New York. Memorials on behalf of recognition were
presented to Congress from the citizens of Philadelphia and
the legislature of Connecticut; pro-Texas sentiment was by no
means restricted to New Orleans and the Southwest. Most
leading Senators--including Clay, Webster, Buchanan, and
Benton--favored recognition. In the House, though, John
Quincy Adams led a bitter attack on recognition, charging that
it would benefit the slaveholders, and that Mexico, not Texas,
was upholding the cause of freedom. Despite the fact that
Adams himself regarded this as "the most hazardous" speech
he had ever made, he observed in his Memoirs (perhaps with
exaggeration) that it was greeted by "a universal shout of
applause" in the North. But by the beginning of 1837 many
members of Congress other than Adams, from New England,
New York, Pennsylvania, and New Jersey, were beginning to
take stands similar to that of the former President, as the
excitement over the Siege of the Alamo and the Battle of San
Jacinto began to wear off. Thus when annexation was proposed in the fall of 1837, the Texan minister in Washington
complained, "Petitions upon petitions still continue pouring in
against us from the North and East. "

   During the next half-dozen years independent Texas
considered as alternate future courses American annexation
and British protection. Great Britain was unhappy both with
southern control of its cotton supply and the American tariff
on British manufactured goods; as a result, she proposed to
Texas that in return for the latter agreeing to a British protectorate she would straighten out Texan finances, obtain
Mexican recognition of independence, and fix the Rio Grande
as the southern boundary. Despite French support for this
plan, a special convention held in Texas in July 1845 voted
overwhelmingly for American annexation.

   Back in the United States sectional attitudes towards
Texas had crystallized even farther by 1843. On March 3 of
that year, the closing day of Congress, John Quincy Adams
and a dozen other members, mostly New Englanders by birth

or ancestry, published a manifesto declaring that the annexation of Texas was a southern plot to "attempt to eternalize an
institution and a power of nature" that were both unjust. At
the state level, the legislature of Maine resolved that annexation would encourage slavery, that it was unconstitutional,
and that it would "tend to drive the states into a dissolution
of the Union"; Massachusetts later took the position that the
Congressional act of annexation was not legally binding on the
states, another New England variation on Southerner John C.
Calhoun's Nullification Doctrine.

Among the leading northern critics of annexation was
William H. Seward of New York, two decades later an expansionist Secretary of State under Lincoln, who declared:
"To increase the slaveholding power is to subvert the Constitution, to give a fearful preponderance which may and probably will be speedily followed by demands to which the democratic free labor states cannot yield and the denial of which
will be made the ground of secession, nullification, and dis-
union. " Equally unenthusiastic was Daniel Webster of Massachusetts, who while Secretary of State from 1841 to 1843
blocked positive action on Texas annexation. Nevertheless,
there were those in the North who did favor annexation, including speculators in Texas securities or lands, commercial
developers, and defenders of the national honor.

The South generally favored annexation for a number
of reasons. In the first place, there was the distinct possibility that England might ally itself with Texas in return for
the abolition of slavery there; the presence of an independent
country free from slavery on the southern border would pose
a distinct threat. Secondly, the South was losing strength in
Congress and in the Electoral College, and the admission of
Texas into the Union as a state would offset this decline.
Then there was the problem of soil exhaustion from cotton
growing in the South, which caused southern planters to seek
new lands in the Southwest. One might cite a number of
other reasons as well.

Too weak in numbers to achieve victory in Congress
through its own efforts, the South proposed to gain its objective by forging an alliance with Thomas Hart Benton and the
West. The elevation of John C. Calhoun to the Secretaryship
of State in 1844 brightened the South's prospects; Calhoun,
however, bungled matters somewhat by publicly linking the
annexation of Texas with a defense of slavery in an anti-
British tirade, thus alienating in part the antislavery Middle

West.   More sophisticated in his analysis was Robert Walker
of Mississippi, who published a letter in the press in February 1844 which took the position that slavery was self-des-
tructive, that the annexation of Texas would attract slaves
there from the rest of the South, and that from there they
would migrate as emancipated Negroes to Mexico, Central
America, and South America.   On the other hand, fear of war
with Mexico and of Texas cotton competition led a few Southerners, such as the Whig planter Waddy Thompson of South
Carolina, to oppose annexation.

On June 8, 1844 the Texas annexation treaty came before the Senate, where it received a more than two-thirds
majority--in the negative.   Only 16 Senators favored the treaty,
as contrasted with 35 who opposed it.   Except for Democrat
Levi Woodbury of New Hampshire, every New England Senator
voted nay; every southern Whig, too, voted against annexation
except John Henderson of Mississippi, as did seven Democrats in violation of their party platform.   Earlier that year
Henry Clay, the likely Whig Presidential nominee, and Martin
Van Buren, the likely Democratic Presidential nominee, also
had taken stands against annexation.   It is generally agreed
that Clay and Van Buren at an earlier date had reached an
agreement to eliminate the annexation issue from the 1844
Presidential campaign.

Despite the vote in the Senate, the opposition of Van
Buren and Clay to annexation was instrumental in denying both
the Presidency.   Handicapped by the two-thirds majority rule
that has wrecked the dreams of more than one Democratic
Presidential hopeful over the years, Van Buren lost his party's
nomination to the first "dark horse" Presidential nominee,
James K. Polk of Tennessee, who had the backing of pro-
annexation Andrew Jackson.   (Walker also played a key role
in sabotaging Van Buren's candidacy.)   Three-time loser Henry
Clay did obtain his party's Presidential nomination, but he
was edged in the general election by Polk.   Here the electoral
vote of New York was decisive, as Liberty Party candidate
James Birney took enough votes away from Clay to cost him
the state and the election.   Significantly, in a total southern
vote of more than 700, 000, Polk's majority over Clay was
less than 14, 000, strong evidence that this section was not
unanimously in favor of annexation.   As for the West, Clay
did carry Ohio, but Polk carried Michigan, Indiana, Illinois,
Missouri, Arkansas, and Louisiana; thus in this election his
own section dealt Clay's Presidential chances a mortal blow.

Faced with the impossible task of obtaining a two-
thirds majority for a treaty annexing Texas, the managers of
the cause now decided to go the joint resolution route, a much
easier though constitutionally dubious course. (Joint resolutions, of course, only require a simple majority.) One of
the leading supporters of the annexation resolution in the House
was the young Stephen A. Douglas of Illinois. Resolutions
were received from the legislatures of Vermont, Massachusetts, New Jersey, and Ohio against annexation, from those
of Maine, New Hampshire, Illinois, Michigan, Missouri, Alabama, and Louisiana in favor; there even was some talk in
Vermont, Massachusetts and New York of a dissolution of the
Union should annexation carry.

The annexation resolution passed the House on January
25, 1845 by a 120 to 98 vote, with 112 Democrats and 8
Southern Whigs in favor, 70 Whigs and 20 Northern Democrats
opposed, while an amended version cleared the House by a
132 to 76 vote on February 28. Much more narrow was the
margin of victory in the Senate, where the vote on February
27 was 27 for, 25 against. Here, as in the second House
vote, party considerations predominated over sectional ones.
Both Senators from New Hampshire, New York, Pennsylvania,
Ohio, Illinois, Missouri, Arkansas, South Carolina, and Mississippi voted in favor of annexation, both Senators from New
Jersey, Delaware, Michigan, Kentucky, Tennessee, Virginia,
and Louisiana against it. Thus the old North/South alignment
of opinion broke down on this particular vote. On March 1,
1845, three days before President John Tyler left office,
Texas joined the Union as a state; it was the last great triumph of the slavocracy.

According to Frederick Merk, it was the Walker Let-
ter--which had enjoyed a circulation of millions in newspapers
and pamphlets--that played the key role both in holding wav-
ering anti-slavery Democrats in the North to party loyalty on
the occasion of Polk's election and in switching enough votes
in the Senate to enable the joint resolution annexing Texas to
pass a half-year later. This estimate was shared by such
contemporary observers as the expansionist Democratic Review ("That letter has been more extensively read and circu-
lated, and produced a more powerful and decided effect upon
the popular mind, than any publication of any American statesman of the present day."), by Democratic elder statesman
Richard Rush of Pennsylvania, by Vice President-elect George
M. Dallas (who recommended Walker for appointment as Secretary of State), and by future President James Buchanan.

In any event, regardless of its actual impact in 1844-5, the
Walker Letter remains a significant precursor of the "safety-
valve" thesis of Frederick Jackson Turner.

The Oregon Question and Manifest Destiny

Before we turn to the circumstances surrounding the
acquisition of Oregon, let us analyze briefly sectional attitudes
towards "Manifest Destiny." Although this concept appears to
have emerged as early as the decade following the termination
of the War of 1812, the actual expression was of much later
vintage; the first individual to employ the term was probably
John O'Sullivan, who, in an unsigned editorial in the expan-
sion-oriented United States Magazine and Democratic Review
for July-August 1845, included a reference to "Manifest Destiny." The following year, on January 3, 1846, Representative Robert C. Winthrop of Massachusetts introduced the expression for the first time into a Congressional debate, proclaiming "the right of our manifest destiny to spread over
this whole continent." While the origins of the concept (as
distinguished from the precise terminology) are lost in the
mists of our past, there also is disagreement among historians as to whether "Manifest Destiny" was a widespread if not
nearly universal sentiment, or whether it was the product of
an elitist corps of propagandists. The traditional interpretation, set forth by Albert Weinberg in his Manifest Destiny,
first published in 1935, took the former position, while a
specialist on the Oregon question, Frederick Merk, published
several books during the 1960's supporting the latter hypothesis, of which Manifest Destiny and Mission in American
History is the most pertinent to our analysis.

Unfortunately, Weinberg in his study fails to set forth
an extensive breakdown of sectional attitudes towards "Manifest Destiny," so that it is necessary to rely wholly on Merk
for this data. (The employment of the latter here in no way
constitutes an endorsement of his hypothesis.) According to
Merk, "Manifest Destiny" sentiment was particularly vigorous
in the Northeast and Old Northwest, with New York City having the greatest concentration of expansionist journals in the
nation. Almost every newspaper of consequence in the city
editorialized on behalf of "Manifest Destiny" to a greater or
lesser degree: the Morning News, the Herald, the Sun, the
True Sun, the Daily Plebeian, the Daily Globe, the Evening
Post. In New York State the Albany Argus and the Atlas

preached expansion, while in New England the Boston <u>Bay</u>
<u>State Democrat,</u> the Hartford <u>Times,</u> and the <u>New Hampshire</u>
<u>Patriot and State Gazette</u> were advocates of this cause.

Equally enthusiastic were many midwestern newspapers,
including the <u>Ohio Statesman,</u> the Cincinnati <u>Daily Enquirer,</u>
the <u>Indiana State Sentinel,</u> the Chicago <u>Democrat,</u> and the
<u>Illinois State Register.</u> Merk finds Illinois to have been the
most expansionist of the midwestern states; generally speaking,
newspaper editorials from the Middle West tended to be more
belligerent than their northern counterparts on the Oregon
question and towards Mexico. Less enthusiastic was the
South, which was more concerned about Texas than Oregon,
and divided on the issue of absorbing the whole of Mexico.
One prominent southern expansionist organ, according to
Merk, was the Baltimore <u>Sun,</u> but technically (at least according to our analysis) Maryland falls into the Border State category rather than into the South. In terms of political parties, Democrats were more enthusiastic towards "Manifest
Destiny" than were the Whigs, and it was thus appropriate
that the war with Mexico erupted during the Presidency of a
Democrat.

Returning to Oregon, no less than four countries at
one time or another claimed this area: the United States,
Great Britain, Spain, and Russia. This nation concluded
agreements with the latter two countries (in 1819 and 1824,
respectively) under which they surrendered their claims to
Oregon; in 1818 England and the United States signed a convention providing for the joint occupation of the area between
the Rocky Mountains and the Pacific Ocean and between the
42nd parallel and 54° 40'. One provision of this convention
was that either party might terminate the joint occupation
agreement upon a year's notice. Three years later, however,
Czar Alexander of Russia signed a proclamation which
"sealed off" the entire northern Pacific from the Kurile Islands
off Siberia to the 51st parallel of the American continent, thus
interdicting foreign trading and fishing in this area. This
edict was an important consideration underlying the issuance
of the Monroe Doctrine in 1823.

The Russian menace faded with that nation's renuncia-
tion of its claims to Oregon in 1824, the United States Senate
ratifying this treaty by a margin of 41 to 1, but in the three
years between 1821 and that date American interest both in
and out of Congress turned towards Oregon. Western Congressmen, for example, had a resolution pushed through de-

manding information on foreign claims to the Pacific Coast. By 1822 Boston merchants engaged in the Chinese fur trade and the Massachusetts whaling interests also had begun to take militant stands on Russian expansion southwards into Oregon, and at the end of 1822 a Massachusetts Congressman came out in support of western demands for immediate action. The bill authored by John Floyd of Virginia for the occupation of the "borders of the Columbia" and a settlement there, however, did not pass the House, despite Floyd's speech describing the American "ball of Empire" rolling westward; by a 100 to 61 vote manufacturing and frontier sections united against commercial and small farming constituencies to defeat the measure. Among the more ardent "Oregonites" in the Senate was Thomas Hart Benton of Missouri, who lambasted Secretary of State John Quincy Adams for allowing Great Britain into Oregon south of the 49th parallel under the 1818 agreement in return for British continuation of American fishing rights in the North Atlantic.

Following this Congressional debate, the Oregon issue lay more or less dormant for the next fifteen years until 1838, when Senator Lewis Linn of Missouri, the colleague of Benton, introduced a new bill for the occupation of the Columbia Valley into Congress. Not surprisingly, much of the opposition to this measure came from the South; Senator William Archer of Virginia was of the opinion that Oregon was more fit to be an Asiatic than an American dependency, while Senator McDuffie of South Carolina maintained that it was so utterly useless that he would not give a pinch of snuff for the entire territory. Linn's measure did not pass at this time, nor did it when he reintroduced it in 1841. Nevertheless, although the West may have lacked the votes to enact Linn's bill, the frontier section did manage to block an appropriation bill before the House of Representatives which would have paid Secretary of State Daniel Webster's way to England. Webster had proposed that this nation relinquish Oregon north of the Columbia River to Great Britain, in return for which the latter was to pressure Mexico into selling to the United States all the land north of the 35th parallel, including the San Francisco Bay area. Designed to appeal to the commercial interests of New England, it proved anathema to the West.

By 1843 expansionists outside of Congress were holding conventions in support of their cause in such cities of the Middle West as Pittsburgh, Cincinnati, and St. Louis. The most climactic of these was the one held at Cincinnati in the summer of 1843, at which ninety-six delegates from six states

of the Mississippi Valley were present.   Far from accepting
compromise on Oregon, these delegates demanded the entire
western coast, the construction of a string of forts across
the continent, and an official reaffirmation of the Monroe Doctrine.   In 1843, for the first time, the Monroe Doctrine was
invoked in a Congressional debate on Oregon.

The 1844 Presidential election, as we have noted at
some length, pivoted on the annexation of Texas.   But Oregon,
too, was an issue to a lesser degree.   While southern "cotton" Democrats opposed any expansion into the Northwest that
would lead to war with Great Britain, Democrats from the
Middle West spearheaded the drive into that area at the Baltimore convention; the resolution they adopted there asserted
"that our title to the whole of the territory of Oregon is clear
and unquestionable; that no portion of the same should be
ceded to England or to any other power...."   Among the
leading exponents of "54°40' or fight" in Congress at this
time were such Middle Westerners as Representative Stephen
A. Douglas of Illinois and Senators William Allen of Ohio,
Lewis Cass of Michigan, and Edward Hannegan of Indiana.
According to Allen, "the United States must be a conquering
Republic, " and "...step by step we have advanced until the
idea of controlling the whole continent is what every village
voter discusses. "   Even more cosmic in his thinking was the
editor of the Western Review, who proclaimed: "Shall Democracy or shall Aristocracy be the governing principle of
the World?   That is the question which must be decided by
the settlement of the rival claims to Oregon...."

Although the final vote tally was too close to constitute
a mandate, the Democrats did win the Presidential election
of 1844 on a "reoccupation of Oregon and reannexation of
Texas" platform.   Even before Polk took office on March 4,
1845, Congress had passed a joint resolution on February 27-
28 providing for the annexation of Texas, while on February
3 the House of Representatives had overwhelmingly endorsed
an "All Oregon" bill by a 140 to 59 vote.   Of the 140 affirmative votes, 125 were cast by Democrats; of the 59 negative
ones, only 4 came from the party of Polk, all of them from
the South.   The scattering of Whig votes for the measure
came from such areas as the Ohio Valley, Pennsylvania, and
the Old Northwest.   It seemed as if the "All Oregon" forces
were on the verge of victory.

This bill, however, did not pass the Senate, and by
the beginning of the following year moderation had replaced

extremism as the key sentiment in Congressional thinking on
Oregon. The South, which never had been willing to risk war
to obtain all that territory north to 54°40', now became even
more cautious in its demands. Here the key figure was the
aging John C. Calhoun, who was able to persuade both President James K. Polk and expansionist Senator Thomas Hart
Benton to settle for half a loaf; enraged by the "treachery" of
the South, Senator William Allen resigned as chairman of the
Senate Committee on Foreign Relations, declaring of Calhoun
that "there never was a solitary grain of democracy in him
and his clannish state." Equally disturbed was Senator Edward Hannegan, who complained of the South's "Punic faith,"
charging that "if it (the Oregon territory) was good for the
production of sugar and cotton it could not have encountered
the opposition it has done...." Actually the defection of the
South should have been no surprise, for as we have demonstrated, as early as 1838 southern voices had been raised
against the "All Oregon" program in the halls of Congress.

While the commercial spokesmen for the South were
coming around to the position by the beginning of 1846 that a
compromise settlement of the Oregon question at the 49th
parallel would be adequate to safeguard their interests, their
counterparts in New York and New England were similarly
concluding that they had gone too far in backing "54° 40' or
fight." Thus in January 1846 the North American Review
characterized Oregon as a wilderness, and such New York
newspapers as the Journal of Commerce (which always had
been moderate in its attitude towards expansion), the Herald,
and the Sun began to editorialize in favor of a settlement at
the 49th parallel. One of the major targets of the Journal of
Commerce was John Quincy Adams, who had opposed the "All
Oregon" program during the lame duck session of Tyler's
Congress, but had switched his stand after Texas had joined
the Union, now feeling that there was a need for the United
States to acquire additional territory where slavery could not
flourish.

Polk's first annual message to Congress, which was
delivered on December 2, 1845, recommended the termination
of Anglo-American joint occupation, as well as claiming the
whole of Oregon. (This was before Polk was converted to
moderation.) The termination resolution, which authorized
the President to give the required year's notice, passed the
House and Senate by the decisive margin of 142 to 46 and 42
to 10, respectively, prior to Polk's signing it on April 27.
(Every Senatorial nay vote was Democratic, five coming from

the Middle West.) Originally more extreme in tone, it was
amended by southern Democrats and Whigs so as to facilitate
negotiations with Great Britain; among the leading critics of
a more moderate approach in the Senate were Lewis Cass and
William Allen. An analysis of the Senatorial vote on the
Presidential discretion provision, which passed by the narrow
margin of 30 to 24, reveals that the bulk of the nay vote
came from Democrats representing the North Central and South
Central States. Not a single Whig opposed this amendment.

Great Britain, like the United States, was also undergoing a change of heart towards the Oregon question around
this time, thanks in part to a change in ministry which brought
Lord John Russell to power. By the summer of 1846 the
British and American negotiators had worked out a treaty
which established the 49th parallel as the boundary between
American Oregon, now the states of Washington and Oregon,
and British Oregon, now the Canadian province of British Columbia. (The water boundary was not fully settled until
1873.) Polk placed this agreement before the Senate, which
advised its acceptance on June 12 by a 37 to 12 vote, and
ratified it by a 41 to 14 vote on June 15. The main opposition, as one might have expected, came from the irreconcilable expansionists of the Old Northwest, who accused Polk of
deception and betrayal; among the nay votes were those of
Cass, Hannegan, and Allen. Like the Webster-Ashburton
settlement a compromise that roughly halved the area in dispute, the Oregon treaty eased our tense relations with England at a time when the American annexation of Texas was
about to plunge the nation into the Mexican War.

Before leaving the Oregon question, it perhaps should
be pointed out that, although as a section the South favored
moderation on this issue, there was a minority there which
vigorously championed expansion. The legislature of Mississippi, for example, adopted a resolution in 1846 supporting
the claim of the United States up to 54° 40', while about
twenty members of Congress from the South were hard-core
expansionists. Thanks to the influence of Calhoun, there
were none from South Carolina; twelve were serving their
first term in Congress in 1846, four their second. Most
were small-town lawyers and farmers, and all but Henry Hilli-
ard of Alabama were Democrats who placed party loyalty first.
Among the other southern expansionists was Andrew Johnson,
the Tennessee tailor, who opined that he was for the whole of
Oregon up to 54° 40' and "far enough on the other side to
deaden the timber on beyond, that we may know where the

line is. "

Finally, let us examine the relationship between the repeal of the British Corn Laws in 1846, which had protected British grain from foreign competition, and the course of Anglo-American diplomacy on the Oregon question. As Norman Graebner has pointed out, Calhoun and low tariff advocates in the United States sought to compromise on the Oregon issue, not only to prevent a war with England but also to facilitate the acceptance of low tariff policies both here and in Great Britain. Despite general eastern and southern enthusiasm, however, the West was far from receptive; in the past it had shipped its grain to the British Isles via Canada, and now upon repeal it had to face formidable European competition. Typical was the observation of Senator Hannegan, who observed that: "Free trade I love deeply, but it will never be bought by me by the territory of my country. " This negative western reaction did not escape the British, and in closing one might quote the Washington correspondent of the Manchester Guardian, whose observation sums up most caustically western attitudes both towards repeal of the Corn Laws and compromise on the Oregon question:

> The news of Sir Robert Peel's great economical scheme has not tended to allay the zeal of the western members for war as much as might have been expected. The constituents of these gentlemen, it must be remembered, are about the most reckless and dangerous population under the sun, just civilized enough to read the paltry village newspaper, which panders to their vanity....

The Mexican War and the Polk Corollary

Even before the Senate ratified the Oregon treaty, both houses of Congress had adopted a declaration of war against Mexico. There were many areas of disagreement between the latter nation and the United States, but three issues stand out as being of primary importance: 1) the dispute over whether the Nueces or the Rio Grande was to be the southwestern boundary of Texas; 2) the suspension by Mexico of the payment of more than two million dollars in adjusted damages to American nationals; 3) the status of California, from which Mexico had expelled American settlers and barred further immigration. Mexican hostility towards the United States, of

course, had been aggravated by the American annexation of
Texas; when the Mexican government refused to receive John
Slidell, whom President Polk had sent to Mexico in an attempt to settle the major differences outstanding between the
two nations, the eventual outbreak of war became almost inevitable. After Mexican forces attacked American troops under General Zachary Taylor near Matamoros, on April 24,
1846, Polk recommended war, declaring that: "Mexico has
... shed American blood on the American soil. "

    We have previously discussed the historical evolution
of American interest in Texas, so that it is not necessary to
recapitulate here. On the other hand, a similar résumé for
California is in order. As early as 1796, a New England
vessel engaged in the fur trade arrived at Monterey, thus in-
augurating a continuing commerce, while from the early part
of the Nineteenth Century onwards New England whalers began
stopping at California ports for supplies; around 1820 New
England merchants started to purchase California cattle hides
for the shoe industry back East. Thus, as was the case with
Oregon, the commercial interests of New England played a
key role in opening up California. Similarly enthusiastic were
the agrarian interests of the West, whose press by the 1840's
was describing California as a new Eden. As was pointed
out in the section on Oregon, it was this section which blocked
Secretary of State Daniel Webster's proposal that the United
States relinquish Oregon north of the Columbia to Great Britain, in return for which the latter was to pressure Mexico
into selling to this nation all the land north of the 35th parallel, including the San Francisco Bay area.

    To some Americans, however, annexation of the entire
Southwest was not enough; as there was an "All Oregon" group
of expansionists, so there also was an "All Mexico" one,
equally committed to the tenets of "Manifest Destiny. " While
the latter brotherhood included such ardent midwestern "Oregonites" as Edward Hannegan of Indiana, Lewis Cass of
Michigan, William Allen of Ohio, and Stephen A. Douglas of
Illinois, both Senators from commercially-oriented New York
were also members, as were Sam Houston of Texas and a
number of prominent Mississippians: Robert Walker, Jefferson Davis, and Henry S. Foote. As was the case with "Manifest Destiny, " the metropolitan communities of the North
Atlantic Seaboard spearheaded the "All Mexico" drive; aside
from an interest in speculation, trade, and investment, many
of these expansionists were motivated by idealism, humanitarianism, and patriotism. Tammany Hall itself sponsored

the greatest "All Mexico" rally, a significant barometer of the prevailing climate of opinion.

On the other hand, in the South there was considerable opposition to "All Mexico," especially among the southern Whigs who represented the large slaveholders of the Lower South, and many of the leading Democrats of such Atlantic Seaboard States as South Carolina and Virginia, including John C. Calhoun. Calhoun ironically argued--aristocrat that he was--that the annexation of all of Mexico would tend to subvert our democratic institutions, while the abolition of slavery by Mexico was disturbing to a number of proslavery Southerners. Even such southwestern newspapers as the New Orleans <u>Delta</u>, the New Orleans <u>Mercury,</u> and the St. Louis <u>Union</u> sought no more of Mexico than that part north of the Sierra Madre Mountains. In the Old Northwest, one finds considerable support for the "All Mexico" movement, but with the exception of such newspapers as the <u>Illinois State Register</u> the level of enthusiasm was several degrees cooler than it was back East. (We noted in our discussion of Oregon that Illinois was probably the most expansionist of the northwestern states.) According to Frederick Merk, the "All Mexico" cause was supported with less ardor by midwestern expansionists than its "All Oregon" counterpart, while New York City Democrats were unwilling to risk war over Oregon for 54º 40', yet were uncompromising in their Mexican demands. Many such minor variations in sectional attitudes, it would seem, characterize the historical evolution of "Manifest Destiny" during this period.

One must, of course, distinguish carefully between sectional attitudes towards the "All Mexico" drive, which was a significant aspect of "Manifest Destiny," and those towards the declaration of war against Mexico. There were many moderates on expansion in every section who came to favor the latter course of action when it became apparent that it was not possible for the United States and Mexico to resolve their differences peacefully. At least at the time of the declaration of war there was general Congressional unanimity that there was no alternative to fighting; the war resolution passed the House 174 to 14 on May 11, 1846, with Ohio and Massachusetts casting five nay votes apiece. It cleared the Senate by an even more decisive 40 to 2 margin the following day, with the two nay votes cast by Whigs from Massachusetts and Delaware. Among the three abstentions was John C. Calhoun; Daniel Webster was absent.

Before long, though, support for the war began to
crumble in Congress and throughout the country as a whole,
with opposition being especially pronounced in the Northeast.
Here the Massachusetts legislature enacted a resolution declaring the war to be one of conquest, "hateful in its objects,"
and "wanton, unjust, and unconstitutional. " Even more venom-
ous was James Russell Lowell, the author of the Bigelow
Papers, who lamented: "But my narves it kind o' grates/
Wen I see the overreachin'/ O' them nigger-drivin' States. /
Ez for war, I call it murder. " New England, it must be remembered, harbored many abolitionists and peace society enthusiasts, while its high tariff manufacturing interests opposed
the enlargement of the low tariff South via expansion into the
Southwest.

The Whig Party throughout the North was sharply divided between the radicals and conservatives. In opposing
the war the former, or Conscience Whigs, charged that the
primary objective of the Polk Administration was to extend
slavery; among their ranks from Massachusetts alone were
John Quincy Adams, Charles Francis Adams, Charles Sumner,
Henry Wilson, and John G. Palfrey. More cautious (as well
as more numerous) were the Cotton Whigs, a faction that included such political leaders as Daniel Webster and such
wealthy businessmen as Abbott Lawrence and Nathan Appleton,
who were reluctant to alienate their southern counterparts by
debating the merits of slavery and to destroy the unity of the
Whig Party. Instead of emphasizing the slavery aspect, they
stressed the fraud and aggressiveness of the war.

Yet southern support for the Mexican War was by no
means unanimous, especially along the Atlantic Coast; public
opinion there was sharply divided, with southern Whigs decidedly antagonistic. South Carolina Democrat John C. Calhoun stated with reference to the declaration of war that "it
was just as impossible for him to vote for that preamble as
it was for him to plunge a dagger into his own heart, and
more so. " As for midwestern opposition, Representative
Abraham Lincoln of Illinois, unlike Calhoun at the beginning
of his national career, introduced his famous "Spot Resolution" into Congress, demanding that President Polk should
indicate the spot on which Mexico had shed American blood
upon American soil. Lincoln, however, was not representative
of the majority sentiment of his section, which alone furnished
more than half of the total number of volunteers during the
war, and had previously sent such expansionists as Douglas,
Allen, Cass, and Hannegan to Congress. In fact, Lincoln

failed to gain re-election. The Southwest, like the Old Northwest, also was generally in favor of war, the urge for expansion being exceptionally strong there. Summarizing the drive for annexation, John D. P. Fuller has concluded that: "... the chief support for the absorption of Mexico came from the North and West and from those whose pro-slavery or anti-slavery bias was not a prime consideration. "

As polling techniques had not been invented in 1846, it is impossible for us to cite percentages measuring sectional attitudes towards the Mexican War. Nevertheless, an examination of the number of troops which each section furnished is highly revealing. According to Henry Hubbart, Illinois rounded up five times as many volunteers as pro-slavery South Carolina. William Dodd, moreover, points out that the whole North from Maryland to Maine, with a population of 9, 300, 000, sent only 27, 000 soldiers to the front, while the Southwest, with a population of less than ·5, 000, 000 cheered more than 45, 000 troops into battle. Similar statistics are set forth by John Hope Franklin, who notes that Tennessee answered a call for 3, 000 men with 30, 000, thus exceeding its quota ten times. In contrast, New York furnished only 1, 700 troops, while Massachusetts sent only one-seventh as many men as Louisiana. Even if one challenges the accuracy of some of the above statistics, the general trend is nevertheless apparent.

Sectional attitudes towards the Mexican War were complicated even further by the Wilmot Proviso, which Representative David Wilmot of Pennsylvania introduced into the House on August 8, 1846, prior to the flowering of the "All Mexico" movement. In brief, Wilmot's amendment to a military appropriation bill provided that any territory acquired from Mexico should be closed to slavery. Although his amendment never passed the Senate (it did clear the House, thanks to strong northern support), it had a profound impact on the course of American history between that date and the Civil War. The South had been thrown on the defensive, and John C. Calhoun countered with a series of resolutions on the slavery question, which he introduced into Congress on February 19, 1847. By this time many Southerners had begun to conclude that, Wilmot Proviso or no Wilmot Proviso, slavery could not exist in California and New Mexico, and as a result "All Mexico" sentiment never firmly established itself in the South. This lessening of enthusiasm was reflected in the peace settlement with Mexico that came before Congress the following year. On the other hand, the Northern aboli-

tionists' appetite for Mexican territory was whetted by the
possibility of adding this area to the Union without increasing
the number of slave states, an outcome not previously anticipated by them.

In the Fall of 1847 President Polk dispatched Nicholas
P. Trist on a secret mission to Mexico in an attempt to negotiate peace. On November 16 Trist received an order from
Washington notifying him of his recall, but he stayed on there
nevertheless, eventually signing a treaty with Mexico at Guadeloupe Hidalgo on February 2, 1848. Incensed by Trist's in-
subordination, Polk grudgingly submitted the treaty to the
Senate for consideration, as its terms were reasonably favorable to the United States, if not more so. Trist had secured
the entire Southwest minus the later Gadsden Purchase for the
United States, at a cost of only 15 million dollars, plus
American assumption of the adjusted claims of its citizens
(totalling $3, 250, 000) against the Mexican government. The
Rio Grande, moreover, was established as the southern
boundary of Texas, thus settling a long-standing dispute.

Less enthusiastic was the five-man Senate Committee
on Foreign Relations, which included among its members such
prominent figures as Daniel Webster, Thomas Hart Benton,
and Edward Hannegan. This body reported the treaty without
recommendation, whereupon Polk observed that "Mr. Webster
is for no territory and Mr. Hannegan is for all Mexico, and
for opposite reasons both will oppose the treaty. " When the
Guadeloupe Hidalgo document was before the Senate, expansionist Senator Jefferson Davis of Mississippi proposed an
amendment annexing the greater part of Tamaulipas and Nuevo
Leon, the whole of Cohuila, and a large part of Chihuahua to
the United States, but his proposal lost 44 to 11. Texas was
the only state which cast the votes of both its Senators in
favor of this amendment, which received only one vote from
the entire South Atlantic Seaboard, that of a Florida Senator;
as we have already pointed out, the "All Mexico" drive waned
in the South following the introduction of the Wilmot Proviso.
On the other hand, an attempt by Senator George Badger of
North Carolina to exclude New Mexico and California from
the annexed area was defeated by a 35 to 15 vote, with four
Democratic Senators from New England, much to the disgust
of Daniel Webster, voting in opposition. Finally, an attempt
by Senator Roger Baldwin of Connecticut to include the Wilmot
Proviso in the treaty failed by 38 to 15, twelve northern Whigs
and three northern Democrats casting the entire affirmative
vote.

Unlike the vote on the Wilmot Proviso amendment, which was highly sectional, the vote on the ratification of the treaty (38 in favor, 14 in opposition) was neither partisan or sectional. There were those like Webster who opposed it because the United States had acquired too much territory; others, like Benton and Douglas, opposed it because the United States had acquired too little territory. Twenty-six Democrats and twelve Whigs voted in favor of the treaty, seven Democrats and seven Whigs against it. Seven of the fourteen votes in opposition to the treaty came from the Old Northwest and Missouri, four from New England and the Middle Atlantic States. Such examples as these illustrate the danger of generalizing in black and white terms about the division of opinion on the Guadeloupe Hidalgo document.

As President Polk did not choose to run for re-election in 1848, it is impossible to interpret the results of the election held that fall as a mandate on his handling of the Mexican War and related issues. The Democrats instead nominated Lewis Cass as their candidate, whose enthusiasm for expansion has been thoroughly noted, while the Whigs selected military hero Zachary Taylor of Louisiana as their standard-bearer. A third party entry was former President Martin Van Buren, who ran on the Free Soil Party ticket and deprived Cass of New York's 36 electoral votes, as Liberty Party nominee James G. Birney had similarly done to Henry Clay four years earlier. Significantly, the Presidential vote in 1848 did not divide along sectional lines, as Taylor carried eight slave states and seven free ones, while Cass carried eight free states and seven slave ones. Like the Senatorial vote on the Treaty of Guadeloupe Hidalgo earlier that year, the election returns revealed none of the confrontation of sections that would characterize Presidential voting a dozen years later.

FOR FURTHER READING

Unquestionably the most comprehensive study of the flowering of anti-war sentiment in New England and elsewhere after the War of 1812 is Merle Curti, The American Peace Crusade 1815-1860. This should be supplemented by such works as the survey by James Truslow Adams, New England in the Republic 1776-1850.

Of all those books that touch upon the American acquisition of Florida, Charles C. Griffin's The United States and the Disruption of the Spanish Empire is particularly useful, although the pertinent data is scattered; Hugh C. Bailey's "Alabama's Political Leaders and the Acquisition of Florida" also merits inspection, despite its much more limited scope. For American interest in Cuba, see Arthur P. Whitaker, The United States and the Independence of Latin America 1800-1830; for American interest in Haiti, consult Rayford W. Logan, The Diplomatic Relations of the United States with Haiti 1776-1891.

The two volumes by Griffin and Whitaker likewise contain a great deal of information on emerging American interest in Latin America, with Whitaker being especially helpful on commerce, but here again there is little consecutive treatment of sectional attitudes. The authority on the Monroe Doctrine, of course, is Dexter Perkins, who has penned three rather specialized volumes covering the years 1823-1826, 1826-1867, and 1867-1907, as well as a more recent survey volume (later revised) bringing his treatment of this topic up to date. Also of value is the article by Stanley L. Falk, "Some Contemporary Views of the Monroe Doctrine." With regard to the 1826 meeting at Panama, one should turn to the Perkins Monroe Doctrine volume for the years 1823 through 1826, and to Ralph Sanders' article, "Congressional Reaction in the United States to the Panama Congress of 1826."

As for the Aroostook War and the Webster-Ashburton Treaty, one may find a great deal of information on both in James Morton Callahan, American Foreign Policy in Canadian Relations, and in Albert B. Corey, The Crisis of 1830-1842 in Canadian-American Relations. Similarly useful is David Lowenthal's article, "The Maine Press and the Aroostook War." Those interested in sectional attitudes towards the Webster-Ashburton Treaty should consult the summary by Thomas A. Bailey in his A Diplomatic History of the United States.

Unlike most of the topics discussed in this bibliographical note, where several books or articles may be cited as basic sources, the treatment of sectional attitudes towards the annexation of Texas presented in the narrative was pierced together from the rather limited accounts that appear in a dozen or so books. For early American interest in Texas, see James Morton Callahan, American Foreign Policy in Mexican Relations (not to be confused with his previously mentioned volume on Canada), and George Lockhart Rives, The

United States and Mexico 1821-1848. Generally speaking, the
Rives work is perhaps the most useful one on this subject,
but there is a rather extended summary in Wayne S. Cole,
An Interpretive History of American Foreign Relations. The
Walker Letter is treated at length in Frederick Merk's recent
Fruits of Propaganda in the Tyler Administration.

    Although Albert Weinberg's Manifest Destiny was long
the classic work in its field, it lacks an extended treatment
of sectional attitudes. Consequently, one must turn to three
books published by Frederick Merk during the 1960's: Manifest Destiny and Mission in American History; The Monroe
Doctrine and American Expansionism 1843-1849; and The
Oregon Question: Essays in Anglo-American Diplomacy and
Politics. As we have noted, Merk's basic interpretation of
"Manifest Destiny"--that it was the product of an elitist corps
of propagandists--is a highly controversial one. There is material on early American interest in Oregon in such works as
Samuel F. Bemis' John Quincy Adams and the Foundations of
American Foreign Policy and William A. Williams' American-
Russian Relations 1781-1847, and on the Oregon question during the years of its greatest intensity in the last of the three
books by Merk listed above, as well as in the study by Norman Graebner, Empire on the Pacific. Merk's volume is also
valuable for its treatment of the repeal of the Corn Laws,
while John Hope Franklin in his article, "The Southern Expansionists of 1846, " examines a somewhat neglected phenomenon.

    Early American interest in California is touched upon
by Callahan in his Mexican study, and by Merk in his The
Monroe Doctrine and American Expansionism 1843-1849.
Merk's Manifest Destiny and Mission in American History contains an extended discussion of the "All Mexico" drive, while
John D. P. Fuller's The Movement for the Acquisition of All
Mexico 1846-1848 focuses on this phenomenon; Rives' volume
is especially useful for its analysis of the Wilmot Proviso and
the Treaty of Guadeloupe Hidalgo. For the Polk Corollary
and the proposed annexation of Yucatan, see the Monroe Doctrine monograph by Perkins for the years from 1826 through
1867, and the last-mentioned work by Merk. An old article
which nevertheless includes a great deal of interesting material is that by William E. Dodd, "The West and the War
with Mexico. " A much more recent effort on the war is the
chapter by Merk in Dissent in Three American Wars.

CHAPTER 3

FROM THE MEXICAN WAR
TO THE CIVIL WAR

Introduction

In the dozen years between the ending of the Mexican War and the election of 1860 the Democrats retained control of the Senate, achieving a two-thirds majority during the last half of the Pierce Administration. Despite the fact that the Whigs had begun to disintegrate following the Presidential election of 1852, the newly established Republicans outnumbered the Democrats in the House the last two years of the Pierce Administration and the last two years of the Buchanan one. A complicating factor was the nativist American Party, whose 43 members played a key role in the House during the 34th Congress (1855-7) and who remained a factor of some consequence there down to the Civil War. No party, in fact, had a clearcut majority in the lower house of Congress during the last half-dozen years prior to the outbreak of conflict, a factor which in conjunction with the collapse of the party system and a string of weak Presidents led to a breakdown of national unity.

Three of the most important treaties ratified during this period were the Clayton-Bulwer Treaty of 1850 with Great Britain providing for the joint construction of a canal across Central America, the Gadsden Purchase of 1853 from Mexico ceding the area south of the Gila River to the United States, and the Elgin-Marcy Treaty of 1854 with Great Britain establishing commercial reciprocity with Canada. While the Whigs backed the Clayton-Bulwer Treaty, approximately one-third of the Senatorial Democrats opposed it; support for this treaty was strongest in New England and the Middle Atlantic States, with the opposition coming almost entirely from the South and Middle West. On the other hand, the South unanimously favored the Gadsden Purchase; here partisan opposition was more equally balanced. As for the Elgin-Marcy Treaty, unfortunately for purposes of analysis there was no official roll-call, although one unofficial tally placed the vote at 32 to 11.

While a dozen or so Senators opposed each of these treaties, an 1858 commercial treaty with China passed the Senate unanimously, as did the 1854 and 1857 treaties with Japan. The only Far Eastern treaty during this era, in fact, against which votes were cast was the 1858 one with Japan; here two Southern Democrats and one New York Republican bolted the majority to oppose it. In the case of Europe, a resolution congratulating the French on their revolution of 1848 won unanimous Senatorial approval, as well as an over-whelming endorsement from the House, aside from a scatter-ing of die-hard Whigs. Various resolutions favorable to the Hungarian revolutionary Louis Kossuth also passed Congress several years later by lopsided margins. Generally speaking, the Democrats tended to be more friendly to Kossuth than the Whigs, with Southerners casting most of the nay votes against these resolutions. A far more significant defeat for the South was the successful attempt by a minority bloc of Republicans from the North and West to prevent the Thirty Million Dollar Bill for the purchase of Cuba from coming to a vote in 1859. Republicans also cast two-thirds of the nay votes when the Senate rejected by an 18 to 27 vote in 1860 the McLane-Ocampo Treaty with Mexico providing for transit privileges, but here it was New England that led the opposition with 10 nay votes.

Following the outbreak of the Civil War Southern Sena-tors and Representatives withdrew from Congress, leaving the North in control of that body along with the West, and en-abling those sections to write into law measures whose pas-sage the South had blocked the previous decade. The black republics of Liberia and Haiti were finally recognized in 1862, while an 1862 treaty with Great Britain regulating the slave trade was ratified by the Senate without dissent. An 1864 treaty with Japan dealing with indemnities likewise won unani-mous Senatorial approval. Thus, despite the fact that a num-ber of Northern Democrats remained in Congress during the Civil War, some of them War Democrats and some "Copper-heads," and despite the fact that some of the majority party Republicans were moderates and some radicals, the Lincoln Administration managed to obtain a surprising degree of un-animity from Congress on at least several diplomatic issues during the Civil War years. More controversial was the measure repealing the Elgin-Marcy Treaty, which passed the House in 1864 by a margin of only 85 to 57 before clearing

the Senate by a more substantial 33 to 8 vote the following
year.   Even in this case there was no marked political or
sectional opposition, although New England was unanimously
favorable to repeal.

Cuba, Nicaragua, and Mexico

During the decade between the ending of the Mexican
War and the beginning of the Civil War, southern imperialists
turned their covetous eyes towards Cuba, Nicaragua, and
Mexico, hoping to add these Spanish-speaking nations to the
United States.   But the mountain labored and brought forth a
mouse.   All the South had to show for its efforts by 1861 was
the Gadsden Purchase of December 30, 1853, under which
Mexico agreed to cede a rectangular strip of territory in the
Mesilla Valley south of the Gila River for 15 million dollars
(later reduced to 10).   This area now constitutes the southern
portions of Arizona and New Mexico.   The Gadsden Purchase
definitely had a southern flavor, as the area bought was under
consideration as part of the route for a railroad to the Pacific,
and Gadsden himself was a prominent railroad man as well
as our minister to Mexico.   Antislavery agitators attacked
the treaty in the Senate, as did Senator Thomas Hart Benton
of Missouri, who quoted "Kit" Carson to the effect that "a
wolf could not make a living upon it. "   Nevertheless, with
unanimous southern backing the U. S. Senate approved this
document by a vote of 33 to 13, while its Mexican counterpart also endorsed it; Santa Anna, who was back in power
again in Mexico, was in need of the money.

In our discussion of the Mexican War we pointed out
that in the South there was considerable opposition to "All
Mexico, " especially among the southern Whigs who represented the large slaveholders of the Lower South, as well as
among many of the leading Democrats of such South Atlantic
Seaboard states as South Carolina and Virginia, including
John C. Calhoun.   One important reason for this restraint
was that many Southerners were convinced that Wilmot Proviso or no Wilmot Proviso, slavery could not exist in California or New Mexico.   On the other hand, slavery was still
flourishing in the Spanish island colony of Cuba, and continued
to do so until 1886, Cuba being the next-to-the-last nation in
the Western Hemisphere to abolish slavery.   It has been noted
that as early as March 1820 the St. Louis Enquirer published
an article declaring that the acquisition of Cuba by the United

States was essential to the preservation of the Union, while
in August 1819 a Philadelphia editor suggested that this nation
should seize the West Indies island. Even those who did not
advocate annexation, including such an unlikely pair as John
Quincy Adams and John C. Calhoun, recognized the commercial significance of the "Pearl of the Antilles. " A general
movement in the South for the annexation of Cuba, however,
did not materialize until a much later date.

According to Basil Rauch, the suppression of the revolutionary Conspiración de la Escalera in Cuba during 1844
polarized sectional sentiment in this country towards this
West Indies island. As Rauch has pointed out, "La Escalera
made the apparition of a Negro republic under British protection and dangerously close to the cotton states seem real and
imminent. The South consequently became the chief advocate
of annexation.... " It was at this time that John C. Calhoun,
who had just been sworn in as Secretary ,of State, complained
to Great Britain about the latter's sworn objective of effecting
universal abolition.

During 1845 Senator David Yulee of Florida introduced
a resolution into the United States Senate providing for the
purchase of Cuba, but withdrew this before it came up for
debate, having seen that this was an idea whose time had yet
to come. A similar proposal was offered by Representative
Robert Smith of Illinois the following year in response to a
public meeting in Springfield, again without success. Within
three years, though, annexation had won the backing of such
ideologically divergent Senators as Jefferson Davis of Mississippi, Lewis Cass of Michigan (a northern annexationist who
was a "doughface"), and Stephen A. Douglas of Illinois, as
well as such southern cabinet members as Secretary of the
Treasury Robert J. Walker and Secretary of the Navy John
Y. Mason. New York trading, shipping, and financial interests also cast eager glances at Cuba, the New York Sun initiating its annexation campaign in 1847. Thus in 1848 the Polk
Administration made an attempt to buy Cuba for 100 million
dollars, while Franklin Pierce's Secretary of State, William
L. Marcy, authorized Pierre Soule to offer Spain as much as
130 million dollars for its island colony. Less enthusiastic
were the two intervening Whig administrations; thus Zachary
Taylor's Secretary of State, John M. Clayton, took the position that "should Spain desire to part with the island, a proposition for its cession to us should come from her. " While
such a stand may have been acceptable to the northern and
southern commercial wings of the party, it hardly reassured

many southern slave holders.

Frustrated in their attempt to annex Cuba legally, southern expansionists now turned to the Cuban revolutionary and adventurer, Narciso Lopez. This ill-starred individual attempted to launch three filbustering expeditions against Cuba in 1849, 1850, and 1851, respectively. The first of these was blocked from leaving by President Zachary Taylor, while the second was driven back after a landing at Cardenas; even more disastrous was the final one, which led to the defeat, capture, trial, conviction, and execution of Lopez, William Crittenden of Kentucky, and some 50 other southern volunteers. One hundred and sixty-two additional supporters (half of whom were Americans) were eventually released by the Spanish government after Congress had voted a $25, 000 indemnity for the wrecking of the Spanish consulate at New Orleans by an angry mob.

Examining sectional attitudes towards Lopez, it is not surprising that practically all of his support came from the South. John C. Calhoun was one of his more enthusiastic advocates, while Governor John A. Quitman of Mississippi, of whom we will hear more later, also strongly backed him. Among those states that contributed regiments in the Spring of 1850 were Mississippi, Kentucky, Louisiana, and Texas; a special school for military tactics was established in Arkansas, while a Georgia contingent was equipped by the governor with arms from the state arsenal. New Orleans also was a focal point of filibustering activity, organizational meetings for the third expedition being held there, in several communities in Florida, and in Savannah, Georgia, during the winter of 1850-1851. An attempt to enlist support in New York City by John O'Sullivan, the prominent expansionist, and Louis Schlesinger, a Hungarian refugee, fizzled when the district attorney seized the filibustering steamer Cleopatra and arrested O'Sullivan, Schlesinger, and several others in April 1851. Lopez, it should be noted, showed little interest in this northern recruiting, having set up his third expedition as basically a southern operation.

And it was the South that protested most loudly and lamented the most bitterly when Lopez met with defeat and death. We have referred previously to the wrecking of the Spanish consulate in New Orleans; the Courier of that city trumpeted: "American blood has been shed. It cries aloud for vengeance ... blood for blood! Our brethren must be avenged: Cuba must be seized. " Likewise, at Mobile an in-

furiated mob was barely restrained from assaulting the crew
of a Spanish ship that had just arrived in port, while at Baltimore a procession of mourners burned in effigy the American consulate at Havana. On the other hand, the defeat and
death of Lopez also resulted in many one-time southern enthusiasts for the annexation of Cuba becoming more skeptical
and restrained towards this project. Thus Ambrosia Jose
Gonzales, a friend of Lopez, noted a waning of interest on
the part of John C. Calhoun, who now felt "that the Cuba
question would draw the minds of the people from an internal
to an external issue and would threaten to divide them even
more. " W. J. Sykes published an article in De Bow's Review
which argued that 1) Cuba could not become a slave market
since she had sufficient slaves; 2) the island would offer
commercial rivalry to the Gulf States; 3) the slavery controversy would be worsened; and 4) the North would attempt to
take Canada.   Louisiana sugar planters remained fearful that
annexation would ruin them until John Thrasher had a long
letter published in 1854 offering arguments to the contrary.

        Nevertheless, annexation sentiment in the South still
persisted, despite the above defections.   Governor P. O. Herbert of Louisiana, for example, sent a message to the state
legislature in 1854 on the "Africanization of Cuba, " blaming
this agitation on British abolitionists.   The foreign relations
committee of the state senate followed suit with a report, and
the Louisiana legislature itself adopted a resolution calling
upon the federal government to take the necessary and appropriate steps to thwart this movement towards "Africanization."
Even more militant was former Governor John A. Quitman
of Mississippi, a self-proclaimed Don Quixote, a "knight
arrant of old" taking up arms "to redress the wrongs of the
weak and helpless. " In 1853 Quitman visited New York,
Philadelphia, Baltimore, Washington, and other cities, soli-
citing assistance for an expedition of liberation.   It is not
known how many individuals enlisted their services on behalf
of his cause, although one terrified Ohioan wrote the British
Prime Minister, Lord Palmerston, in September 1854 that
Quitman proposed to raise 200, 000 men, of whom 150, 000 had
already been enrolled.

        More effective as a spur to annexation was the sense
of national indignation that followed in the wake of the seizure
of the American merchant vessel Black Warrior by authorities
at Havana on February 28, 1854.   It was charged by the latter
that there was an error in the Black Warrior's manifest.
Among those who most strongly favored a firm stand against

Spain was the American minister to that nation, Pierre Soule
of Louisiana. Soule met with John Y.
Mason of Virginia,
the American minister to France, and James Buchanan of
Pennsylvania, the American minister to England, at Ostend,
Belgium on October 9 at the instruction of Secretary of State
William Marcy to formulate a policy relative to the acquisition of Cuba. Soule and Mason, it will be noted, were
Southerners, while Buchanan was a southern sympathizer.
The so-called Ostend Manifesto (which was dispatched from
Aix-la-Chapelle) provided that the American government should
attempt to purchase Cuba, but if this effort failed, "then by
every law human and divine, we should be justified in wrest-
ing it from Spain, if we possess the power." When Marcy
received his handiwork with little enthusiasm, Soule resigned
on December 17.

      The Ostend Manifesto, however, was not published un-
til March 3, 1855. As one might expect, editorial reaction
was sharply divided along North/South lines. In the North
only the Philadelphia Pennsylvanian supported the plan wholeheartedly, describing it as "a dignified and powerful paper, "
while even in expansionist New Orleans journalistic sentiment
ranged across a broad spectrum. Perhaps the most vehement
critic of the document was Horace Greeley, editor of the New
York Tribune, who opined afterwards that:

            The coarseness, the effrontery, and the shameless-
            ness of the Ostend Manifesto seemed to carry the
            world back to the days of Attila or Genghis Khan,
            and to threaten the centers of civilization and re-
            finement, the trophies of art, and the accumulations
            of wealth with a new irruption of barbarians from
            the remote, forbidding West.

      As for editorial partisanship and the Ostend Manifesto,
it is noteworthy that only one Whig journal (the New Orleans
Bee) supported it, while many Democratic organs attacked it.
One prominent northern Democratic member of Congress who
favored the annexation of Cuba was the "doughface" expansionist, Lewis Cass of Michigan, who valued Cuba for its
strategic position, but insisted that the transfer be made with
honor. From the purely practical point of view, too, this
was a most propitious time for the United States to issue the
Ostend Manifesto, since England and France were involved in
the Crimean War at this time, and thus were in no position
to come to the aid of Spain.

Following the turmoil over the Ostend Manifesto, the attention of the expansionists shifted to Nicaragua and the activities of the "Grey-eyed Man of Destiny, " William Walker. Unlike Cuba and like Mexico, Nicaragua had abolished slavery, but in the eyes of a number of Southerners there was no reason why it could not be re-established; Walker, in fact, revived slavery in Nicaragua in 1856 during his brief Presidency. In this connection the New Orleans Louisiana Observer noted the following year that:

> A civilized people may exterminate their inferiors and reduce a once savage region to order, but a barbarous people can never become civilized without the salutary apprenticeship which slavery secures. It is the duty of civilized nations to furnish masters to savages. The exodus from bestial barbarism to enlightenment is through slavery, and the sooner civilized men learn their duty and their right the sooner will the real progress of civilization be resumed.

Walker's apprenticeship in filibustering had been served in Lower California, which he made an unsuccessful attempt to seize in 1853. Shifting his base of operations to Nicaragua two years later, then divided by civil war, he managed to subjugate the Central American nation and set himself up as a dictator, becoming President in July 1856. Back in the United States, President Franklin Pierce rather tardily issued a proclamation against the invasion, while railroad magnate Cornelius Vanderbilt, who had obtained control of American isthmian transit interests, promoted the formation of a coalition of neighboring republics which drove Walker from power in the Spring of 1857. By the end of the year, though, Walker had raised a new expedition in the United States and had landed at Greytown, although this time it was the American navy which brought his filibustering activities to an end. Like Lopez in Cuba, Walker launched still a third expedition; like Lopez, he was captured, tried, convicted, and executed when his third expedition failed.

As was the case with Lopez, too, the roots of Walker's support were firmly anchored in the South. Thus when his first expedition composed of fifty-eight men sailed from San Francisco in May 1855, a notice in the New Orleans newspaper was quite open and frank, but an advertisement in a New York one was vague and mysterious: "Wanted--ten to fifteen young men to go on a short distance out of the city."

Walker's second expedition was composed mainly of volunteers from the South and the Southwest; prior to his third expedition demonstrations were held on his behalf in Memphis and Louisville, and recruiting was promoted in Mobile, Nashville, Savannah, and Charleston. (Walker also received a warm but brief welcome in New York City.) In February 1858 the Alabama Legislature chartered the Mobile and Nicaragua Steamship Company, while in March of the same year the Southern Emigration Society began operations, with branches in Alabama, Mississippi, South Carolina, and other southern states. Despite these varied and widespread expressions of support for Walker in the South, we also should note that a number of prominent southern Congressmen, including John Slidell of Louisiana and Lucius Q. C. Lamar of Mississippi, did uphold the right of the American government to arrest Walker.

When Walker met his death in 1860, most of the southern press wept for its hero. Less moved were such northern newspapers as the Washington Daily National Intelligencer, which commented on September 26, 1860, upon learning of his execution:

> He has created a deep distrust of all North Americans throughout the entire Isthmus. Our Government is regarded as ambitious, deceitful, and treacherous by those who, before General Walker visited them, looked upon our Republic for imitation. He has prepared the way for the predominance of European, particularly English, influence from the Gulf of Panama to the southern boundary of Mexico. It is well that expeditions with such results should end.

Of greater permanent significance was the Clayton-Bulwer Treaty of 1850 between the United States and Great Britain. This provided for the joint construction of an unfortified canal through Central America at some unspecified point; a half-century later the American government was to renegotiate this agreement, building a canal through Panama on its own and then fortifying it. Despite the fact that in the latter half of the Nineteenth Century this proved to be one of the most unpopular treaties ever ratified by the United States the Clayton-Bulwer Treaty did pass the Senate by the rather comfortable margin of 42 to 11. Southerners cast five nay votes and Midwesterners also five; among the more vocal critics was Stephen A. Douglas of Illinois, the leader of the

faction bent on driving the British completely out of Central
America.

Several years before the outbreak of the Civil War,
there was also a revival of expansionist interest in Mexico.
President James Buchanan's December 1858 message to Congress, in fact, expressed a desire for the United States not
only to assume a protectorate over the northern part of Mexico, but also to purchase Cuba. In February 1859 this southern sympathizing chief executive requested authorization from
Congress to use the armed forces to prevent "lawless violence" from obstructing the transit route across Central
America, while in December 1859 he requested an invasion
of Mexico to restore order there. One of the leading supporters of Buchanan's Mexican policy was Sam Houston, who introduced a bill into the United States Senate in 1858 to establish a protectorate over Mexico, and who in 1859 as governor
of Texas asked the federal government to supply him with
military equipment for 5, 000 rangers, ostensibly to counter
Indian depredations, but actually to form the nucleus for an
invasion force. Despite the fact that slavery had been abolished in Mexico, a number of Southerners were attracted to
that nation by its mineral resources; throughout the 1850's
De Bow's Review had published article after article on Mexico
and particularly about its mines. At the start of the Civil
War, moreover, Confederate troops marched into New Mexico
with the intention of swinging south to take Sonora, Chihuahua,
Durango, and Tamaulipas, and the Confederate government
entered into negotiations with Santiago Vidaurri, the strong
man of Coahuila and Nuevo Leon, in an attempt to bring
northern Mexico into the Confederacy. Unfortunately for the
South, both of these projects came to naught.

Buchanan's proposal to annex Cuba, repeated also in
his messages of December 1859 and December 1860, met with
as little success as his plan to establish a protectorate over
northern Mexico. John Slidell of Louisiana did introduce a
"Thirty Million Dollar Bill" into the Senate in January 1859,
but the Republicans of the North and West (who held only 20
of the 62 seats) were able to keep the measure from coming
to a vote. In addition, Buchanan's assertion that the annexation of Cuba would lead to the termination of the African
slave trade alienated some Southerners.

During the tumultuous Presidential election of 1860 both
wings of the split Democratic Party advocated acquiring Cuba,
Northern Democratic Presidential nominee Stephen A. Douglas
proposed to extend his concept of "popular sovereignty" to the

West Indies island. Nevertheless, the newly elected Republican chief executive, Abraham Lincoln, refused to accept the
Crittenden Compromise, which would have permitted slavery
in all territory "now held or hereafter acquired" south of 36°
30', while the newly independent Confederacy was forced to
disavow all designs on Cuba in its attempt to obtain European
recognition and assistance. By the time of the outbreak of
the Civil War, too, a number of Southerners were becoming
suspicious that Buchanan's support of Cuban annexation was
based on ulterior motives; thus a Charleston Mercury editorial
of February 26, 1858 entitled "The Red Rag of Cuba for the
South" stated that the various annexation proposals were
"pleasing deceits--baits manufactured for party purpose--to
quiet the South in the progress of the North to mastery in the
Union. "

If the Civil War did not secure the annexation of Cuba,
Nicaragua, and Mexico for the South, it did enable the federal
government finally to obtain the recognition of the black republics of Haiti and Liberia, southern Congressmen no longer
being able in their absence to block the passage of the necessary legislation. One of the main reasons that the South had
opposed American participation in the Panama Congress of
1826 was that it feared the latter would be sympathetic towards
Haiti; at the time of the fight over the "Gag Rule" in the
House of Representatives a dozen or so years later, John
Quincy Adams introduced numerous petitions from both merchants and abolitionists on behalf of recognition. When the
Dominican Republic revolted from Haiti in 1844, the insurgents
went to great lengths to represent themselves to the United
States as a white population struggling to escape from Negro
domination.

But recognition was not obtained at that time, and by
1854 such northern newspapers as the New York Tribune and
the New York Evening Post, both of which were hostile to
southern filibustering, published editorials opposing the recognition of the Dominican Republic and the annexation of Samana
Bay. Even in 1862 both Senators from the border states of
Kentucky and Delaware opposed the recognition of Haiti, but
the temporary Spanish occupation of the Dominican Republic
(at the invitation of the latter) posed a sufficient threat to enable Charles Sumner of Massachusetts to rally his forces and
obtain the recognition of both Haiti and Liberia during that
year. By the end of the Civil War (1865) revolt and fever
had dampened Spanish interest in the Dominican Republic as
it had Napoleon's imperialistic dreams two generations pre-

viously, and Madrid withdrew its forces without a confrontation with the United States.

Canada and Reciprocity

        Hardly had the excitement died down following the termination of the Mexican War, with the United States acquiring an enormous bloc of land in the Southwest under the Treaty of Guadaloupe Hidalgo, than sentiment for expansion into Canada began to mushroom at various points along the northern boundary. Among those backing this movement were the legislatures of New York and Vermont; the latter resolved in 1849 "that the peaceful annexation of Canada to the United States, with the consent of the British Government, and of the people of Canada, and upon just and honorable terms, is an object in the highest degree desirable ‚to the people of the United States. " Commercial organizations in such cities as New York and Boston also were not adverse to the idea, while there was great enthusiasm for this project in the area surrounding Minnesota, which desired both a lowering of freight rates and access to Canadian waterways. Among ethnic groups the French-Canadians were especially active, setting up a society in Woonsocket, Rhode Island which favored the political union of the two countries, with lesser bodies in Nashua, New Hampshire and Worcester, Massachusetts. Nevertheless, one does not find the reckless willingness to risk war that so frequently manifested itself in the disputes over the Maine and Oregon boundaries earlier in the decade. Expansion northwards by now had become tempered with moderation.

        Less enthusiastic were the slave states of the South, which favored the annexation of Cuba, but opposed that of Canada. In 1848 a bill was introduced into Congress providing for commercial reciprocity between this nation and Canada; although it passed the Canadian Parliament and the United States House of Representatives, it bogged down in the United States Senate, thanks in part to poor management, thanks in part to the hostility of the South. J. C. Wescott of Florida, in fact, virtually accused his southern colleagues of banding together against it, many of the latter apparently being of the opinion that reciprocity would constitute the first step to annexation. Yet one also found protectionists in the North, especially in the Whig Party and among the coal and lumber magnates.

By 1854, however, negotiations between the American
and Canadian governments had progressed to the point where
it was possible for the former to present a reciprocity measure to the United States Congress which contained provisions
that appealed to every section.   Thus the North American Review commented that "Sectionalism vanished for the time, and
the act swept through Congress, with an irresistible enthusiasm,
of which our history affords no parallel." Considering the
sectional tensions that heightened the debate when the Kansas-
Nebraska Act of 1854 was under consideration, the smooth
sailing that the Elgin-Marcy Reciprocity Treaty with Canada
enjoyed is in retrospect even more surprising.   (It passed
the Senate by an official vote of 32 to 11.) Far from blocking its passage, as it had done in the case of the reciprocity
proposal of 1848, the South strongly backed the 1854 measure.
According to Ephraim D. Adams:

> In 1854 it was Southern opinion that carried through
> Congress the reciprocity treaty with the British
> North American Provinces, partly brought about,
> no doubt, by a Southern fear that Canada, bitter
> over the loss of special advantages in British mar-
> kets by the British free trade of 1846, might join
> the United States and thus swell the Northern and
> free states of the Union.

Actually, when one examines the provisions of the
treaty, it is not surprising that southern leaders such as
John Mason and Robert Toombs cooperated with northern
leaders such as Stephen A. Douglas and William H. Seward
in effecting its passage.   Among the items included on the
free list were such southern specialties as rice, pitch, tar,
turpentine, and tobacco.   To further consolidate southern
backing, the British legation gave a ball from which the company went home "pleased with each other, themselves, and
the rest of mankind." (The British Consul in Charleston
labored mightily on behalf of reciprocity.) But the lumbermen of Maine also benefitted from the treaty, as they were
allowed free passage for their lumber down the St. John River,
while the fishermen of New England (who had spearheaded
the movement for the negotiation of a reciprocity treaty) won
reciprocal free access to the fisheries of the Atlantic Coast
north of 36º.   As for the Old Northwest, it won the opening
of Canadian canals and waterways in return for the free navigation of Lake Michigan.   The Elgin-Marcy Reciprocity
Treaty was to run for a minimum term of ten years, after
which either party might terminate it on a year's notice, a

provision which appealed to those who preferred a "trial run" type measure to a more permanent one.

Within three years, though, Canadian complaints against the American cod fishing bounty had mounted to the point that an unsuccessful attempt was made to introduce a bill into Congress repealing the act of 1816 which had established this system. Both the legislature of Massachusetts and that of Maine opposed this effort. A similar measure did pass the Senate by a 30 to 24 margin in 1858, with only four Senators from the Northeast voting in its favor, but it did not clear the House at this time. Nor did the proposed repeal make any further progress through Congress while the Canadian Reciprocity Treaty was still in effect.

By the time of the outbreak of the Civil War a movement was under way, centered in the East, to terminate or to alter drastically the Elgin-Marcy Treaty. The New York legislature, for example, requested a new set of terms which would render trade "reciprocally beneficial and satisfactory, as was intended and expressed by the treaty"; interests in this state apparently were upset at the construction of the Grand Trunk Railway. On the other hand, James W. Taylor of Minnesota affirmed in 1860 that public opinion west of Buffalo was opposed to termination, and during the same year a committee of the Chicago Board of Trade praised the treaty, complaining that the opposition had been "fostered by railway monopolies to force trade over their routes to the seaboard."

The anti-treaty movement nevertheless continued to gather momentum in this country, and during the Congressional session of 1863-1864 three bills were introduced pertaining to the Elgin-Marcy document. New Yorker Elijah Ward's measure would have authorized the appointment of a commission to negotiate a new treaty, while Vermonter Justin S. Morrill's would have terminated the treaty at once; still another bill, Joint Resolution No. 56, left the latter to the discretion of the President. The boards of trade of such border cities as St. Paul, Milwaukee, Chicago, Detroit, Cleveland, and Ogdensburg still favored ideal reciprocity, however, and Isaac N. Arnold of Illinois spoke on behalf of the Canadian treaty in the House of Representatives. On the other hand, Portus Baxter of Vermont sarcastically proposed the establishment of "a commission to arrange terms for continuing, in a dignified position, the wet nurse of the sick British colonies." Another New England defector was Frederick Pike of Maine, who asserted that he wanted the treaty "to draw its last breath as soon as possible, " declaring that Maine's fishermen derived little profit from the inshore fisheries.

Although at least at the inception of the Civil War Canadian public opinion was pro-Northern, many Northerners resented England's recognition of the Confederacy as a belligerent power and the building of ships there destined for use by the South. To make matters even worse, a local magistrate in Montreal released the Confederate St. Albans Raiders late in 1864, contrary to the wishes of the Canadian government. When the repeal measure, which had cleared the House 85 to 57, came up for a final vote before the Senate, it passed by a decisive 33 to 8 margin, with only three northwestern Senators opposing it; American farmers were obviously resentful about Canadian peas and other crops. (The low-tariff South, of course, was absent from the balloting.) President Abraham Lincoln signed the bill into law late in March, and reciprocity came to an end a year later. The Republican Party, it must be remembered, had won the Presidency in 1860 with a platform that included a protective tariff plank, and since then the southern voting bloc (which had supported reciprocity in 1854) had been absent from Congress.

While reciprocity was dying, annexation talk was again flourishing, with Minnesota spearheading the movement to acquire Indian lands in the Red River Valley. But there was annexationist sentiment back East, too; the consistently annexationist New York Herald, for example, talked of seizing the British provinces as "compensation" for the loss of the South, asserting that the United States would become a third or fourth-rate power if it did not annex Canada. (James Gordon Bennett was a bitter Anglophobe.) Other prominent supporters of "compensation" included Charles Sumner of Massachusetts, Chairman of the Senate Foreign Relations Committee; Senator Benjamin Wade of Ohio; Salmon P. Chase of Ohio, Secretary of the Treasury; Governor Andrew of Massachusetts; and Cassius M. Clay of Kentucky, soon to be minister to Russia. How "sincere" this annexation talk was is subject to dispute. According to Robin W. Winks, "In 1864 the Republican Party used annexationism to secure the Irish vote, and in 1865-1866 annexationism was a means of reconciling the West and New England to the abrogation, engineered by the protectionist Middle Atlantic states, of the reciprocity treaty. " But despite the fact that quite a few individuals apparently exploited the annexation issue for personal political gain, there were a number of genuine expan-

sionists, especially in Minnesota. Thus it came as no surprise that William H. Seward was loudly applauded when he
delivered a speech in St. Paul in 1860 affirming that this city
would be the ultimate seat of power in North America. Such
is the stuff of which dreams are made.

The Pacific, Africa, and Commerce

While American merchants were engaging in commerce
with Europe, the West Indies, Latin America, and the Pacific
Coast, they also were actively trading with Hawaii, China,
and Africa. Among the Atlantic Coast ports that played a
leading role in the East Indian trade were Salem and Boston,
Providence, a few of the towns of Connecticut, New York City,
Baltimore, and Norfolk. Of these ports, New York City
could claim the distinction of the first completed voyage,
while Philadelphia for a while had the largest tonnage, although eventually the trade tended to concentrate in the former
port. During the early national period, moreover, both
Pennsylvania and New York adopted protective duties in support of the China trade, and by 1791 the federal government
itself had begun to extend favors to this particular commerce.

The trade pattern between the Atlantic Seaboard and
the Far East did sometimes vary, but probably the most basic
one had New England ships picking up furs from the Indians
along the Pacific Northwest coast, and after a stopover in the
Hawaiian Islands for provisions, then proceeding to Canton
where they exchanged these furs for the products of the Orient. Significantly, Hawaii itself, despite the fact that it was
not an American possession, soon became a gathering place
for American expatriates; the Pacific Northwest had yet to be
settled, while California remained in Mexican hands. After
1820 New England missionaries, led by the Congregationalists,
began arriving in Hawaii. Imbued with a sense of the "white
man's burden, " these missionaries later played an important
part in the revolt at the end of the century, which led to
American annexation shortly thereafter.

By this time, too, sandalwood had begun to replace
furs (which were becoming scarcer) as the principal item in
the cargoes of the traders, but by the close of the decade
the sandalwood commerce also experienced a decline, thanks
to a deterioration in the quality of this product. After 1830
American whalers came to play a more and more important

role in Hawaiian economic life.   In 1834, on the other hand,
the Russian American Company began a movement to exclude
American vessels from Alaska (then still in Russian hands),
while further south the Hudson's Bay Company attempted to
effect the same objective for the coastal area between Alaska
and California.   By this time, however, American settlers
had begun to pour into the Willamette Valley of Oregon, thus
opening up a new trade between the Pacific Northwest and
Hawaii; lumber, salmon, and wheat from the former were exchanged for sugar and hides from the latter.

Despite the enthusiasm of New England traders, whalers, and missionaries for increased American contacts with
Hawaii, the Pacific, and China, the South remained lukewarm,
if not hostile.   Admittedly President James Monroe of Virginia had taken steps in 1820 to use the United States navy to
protect and extend American commerce in the Pacific, but in
1829 Senator Robert Hayne of South Carolina, a states' rights
advocate who also engaged in a famous debate with Daniel
Webster during that year, made a report which attacked a
proposed naval expedition to the Pacific.   A quarter of a century later, in 1855, the "sugar cane" Senators from Louisiana, Judah P. Benjamin and John Slidell, led a movement in
the Senate to block passage of a reciprocity treaty with Hawaii,
which would allow sugar to enter the United States duty-free.
For the remainder of the century, Louisiana spearheaded the
movement against the annexation of Hawaii.

Following the acquisition of California from Mexico
under the Treaty of Guadeloupe Hidalgo in 1848, San Francisco
succeeded Honolulu as the commercial and financial center of
the northwestern Pacific.   Nevertheless, American interest in
Hawaii continued.   According to a report dated January 26,
1850, "about 150 Americans from San Francisco have landed
at Honolulu within the last six weeks, many of them with the
intention of purchasing land and settling on these Islands."
The following year, Samuel Brannan attempted to emulate
Narciso Lopez and William Walker by mounting a filibustering
expedition against Hawaii.   When Brannan, who was a political
power at the Golden Gate, arrived aboard the Game-Cock on
November 15, 1851, though, the Hawaiian government boy-
cotted him, and his filibustering effort fizzled.

Two years later, in 1853, the legislature of Washington Territory passed a resolution stating that "great advantage
would result to this Territory and to the United States of
America, by the annexation of the Sandwich Islands."   Rumors

also began to circulate that new filibustering expeditions
against Hawaii were being organized in California. Even back
East there was some enthusiasm for Hawaiian annexation; the
New York Herald, for example, declared: "Let us have the
Sandwich Islands, small pox, missionaries, volcanoes, and
King Kamehameha, admitted into the Union without delay."
Perhaps the strongest advocate of annexation in Congress was
Representative Israel Washburn of Maine, who stressed the
commercial and naval importance of Hawaii, and the immi-
nent danger of its seizure by some other power.

A decade previously American involvement in China
had reached a climax with the signing of the Treaty of Whangia
in 1844; sometimes known as Cushing's Treaty, it contained
both extraterritorial rights and most-favored-nation clauses.
Between 1839 and 1842 England and China had been involved
in the First Opium War, and under the Treaty of Nanking
(1842) the victorious British wrung certain concessions from
the Chinese, many of which were extended to the Americans
two years later. New England traders and missionaries long
had been active there; in 1840 the merchants of Boston and
Salem presented a memorial to Congress suggesting that the
time for sending an envoy to China had not yet come, but
that a naval force should be sent there sufficient to protect
American interests. This group, along with a number of New
England Whigs, also was active four years later at the time
of the Treaty of Whangia. As Wayne S. Cole points out in
his An Interpretive History of American Foreign Relations,
Massachusetts spearheaded the drive for increased American
involvement in China:

> Abbott Lawrence, a Whig Representative from
> Massachusetts, submitted a memorial from Ameri-
> can merchants in China asking Congress to provide
> naval protection and a trade treaty with China.
> Secretary of State Daniel Webster of Massachusetts
> wrote President Tyler's message urging Congress
> to appropriate the necessary funds. The chairman
> of the Committee on Foreign Affairs who led the
> move in the House of Representatives was John
> Quincy Adams of Massachusetts. The man appointed
> to lead the mission was Caleb Cushing, a Whig and
> the son of a shipowner from Newburyport, Massa-
> chusetts.

In breaking down the geographical origins of the first
United States consular officers in China, one finds that ten

came from Massachusetts, eight were from New York, three
from Pennsylvania, and two each from California, Connecticut, and Maryland.

Nevertheless, it is quite significant that the treaties
which the United States negotiated with various Far Eastern
nations during the middle third of the Nineteenth Century encountered little, if any, sectional or partisan opposition. The
1833 commercial treaty with Siam won unanimous Senatorial
approval, as did the abovementioned Treaty of Whangia and
the 1858 commercial treaty with China with its new and more
sweeping most-favored-nation provisions.   Commodore Matthew C. Peary's treaty of 1854 opening up Japan to the United
States likewise passed the U. S. Senate without a dissenting
vote; this also was the case with the convention of 1857, which
obtained for this nation various extraterritorial rights, and
the convention of 1864, which committed the Japanese government to pay an indemnity of $3 million after a Japanese
feudal lord at the Straits of Shimonoseki had fired upon a
number of foreign ships.   Only the commercial treaty of 1858
encountered scattered Senatorial opposition in the form of
three nay votes.

New England likewise assumed a key role in the opening up of Africa commercially.   In 1788 both Rhode Island
and Massachusetts passed legislation making the slave trade
illegal; following this, a number of New England vessels began engaging in legitimate trade along the west coast of Africa.
The outbreak of the Napoleonic Wars aided the growth of
American commerce there, as it tended to remove their
British and French competitors from the scene.   After the
termination of this conflict in 1815, American West African
trade continued to flourish, despite British and French resentment.   Around the middle of the Nineteenth Century the
main cargoes of New England traders for this market were
tobacco, rum, cheap cottons, guns, and ammunition, with
palm oil being the most important West African export.

Even more important, the merchants of Salem led the
movement to open up Zanzibar, a small but commercially
important island off the eastern coast of Africa, from 1825
onwards; Salem was able to dominate this commerce because
the waters of Zanzibar were not suited to large craft, and
its own small and shallow harbor could accomodate only small
vessels.   The first American consul to Zanzibar was Richard
P. Waters of Salem; of the first twenty American consuls to
Zanzibar, all but four came from Massachusetts, most of

them from Salem. The United States enjoyed a thriving commerce with Zanzibar for a generation, American calico or
cotton cloth being traded for African ivory (legally) or slaves
(illegally). Following the end of the Civil War, though, there
was a sharp decline in American interest in, and commerce
with Zanzibar, in part due to the growing Anglo-German rivalry there with its concomitant shouldering aside of the
Americans, in part due to the replacement of small clipper
ships by large steamships unsuitable for the Zanzibar-Salem
run.

The South, too, was interested in Africa prior to the
Civil War, but for different reasons. Although there was
considerable sentiment for African colonization in the southern
states, southern members of Congress managed to block recognition of the black republic of Liberia from 1847 down to
1862, by which time the South was out of the Union. There
also was some enthusiasm in the South for the re-opening of
the slave trade, which peaked at several conventions held
there during the 1850's, but even the Confederacy dared not
take this step for fear of alienating possible European support.
Unlike abolitionist New England, the ante-bellum South was
forced to view Africa through the eyes of a slave society
whose attitudes were colored by a generally defensive stance
on the race question, if not by subconscious guilt feelings.
During the Civil War, in 1862, the U. S. Senate unanimously
approved a convention with Great Britain effectively stifling
the trans-Atlantic slave trade, thanks to its provision for the
mutual right of visit and search.

European Revolutions and Wars

In 1848 a series of revolutions shattered Europe, breaking the generation-long stranglehold of conservatives on government there, even ending the political career of Metternich
in Austria. Among the other countries affected were Germany, Italy, and France. This time Louis Philippe was
driven from power instead of being elevated to it; the victorious alliance of republicans and socialists, however, was
shattered when the latter was repressed. "In every section
of the United States, " observes Merle Curti, "the early republican phase of the revolutions was generally greeted with
sympathy and even enthusiasm. " Monster mass meetings
celebrating their outbreak were held in such cities as Boston,
New York, Philadelphia, Baltimore, Washington, Richmond,

New Orleans, and Cincinnati.   Among the factors underlying
American support were a hatred of monarchy, a love of republicanism, a belief in national unity and self-determination,
and a desire for trade.

On the occasion of an earlier uprising--the French
Revolution of 1830--a majority of Americans both North and
South viewed the event with approval as a step in the direction of democracy.   At that time public opinion in this country
was particularly receptive to the news of foreign revolutions,
as western frontier democracy had swept to power nationally
in the Presidential election of 1828 with the triumph of "Old
Hickory, " Andrew Jackson.   The French Revolution of 1848,
in contrast, fell approximately in the middle of the twenty-
year conservative era that bridged the gap between the Jack-
sonian era (1829-1841) and the Civil War and Reconstruction
era (1861-1877).   Thus it is not surprising that enthusiasm
in the United States was more restrained than it had been in
the case of its 1830 counterpart.   Donald C. McKay, who has
studied American relations with France over the years, observes relative to the three French revolutions of 1830, 1848,
and 1870 that:

> It is worth noting also that the three revolutions
> were received with diminishing public interest, re-
> flecting a certain feeling of skepticism concerning
> the usefulness of repeated revolutions and a certain
> growing sophistication in this country, which in
> some quarters was even willing to admit that mon-
> archic rule might be a good thing under certain
> conditions.

Skepticism was especially pronounced in the increasingly conservative South, which was alienated by the temporary
victory of the socialists in France and by the more permanent
abolition of slavery throughout the French Empire in 1848.
This, it will be remembered, was the South of John C. Calhoun rather than that of Thomas Jefferson.   Thus the Southern Whig J. P. Kennedy wrote a British friend in April 1848:
"You see that gentlest of suckling doves, the mob of Paris,
sacking the Tuileries; and for the sake of sentiment and the-
atrical effect, bearing away the throne to burn it at the base
of the column of July ! !"   As for Calhoun himself, this exponent of a "Greek" democracy led by a master class lamented: "Indeed, I have no hope, that (France) will ever be
able to establish any government deserving to be called a re-
publick. "   Exuberant at the failure of the reform-minded

Chartists to gain power in England, Calhoun looked upon that nation with its relatively rigid class structure as the chief bulwark of Europe, although he also entertained high hopes for German federalism. With regard to the latter, Calhoun was of the opinion that it would be a mistake to base the new German constitution on national unity, the German states being too highly diverse for such an approach.

Likewise, in the case of New England, one encounters numerous criticisms of the new French regime. Such intellectuals as Edward Everett and George Ticknor feared privately that "the revolution will prove no boon for France and Europe." Equally unenthusiastic was Daniel Webster, an Anglophile; like Calhoun, the New England statesman was of the opinion that a constitutional government could never last long there, the rulers of France being poets and editors rather than men of affairs. The most vocal newspaper critic of the French revolution, however, was not a New England organ but the Washington National Intelligencer, formerly the official Whig paper.

A further development which lessened American enthusiasm for the French Revolution of 1848 was the elevation of Louis Napoleon to the Presidency. In this case the press of this country was generally hostile, with the New York Commercial Advertiser complaining that: "As mediocre in point of talent as he is ambitious in character, no illusion was possible respecting him, except among the most ignorant of the inhabitants of the provinces, who are stupid enough to be accessible to the grossest of deceptions." This suspicion and distrust lingered in the minds of many Americans even after Louis Napoleon had consolidated his hold on the French government. Many Hungarians particularly disliked him for his suppression of the Roman Republic, while between ten and fifteen thousand persons attended a mass protest meeting at Cincinnati in the summer of 1849. The coup d'etat of 1851 by which Louis Napoleon became Napoleon III also incurred the wrath of the American press.

Regardless of what many Americans thought of him, however, Louis Napoleon (or Napoleon III) did hold and maintain power in France for over two decades. This was not the case with an American "favorite," the Hungarian Louis Kossuth, who played a key role in the Austrian Revolution of 1848 which drove Metternich from power. Unable to crush the revolution by himself, the emperor of Austria turned for assistance to Nicholas I of Russia, who moved in and brutally

smashed the revolt. Kossuth then fled to Turkey, where he
was arrested and thrown into prison.

Fortunately for Kossuth, his noble exploits had won him
many admirers in this country, including Senator Henry S.
Foote of Mississippi, who introduced a resolution in February
1851 that passed without a roll call affirming sympathy for
Kossuth's cause and offering him transportation to this country.
Among Kossuth's other admirers in the Senate were Charles
Sumner of Massachusetts, who described him as "grandly his-
toric, a living Wallace, a living Tell," and Daniel Webster of
Massachusetts, who observed that "the world has waited for
nearly nineteen hundred years to see his like"; to Lewis Cass
of Michigan he was "the representative of a sacred cause--of
a great and glorious cause, involving human rights in every
nation of the globe." In the House of Representatives, on the
other hand, the vote on the resolution was 126 in favor to 42
against, with 38 of the negative ballots coming from states
east of the Alleghenies and south of the Ohio River.

A similar voting pattern manifested itself in the vote
on the Senate resolution introduced by Senator Foote in December 1851 providing for the appointment of a reception
committee to welcome Kossuth. According to Foote, Kossuth
was the most illustrious person, in all respects, that the present generation had produced in any quarter of the world. Of
the 6 Senators who voted against this resolution (as compared
with 33 in favor), one each came from North Carolina, Arkansas, Alabama, Georgia, Florida, and Kentucky. In the House,
a western Congressman (John Robinson of Indiana) brought up
the resolution; of the 16 votes against it, 15 were cast by
members living east of the Alleghenies and south of the Ohio
River. Still another resolution was passed by a 123 to 54
margin calling for Kossuth to appear before the House, with
48 of the nay votes again coming from the usual geographical
area. As was the case with the French Revolution of 1848,
Democrats generally were more in favor of Kossuth than were
the Whigs.

Having become increasingly conservative over the years,
the South no more favored a revolution on behalf of "oppressed
peoples" engineered by a Louis Kossuth than they did one directed by a Louis Napoleon. In contrast, northern abolitionists such as Senator John P. Hale of New Hampshire and
William H. Seward of New York strongly backed the Hungarian
cause, respectively suggesting that the United States suspend
diplomatic relations with both Russia and Austria, and grant

public lands to refugees from Hungary. Yet other abolitionists were repelled by Kossuth's failure to take a firm stand
on the slavery issue, while many Catholics were alienated by
the generally anti-clerical nature of the European revolutions.
At the state level, the legislatures of Massachusetts, New
Jersey, and Delaware passed pro-Hungary resolutions, while
that of Iowa named a county for Kossuth.

But it was the Middle West (in particular Ohio) rather
than New England which gave Kossuth his warmest reception
when he was touring the United States in the winter of 1851-
1852. Among the American cities that he visited were Pittsburgh, Cleveland, Columbus, Cincinnati, Louisville, Indianapolis, and St. Louis. Curiously, the dying Henry Clay
showed only a lukewarm interest in Kossuth. After stopping
off at New Orleans and Mobile, the Hungarian patriot docked
at New York, after which he went on a brief tour of New
England and western New York State. According to Horace
Mann, Kossuth's midwestern tour was "one such as no Roman
Consul returning from foreign conquests and laden with the
spoils of war had ever known. "

While many liberal-minded Americans disliked both
Napoleon III of France and Nicholas I of Russia, they were
forced to choose between the two by the series of events sur-
rounding the Crimean War of 1854-1856, or otherwise remain
neutral. This conflict, an episode in which inspired Alfred
Lord Tennyson's famous poem "The Charge of the Light Bri-
gade, " flared up after a quarrel over the protection of the
Holy Places in Palestine gave the Russians an excuse to declare war against Turkey. France, Great Britain, and
Cavour's Sardinia now came to the assistance of "the Sick
Man of Europe, " and after a sharply fought campaign in the
Crimea imposed a humiliating peace upon Russia. The official position of the American government during the Crimean
War was one of neutrality, Congress not even adopting any
resolutions pertaining to the conflict. Three hundred Kentucky
riflemen, however, did ask to be sent to the Crimea.

Before examining sectional attitudes towards the Crimean War, we should point out that American newspapers as
a rule tended to be highly anti-Russian in their editorial sentiments. One reason for this was that a number of imported
and translated works on Russia by European authors were
published in the United States around this time; according to
L. Jay Oliva, without exception they presented an unflattering,
if not condemnatory, picture of the Russian Empire. On the

other hand, the American people tended to be friendly and
sympathetic towards the kingdom of Nicholas I. Aside from
a widespread dislike of Napoleon III, whose France was at
war with Russia, many Americans had yet to forgive the English for the War of 1812, while Irish-Americans harbored a
deep resentment against Great Britain which dated back cen-
turies. Thus Thomas A. Bailey has concluded that "the feeling of the American people on the whole was probably more
anti-British than pro-Russian. " As for Turkey, few Americans had strong feelings one way or another towards the Sub-
lime Porte during the 1850's, although a generation earlier
the erratic John Randolph of Virginia had defended it at the
time of the struggle for Greek independence.

Turning to the South, Andrew D. White once observed
that pro-Russian sentiment at this time was the strongest
among the pro-slavery men of the North, and particularly
among the southern states.   Southerners, in fact, felt that
their section and Russia had much in common, deeply lamenting the death of Nicholas I in 1855; one indeed might draw
certain valid parallels between Russian serfdom and southern
slavery.   In this connection we might cite the example of
Senator William H. Gwin of California, who had once represented Mississippi in Congress and hoped to see his adopted
state divided into two parts, with the southern segment to be
admitted as a slave state.   During his re-election campaign
of 1855 he made the Crimean War one of his major issues.
Southern commercial interests were admittedly somewhat apprehensive about war, as Great Britain was one of the chief
importers of southern cotton, but southern resentment against
the former country because of the latter's militant abolitionist
and anti-slave trade stance outweighed the commercial aspects
in the minds of most.   Thus a study of southern newspapers
for the years 1854 through 1856 reveals that pro-British articles were a rarity.   As was the case with its support of the
Embargo a half-century earlier, the following statistics demonstrate that the South has on more than one occasion sacrificed its economic self-interest when other considerations
seemed more important to it:

Year	Total Imports into Great Britain	Imports from the American South
1853	£895, 279, 749	£658, 451, 796
1854	£887, 333, 149	£722, 151, 346
1855	£891, 751, 952	£681, 629, 424

European Diplomacy and the American Civil War

     While Europe experienced a period of revolution in 1848 and in the years that followed, civil war did not erupt until more than a decade later in the United States. During these years the South sought recognition and assistance from England, France, and various other European powers; in contrast, the North was content with Europe remaining neutral, successfully blocking the diplomatic maneuverings of the South. A number of ships destined for service in the Confederacy, however, were built in France and England during the early part of the war, which not only inflicted considerable damage on northern shipping, but also laid the French and British governments open to damage suits following this conflict. In 1863 the North received a much-needed boost in morale when a Russian fleet paid visits to both New York City and San Francisco, Russia being the only major European power to ally itself with the Union government during the American Civil War.

     Generally speaking, as H. C. Allen points out, "the events of the war left a considerable legacy of mistrust and even hatred of Britain in the North, and of disillusion and bitterness towards her in the South." Or, as Henry Cabot Lodge observes, "The North was left with a bitter sense of wrong and outrage, and the South with a conviction that they had been uselessly deceived and betrayed." At the outset of the war, one might add, there had been conflicting attitudes in the South towards the former mother country. A close affinity between the British aristocracy and that of the South did exist, while Great Britain was the best market for southern cotton; on the other hand, the South did not care for England's militant abolitionist and anti-slave trade stance, and had largely sided with Czarist Russia against Great Britain during the recent Crimean War. In the North, apart from the commercial interests of New York City and other ports which preferred friendly relations with England, New England long had been a hotbed of pro-British sentiment, being that section which was the most opposed to the War of 1812.

     The widespread dislike of Napoleon III, which was prevalent in every section of this country prior to the American Civil War, precluded a serious erosion of his image here, as it had already hit rock bottom. The South, moreover, had not particularly cared for the French Revolution of 1848 in its earlier, more idealistic stage, while France had been the ally of Great Britain against Russia (with whom the South tended

to side) during the Crimean War. Nevertheless, there was a
certain affinity between France and the South, motivated in
part by the Latin and Catholic elements present in the latter,
in part by a similarity in temperament. Napoleon III personally disliked the North, and privately favored secession; a
divided United States would make easier the implementation of
his imperialistic schemes in Mexico. The French monarch
also was unable to rely on a pocket of pro-French sentiment
in the North, such as Great Britain had in New England.

There have been times in its history when the South
has sacrificed economic self-interest when other considerations
seemed more important to it, but during the American Civil
War many Southerners were of the opinion that cotton was
their greatest diplomatic weapon. Thus Benjamin H. Hill
once observed that "we point to that little attenuated cotton
thread, which a child could break, but which, nevertheless,
can hang the world, " while the editor of the Montgomery Daily
Post commented that: "Cotton can be made to sustain our
Government, support our army, supply our people, and secure
our independence. " Thus it is perhaps appropriate that the
standard secondary work in its field is labelled King Cotton
Diplomacy. Yet in the absence of Confederate cotton the mills
of England and France did not fold; England had a large surplus of both raw cotton and finished cloth on hand, while India
and Egypt emerged as new sources of raw cotton. The South
had lost its trump card.

While Napoleon III of France was unwilling to take the
risk of recognizing and assisting the South unless Great Britain took these steps first, he still pursued his own imperialistic designs in the New World, occupying Mexico City with
a French army on June 7, 1863, and placing Archduke Maximilian of Austria on the throne as emperor on April 10, 1864.
Public opinion in the South, it will be recalled, was divided
on the "All Mexico" issue around the time of the Civil War.
Nor was there universal enthusiasm in that section now for
the French intervention, although some Southerners regarded
it as being a possible key to their recognition by foreign
powers. Among those who backed the Maximilian plot were
former Senator William H. Gwin, who proposed that California
be annexed to Mexico, and Matthew Fontaine Maury, who had
plans for developing the Sonora mines. In contrast, the con-
demnation of Napoleon's Mexican caper was well-nigh universal throughout the North, with such newspapers as the Chicago Tribune and the New York Herald bitterly flogging the
French.

Towards the end of the Civil War, late in 1864, a fantastic scheme began to unfold in the minds of Francis Blair and other influential Northerners which would have reunited the North and the South by arranging an armistice, under the cover of which the Confederate forces would join ranks with the liberal Mexican faction led by Benito Juarez and drive the French from Mexico. General Lew Wallace proposed a similar project early in 1865. This scheme did not bear fruit, but following the end of the Civil War several thousand Confederates did emigrate to Mexico and settled there; while Confederate engineers were initiating a system of land surveys, Confederate immigration agents were active on both coasts and in the interior. Within a year, however, Maximilian had begun to sour on the colonization project; by this time, too, the Union government was in a position to place pressure on France into withdrawing from Mexico, claiming that Napoleon III's intervention constituted a violation of the Monroe Doctrine. The French withdrawal from Mexico in the spring of 1867 was followed shortly by the defeat, capture, and execution of Maximilian, who lacked the intelligence or common sense to abdicate and flee when his benefactors pulled out.

A review of sectional attitudes towards Russia, the one European power that was friendly to the North during the American Civil War, is in order here, as we have presented no extended treatment of this subject so far. It is significant that diplomatic relations between the two countries were established at the insistence of the Boston merchants, and thus had a decidedly commercial orientation for a number of years. At the time of the Napoleonic Wars there was considerable pro-Russian sentiment throughout New England, as Russia was lined up with Great Britain against Napoleonic France; the Federalists of this section, it will be recalled, had long been friendly to England, and looked upon the French Revolution with extreme disfavor. Following the War of 1812, moreover, there was also considerable enthusiasm in New England for Alexander I and his Holy Alliance, but little outside that section. Russian encroachments down the Pacific Coast from Alaska southward around this time also had a rather deleterious effect on the Russian image throughout this country, and were among the factors leading to the promulgation of the Monroe Doctrine. A generation later, at the time of the Crimean War, there was considerable pro-Russian sentiment in the South, for reasons that we recently explored.

One of these--that there were certain parallels between Russian serfdom and southern slavery--serves as a fitting

point of departure for an examination of sectional attitudes
towards Russia during the American Civil War. In 1861 Czar
Alexander II issued a manifesto freeing some twenty million
white serfs from the overlordship of their masters. Although
this action was praised by such northern newspapers as the
New York Tribune, it was attacked by such southern ones as
the Richmond Examiner, which took the position that as Abraham Lincoln was trying to free black slaves while subjugating
white Southerners, Alexander II was enslaving Poles while
emancipating serfs. Conversely, the Polish Insurrection of
1861 was greeted with little enthusiasm by the northern press;
the New York Times, for example, commented that: "the
same Czar who glorifies his dynasty by the emancipation of
45,000,000 [sic] serfs, claims additional lustre for it by be-
stowing a separate Council of State upon the Kingdom of Poland. " Many Northerners also were alienated from the Polish
cause by the sympathetic attitude taken by England and France
towards this uprising. In addition, the leading Polish propa-
gandist in this country during the 1840's and 1850's, one
Caspar Tochman, had taken the side of the Confederacy during
the American Civil War, and this had a predictable impact on
northern opinion.

During 1863 another rebellion broke out in Poland
against Russian rule. Many northern newspapers, in particular those of New York City, speculated that this uprising
would so occupy the attention of the British and the French
that it would forestall their intervention on the side of the
Confederacy. In this connection one southern newspaper, the
Petersburg Daily Express, sarcastically commented that had
the Polish Insurrection broken out ten years previously,
"every northern rostrum would have thundered with plaudits
to the gallant Poles, and every victory which they would have
achieved over the Russian forces would have awakened the
most gratifying emotions in the popular bosom of Yankeedom."
Thus, despite the aid which Kosciuszko and Pulaski had given
our government during the American Revolution, when the
Poles themselves revolted during the early 1860's, the United
States officially turned a cold shoulder to the insurgents. Especially frosty was the American minister to Moscow, Cassius
Clay, who was of the opinion that "our interests and my sympathies are on the side of Russia--liberal Russia--against
reactionary Catholic and despotic Poland. " The Central Polish
Committee did make an attempt to raise funds for their cause
in this country, but it collected only $16,000, of which half
came from the San Francisco area.

On September 24, 1863 two Russian warships made their appearance off New York City.   Unprecedented as this visit was, it was an even more welcome sight in that four French and three British warships were already present, with crews of some 5, 000 men.   Many Americans interpreted this action as an attempt by Alexander II to prevent a combined Anglo-French attack on the North, although this consideration was not the foremost one in the Russian monarch's mind; the French and the British, on the other hand, apparently were not planning to launch an attack on this country, despite the presence of their ships off New York.   Three weeks later, on October 12, 1863, a Russian fleet of six warships began to congregate in San Francisco Bay under Rear Admiral Popov, who was no stranger to the area.   This visit created less of a sensation than its New York counterpart.   Whether there was a connection between the appearance of the Russian ships off San Francisco and the existence of a pocket of pro-Polish support there (alluded to above) is not clear.

Various theories have been set forth in an attempt to explain these naval visits.   Frank A. Golder, for example, suggested in 1915 that the eruption of the Polish crisis had led the Russian government, which was faced with the strong probability of war with both England and France, to transfer its fleet to neutral ports.   Another hypothesis, more prevalent at the time of the event, was that the Russians were desirous of obtaining our friendship and forging an alliance with us.   In any event, a comprehensive survey of American newspapers by Thomas A. Bailey has revealed that the contemporary press of this nation paid less attention to the Russian presence than one might have expected from later accounts. Journalistic interest, far from being geographically uniform, noticeably waned once one crossed the Alleghenies, and news releases on the Russian fleet were not regarded as being of sufficient importance to telegraph across the mountains.

Despite this indifference on the part of the interior, delegations from various states began making their way to New York City to pay the Russian fleet their respects.   In this connection General Hiram Wallbridge declared there that: "Providence has decreed that there shall be two great hemispheres, one the Eastern and the other the Western.   The one shall be represented by Russia, and the other by the United States. " Conversely, the South was not pleased by the Russian naval visit, and some editors even drew comparisons between Alexander II and "Abraham I. " By 1864, though, when the tide of battle had begun to turn in favor of the North,

stories of Russian atrocities against Poland started to appear
more frequently in the press of that section; according to
Martin Kaufman, as a whole the American people favored
Polish independence, and under different circumstances might
have come to the latter's assistance. But regardless of the
seemingly tenuous nature of Russian-American friendship during these years, a tradition has grown up that at this time
the Russian bear and the American eagle swore eternal
friendship, and even today those desiring to thaw out the
"Cold War" frequently point back to this "Golden Age" when
these two giants were allies.

FOR FURTHER READING

          The topic of southern expansion during the 1850's has
generated a surprisingly large amount of scholarly writing.
For a general survey, John Hope Franklin's The Militant South
1800-1861 is outstanding; a more technical study worth con-
sulting is Amos Ettinger's The Mission of Pierre Soule to
Spain 1853-1855.   More leftist in orientation are Philip S.
Foner, A History of Cuba and Its Relations with the United
States, and Eugene Genovese, The Political Economy of Slav-
ery, the latter work being particularly valuable for its com-
ments relating slavery to southern expansion.   Still another
study, this one quite specialized, is Basil Rauch, American
Interest in Cuba: 1848-1855.   The more noteworthy articles
dealing with this southern expansion include Earl W. Fornell,
"Texans and Filibusters in the 1850's"; Gavin B. Henderson,
"Southern Designs on Cuba, 1854-1857 and Some European
Opinions"; Durwood Long, "Alabama Opinion and the Whig
Cuban Policy, 1849-1851"; J. Preston Moore, "Pierre Soule:
Southern Expansionist and Promoter"; and C. Stanley Urban,
"The Ideology of Southern Imperialism: New Orleans and the
Caribbean, 1845-1860. " For American recognition of the Do-
minican Republic and Haiti, one should turn to Rayford W.
Logan, The Diplomatic Relations of the United States with
Haiti 1776-1891; Ludwell Lee Montague, Haiti and the United
States 1714-1938; and Charles C. Tansill, The United States
and Santo Domingo, 1798-1873.

          Northern expansion into Canada during this period, along
with American commercial reciprocity, has generated less
scholarly writing in comparison.   Some authors touch on the
former topic, some on the latter, some on both.   Perhaps the
most extensive discussions are those found in James Morton

Callahan, American Foreign Policy in Canadian Relations; Alvin C. Glueck, Jr., Minnesota and the Manifest Destiny of the Canadian Northwest; and Lester B. Shippee, Canadian-American Relations 1849-1874. Also of value are Donald F. Warner, The Idea of Continental Union: Agitation for the Annexation of Canada to the United States 1849-1893, and Robin W. Winks, Canada and the United States: the Civil War Years. Warner plays down both northern support for annexation and northern opposition, while Winks points out that annexation talk was frequently a political subterfuge.

Turning to American commerce with the Far East, two of the best general surveys dealing with American relations there that contain material on this topic are Lawrence H. Battistini's The Rise of American Influence in Asia and the Pacific, and Tyler Dennett's Americans in Eastern Asia. For articles, one should consult Harold Whitman Bradley, "Hawaii and the American Penetration of the Northeastern Pacific, 1800-1845, " and Andrew F. Rolle, "California Filibustering and the Hawaiian Kingdom. " On the other hand, the introduction to Norman R. Bennett and George E. Brooks, Jr. , ed. , New England Merchants in Africa: A History through Documents 1802 to 1865, is especially useful for its treatment of American commerce with the so-called "Dark Continent. " This subject also is covered in the author's recently published survey of American relations with Africa, including a discussion of American attitudes towards the slave trade. Other books dealing with the slave trade include Frederic Bancroft, Slave Trading in the Old South; Sir Reginald Coupland, The British Anti-Slavery Movement; Peter Duignan and Clarence Clendenen, The United States and the African Slave Trade 1619-1862; Warren S. Howard, American Slavers and the Federal Law 1837-1862; Daniel P. Mannix, Black Cargoes: A History of the Atlantic Slave Trade 1518-1865; and James Pope-Hennessy, Sins of the Fathers: A Study of the Atlantic Slave Traders 1441-1807.

With regard to Europe, those desiring additional information on American attitudes towards the French Revolution of 1848 and Louis Napoleon should turn to the monograph by Henry W. Casper, American Attitudes towards the Rise of Napoleon III. Key articles on this subject include Merle E. Curti, "The Impact of the Revolutions of 1848 on American Thought"; Eugene N. Curtis, "American Opinion of the French Nineteenth-Century Revolutions"; and Charles M. Wiltse, "A Critical Southerner: John C. Calhoun on the Revolutions of 1848. " Curtis, who pictures Charles Sumner as pro-revolu-

tion, is in conflict with Henry Blumenthal, who portrays him
as anti-revolution. For Louis Kossuth, see Malbone W. Gra-
ham, American Diplomacy in the International Community, and
John W. Oliver, "Louis Kossuth's Appeal to the Middle West
--1852." Briefer but still of interest is the article by Curti,
"John C. Calhoun and the Unification of Germany." Among
the leading studies of American attitudes towards the Crimean
War, one might cite such articles as Horace Perry Jones'
"Southern Opinion of the Crimean War"; Howard R. Marraro's
"American Opinion on Sardinia's Participation in the Crimean
War"; and L. Jay Oliva's "America Meets Russia: 1854."
Probably the most comprehensive overview is the doctoral
dissertation of Arthur James May, Contemporary American
Opinion of the Mid-Century Revolutions in Central Europe.

One of the best brief surveys of Confederate diplomacy
is that found in E. Merton Coulter, The Confederate States of
America 1861-1865. For England and the Civil War, see
H. C. Allen, Great Britain and the United States; for France
and that conflict, Henry Blumenthal, A Reappraisal of France-
American Relations 1830-1871. The Maximilian episode is
treated by Kathryn Abbey Hanna in her article, "The Roles of
the South in the French Intervention in Mexico." Curiously,
a number of studies have appeared on American relations with
Poland during the Civil War, including Arthur Prudden Cole-
man's book The Polish Insurrection of 1863 in the Light of
New York Editorial Opinion, and the following articles: Mar-
tin Kaufman, "1863: Poland, Russia, and the United States";
Joseph W. Wieczerzak, "American Opinion and the Warsaw
Disturbances of 1861"; and, by the same author, "American
Reactions to the Polish Insurrection of 1863." For the more
important visit of the Russian fleet, see Thomas A. Bailey,
America Faces Russia and "The Russian Fleet Myth Re-
Examined"; also useful is Alexandre Tarsaidze, Czars and
Presidents.

CHAPTER 4

FROM THE CIVIL WAR
TO THE SPANISH-AMERICAN WAR

Introduction

The period between the Civil War and the Spanish-American War might be broken down in a number of different ways for purposes of analysis, but for the following discussion a four-fold division is perhaps most advisable. The era of Reconstruction (1865-77) witnessed the gradual return of the southern states to the Union; during this period Republicans and even Negroes won election to Congress from Dixie. The Republicans maintained a two-thirds majority in the Senate down to the last two years that Ulysses Grant served as President, although the Democrats controlled the House the last two years of each term that he functioned as chief executive.

Despite the fact that he escaped conviction on impeachment proceedings by only a single vote when he was on trial before the Senate, Andrew Johnson fared amazingly well in obtaining Senatorial approval for his foreign policy schemes. The 1867 treaty with Russia annexing Alaska passed the Senate with only two New England Republicans in opposition, while the 1868 Burlingame Treaty with China won unanimous Senatorial approval. During the term of his successor, Grant, the 1871 Treaty of Washington with Great Britain cleared the Senate by a 50 to 12 vote; here there were 10 Democrats opposed in a vote devoid of sectional trends. But the 1869 treaty annexing the Dominican Republic could only muster a 28 to 28 tie vote when it came before the Senate a month later. Significantly, Republicans cast two-thirds of the nay votes in another roll-call that failed to manifest a noteworthy sectional pattern, with Foreign Relations Committee Chairman Charles Sumner of Massachusetts spearheading the opposition. As for commercial reciprocity with Hawaii, an 1867 treaty negotiated while Johnson was President went down to a 20 to 19 defeat, with Midwesterners casting half of the nay votes,

all but one of which were Republican.   On the other hand, an
1875 reciprocity treaty won Senatorial approval by a 50 to 12
vote, with the Middle West again the most hostile section; here
8 opponents of the treaty were Republicans, despite the fact
that a member of their party was sitting in the White House.

The eight years that followed the termination of Reconstruction (1877-85) witnessed continued Republican control of
the Presidency.   The Democrats had a majority in the House
during six of these years, but were able to win clear-cut control of the Senate during only two, despite the fact that with
the ending of Reconstruction the Republican Party experienced
a sharp decline in political strength throughout Dixie.   During
the Hayes Administration an 1878 commercial treaty with
Samoa was ratified by the Senate without dissent, while an
1880 immigration treaty with China was approved with only
four Republicans in opposition, three of them from New England, after Hayes had vetoed a measure passed by Congress
the previous year repealing the Burlingame Treaty.   When
Chinese exclusion finally passed Congress in 1882 with Chester
Arthur President, over two dozen Senators absented themselves
on both occasions when the Senate voted on it; the second time
around the nay vote was unanimously Republican, with New
Englanders leading the opposition on both occasions and Southerners and Westerners almost unanimously favorable.   A
slightly different pattern emerged when the 1884 reciprocity
treaty with Hawaii came to a vote, as here the opposition was
almost completely divided between the Republicans and Democrats in a roll-call devoid of sectional trends such as Midwestern hostility.

As for Latin America, Democrats and Republicans like-
wise were equally opposed to the 1884 reciprocity treaty with
Mexico, which won narrow Senatorial approval with Southerners leading the opposition against its western supporters.   In
contrast, for only the second time since the Civil War the
Democrats provided the bulk of the opposition to a major diplomatic proposal when they held the 1884 Frelinghuysen-Zavala
Treaty with Nicaragua to an inadequate simple majority.
Thanks largely to the opposition of President-elect Grover
Cleveland, 14 Southerners (all of them Democrats) voted nay;
one may cite this as one of the first examples, along with the
votes on Chinese exclusion, of Southern Democratic bloc voting on diplomatic proposals.   It, moreover, antedates by a
generation American involvement in World War I and Woodrow
Wilson's Fourteen Points, when Southern Democrats played a
key role by supporting the foreign policy of only the second

Democrat to be elected President since the Civil War.

During the next twelve years (1885-97) Democrat Grover Cleveland was President for eight, but the Democrats controlled the Senate only during the first two years of his second term, although they had a majority in the House during eight of these twelve years. Unquestionably the most significant diplomatic vote in Congress during Cleveland's first term was the rejection of the 1888 Bayard-Chamberlain Treaty with Great Britain on a 27 to 30 vote. This, it should be firmly emphasized, was one of the most partisan votes in American history, all of the nay votes being Republican; it also was one of the most sectional, in that every Southerner who voted supported the treaty, while every New Englander who voted opposed it. The following year, with Republican Benjamin Harrison sitting in the White House, 12 Democrats, 7 of them from the South, made a futile attempt to block the Samoan treaty, although the 1892 fur seals treaty with Great Britain won unanimous Senatorial approval. With respect to now independent Hawaii, during the Second Cleveland Administration the Senate gave its unanimous approval in 1894 to a "hands off" resolution, but only passed a measure the following year endorsing the President's handling of the Hawaiian situation by a narrow 24 to 22 vote. Nineteen of the nay votes were Republican, and only one of them was from the South.

In the Presidential election of 1896 free silverite William Jennings Bryan seized control of the Democratic Party from "gold bug" Cleveland in a confrontation of West and South against North and East. (Bryan and Cleveland, who were miles apart on financial policy, nevertheless shared common ground in their mutual anti-imperialist stance.) Victory at the polls, however, went to the Republican nominee, William McKinley, while the G. O. P. also gained control of Congress for the next four years (1897-1901). When the 1897 aribtration treaty with Great Britain came up for a Senatorial vote two months after McKinley was sworn in as President, it failed to obtain the necessary two-thirds majority. Although the Republican nay vote was almost as large as the Democratic, sectional opposition was strongest in the South, the Great Plains, and the Pacific Coast; conversely, New England, the Middle Atlantic States, and the Middle West voted heavily for the treaty, the Northeast being pro-gold like Great Britain. The following year, when the United States annexed Hawaii, Democrats cast 17 of the 21 nay votes, over half of the latter coming from the South.

Unfortunately for purposes of analysis, there was no
official roll-call on the declaration of war against Spain in
either house of Congress, but the Treaty of Paris officially
ending this conflict barely cleared the Senate in 1899 by a 57
to 27 vote. Again, as was the case with the annexation of
Hawaii, the nay vote was overwhelmingly Democratic, with
the South again leading the opposition with 14; Democratic
President Grover Cleveland, it will be recalled, had been unfavorable to this action a half-dozen years previously. Conversely, Middle Western Republicans, who had been highly
enthusiastic about the declaration of war, were similarly favorable towards the treaty of peace acquiring the Philippines.
But within two decades this section was to execute an ideological volte face and spearhead the opposition against U. S.
entry into World War I, in one of the great opinion shifts of
American history.

Relations with Europe

As we have noted, there was a North/South division
of opinion concerning Napoleon III at the time of the American
Civil War, and it is not surprising that several years later
the North generally sided with Bismarck against him when
Prussia attacked France. Pro-Prussian sentiment was especially strong in New England. Charles Goethe Baylor, for
example, composed a poem, "America to Germany," which
began with the words "All hail: O Bible land"; then there was
Bayard Taylor, the translator of Faust, who wrote the "Ju-
bellied eines Amerikaners." Novelist Louisa M. Alcott, too,
observed in a similar vein: "I side with the Prussians, for
they sympathized with us in our war. Hooray for Old Pruss."
When Napoleon III fell from power, New York City newspaper
editor Horace Greeley sneered in the Tribune: "No fraud so
gigantic ever perished so swiftly and so utterly. The fall of
the first Napoleon seems august by comparison.... The last
Napoleon is a bad copy of his supposed uncle with the heart
and brain left out.... "

In contrast, aside from the carpetbag newspapers,
most Southerners looked upon the newly established Second
German Empire with considerable disfavor. Among their
American targets, German immigrant and Missouri Senator
Carl Schurz seems to have been their favorite whipping boy,
although the one-time revolutionary had settled in the U. S. in
1852. The Charleston Daily Courier, for example, described

Schurz as a "muddle head, " the "greatest of political scamps,"
and "that renegade ... whose head would have been chopped
off if he had remained in Prussia in 1848"; the Savannah
Morning News similarly lamented his membership on the Committee on Foreign Relations, observing that his presence there
would cause foreign powers to "look on this blatherskite as
the mouthpiece of public opinion. " Schurz's support of the
Union during the Civil War also may have been a factor in
these attacks.

Among those factors responsible for the presence of
strong pro-Prussian sentiment in this country in 1870-1871,
perhaps none was more important than the fact that there were
fifteen times as many German-born immigrants here as French
ones. As Henry Blumenthal points out, "Many of them had
volunteered in the Union army and, in contrast to France,
their fatherland had lent moral and financial support to the
Northern cause. " Like the North, too, Prussia favored national unity over sectional disunity; in this connection the
Providence Press observed that "Prussia fights for nationality, Napoleon for empire. " In addition, most Americans
both North and South were Protestants, and it was Napoleon
III, not Bismarck, who sided with the Pope, leading to the
charge that the French monarch was backed by Jesuits, ultra-
montanes, and infallibilists.

On the other hand, Napoleon III did enjoy considerable
support in the South and among the Democrats and Catholics
of every section. Thus the Chicago Times commented that
the "majority of the brains, conservatism, and decency of the
country" were in favor of France, praising French civilization and character as being far superior to Prussian despo-
tism, greed, and selfishness. Southerners also sympathized
with the French because the French were playing a defensive
role in the Franco-Prussian War, as they had done during the
American Civil War. The French in this country, if only for
the reason that they were fewer in numbers, lacked the effective organization for propaganda that the Germans possessed,
but they did set up "L'Union Republicaine de Langue Fran-
çaise" in New York City. This organization pictured the
Prussian king as the merciless conqueror of the recently established French republic.

Following the fall of Napoleon III the Third French
Republic was established. With the controversial French
monarch eliminated, public opinion in the North began to veer
in the direction of France and away from Germany, especially

after the Second German Empire had annexed Alsace-Lorraine.
In contrast, the South, which was politically more conservative than the North, received the new French republic with a
general lack of enthusiasm. The setting up of the Paris
Commune in 1871, moreover, also tended to alienate American public opinion in general from France, as its radical
character was anathema to most Americans.

It is perhaps appropriate that the few significant controversies involving the United States and various European
nations during this period were basically economic, centering
around such issues as the tariff and reciprocity. At this
time France was importing American cotton and tobacco and
exporting such luxuries as silks, wines, and brandies. The
French, who had been suffering a gradual decline in exports
to this country over the years because of high American
tariffs, especially on silk, sent a group of representatives to
the United States during 1878 in an abortive attempt to persuade us to negotiate a reciprocity treaty. Californians,
though, were fearful that reciprocity would adversely affect
their wine industry, and the San Francisco Chamber of Commerce issued a pamphlet the following year attacking reciprocity.

On the other hand, the attempt by Germany and other
European nations during the 1880's to restrict or even to prohibit the importation of American pork on health grounds alienated the hog raisers and meat packers of the Middle West,
who complained to Congress and the State Department. (Many
of these hog raisers were of German stock.) After Congress
had imposed a duty on German sugar in 1890, Germany agreed
to lift its ban on American pork the following year; in 1886
Congress had enacted legislation subjecting meats to rigid inspection before export.

As for American relations with Italy, on October 15,
1890 the police chief of New Orleans, who at that time was
investigating alleged Mafia activities there, met his death at
the hands of unknown assassins. After a number of Italian
suspects had been tried and acquitted, an enraged mob broke
into the local jail on March 14, 1891 and lynched eleven persons, three of whom were Italian nationals; the Italian government thereupon demanded an indemnity for the victims, and
the prosecution of those responsible. Unlike the unification
of Italy, this incident firmly solidified American public opinion
against Italy, regardless of section. According to the Louisville Courier Journal, "there has not been a time, since

Washington bade farewell to the Continental Army, when the people of this country were so one with themselves, and with one another, as they are at this present moment. " Not only did a number of volunteers, especially from the West and the South, offer their services to the Secretary of War, but even the rabidly anti-Southern Chicago Inter-Ocean, which had been critical of the lynchings, proclaimed that an Italian attack on New Orleans would be met by "Uncle Sam and the flag, " since "this is a Nation with a big N. " This incident was resolved peacefully the following year when the American government offered its Italian counterpart a 25 thousand-dollar indemnity, a settlement which the latter agreed to accept.

Quite different in nature was the reaction in this country to the arbitration treaty of 1897 between the United States and Great Britain, drawn up by Richard Olney and Sir Julian Paunceforte in the aftermath of the Venezuelan boundary controversy. (We will examine this dispute in our discussion of Caribbean affairs.) Initially, there seems to have been considerable support for this treaty throughout this country. Among its backers were the legislatures of Massachusetts, Connecticut, Maine, Vermont, New York, Delaware, South Carolina, Alabama, and Minnesota, as well as the Merchant's Association of Boston and the New York City and Chicago chambers of commerce; mass meetings also were held on behalf of the treaty in such cities as New York City, Boston, Philadelphia, Pittsburgh, and Cincinnati. But arbitration also had its enemies: the New York Journal and Sun, the Chicago Tribune, most Irish-Americans, expansionist Senator John Morgan of Alabama, and the silver Senators from the Rocky Mountain states. The latter were Anglophobic in outlook because Great Britain was then the leading champion of the gold standard in the entire world, and the Rocky Mountain states led the nation in the production of silver. The treaty thus mustered only a 43 to 26 majority when it came up for a final vote on May 5, 1897, a shift of three votes being necessary to effect its passage. Opposition was centered west of the Mississippi River and south of the Mason-Dixon Line.

More continuous was American interest in Russia during this period. As we have pointed out, the visit of the Russian fleet to New York City and San Francisco in 1863 was received with far greater approval in the North than in the South. When Grand Duke Alexis toured America in the winter of 1871-1872, it thus is not surprising that he encountered small crowds and restrained enthusiasm in Dixie, particularly at Memphis. Although Alexis received a rather lukewarm reception in Washington, he was greeted with a royal welcome at New York, while police had to use bayonets to hold back the crowd in Milwaukee, which boasted a considerable Russian population. Alexis also contributed to the relief of burned-out Chicago, and went on a buffalo shoot at Omaha.

By the end of the decade, though, Russian anti-Semitism was becoming an issue in the United States, gradually eroding the favorable image of the Czarist regime that had built up over the years in the North. After Theodore Rosenstrauss of Rochester, New York had experienced discrimination in his business operations upon his return to Kharkoff, Representative Samuel S. Cox of New York took up his cause (1879), while public meetings were held on his behalf in New York, Philadelphia, and other cities. From 1882 on resolutions were introduced into Congress making inquiries about discrimination against American Jews as a group in Russia, or protesting against their mistreatment. But it was not only the Jews who were persecuted there. In 1899 the Michigan legislature passed a concurrent resolution petitioning President William McKinley to come to the assistance of the Finns; this resolution attacked "the policy of the Russian Government in its present administration of the civil and military affairs in Finland." We will have more to say in the next chapter about alleged Russian mistreatment of minority groups following the turn of the century.

Lest one assume on the basis of this discussion that the United States thought of Europe only in diplomatic terms in the years between the American Civil War and the Spanish-American War, let us not forget the impact of the ethnic vote on certain Presidential elections, in particular that of 1884. Just prior to this election a certain Reverend Samuel D. Burchard made a speech accusing the Democratic Party of being the organ of "rum, Romanism, and rebellion;" this attack drove many of the Irish voters of New York into the arms of the Democratic Presidential candidate, Grover Cleveland, despite the fact that his Republican opponent, James G. Blaine, was a notorious Anglophobe. By this time a number of northeastern cities had accumulated large Irish populations. Aided by a rainstorm in upstate New York, Cleveland took the state's 36 electoral votes with a popular vote margin of 1, 143 out of a total of 1, 167, 175 votes cast, winning the Presidency over Blaine in the Electoral College, 219 to 182. The memory of Burchard's faux pas led both the Republicans and Democrats to insert planks in favor of home rule for Ireland in their national platforms both during 1888 and 1892.

The Northern Frontier

Two years following the close of the Civil War, in
1867, the United States purchased Alaska from its Civil War
ally, Russia, for $7, 200, 000; by this date the Russian Amer-
ican Company, which had ravaged its resources, was facing
bankruptcy. It is quite appropriate that Secretary of State
William H. Seward of New York was the individual who han-
dled these diplomatic negotiations, since he long had been a
devotee of expansion. As early as 1846 Seward had declared
that America's population was destined "to roll its resistless
waves to the icy barriers of the North, and to encounter oriental civilization on the shores of the Pacific. " We have
previously mentioned Seward's speech at St. Paul in 1860 advocating expansion to the North, in which he observed that the
outposts which Russia was building would yet be the outposts
of America. In Congress Seward had a powerful ally in Senator Charles Sumner of Massachusetts, who also favored the
acquisition of Alaska, not out of expansionist sentiment per
se, but because it would bring about "amity with Russia" and
would "dismiss another European sovereign from our continent. " Sumner's scholarly address in support of Seward was
widely quoted in the press, and probably had a marked effect
on the thinking of Sumner's fellow-Senators, who gave the
treaty a large majority (37 to 2) when it came up for final
passage on April 9, 1867. The southern states did not vote
on this treaty, being absent from Congress; William Pitt
Fessenden of Maine and Justin Morrill of Vermont were the
only dissenters.

Actually, American interest in Alaska had been growing since before the Civil War. Thus Senator William M.
Gwin of California, a former resident of Mississippi, suggested during the Buchanan Administration that the United
States offer Russia five million dollars for Alaska. By the
time of its purchase the inhabitants of both California and
Washington Territory had developed a vital interest in Alaska,
especially in its fisheries and fur seals; in this connection a
number of citizens of Washington Territory petitioned the
United States government to survey the fishing grounds in the
Bering Sea region, while a group of California fur traders
headed by Louis Gladstone expressed interest in acquiring the
expiring rights of the Hudson's Bay Company in Russian
America. Similarly enthusiastic were West Coast journalists.
In 1934 Thomas Bailey published an article in which he
sampled contemporary editorial opinion in six Pacific Coast
newspapers and reached the conclusion that the press of that

region was definitely in favor of the Alaska treaty.   One exception to this general chorus of approval was the San Francisco Alta California, which concluded at first that Russian
America "is intrinsically of no value to us whatever," but
began changing its tune two days later, after having done some
hasty research.

    Also enthusiastic towards the acquisition was Charles
Sumner's New England, which had a decided commercial interest in the area.   Whalers from this section, for example,
were eager for Alaskan seal furs and walrus ivory, as well
as sperm oil and ambergris.   Even more grandiose in his
thinking was Nathaniel P. Banks, Chairman of the House Foreign Relations Committee, who observed: "If this transfer is
successful, it will no longer be an European civilization or
an European destiny that controls us.   It will be a higher
civilization and a nobler destiny.   It may be an American
civilization, an American destiny of six hundred million souls."
During the Congressional debate the Boston press was almost
uniformly favorable towards the purchase, while no New England newspaper of any consequence opposed annexation.   It is
especially noteworthy, too, that no editorial at this time emphasized the possible threat of the Alaskan fishing grounds.

    Despite the fact that William H. Seward, the individual
most responsible for the negotiation of this treaty, was from
New York, his pet proposal did run into some criticism from
Horace Greeley's New York Tribune, then radical Republican
in its politics.   The Tribune made reference to "deserts of
snow" and the lobbying activities of Seward and his "Esqui-
maux ring."   "Go West, Young Man" Greeley apparently was
concerned about the adverse impact of the purchase on American relations with Great Britain, although he personally disliked both Seward and President Andrew Johnson.   In fact,
such New York City newspapers as the Independent and the
Sun also opposed the acquisition, while the World, Commercial Advertiser, Times, and Herald favored it.   Even the pro-
treaty World headlined one of its articles: "Tropical Disad-
vantages Offset by the Value of the Ice Trade--Secretary
Seward's New Ice-other-mal Line--A Great Opening for Soda-
Water Fountains and Skating Ponds."   On the other hand,
there was little journalistic hostility to Seward's treaty in
nearby Philadelphia, and the press of Washington and Baltimore was generally favorable.

    The South, too, was by no means unfavorable, a most
curious reaction in light of that section's longtime lack of en-

thusiasm for Canadian annexation. Of 16 southern newspapers examined by Richard E. Welch, Jr., only two were outright opponents of the purchase of Alaska. Such newspapers as the Louisville Daily Journal and the Memphis Daily Post justified the purchase on commercial grounds, as did the New Orleans Commercial Bulletin, which apparently had visions of an economic alliance between the Northwest and the South:

> The demands for cotton goods in the new region of the Northwest will be enormous, and there is no reason why these goods should not be manufactured in the South, thereby employing our poor and industrious population, and adding greatly to our resources ... it will be seen that the South will be greatly advanced by the acquisition and settlement of the Russian American possession.

More divided in its reaction was the midwestern press, which is also somewhat puzzling in that around the time of the American Civil War St. Paul was spearheading the drive to annex Canada. Alaskan and Canadian annexation, it would seem, were not favored by the same interests or sections. While the Chicago Evening Journal strongly approved the purchase of Alaska, the Chicago Republican was split, the editor being tepidly favorable, its Washington correspondent vehemently anti-treaty; likewise, the Cincinnati Commercial supported the acquisition, while the Cincinnati Daily Gazette did not. Generally speaking, the Alaskan treaty does not seem to have interested midwestern editors as much as it did those on the East and West Coasts.

Within a year, sectional attitudes towards Russian America began to change perceptibly. When the appropriation bill that accompanied the treaty was passed by the House, 113 to 43, on July 14, 1868, only five of the nay votes came from a trans-Mississippi state, and only one from a trans-Rocky Mountain state. Yet there was considerable opposition to the appropriation in New England, where fishing interests apparently felt threatened, and in the upper Mississippi Valley, where isolationism was on the rise. In opposing the appropriation Representative C. C. Washburn of Wisconsin observed "that we could have bought a much superior elephant in Siam or Bombay for one hundredth part of the money, with not a ten thousandth part of the expense incurred in keeping the animal in proper condition." Although the Midwest had been rather lukewarm towards the purchase itself a year previously, New England generally had been enthusiastic, and thus its reduced support for the appropriation is quite significant.

At the time of the purchase San Francisco was perhaps the West Coast city which was most interested in Alaska,
salmon fishermen becoming increasingly active in salting as
well as canning their catches there. The great gold rush of
1897-1898 into the Klondike and the Yukon, though, later
shifted the principal American connection to Seattle, which
had by this time become a railroad terminus as well as a
port. Another West Coast city interested in Alaska was Portland, which also claimed to be the natural gateway to the
North, but never was able to usurp the role of either San
Francisco or Seattle.

Shifting to neighboring Canada, two key events that
occurred in the years following the American Civil War were
the British North America Act of 1867, which established the
Dominion of Canada, and the Riel Rebellion of 1870, an uprising of the metis, or half-breed French-Canadians, under
the leadership of Louis Riel. Far from greeting the former
development with unanimous enthusiasm, American public
opinion was by no means favorably disposed to the establishment of the Dominion of Canada. The House of Representatives, in fact, even approved a resolution on March 27, 1867
attacking this measure as a violation of the Monroe Doctrine
and a step in the direction of monarchy. During the same
year, too, the legislatures of Maine and Massachusetts passed
resolutions denouncing the formation of the Dominion. When
Louis Riel revolted against the Dominion in 1870, therefore,
it is not surprising that his movement met with sympathy and
even enthusiasm, especially among the more ardent expansionists in ths country.

Any reasonably complete roster of these expansionists
would consume as much space as this discussion, but the top
rank of leaders included James W. Taylor, formerly state
librarian of Ohio and the greatest American authority on
western British America, Senator Alexander Ramsey of Minnesota, Senator Zachariah Chandler of Michigan, Representative Nathaniel P. Banks of Massachusetts, and Philadelphia
financier Jay Cooke. Although Ramsey and Chandler were
apparently motivated by commercial considerations, Cooke
was interested in the route of the proposed Northern Pacific
Railroad; in contrast, Nathaniel P. Banks supported annexation in an effort to win the votes of his Irish constituents,
introducing a bill calling for continental union into the House
on July 3, 1866 that died in his own Committee on Foreign

Affairs. Expansion sentiment was especially strong in St. Paul and in Pembina, Dakota Territory; there was at least an informal alliance on this issue between the East and the Middle West.

On the other hand, American interest in acquiring the Pacific province of Canada, British Columbia, was largely confined to the West, in particular San Francisco. Various California interests not only desired to exploit the goldfields of British Columbia, but also feared that the construction of a transcontinental railroad would have an adverse effect on American trade with the Orient, Victoria being closer to the Far East than San Francisco. Even more aggressive was the Portland Herald of neighboring Oregon, which proposed a filibuster to liberate British Columbia; unlike those of Narciso Lopez and William Walker, in the words of Donald Warner, "the expedition did not leave the columns of the paper." Nevertheless, it was a member of the House from Pennsylvania, George F. Miller--not a Pacific Coaster--who introduced a resolution proposing the annexation of British Columbia on terms mutually satisfactory to Great Britain and the United States.

In 1885 Louis Riel attempted to stir up another revolution against the Canadian authorities, centering his activities in the province of Saskatchewan; this time Riel was captured, tried, convicted, and executed. (During the same year the Canadian Pacific Railway was completed, a technological triumph which united the country.) Yet despite Riel's defeat, outpourings of expansionist sentiment still erupted in the United States on occasion. Three annexation resolutions, for example, were introduced into Congress between 1888 and 1891, although none of these emerged from committee, nor were they discussed on the floor; only ten members of Congress, who represented the border states of Maine, New Hampshire, New York, Ohio, and Michigan, expressed sympathy for expansion. In 1893 Representative Jacob Cummings of New York also introduced a pro-annexation resolution into the House, and in 1894 Senator Jacob Gallagher of Vermont followed suit in the Senate. Again, neither resolution was debated.

Thus the attempt to join Canada, or at least a part of it, to the United States, ended in failure. In retrospect, the movement never had much support in the South, while even the western and mountain states were lukewarm, aside from the agitation over British Columbia following the Civil War;

it was the East and the Middle West, and these sections alone, which showed a consistent interest in annexation. Nevertheless, it was the western and mountain states which spearheaded the actual American involvement in Canadian affairs. In this connection one might cite at least several examples: the role of Spokane as the metropolis of the "Inland Empire" in southeastern British Columbia; the processing by American smelters in Washington and Montana of the ore from the Kootenay mines; and the migration of Mormons from Utah to southern Alberta from 1887 on, where they raised sugar beets. If not in fact annexed, Canada became more Americanized.

While annexation may have eventually died out as a significant issue in Canadian-American relations, the same thing does not hold true of reciprocity. It will be recalled that the Elgin-Marcy Treaty with Canada, originally ratified in 1854, was repealed by Congress ten years later. During the following year, in 1865, a convention was held at Detroit which was to consider Canadian-American economic relations; here the 450 delegates representing cities from Bangor, Maine, to St. Paul, Minnesota, unanimously adopted a resolution urging the negotiation of a new reciprocity treaty. Congress, though, failed to take action at this time.

The abrogation of the Elgin-Marcy Treaty did have a considerable impact on the economic life of this country. Among those who suffered as a result were the gas companies of northern cities which used Nova Scotia coal, and the railroad and shipping interests of New England. Conversely, Ohio Republican Ben Wade sought to protect grindstone makers. During 1869 the Michigan legislature (which was stimulated into action by difficulties in moving western crops), the Boston Board of Trade, and the New York Chamber of Commerce came out in support of liberalized trade with Canada. Kentucky and Kansas stud farmers also wanted duty-free breeding cattle. When reciprocity was again before Congress in 1870, some members (such as William Lawrence of Ohio) supported it because it would hasten annexation, others (such as Thomas Perry of Michigan) opposed it because it would impede annexation. This example is only one of many which might be cited to demonstrate that it is impossible to separate these two issues totally.

The following year, in 1871, the Senate ratified the Treaty of Washington, which we have previously discussed relative to the Alabama claims. Aside from its other provisions, this document granted American fishermen much more extensive fishing privileges than they had enjoyed under the Convention of 1818, in return permitting British subjects to fish as far south as Delaware Bay. This was indeed a generous settlement, and was so recognized by most of the American press; even the Boston Advertiser compared the Treaty of Washington favorably with the Webster-Ashburton Treaty of 1842, concluding that: "Each treaty may be regarded as successful, but the second is much the greater success of the two. " New England fishermen, however, remained skeptical.

For the next decade the fisheries question remained in the background of American diplomacy, but by 1883 it had again become a focal point of controversy.   "... I was told by an official of the State Department, " a member of the British legation in Washington wrote in February, "that letters were received daily from the Eastern States advocating the repeal of the Articles in question on the ground that no fish worth speaking of had been caught by American fishermen in British waters for the last two years. " Led by Senator William P. Frye of Maine, Congress passed and President Chester A. Arthur signed a resolution giving notice that in two years the fisheries articles of the Treaty of Washington would no longer be binding.   In fact, on the day after the latter became inoperative, July 2, 1885, Congress passed a new tariff law imposing duties on mackerel and other fish.

Pro-reciprocity sentiment admittedly remained strong in some quarters.   The New York Chamber of Commerce, for example, adopted a resolution in November 1887 favoring an "early adjustment of the fishery question, " while the Chicago Tribune came out in support of commercial union with Canada at this time; even the Boards of Trade of Bath and Portland, from the great fishing state of Maine, expressed similar sentiments.   Nevertheless, when Senator George F. Edmunds of Vermont introduced a retaliation bill into the Senate in 1887, directing the President to ban fresh and salt fish from Canada at his discretion, in the event that American fishermen were unjustly treated, his measure passed that body by an overwhelming 46 to 1 margin.   After the Canadians had seized several American fishing boats, moreover, Representative Henry Cabot Lodge of Massachusetts, then at the beginning of his long and illustrious Congressional career, asserted: "Whenever the American flag or an American fishing smack is touched by a foreigner, the great American heart is touched. "

Dissatisfied with retaliation as a solution, President
Grover Cleveland (who signed the above measure) had his
Secretary of State, Thomas F. Bayard of Delaware, enter
into negotiations with Joseph Chamberlain, who was representing Great Britain. The result was the Bayard-Chamberlain Treaty of 1888, providing for a reciprocal tariff, and a
modus vivendi. Attacked by Republican partisans eager to
discredit Cleveland, by the Anglophobic Irish, and a number
of western Populists resentful of Great Britain's role as a
creditor nation, as well as by such spokesmen for the New
England fisheries as Senators Frye, Edmunds, and George
Frisbie Hoar of Massachusetts, this treaty mustered only 27
votes for passage (to 30 against) when it came up for a final
vote on August 21, 1888. Not a single New Englander favored
it, not a single Southerner opposed it. Among its other
critics were the once favorable New York Chamber of Commerce and the New York Board of Trade and Transportation,
which attacked it respectively on the grounds that it favored
Canada at the expense of the United States, and was unjust
and inequitable.

President Cleveland, himself now playing the game of
partisan politics to the hilt, countered with a drastic proposal
for commercial war with Canada, a move designed to appease
the Irish whom he had alienated by his support of the Bayard-
Chamberlain Treaty; the chief executive was to be given "the
power to suspend by proclamation the operation of all laws
and regulations permitting the transit of goods, wares, and
merchandise in bond across or over the territory of the United
States to or from Canada." This politically inspired measure,
which would have seriously damaged New England railroads
economically had it been adopted, fortunately never passed
Congress. In any event, the modus vivendi drawn up at the
same time as the Bayard-Chamberlain Treaty became the
basis for the use of the fisheries, and remained so until
Canada abrogated it in 1923 in retaliation against the highly
protective Fordney-McCumber Tariff which Congress had
passed the previous year.

While New England fishermen were successfully attempting to undercut Canadian reciprocity, Pacific Coasters
were complaining about the Canadian (later Japanese) poachers
who were threatening the fur seals of Alaska with extinction.
In 1886 American revenue cutters seized Canadian pelagic
sealers in the Bering Sea, while in 1889 Congress declared
American dominion over its waters. When Great Britain
charged that the American position on this question was a

violation of international law, the United States signed an
arbitration treaty with England in 1892, which the Senate unanimously endorsed, referring the question to a mixed international tribunal. That body eventually ruled in 1893 that
this nation could not claim exclusive rights to a closed sea,
assessed damages against the United States, and established
seasonal prohibitions on pelagic sealing around the Pribilof
Islands. The American eagle, now nesting in Alaska, was
not to flap its wings over a mare clausum.

The Caribbean Basin

    While expansionist Secretary of State William M. Se-
ward was casting his covetous eyes upon Alaska, he also was
formulating imperialistic projects relative to the Caribbean.
The first of these called for the purchase of the Danish West
Indies for $7,500,000, a sum comparable to that expended
on Alaska; an 1867 treaty with Denmark providing for the acquisition of the future Virgin Islands, however, languished in
the Senate, and President Ulysses S. Grant eventually abandoned it upon assuming office. On the other hand, Grant was
interested in acquiring the Dominican Republic, or Santo Domingo, now again independent from Spain, and he dispatched
his personal secretary, General O. O. Babcock, there to
make final arrangements.

    Since the close of the Civil War, the Dominican Re-
public had become increasingly attractive to American speculators and promoters. When two individuals from Baltimore
expressed an interest in the island of Alta Vela, the Maryland
legislature passed a resolution upholding their claims, as did
Pennsylvania. Grant, though, was much more interested in
obtaining the entire Dominican Republic. A number of prominent Senators and Representatives likewise favored its acquisition; among these were Senators Roscoe Conkling of New
York, Oliver P. Morton of Indiana, and James W. Nye of
Nevada and Representative Nathaniel P. Banks of Massachusetts and Godlove Orth of Indiana.

    But Congress was by no means unanimously in favor
of this project. One southern sympathizer, Representative
Fernando Wood of New York, reluctantly spoke out against
annexation on the grounds that it would add to the country's
Negro population. Even more formidable was the opposition
of Senator Charles Sumner of Massachusetts, chairman of the

Committee on Foreign Relations; Sumner, who earlier had
supported the purchase of Alaska, employed the racist argument that annexation of the Dominican Republic would menace
this nation's great heritage by "taking into this country any
of the Latin race, with its treacherous blood and its notions
of superstition and bigotry. " Sumner apparently was also
apprehensive that its acquisition might eventually lead to an
American take-over of neighboring Haiti, he having led the
fight to recognize that black republic in 1862 after years of
southern obstruction. Both Sumner and prestigious German-
American Senator Carl Schurz of Missouri also attacked the
annexation of the Dominican Republic on the grounds that Manifest Destiny should not extend beyond the North American
continent.

Although a number of Republicans favoring annexation
did come from the states of the Middle West and Far West,
this issue did not lead to a sectional division of opinion in
Congress. Nor, for that matter, did the voting split along
partisan lines, as no less than 19 Republican Senators cast
their ballots against the treaty when it came up for a final
vote on June 30, 1871, the tally being 28 in favor, 28 against.
With the exception of the New York Herald, no newspaper
that gave extensive coverage to foreign news supported the
treaty, with most of the Boston and Philadelphia press, the
Springfield Republican, the New York Tribune, and the New
York Times opposing it. In addition, one poll of Massachusetts sentiment had those interviewed nine-to-one against annexation, while the Indiana legislature passed a resolution
condemning Senator Oliver P. Morton for supporting the treaty.

Similarly abortive was the attempt to achieve com-
mercial reciprocity with Mexico. On November 26, 1876
Porfirio Diaz seized control of the Mexican government, hold-
ing power down through 1911. Two years later, in 1878, the
United States officially recognized Diaz, with the leading Congressional supporters of recognition including Senator Roscoe
Conkling and Representative S. S. "Sunset" Cox, both of New
York. At this time, too, a prominent southern member of
Congress, expansionist Senator John T. Morgan of Alabama,
began showing interest in connecting Mexico City with the
American railway system; Porfirio Diaz also encouraged
foreign investment, especially in railroads. During the following year, in 1879, Senator-to-be George Hearst of California acquired a gold and silver mine in Durango, and soon
afterwards purchased timberlands stretching from Vera Cruz
to Yucatan; in 1892 the Southern Pacific started buying up

major railroad lines in Mexico, including one extending from Piedras Niegras to Durango.

Early in 1883 a commercial reciprocity treaty was concluded by Matias Romero, representing Mexico, and Secretary of State Frederick T. Frelinghuysen of New Jersey. Romero later was the guest of honor at a gala banquet hosted by the prominent merchants of Philadelphia, while Porfirio Diaz spent three weeks on the East Coast of this country talking and socializing with railroad barons and commercial leaders. Senator John T. Morgan proclaimed that "We are ... beginning a new and greater career, hand in hand with Mexico"; reciprocity also found a strong supporter in the Foreign Mission Board of the Southern Baptist Convention, which wanted to protect its missionaries in Mexico against attacks by unfriendly Indians. But the general reaction to the treaty was by no means universally favorable. Some critics, for example, maintained that it would line the pockets of the southwestern railroads and St. Louis sugar refineries at the expense of the Treasury. Cruelly torn was Louisiana, which desired more trade with Mexico, but not at the expense of the sugar planters of the state.

When the reciprocity treaty came up for a final roll call in January 1884, sugar Democrats and protectionists were able to block its approval, but two months later a slight shift in Senatorial sentiment enabled its proponents to obtain passage, 41 in favor to 20 against. In terms of a sectional breakdown, this treaty was supported by the West, and opposed by the two Louisiana Senators and a half-dozen other Southerners, as well as by the importing, sugar refining, banking, and sea transport interests of the East. An amendment requiring implementary legislation, though, eventually rendered the treaty a dead letter; it was impossible to pass such legislation through the House of Representatives at this time, despite the efforts of such key members as Abram S. Hewitt, a low tariff Democrat from New York. In June 1886 the House of Representatives tabled the reciprocity bill by the overwhelming majority of 162 to 51, with traditionally low tariff southern Democrats supporting reciprocity and Northerners of both parties generally opposing it.

Still another project dating from this period which involved the United States and a Caribbean nation that never reached fruition was the proposed Nicaraguan Canal. In retrospect this failure is difficult to explain, as during that period there was considerable support for this project in every

section of the country. As one might expect, the leading
Congressional proponent of the Nicaraguan Canal was Senator
John T. Morgan of Alabama, who continually attempted to
pressure Congress into taking action down to the time of the
Spanish-American War, by which time the alternate Pana-
manian route had begun to gather widespread support.

Merely to list the various members of Congress, state
legislatures, prominent individuals, and private groups that
endorsed the Nicaraguan Canal at one time or another would
consume a page or two. In any event, some of those that
took an affirmative stand during the decade of the 1880's included the Chambers of Commerce of Boston, Charleston,
Denver, Duluth, San Francisco, San Diego, and Wheeling,
and the Boards of Trade of Chicago, Cincinnati, Indianapolis,
Kansas City, Los Angeles, New Orleans, Philadelphia, Portland (Oregon), Providence, San Francisco, and Savannah.
During the following decade national canal conventions were
held at St. Louis and New Orleans in 1892, a more localized
one in San Francisco in 1894. This project also was endorsed by the legislatures of California, Alabama, Oregon,
Nevada, Washington, Florida, Georgia, and Idaho. Among
the many endorsements that one might cite, that of the Virginia Organization to Promote the Nicaragua Canal is perhaps
typical; in the words of that body, it "would be of more value
and importance than a dozen Samoas or Samana Bays and
without their entanglements would ensure to the United States
as many advantages as Gibraltar and Bermuda offered Great
Britain. "

Opponents of the proposed canal seemingly were few
and far between. Among those of consequence were two New
York commercial journals, the Journal of Commerce and the
Commercial and Financial Chronicle, both regarding it as
overly expensive and potentially troublesome. At one time,
in fact, the House of Representatives voted 127 to 76 in favor
of the Nicaraguan route. On the other hand, the Frelinghuysen-Zavala Treaty of 1884, under which the United States
secured exclusive construction rights in Nicaragua, failed to
receive a two-thirds majority in the Senate, 32 Senators favoring it and 23 opposing it. Thanks largely to the opposition of President-elect Grover Cleveland, Southern Democrats
cast 14 of the nay votes.

Other factors, too, militated against the success of
this project. Prior to the emergence of the alternate Panama
route as a serious competitor, the Nicaraguan canal had a

formidable rival in the Eads ship-railway project involving
the Isthmus of Tehuantepac.   The latter scheme, in fact, had
considerable backing among the residents of the Mississippi
Valley, especially those of New Orleans and Missouri.   In
addition, it was feared that an American-built canal through
Nicaragua might violate the Clayton-Bulwer Treaty of 1850,
while the potential expense of the canal project discouraged
the economy-minded.

At the same time that these various canal and ship-
railroad projects were being debated, the American navy was
growing to formidable size.   Thus it was no longer necessary
for the United States to rely heavily on the support of the
British navy when the American government invoked the Mon-
rone Doctrine against some European power that was encroach-
ing upon the sovereignty of some Latin American country, and
even enabled this nation to stand up to Great Britain on occasion.   In 1895 England, already burdened by a number of
problems arising from its imperial ventures in Africa, had
threatened to settle by force the dispute over the gold-rich
boundary between Venezuela and British Guiana.   Successfully
proposing arbitration, Secretary of State Richard Olney observed that: "Today the United States is practically sovereign
on this continent, and its fiat is law upon the subjects to
which it confines its interposition. "   Ironically, the final
awards of the Venezuelan boundary commission handed down
in 1899 were substantially in accord with the British claims,
but the principle established by President Grover Cleveland
and Olney was none the less highly significant.

After surveying public opinion towards Cleveland's
stand vis-à-vis the Venezuelan boundary dispute, Theodore
Roosevelt wrote to Henry White: "Outside of the moneyed interests of New York and Boston, the American people, like
Congress and the press, are solidly behind the President in
defense of the Monroe Doctrine. "   On the other hand, as
Henry Cabot Lodge pointed out in a letter to a friend, Great
Britain's hostility to silver caused the South and the West to
dislike her, these two sections regarding the former mother
country as an ally of the northeastern gold interests.   "The
bottom of the trouble in recent times, " wrote Lodge, "is
England's attitude on the money question and the way in which
she has snubbed all our efforts to do anything for silver. "
Also taking into consideration the chronic Anglophobia of the
Irish, it is evident that public opinion in this country was
basically pro-England or anti-England, not pro-Venezuela or
anti-Venezuela.

Actually, as Dexter Perkins points out, sectional considerations were only of minor importance relative to support for Cleveland on this issue. "Never, perhaps in the history of American foreign policy, " writes the author of The Monroe Doctrine, "was there a more remarkable example of unanimity among the politicians than that displayed in these December days of 1895. " Among the few newspapers to criticize the chief executive were the Baltimore Sun, the Boston Herald, the New York Journal of Commerce, and the New York World, which referred to the whole affair as a "jingo bugaboo. " As for the political leaders, when the governors of 28 states were asked by the New York World to take a stand, 26 affirmed their support of the President. Governor John Peter Altgeld of Illinois did view the administration's position on Venezuela negatively, but Altgold also disagreed with Cleveland's domestic policy as well. More typical was the reaction of such imperialists and jingoists as John T. Morgan, Henry Cabot Lodge, and Theodore Roosevelt, all of whom strongly backed Cleveland's stance towards Great Britain.

Expressions of approval at this twisting of the British lion's tail took many forms, but certainly among the most spectacular was the reaction of certain employees of the Kansas City Board of Trade; a number of these garbed themselves in Revolutionary War costumes and, singing patriotic songs and banging tin pans, marched up five flights of stairs, demanding the surrender of the British consulate. Business groups also were sympathetic to Cleveland's position in such cities as Pittsburgh, Buffalo, Baltimore, Trenton, St. Paul, Milwaukee, Indianapolis, Cleveland, Cincinnati, Memphis, Atlanta, San Francisco, and Helena. Chicago was apparently divided, with the bankers attacking Cleveland, the industrialists and merchants supporting him; there was even some pro-Cleveland sentiment among the business interests of Boston. The significance of this general solidarity of business sentiment, outside of New York City, against Great Britain relative to the Venezuelan boundary dispute is of more than passing interest; it was the commercial elite of New York City, perhaps more so than that of any other major metropolis, which was initially unsympathetic towards the acquisition of a colonial empire, despite the trumpetings of the jingoistic New York City yellow press. We will have more to say about this group in our treatment of the Spanish-American War.

The Pacific Basin

Following the Mexican War, American interest in
Hawaii continued to grow, especially on the part of newly-
annexed California, despite the failure of the Brannan filibust-
ering expedition of 1851. By 1871, when most of the whaling
fleet was lost in the ice off the northern coast of Alaska,
New England's trade with Hawaii had begun to decline, but
Hawaiian commerce with San Francisco continued to flourish.
Twice previously, in 1855 and 1867, the Senate had failed to
ratify reciprocity treaties with Hawaii, but in 1875 Hamilton
Fish negotiated a third one; under this agreement the United
States was to abolish its duties on a number of Hawaiian products, including sugar, in return for which Hawaii was to
place additional American products on the free list. This
treaty passed the Senate on March 18, 1875, by a vote of 51
to 12. After a twenty years' battle, the anti-reciprocity coalition of sugar producing and refining states led by Louisiana
had finally lost; as in 1867 the Middle West led the opposition.

Although most California sugar refiners were opposed
to reciprocity with Hawaii, one of the more visionary of them,
Claus Spreckels, himself obtained a sugar plantation in
Hawaii. By the time of annexation (1898) Spreckels had assumed a dominant role in the political and economic life of
Hawaii, was monopolizing traffic between Hawaii and California with his Oceanic Steamship Company, and was refining
most of the sugar from Hawaii at his sugar refinery at San
Francisco. Never perhaps in American history had a treaty
operated so exclusively for the benefit of a single individual.

On the other hand, the movement to repeal the Hawaiian reciprocity treaty was spearheaded by Henry Alvin Brown
of Saxonville, Massachusetts. Brown was a former special
agent of the Treasury Department and special inspector of
customs in the district of Boston and Charleston, Massachusetts. In a series of pamphlets Brown sought to forge an
alliance of eastern sugar refiners, southern sugar producers,
and West Coast sugar consumers against the treaty. By 1881
he had obtained the backing of the San Francisco Chronicle,
the entire press of Louisiana, and at least a half dozen influential newspapers in other parts of the country.

In Congress the anti-reciprocity drive was led by Representative Randall L. Gibson of Louisiana, who along with
several other members of the House introduced several resolutions in the winter of 1881-1882 attacking the treaty. Gibson

soon found a powerful ally in Senator Justin S. Morrill, Chairman of the Finance Committee; Morrill was of the opinion that: "We require no fortified Gibraltar, no halfway houses on any of the highways of the ocean leading to colonial dependencies." Among those groups that petitioned Congress in favor of abrogation at this time were the sugar and rice planters of Louisiana, North Carolina, South Carolina, and Georgia; the sugar refiners of the Atlantic Seaboard States; the New York City and New York State Chambers of Commerce; and the Providence and Philadelphia Boards of Trade. Repeal, however, had a formidable opponent in Senator John T. Morgan of Alabama, whose Foreign Relations Committee buried Morrill's resolution favoring abrogation. According to Morgan, the Hawaiian Islands "may be said to be properly within the area of the physical and political geography of the United States."

Opponents of reciprocity were able to stall for three years the ratification of a new convention, originally concluded on December 6, 1884, which explicitly extended the 1875 convention for seven years, but the Senate finally placed its stamp of approval on this on November 7, 1887 by a vote of 43 to 11. Aside from its reciprocity provisions, Article II of this document, which had been added at the insistence of Senator Morgan, granted to the United States the exclusive right to establish and maintain a coaling and repair station at Pearl Harbor. The roster of opponents of reciprocity at this time was quite similar to its counterpart a dozen years previously, with powerful Senator Nelson W. Aldrich of Rhode Island representing the eastern sugar refiners. One exception was the rice interests of the South, which since 1885 had no longer felt threatened by declining imports of that produce from Hawaii.

Within a decade, though, Hawaii was annexed by the United States, and thus was no longer subject to a tariff. In fact, had this country so desired, it could have acquired Hawaii as early as 1893. During that year the reactionary, anti-foreign queen, Liliuokalini, was overthrown by a coalition led by Sanford B. Dole, the sugar planters of the Hawaiian Islands, and U. S. Minister to Hawaii John L. Stevens. President Benjamin Harrison favored annexation, but before Congress could act on the treaty, his term of office had expired, and the incoming President, Grover Cleveland, withdrew the treaty. (A number of Senate Democrats had previously announced their opposition.) Eight years previously, in 1885, Cleveland had similarly undercut an outgoing Republican predecessor who had proposed American involvement in the Congo.

Examining public opinion at this time towards the annexation of Hawaii in greater depth, the geographically diversified group of supporters included the legislatures of Oregon, California, Colorado, Pennsylvania, Illinois, and New York. Among newspapers favoring annexation were the Washington Post, the New York Tribune, the New York Sun, the Chicago Tribune, the Philadelphia Inquirer, the Boston Evening Transcript, the Detroit Tribune, the San Francisco Morning Call, the San Francisco Bulletin, and the St. Louis Republican. Prominent individuals who backed annexation included author Brooks Adams, Senators Henry Cabot Lodge and George F. Hoar of Massachusetts, former Secretary of State Thomas F. Bayard, and Senator John T. Morgan of Alabama. In summation, Thomas A. Bailey has noted that the pro-Hawaii forces consisted of "missionaries, traders, whalers, sugar planters, big-navyites, and imperialists. "

But sentiment towards Hawaii was by no means unanimously in favor of annexation, opponents including President Grover Cleveland, former Senator Carl Schurz of Missouri, and historian Hermann von Holst. The metropolitan press, in fact, was divided; in the opinion of the Chicago Herald, "We already have Negroes, Chinamen, Greasers, Indians, Jerry Simpson and Mrs. Lease, and we don't want any more in the combination. " Many other leading big city newspapers remained cautious or skeptical, while the provincial press of the South, Middle West, and West generally was opposed to annexation. According to Ernest May, "At no time can the public interest in the issue have been very large. Except in San Francisco, no metropolitan daily reported extended discussion. " Apparently only a minority felt, as did Cleveland, that Queen Liluokalini had been wronged by the American rebels, and that the people of Hawaii did not want annexation by the United States.

Following the outbreak of the Spanish-American War, in 1898, Republican President William McKinley finally obtained the annexation of Hawaii by using the same joint resolution device that had enabled Texas to join the Union a half-century earlier. One prominent opponent of annexation was sugar king Claus Spreckels, who feared that the annexation of Hawaii not only would terminate the importation of cheap contract labor into the Islands from Asia, but also would bring Hawaiian sugar wholly within the American system of tariffs and subsidies. Similarly critical was the powerful speaker

of the House, Thomas Reed of Maine; despite his opposition,
though the annexation resolution passed that body 209 to
91 on June 15.   When this joint resolution came before the
Senate, it did encounter southern opposition on racial and
commercial grounds, as well as scattered northern and western criticism on constitutional ones, but nevertheless cleared
the Upper House with ease, 42 to 21.   According to one analyst, only 2 of the 16 members of Congress from the Pacific
Coast States cast their votes against annexation, and only 30
of the 105 from the former slave states cast their votes for
it.   Thus the United States expanded beyond the continental
confines of North America for the first time, acquiring the
initial piece of its overseas empire aside from its holdings
in Samoa.

Unlike Hawaii, with which it was carrying on a considerable trade, China became something of a bête noire to
California in the years following the Civil War, especially
after Chinese immigration into that state began to reach formidable proportions.   The first Asiatics, in fact, did not enter
California until 1848, the last year of the Mexican War; by
1852, however, the total number of Chinese there had reached
the neighborhood of 25, 000.   Most of these were concentrated
in the city of San Francisco and the mining camps of the
North, although one also found them on farms.   Aside from
their stereotyped employment by restaurants and laundries,
Chinese also were active as workers on railroad construction
projects, often causing resentment among the native whites by
laboring for "coolie wages. "   Nevertheless, their immigration
was frequently encouraged by various commercial elements;
thus in 1856 the refusal of the Commissioner of Immigrants
to implement a special anti-Oriental law, which led to his
dismissal, was praised by a group of 76 San Francisco
merchants and importers.   In the opinion of the latter, the
state's revenue would benefit from a population increase, their
own interests requiring "an unrestricted China trade. "

Despite their support by the abovementioned commercial groups, the Chinese were regarded with hostility by many
politicians.   Thus on April 12, 1852, after the California
Senate had rejected an Assembly measure legalizing contract
labor, Senator Paul K. Hubbs introduced a bill "to prevent
coolie labor in the mines, and to prevent involuntary servi-
tude. "   Four days later, on April 16, seven members of the
Committee on Mines and Mining Interests presented a report
which prophesied relative to the Chinese: "The time is not
far distant when absolute prohibition of entry will be neces-

sary for our own protection. " Even Governor John Bigler was caught up in this anti-Chinese hysteria, proclaiming the need "to check this tide of Asiatic immigration, and to prevent the exportation by them of the precious metals which they dig up from our soil without charge, and without assuming any of the obligations imposed upon citizens. " Governor Bigler was re-elected, although it is not clear whether his anti-Chinese stand aided or hindered his drive for votes.

Six years later, in 1858, the state legislature did pass a measure of an anti-Chinese character, signed by Governor Bigler, which imposed a head tax of fifty dollars on those immigrants "who cannot become citizens. " The California Supreme Court admittedly found this law to be unconstitutional, but previously, in 1854, it had declared inadmissible in court the testimony of "Mongolians" against white persons. Thus within less than a decade after their initial arrival the Chinese in California had become the victims of widespread discrimination, if not outright persecution. The fact that a third of the white population of California between 1850 and 1860 had migrated there from the South probably also contributed to the pro-Aryan intellectual climate of the state.

To some, it would seem, adversity is a stimulus rather than a handicap. By 1867 the Chinese population of the West Coast had increased to 50, 000, twice what it had been in 1852. A demand for cheap railroad labor at the end of the decade also swelled the ranks of the Chinese, nine-tenths of a total of 10, 000 railroad laborers in 1869 being of that nationality, and by 1875 the number of West Coast Chinese had risen to 100, 000. In 1882, the year that Congress passed legislation barring further Chinese immigration, the figure stood at 130, 000.

Political protests against this mushrooming colony of Orientals continued apace in California and other western states. In 1876, for example, the state Senate of California sent a message to Washington appealing for a national policy of exclusion; the new state constitution of 1879 contained a number of clauses directed against the Chinese. But protest frequently took a more violent form. Dennis Kearney, an Irish immigrant who harangued the masses from the sandlots of San Francisco, preached expulsion as well as exclusion, suggesting rioting and lynching as possible alternatives if more peaceful means failed. In 1880 there was an anti-Chinese riot in Denver, while in Tacoma and Seattle five years later a number of Chinese were run out of town. In an article published at the time of this outrage the Seattle Call made reference to "the two-bit conscience of a scurvy opium fiend, " "the treacherous almond-eyed sons of Confucius, " "chattering, round-mouthed lepers, " and "those yellow rascals who have infested our western country. " One of the worst massacres of all occurred at Rock Springs, Wyoming in 1885, where 28 Chinese were killed in a single day.

If Westerners frequently turned to these less peaceful forms of protest against the Chinese, it was partly because Congress had monopolized the right to legislate relative to them, beginning with the Burlingame Treaty of 1868, which gave the Chinese the right of unlimited immigration. Significantly, this won unanimous Senate approval. But the importation of Oriental labor to break strikes in the East, particularly in Massachusetts and Pennsylvania, led to a broadening of the anti-Chinese movement beyond its California-West Coast base, and in 1875 Congress passed a law making the importation of coolie labor a felony. Four years later, in 1879, Senators and Representatives from the West and the South spearheaded a movement to repeal the Burlingame Treaty; generally opposed by the Republicans, this measure was vetoed by President Rutherford Hayes. Among the other defenders of the Chinese were Oliver P. Morton of Indiana, who died during the debate on the abrogation measure, the New York Chamber of Commerce, and a number of eastern newspapers, one of which praised Hayes' veto message as "saving the character of the country from humiliation among the family of nations. " Some Easterners and Midwesterners were apparently disturbed by what they regarded as an exercise in bigotry.

But Chinese exclusion was an idea whose time had come, and three years later, in 1882, both the President and the Congress placed their stamp of approval on legislation effecting this objective. When the Forty-seventh Congress convened, Senator John F. Miller of California introduced a bill barring both skilled and unskilled Chinese laborers from this country for twenty years, and denying citizenship to Chinese residents already present. George F. Hoar of Massachusetts, George F. Edmunds of Vermont, John Sherman of Ohio, and a number of other northern Senators opposed Miller's proposal, partly as a result of strong Abolitionist and free immigration sentiment there, partly as a result of their fear that it might have an adverse impact on American trade with China. Miller's bill, however, passed both houses of Congress, thanks largely to western and southern support;

one southern Senator, in fact, declared that he would protect
"the whole people of the Pacific States ... against a degrad-
ing and destructive association with the inferior race now
threatening to overrun them. " President Chester A.
Arthur vetoed the original version of this bill, thus winning him a
wave of applause in New England and the Northeast, but he
later signed a substitute measure reducing the term of twenty
years to ten. Ironically, despite the enactment of this legislation, a wave of anti-Chinese hysteria engulfed the West
Coast in 1885, several examples of which we have already
cited.

Thanks to the congressional legislation passed in 1882
and in 1888, the Chinese population of the West Coast began
to ebb. During the 1880's that of the six Far Western States
fell from 97, 124 to 89, 422; during the 1890's it further
slipped from 89, 422 to 56, 325. One exception to this rule
was San Francisco, which had come to harbor over a third
of the state's Chinese population by 1890. Following the turn
of the century, in 1904, Congress indefinitely and uncondi-
tionally re-enacted and continued all existing legislation, extending it to include the insular possessions of the United
States; nevertheless, in 1943 this body saw fit to repeal
Chinese exclusion, China being our ally against Japan at the
time.

In direct contrast to the widespread American lack of
enthusiasm for Chinese immigration during the latter part of
the Nineteenth Century was the widespread enthusiasm for
Chinese trade. During the 1890's American exports to China
increased by over 200 per cent, a figure matched only by
Africa. Although in terms of total exports our trade with
China on a percentage basis was relatively insignificant, it
was thought in many quarters that this Oriental nation, with
its 400 million inhabitants, was potentially "the greatest of
the world markets. " West Coast organizations like the San
Francisco Chamber of Commerce were not alone in favoring
the continued expansion of American trade with China; its
Boston counterpart, the Chicago Board of Trade, and the
Southern Cotton Spinners Association, to cite only three examples, were equally enthusiastic. The latter organization,
in fact, approved a grandiose resolution at its 1899 Charlotte
meeting calling for the preservation of the Chinese Empire,
the acquisition of the Philippine Islands, the laying of a Pacific cable, and the construction of an Isthmian canal.

Various European nations were also manifesting in-

terest in China as the Nineteenth Century drew to a close.
In 1894-1895 there was a war between Japan and China from
which the former emerged victorious, while in 1898 several
European nations--Russia, England, Germany, and France--
began carving out spheres of interest along the Chinese coast.
As a result of these developments, the commercial interests
of this country quite naturally felt threatened. Among those
organizations which sent petitions to the State Department attacking this partitioning of China were the chambers of commerce of New York, Boston, San Francisco, Baltimore,
Seattle, and the Philadelphia Board of Trade; equally active
were the New England Shoe and Leather Association, the New
England Cotton Manufacturers' Association, the Trans-Mississippi Commercial Congress, and the Southern Cotton Spinners' Association. The demand for the preservation of
American commercial privileges in China, it is apparent, was
truly national in scope.

        As was the case with the Monroe Doctrine, the Ameri-
can government took a British proposal for joint action relative to China and transformed it into a unilateral declaration:
the so-called Open Door Policy. This important proclamation, as commonly understood, guaranteed the territorial integrity of China and commercial equality there for the United
States and other foreign powers, although technically it was
somewhat narrower in its original form; after the various
European powers involved gave evasive and qualified replies
to an inquiry from our government, Secretary of State John
Hay announced on March 20, 1900 that its acceptance was
"final and definitive." In light of the wide geographical distribution of the abovementioned protests against the European
partitioning of China, and endorsements of increased Americar
trade with that nation, it is not surprising that editorial
opinion in this country, regardless of section, was generally
favorable to the Open Door Policy. There were exceptions
such as the New York Press, the New Orleans Picayune, and
the Springfield Republican, but more representative of general
American sentiment was the observation of the Philadelphia
Press that it was a greater achievement than the Spanish-
American War, and that of the New York Journal of Commerce that it was "one of the most important diplomatic negotiations of our time." Even such anti-imperialist newspapers as the Boston Evening Transcript, the New York
Herald, and the New York Evening Post commended McKinley
and Hay. For once, sectional cross-currents of opinion were
submerged in a sea of national unity.

The Spanish-American War
and the Triumph of Imperialism

Following the American Civil War and the abolition of
slavery in the South, the Cuban annexation movement waned
sharply. After a revolt had broken out in Cuba in 1868,
Secretary of State Hamilton Fish advised President Ulysses
S. Grant in the summer of 1870 even to abstain from recognition of the insurgents. Then in the midst of Reconstruction,
this nation was hardly eager to take on an added racial burd-
en; as the Wilmington, North Carolina Daily Journal observed: "Sooner or later (Cuba) will be annexed. And then
for a harvest of 'reconstruction.'" Five years later, in 1873,
a nation-wide furor arose when Spanish naval authorities captured the arms-running ship Virginius, which was flying the
American flag illegally, and had 53 members of the crew
(some of them Americans) shot as pirates. Fortunately, this
incident was peacefully settled a month later when the Spanish
government paid an indemnity of $80,000 to the families of
the executed Americans.

During the 1880's little of significance occurred in
Cuban-American relations. The Spanish authorities, who
again were in control of the island, paid lip service to the
implementation of liberal reforms; of these, unquestionably
the most important was the gradual abolition of slavery. Commercial relations between the United States and Cuba, however, were severely disturbed in 1890 when the McKinley
Tariff authorized a bounty of two cents a pound on the production of domestic sugar. (This provision was to remain in
effect for fourteen years.) As was the case with Hawaii,
whose economy was similarly disturbed by the bounty, revolution broke out in Cuba shortly thereafter (1895). The Panic
of 1893 in this country likewise had an adverse effect on the
Cuban economy.

Although a number of historians have interpreted the
Spanish-American War in terms of yellow journalism and the
blowing up of the Maine, the fact remains that there was
widespread sympathy for the Cubans throughout this country
as early as the abovementioned revolution of 1895. Even such
isolationist newspapers as the New York Evening Post, the
Springfield Republican, and the Boston Transcript raised their
voices in support of the insurgents. Both the press of this
country and the national Cigar Makers' Union were influenced
by the activities of the pro-Cuban Junta, or committee of
revolutionaries, which operated out of New York City. Among

those metropolises where there were demonstrations on behalf
of the Cubans at this time were New York City, Chicago,
Kansas City, Cleveland, Akron, Cincinnati, Philadelphia, and
Providence; prominent political leaders who backed a strong
stand towards Cuba included Governor John Peter Altgeld of
Illinois, Governor "Pitchfork Ben" Tillman of South Carolina,
the silverite governors of Georgia, Arkansas, and Indiana,
and such prominent members of Congress as John T. Morgan
of Alabama and William V. Allen of Nebraska. The fact that
many southern and western Populists were favorably disposed
to the Cuban cause has led a number of historians to conclude
that the movement was basically agrarian in origin. We will
have more to say about this later when we analyze the reaction of Missouri to the Spanish-American War.

Congress likewise tended to sympathize with the Cuban
cause. Despite the opposition of John Sherman of Ohio,
Chairman of the Senate Foreign Relations Committee, two resolutions emerged from his committee, one threatening intervention, the other recognizing Cuban belligerency. A resolution stressing the latter concept and demanding independence
for Cuba passed both houses of Congress with overwhelming
majorities early in 1896; some Southerners, though, opposed
this resolution because of the racial issue, some New Englanders because their abolitionist predecessors had disap-
proved of the Southern-led movement to annex Cuba during the
1850's. Much to the displeasure of the annexationists and
jingoists, President Grover Cleveland continued to follow a
course of restraint.

There was little discussion of the Cuban issue during
the 1896 Presidential campaign, both parties being largely
preoccupied with the free coinage of silver question. In December, however, a black Cuban general, Antonio Maceo, was
slain by the Spanish General Valeriano "Butcher" Weyler under
suspicious circumstances; Weyler had just taken command of
the Spanish forces in Cuba, and had begun to herd the civil
population into concentration camps. As a result, a sense of
indignation seized the American people. Mobs burned Weyler
in effigy in small towns in New Jersey, Pennsylvania, Illinois,
and Iowa, while there were pro-Cuban rallies in a number of
larger cities, including Atlanta, Dallas, New York, Buffalo,
Jersey City, Wheeling, Chattanooga, Los Angeles, Little Rock,
and Newark. (The latter two were predominantly Negro in
composition.) Memorials in favor of belligerent rights or
Cuban independence also were received by Congress at this
time from the legislatures of Louisiana, Nebraska, South

Carolina, and Wyoming.

The inauguration of William McKinley as President in March 1897 was followed by a temporary cooling of the Cuban issue, thanks in part to the removal of Weyler, thanks in part to the implementation of certain reforms in Cuba. There was a drop in the number of petitions and memorials received by Congress, a reliable indication that the public no longer was clamoring for intervention as it had been a year previously. When the New York Herald polled members of both the House and the Senate, it discovered that a majority was privately opposed to Congressional action.

Had nothing further occurred to agitate Cuban-American relations, it is quite likely that war could have been prevented, despite the trumpetings of the yellow press. Nevertheless, the public was again stirred up by the publication in a New York newspaper on February 9, 1898 of a private letter written by the Spanish minister, Dupuy de Lomé. In this epistle de Lomé castigated President McKinley as "weak and a bidder for the admiration of the crowd, besides being a would-be politician who tried to leave a door open behind himself while keeping on good terms with the jingoes of his party." (More recently, H. Wayne Morgan, among others, has emphasized his decisiveness.) Hardly had the furor died down over de Lomé's indiscretion, the minister being forced to resign, than word arrived from Havana on February 16 that the battleship Maine had been blown up in the harbor there, killing 260 men. War now seemed inevitable, the forces of moderation doomed.

At this point in the narrative we will turn aside from the chronological procession of events and examine sectional attitudes towards Cuba up to and including the blowing up of the Maine. First let us look at the yellow press of New York City, long regarded as the leading jingoist force in this country. By the time that "Butcher" Weyler had begun his reconcentration program, several New York City newspapers had correspondents on the island. Joseph Wisan, writing in 1934, took the position that "... the Spanish-American War would not have occurred had not the appearance of (William Randolph) Hearst in New York journalism precipitated a bitter battle for newspaper circulation," but Meredith W. Berg and David M. Berg, in rebutting Wisan thirty years later, declared that: "Of the major New York City papers, Hearst's Journal alone maintained a consistent pro-war stand from the day news of the 'Maine' explosion first raced across the wires of the news services." According to the latter, Pulitzer's

World steered a moderate course as late as February 26, then
reversed itself and adopted a more jingoist stance when public
opinion began to flow in the direction of war.

Ironically, one of the most vigorous opponents of war
with Spain also had its headquarters in New York City: the
Eastern business establishment. According to the bitterly
hostile Sacramento Evening Bee, Wall Street was "the colossal
and aggregate Benedict Arnold of the Union, and the syndicated
Judas Iscariot of humanity. Whenever the news of the day
presaged war, the stock market inevitably plunged downward.
(Admittedly, a minority of business leaders did favor war.)
It was not until after England, France, Germany, and Russia
began carving out spheres of influence in China early in 1898
that most of the businessmen of New York City, Boston, and
other large Eastern cities came to realize that their interests
would be served by the acquisition of a colonial empire, that
of Spain being the most readily available.

The press of the Middle West was also rather jingoist
in orientation, but this was more the result of the propaganda
activities of the Cuban Junta than of deliberate yellow journalism. According to George W. Auxier, "The basic interests
of the United States in the Caribbean were reflected in the
editorial columns of middle western newspapers ... in terms
of economic imperialism, military strategem, political idealism, and a large measure of humanitarianism. " The business
interests of this section were far less opposed to war than
eastern counterparts; in 1897 the Kansas City Board of Trade
had urged recognition of Cuban independence, while in 1898
the Cincinnati Chamber of Commerce condemned Spanish policy
towards Cuba. Also favorably disposed to the Cuban cause
were many of the business leaders of Pittsburgh, Louisville,
St. Louis, and Chicago. In the opinion of Ray Billington,
"No other section contributed so generously to the cause of
Cuban independence. "

Thus it is not surprising that twenty of the twenty-four
Senators from this section voted or spoke consistently for intervention; Populist Senator William V. Allen of Nebraska announced in Congress that he was "the jingo of the jingoes. "
No less than seventy-four of the seventy-nine petitions directed
to middle western members of Congress were favorable to the
Cuban cause. An examination of public opinion on a state-by-
state basis, however, does reveal slight variations, Michigan
only gradually shifting from an attitude of indifference to
vacillating support for the Cuban cause, and Minnesota form-

ing a wide spectrum ranging from a demand for immediate intervention to absolute opposition to war.

As for the South, it has been observed by more than one commentator that the Spanish-American War helped to heal the North/South split. The Detroit News, to cite only one example, declared at the time that: "Nothing short of an archeological society will be able to locate Mason and Dixon's line after this." In contrast, C. Vann Woodward has pointed out relative to domestic politics that this conflict disrupted the South's preoccupation with reform and cooled the radical temper of the 1890's. "The Spanish War finished us," observed the great Populist leader Tom Watson: "The blare of the bugle drowned the voice of the Reformer."

Like its midwestern counterpart, the press of the South was generally favorable to war over Cuba, partly for the reason that it offered an opportunity to prove southern patriotism and fighting ability. Even the country press was drawn out of its provincialism, if only temporarily. One exception was Florida, which was the only state of the Union in which all the important newspapers were united in opposition to war, mainly for the reason that Florida was confronted with the threat of a possible attack by the Spanish fleet. The business interests of this state also were opposed to war, unlike the Florida Cigar Makers' Union, which visualized a "Cuba Libre" with labor unions. As was the case with the Middle West, an examination of public opinion on a state-by-state basis does reveal slight variations. Mississippi, for example, apparently was far more disposed to war than North Carolina.

Regardless of those variations in public opinion from section to section and from state to state, the sinking of the Maine tended to unite public opinion more firmly behind the jingoists. By this time northern and eastern urbanites had joined southern and western farmers in demanding war. When Senator Redfield Proctor of Vermont delivered an address before that body upon his return from Cuba in mid-March, he concluded that the only feasible solution to the Cuban question was American intervention; it was rumored that Proctor had gone to Cuba as McKinley's observer, with the result that his speech was given nation-wide coverage.

As the pressure for war mounted, the chief executive carefully formulated a war message, two months having elapsed since the Maine had been blown up. A Congressional resolution authorizing the President to intervene in Cuba to stop the

war and establish an independent government cleared the House
173 to 121 on April 18, with only twenty-five Westerners
opposed, and the Senate 67 to 21 on April 16; 19 of the Senatorial nay votes were cast by Republicans, 10 from the
Northeast and 6 from the Middle West. (The declaration of
war passed both houses of Congress on April 25 without roll-
calls being taken.) At the same time, however, Congress
adopted without dissent an amendment offered by Senator Henry
Teller of Colorado, which renounced any intention on the part
of the United States "to exercise sovereignty, jurisdiction, or
control over Cuba. " Although some members of Congress
probably were voting their consciences in supporting this
amendment, Senator Teller himself had the more mundane
objective of protecting the sugar beet interests of his native
Colorado.

The war itself lasted only three months. On May 1
Commodore George Dewey won a decisive victory in the Battle
of Manila Bay, while on July 3 Admiral William T. Sampson
destroyed the Spanish fleet when it attempted to leave Santiago
harbor. Two days earlier the Rough Riders, led by Colonel
Theodore Roosevelt, had played an important role in the Battle of San Juan Hill. That fall peace negotiations began; on
December 10 the Treaty of Paris was signed. Under this
Spain agreed to cede the Philippines to the United States for
twenty million dollars, to surrender all claim and title to
Cuba, and to cede Puerto Rico and Guam to the United States
as an indemnity. Spain's once mighty colonial empire now
lay in ruins.

Public opinion in this country, however, was by no
means unanimously in favor of acquiring the former Spanish
possessions, the Philippines being the main focal point of controversy. A poll of 498 newspapers conducted by the New
York Herald in December 1898 revealed that 61. 3 per cent
were favorably disposed to expansion; the trade-minded West
was overwhelmingly in favor, New England and the Middle
Atlantic States to a lesser extent, and the race-conscious
South opposed by a narrow margin. Unlike the West, commercial advantages did not outweigh social factors here. Among
the leading journalistic critics of expansion were the New York
Evening Post, the Springfield Republican, the Boston Herald,
and the Baltimore Sun. According to Christopher Lasch,
"Southern Democrats were almost unanimous in condemning
'imperialism' on the grounds that Asiatics, like Negroes, were
innately inferior to white people and could not be assimilated
to American life, " but the Atlanta Constitution and the New

Orleans Times-Picayune felt differently. Northerners who
favored acquiring the Philippines on the grounds that the na-
tives were unfit for self-government thus were faced with a
dilemma; they could hardly criticize the South for denying
equal rights to the Negro when they themselves were employing a different version of the Aryan supremacy thesis themselves.

Although most political leaders favored the annexation
of the Philippines, as did their journalistic counterparts, the
ranks of the anti-expansionists did include former President
Grover Cleveland and former Presidential candidate William
Jennings Bryan. Also opposed to annexation was normally
expansionist Senator John T. Morgan of Alabama, who accepted
the abovementioned theory of Filipino racial inferiority, as
well as the one that the acquisition of the Philippines might
lead to a conflict with the other powers. In Congress the
roster of anti-expansionists aside from Morgan ranged across
a wide geographical and political spectrum: conservative Democrats such as Arthur Gorman of Maryland, Stephen White of
California, and Donelson Caffery of Louisiana; silverites such
as George Vest of Missouri, John Jones of Nevada, and Henry
Teller of Colorado; Republicans such as George Frisbie Hoar
of Massachusetts and William Mason of Illinois.

More numerous were the ranks of the annexationists:
Henry Cabot Lodge of Massachusetts, William F. Frye of
Maine, Orville Platt of Connecticut, and such midwestern
Senators as Marcus Hanna of Ohio, John Spooner of Wisconsin, and William Allison of Iowa. The fight for ratification
in the Senate was led by Cushman K. Davis of Minnesota,
while the ablest legal argument in favor of expansion was made
by Joseph B. Foraker of Ohio. Unquestionably one of the
outstanding examples of imperialistic sentiment was the address of Albert J. Beveridge of Indiana in which Beveridge,
who had just returned from a visit to the Philippines, proclaimed:

> The Philippines are ours forever.... And just be-
> yond the Philippines are China's illimitable markets.
> We will not retreat from either.... The Pacific is
> our ocean.... And the Pacific is the ocean of the
> commerce of the future.... The Power that rules
> the Pacific ... is the Power that rules the world.
> And, with the Philippines, that Power is and will
> forever be the American Republic.

Despite such proclamations as that of Beveridge, the annexation of the Philippines would never have been approved by the "lame duck" 55th Congress had not William Jennings Bryan reversed himself and come out for the ratification of the Treaty of Paris. Bryan's reasons for this abrupt volte-face were threefold: he wanted the war ended; a minority should not thwart the will of a majority; the Presidential election of 1900 could become a referendum on imperialism. When the treaty came up for a final vote on February 6, 1899, its margin of victory was narrow, 57 to 27, with only one vote to spare.

As was the case with the declaration of war, the Middle West again heavily favored annexation; it should be noted, however, that most of the Senators from this section were Republicans who backed their President partly out of party loyalty. Democrats and Populists from this section were far less enthusiastic about acquiring the Philippines, while a minority group of New England Republicans was likewise hostile. On the other hand, only a handful of southern Senators favored the unconditional ratification of the treaty with Spain, although a few others also voted for it with reservations. No less than fourteen Southerners openly cast nay ballots. Yet regardless of the narrowness of this victory, Republicans had widened their Senate majority over all other parties combined from two to nineteen in the Congressional election of 1898, and if necessary McKinley could have obtained the ratification of this treaty when the new Congress met. This is a fact often overlooked by historians.

Between the ratification of the Treaty of Paris and the Election of 1900 a number of anti-imperialist leagues were organized in Boston, Springfield, New York City, Philadelphia, Baltimore, Washington, Cincinnati, Cleveland, Detroit, St. Louis, Los Angeles, and Portland (Oregon). Many of the leading anti-imperialists of the 1890's, however, had been from New England, and were rather advanced in age. In this connection one might cite nationally such names as Justin Morrill, Edward Everett Hale, John Sherman, George F. Hoar, George F. Edmunds, Benjamin Harrison, Andrew Carnegie, Thomas B. Reed, Hermann von Holst, Thomas Wentworth Higginson, Charles Eliot Norton, Carl Schurz, E. L. Godkin, Charles W. Eliot, Charles Francis Adams, Jr., Mark Twain, Thomas Bailey Aldrich, William Dean Howells, William Graham Sumner, and William James.

Like another perennial Presidential loser, Henry Clay,

William Jennings Bryan often picked the wrong issue at the
wrong time on which to base his campaign.   This was true
in 1896 when he embraced the free coinage of silver; it was
also true in 1900 when he took a stand on behalf of anti-imperialism in a campaign that was so clouded by free silver
and other issues that it was in effect merely a vote of con-
fidence for McKinley "prosperity. " Bryan's popular vote in
the East did show a gain the second time around, particularly
in the anti-imperialist stronghold of Massachusetts, but Mc-
Kinley offset this improved showing by substantially increasing
his vote in the Rocky Mountain and Pacific Coast States. In
the Middle West, every state except Missouri went for Mc-
Kinley; even Robert La Follette, Sr. , who was to be a prominent isolationist at the time of World War I, embraced imperialism when he was campaigning for governor of Wisconsin.
But the most ardent exponent of expansion during the Presidential election of 1900 was not William McKinley, but rather
his Vice Presidential nominee, Theodore Roosevelt of New
York; T. R. 's frontier experience as a young man later played
a key role in the shaping of his imperialistic philosophy. In
this connection there comes to mind the "psychic crisis"
theory of Richard Hofstadter, who held that there was a direct
connection between the closing of the frontier around 1890 and
the acquisition of an overseas colonial empire less than a
decade later To sum it up succinctly: today the West, to-
morrow the world!

FOR FURTHER READING

        American relations with France in the years following
the U.S. Civil War have been systematically examined by a
number of scholars.   For the French Revolution of 1870, consult Eugene N. Curtis' "American Opinion of the French Nineteenth-Century Revolutions"; for the Franco-Prussian War,
see Henry Blumenthal's A Reappraisal of Franco-American
Relations 1830-1871; Elizabeth Brett White's American Opinion
of France from Lafayette to Poincaré; Jeanette Keim's Forty
Years of German-American Political Relations, and Count
Otto zu Stolberg-Wernigerode's Germany and the United States
of America during the Era of Bismarck.   Blumenthal also
discusses American trade with France, while David M. Pletcher examines the commercial treaty of 1878 in his The
Awkward Years: American Foreign Relations under Garfield
and Arthur.   On the other hand, Alexander de Conde touches
on the German boycott of American pork during the 1880's

in his A History of American Foreign Policy.

Two works that analyze the 1891 lynchings of jailed Italians in New Orleans are Alice Felt Tyler, The Foreign Policy of James G. Blaine, and J. Alexander Karlin, "The Italo-American Incident of 1891 and the Road to Reunion." The Anglo-American arbitration treaty of 1896 is discussed in Ernest R. May, Imperial Democracy: The Emergence of America as a Great Power; Calvin D. Davis, The United States and the First Hague Peace Conference; and Thomas A. Bailey, The Man in the Street. One should turn to Bailey's America Faces Russia for the 1871 visit of Grand Duke Alexis, and to William A. Williams' American-Russian Relations 1781-1947 and Malbone W. Graham's American Diplomacy in the International Community for American public opinion and Russian anti-Semitism.

A leading authority on American relations with Canada during the last half of the Nineteenth Century is Donald Warner, who has written "Drang Nach Norden: The United States and the Riel Rebellion," and The Idea of Continental Union: Agitation for the Annexation of Canada to the United States 1849-1893. Other important studies of the abortive annexation movement include Alvin C. Glueck, Jr., Minnesota and the Manifest Destiny of the Canadian Northwest and Lester B. Shippee, Canadian-American Relations 1849-1874. For an extended treatment of Seward's folly, see Richard E. Welch, Jr., "American Public Opinion and the Purchase of Russian America"; for briefer accounts, consult Albert A. Woldman, Lincoln and the Russians; Foster Rhea Dulles, America in the Pacific: A Century of Expansion; Alexander de Conde and Armin Rappaport, editors, Essays Diplomatic and Undiplomatic of Thomas A. Bailey; and Earl Pomeroy, The Pacific Slope. Among the better discussions of Canadian reciprocity are those found in the abovementioned book by Shippee and Charles S. Campbell, Jr.'s "American Tariff Interests and the Northeastern Fisheries, 1883-1888," and in Robert Craig Brown's Canada's National Policy 1883-1900: A Study in Canadian-American Relations and John A. S. Grenville and George Berkeley Young's Politics, Strategy, and American Diplomacy: Studies in Foreign Policy, 1873-1917. The fisheries question is examined at some length in Charles C. Tansill, The Foreign Policy of Thomas F. Bayard 1885-1897.

As good an introduction as any to southern designs on the Caribbean following the Civil War is O. Lawrence Burnette, Jr.'s "John Tyler Morgan and Expansionist Sentiment in the New South"; more detailed is August Carl Radke, Jr.'s doctoral dissertation, John Tyler Morgan: An Expansionist Senator, 1877-1907. There is considerable material on the abortive attempt to annex the Dominican Republic in Charles C. Tansill, The United States and Santo Domingo, 1798-1873; Ernest May, American Imperialism: A Speculative Essay; and Sumner Welles, Naboth's Vineyard: The Dominican Republic 1844-1924. American relations with Mexico are covered in the abovementioned books by Pletcher on Garfield and Arthur, and by Tansill on Bayard, and in Robert D. Gregg, The Influence of Border Troubles on Relations Between the United States and Mexico 1876-1910. An outstanding treatment of the subject which it discusses is Paul J. Scheips, "United States Commercial Pressures for a Nicaragua Canal in the 1890's." One should consult for the American reaction to the Venezuelan boundary crisis of 1895 such works as Nelson W. Blake's "Background of Cleveland's Venezuelan Policy" (in Armin Rappaport, Issues in American Diplomacy); Walter LaFeber's The New Empire: An Interpretation of American Expansion 1860-1898; Dexter Perkins' The Monroe Doctrine, 1867-1907; and the abovementioned book by Tansill on Bayard.

Turning to the Pacific, Donald Marquand Dozer, "The Opposition to Hawaiian Reciprocity, 1876-1888," is a must for the topic that it explores; the abovementioned book by Pletcher also is of value in this connection. Monographs that deal with annexation include Merze Tate, The United States and the Hawaiian Kingdom; Julius Pratt, Expansionists of 1898; Frederick Merk, Manifest Destiny and Mission in American History (the vote in Congress); and the two abovementioned volumes by Ernest May. A key study of early manifestations of anti-orientalism on the Pacific Coast is Rodman W. Paul's "The Origins of the Chinese Issue in California"; outstanding articles on later ones elsewhere in the West are Roy T. Wortman's "Denver's Anti-Chinese Riot, 1880" and Jules Alexander Karlin's "The Anti-Chinese Outbreak in Seattle, 1885-1886" and "The Anti-Chinese Outbreak in Tacoma, 1885." For California, also consult the abovementioned book by Earl Pomeroy, as well as that by Elmer C. Sandmeyer, The Anti-Chinese Movement in California. Congressional attempts at Chinese exclusion are examined by Tansill in his book on Bayard and by Grenville and Young in their monograph, while American commerce with China during the 1890's is treated by Charles S. Campbell, Jr. in his study, Special Business Interests and the Open Door Policy. Marvin Blatt Young discusses the editorial reaction in this country to the latter in his The Rhetoric of Empire: American China Policy 1895-1901.

Unquestionably the best introduction to American public
opinion and the Spanish-American War are the two abovementioned books by May; those by Pratt, LeFeber, and Perkins
also merit inspection, as do Marcus Wilkerson's "The Press
and the Spanish-American War" and Public Opinion and the
Spanish-American War. Important studies that deal with specific sections and states are Joseph Wisan, The Cuban Crisis
as Reflected in the New York Press (1895-1898); Meredith W.
Berg and David M. Berg, "The Rhetoric of War Preparation:
The New York Press in 1898"; Ray Allen Billington, "The
Origins of Middle Western Isolationism"; William G. Carleton,
"Isolationism and the Middle West"; George W. Auxier,
"Middle Western Newspapers and the Spanish-American War,
1895-1898"; Raymond A. Deter, "The Cuban Junta and Michi-
gan: 1895-1898"; Peter Mickelson, "Nationalism in Minnesota
during the Spanish-American War"; Thomas D. Clark, The
Southern Country Editor; John C. Appel, "The Unionization
of Florida Cigarmakers and the Coming of the War with
Spain"; George H. Gibson, "Attitudes in North Carolina Regarding the Independence of Cuba, 1868-1898"; Donald Brooks
Kelley, "Mississippi and 'The Splendid Little War' of 1898";
and J. Stanley Lemons, "The Cuban Crisis of 1895-1898:
Newspapers and Nativism" (a study of Missouri).

A number of the abovementioned books and articles also
treat at varying lengths imperialism, anti-imperialism, and
the Election of 1900. Key studies that have these topics at
their focal point include Robert L. Beisner, Twelve Against
Empire: The Anti-Imperialists 1898-1900; Fred H. Harrington, "The Anti-Imperialist Movement in the United States,
1898-1900"; Christopher Lasch, "The Anti-Imperialists, the
Philippines, and the Inequality of Man"; Padraic Colum Kennedy, "La Follette's Imperialist Flirtation"; and Richard Hofstadter, "Manifest Destiny and the Philippines" (in Theodore
P. Greene, American Imperialism in 1898). Also see in this
connection Garel A. Grunder and William E. Livezey, The
Philippines and the United States.

CHAPTER 5

FROM THE SPANISH-AMERICAN WAR
TO WORLD WAR I

Introduction

William McKinley was re-elected President in 1900,
but his term in office was cut short by an assassin's bullet
the same year that he took his second oath of office. His
successor, the youthful Theodore Roosevelt, then finished out
McKinley's second term and won re-election on his own. During these eight years the Republicans controlled Congress, the
Senate by decisive margins, although they never obtained a
two-thirds majority in the upper house. Abandoning the isolationist stance that had characterized American foreign policy
during most of the Nineteenth Century, T. R. involved this
nation in European, African, Asian, and Latin American affairs while pursuing his "Big Stick" diplomacy. Nevertheless,
the more controversial treaties which the Senate ratified during his Presidency mainly involved Latin America, especially
the Panama Canal, Cuba, and the Dominican Republic. While
Southern Democrats led the unsuccessful minority against the
two Hay-Paunceforte treaties, the Hay-Harran Convention, and
the Hay-Bunau Varilla Treaty, all pertaining to the canal issue, they also spearheaded the opposition to the Platt Amendment, Cuban reciprocity, and the Dominican pact.

During the Taft Administration the Republicans continued to dominate the Senate, but lost their majority in the
House at the mid-term Congressional election. Under Taft,
"Big Stick" diplomacy gave way to "Dollar Diplomacy," with
its focus on Latin America and the Far East. When Japanese
interest in Magdalena Bay, Mexico led Senator Henry Cabot
Lodge to offer his corollary to the Monroe Doctrine in 1912,
however, only four Senators, two of them Republicans and
two of them Democrats, opposed his resolution in a vote devoid of sectional trends; partisan Southern Democratic hostility was far less in evidence here than it had been in the case
of Roosevelt's Latin American policy. Perhaps the most con-

troversial diplomatic issue that arose during the Taft Administration was Canadian reciprocity, a question which proved
decisive in the Canadian national election of 1911. Curiously,
despite the fact that a Republican was sitting in the White
House, over ninety per cent of Senatorial Democrats voted
for this measure, while Senatorial Republicans split almost
evenly on the question. As for the sectional breakdown of
this roll-call, the Middle West and the Great Plains led the
opposition, with the Eastern Seaboard from New England to
the South Atlantic States generally favorable to this scheme.

The next year, in 1912, Woodrow Wilson became only
the second Democrat since the Civil War to win election as
President, capitalizing on a Republican split between Roosevelt and Taft to capture the Electoral College with a plurality
of the popular vote. The Democrats did control the Senate
for the first six years of Wilson's Presidency, but the Republicans increased their total to 49 seats in the Congressional
election of 1918, thus enabling Wilson critic Lodge to become
chairman of the Senate Foreign Relations Committee. (At
this time the Democrats also lost the majority they had enjoyed in the House for the past eight years.) Reversing the
position they had assumed during the Presidency of Roosevelt,
Southern Democrats generally backed Wilson's Latin American
policy. When the Panama Canal tolls bill came up for a vote
in 1914, two-thirds of the nay vote was Republican, with
Westerners leading the opposition. Republicans also cast
three-fourths of the votes against the 1916 Bryan-Chamorro
Treaty with Nicaragua; here again the West was the most
hostile section. Partisan opposition to Wilson was even more
apparent in the Congressional roll-calls on the Jones Act vis-
a-vis the Philippines. When this measure came up for a vote
in the Senate the same year, every one of the 24 Senators
who answered nay was a Republican, although every Southern
Democrat who cast a ballot supported this measure. In this
particular case New England was less favorably disposed than
any other section.

Turning to Congressional votes pertaining to World
War I, which had broken out in the summer of 1914, three
years before official U. S. involvement, one again finds Southern Democrats firmly backing their chief executive. Together
with Northeasterners they played a key role in the tabling of
the Gore and McLemore resolutions of 1916 that would have
restricted American travel on armed vessels, although there
were two Southern Democrats among the five nays when the
Senate voted on February 7, 1917 to break off diplomatic re-

lations with Germany.   But by the time Congress declared
war on the latter two months later, most sections of the
country and most members of the opposition party had united
behind Wilson, with the exception of the predominantly Republican Middle West, which cast the bulk of the 50 anti-war
ballots in the House after spearheading the forces opposing
the armed ship bill a month earlier.   (In the Senate, the half-
dozen votes against war were devoid of both sectional and
partisan trends.)   Middle Western isolationism had thus already begun to assert itself, even before the debate on the
League of Nations, when Republicans from this section played
a key role in defeating the Treaty of Versailles, with Southern
Democrats, as before, the leading supporters of the Wilson
Administration.

Hemispheric Affairs

Like the mythological phoenix, the Canadian reciprocity
question arose from its ashes again and again, after hopefully
having been disposed of permanently.   In 1898, at the time of
the Spanish-American War, a joint high commission investigated the possibility of negotiating a new Canadian reciprocity
agreement, but as always the New England fishing interests
were adamant in their opposition.   Led by the two powerful
Massachusetts Senators, Henry Cabot Lodge and George
Frisbie Hoar, the anti-reciprocity movement had its headquarters in Gloucester, soon to be represented in Congress
by Lodge's son-in-law; in this connection Lord Herschell
wrote Salisbury, the British Prime Minister, that:

...the opposition ... emanated chiefly from the fishing town of Gloucester, Massachusetts, and that it
seemed strange that it should be regarded as more
important to conciliate a single town in one of the
States than at the risk of giving offence to the inhabitants of that town to ensure a satisfactory settlement with Great Britain.

Surveying public opinion throughout the country as a
whole towards Canadian reciprocity, a number of the leading
newspapers of the eastern and central states did strongly favor
free paper and pulp.   The Senate Foreign Relations Committee, however, included several Senators from the timber
states, and they were no more willing to approve reciprocity
for lumber than were their New England allies to do so rela-

tive to fish. Among the important business groups that futi-
lely endorsed Canadian reciprocity at this time were the
chambers of commerce of Cleveland and Boston.

Four years later, in 1902, Secretary of State John Hay
negotiated a reciprocity agreement with Newfoundland, the
Hay-Bond Treaty. Although the latter was well received by
much of the American press, it was anathema to the fishing
interests of Massachusetts and Maine. Newfoundland even
agreed to include boots and shoes on the free list, but Senator
Henry Cabot Lodge's opposition was so vigorous that the treaty
did not even reach the floor of the Senate until 1905, at which
time it was amended beyond acceptability and finally tabled.
When the government of Newfoundland retaliated against the
New England fishermen on its coast, jingoist Senator Lodge
unsuccessfully requested that President Theodore Roosevelt,
a close friend of his, send a cruiser to the area to protect
American rights.

During 1909, the same year that the United States
agreed to refer the North Atlantic fisheries question to the
Hague Tribunal for final settlement, the highly protective
Payne-Aldrich Tariff was passed by Congress and signed into
law by President William Howard Taft. As this measure
threatened commerce between America and Canada, representatives of the two nations negotiated a reciprocity agreement
on January 26, 1911 which reduced or eliminated the duties
on many Canadian items, in particular agricultural products.
This reciprocity agreement also provided for a lowering of
the Canadian tariff on a number of American manufactured
goods.

The anti-reciprocity movement in this country during
1911 was spearheaded, not by New England fishermen, but
rather by the agricultural interests of the Middle West, who
generally had favored tariff reduction in 1909. Opposition was
especially strong in Minnesota and North Dakota, the two
states whose wheat farmers would be most affected by Canadian
competition, a majority of the newspapers of the latter state
being unfavorable to reciprocity. Representative Halver
Steenerson of Minnesota spoke for the agrarian interests of
his section when he commented in the House of Representatives
on April 11 that "The measure has all the faults of protection
gone mad. . . . It is the Democratic donkey tail end first, and
the rear end of the Republican elephant." There was some
support for reciprocity in this section, though; advocates included newspapers seeking cheap paper, railroad baron James

J. Hill, and the millers of the Twin Cities. (The three urban
Representatives from Minnesota also backed reciprocity). As
for the opposition to reciprocity outside of this section, many
western lumbermen and New England fishermen were unenthusiastic, although the financial interests of the East favored
the 1911 agreement on the grounds that it would facilitate their
endeavors to obtain control of the Canadian market. Despite
these contending forces, the press of this nation generally
adopted a favorable stance towards reciprocity, a factor which
unquestionably helped obtain Congressional approval.

A reciprocity measure was passed by the House of
Representatives on April 21 by a vote of 268 to 89, and by
the Senate on July 22 by one of 53 to 27. Here the Middle
West and Great Plains cast two-thirds of the nay votes. During the debate on this bill President William Howard Taft,
who did sign it, made the observation that: "The amount of
Canadian products that we would take would make Canada only
an adjunct of the United States. " In fact, there was some
talk in this country at the time that reciprocity would lead to
annexation, with the Hearst press spearheading the imperialists. But there was to be no reciprocity, as there was to be
no annexation. Despite the fact that the farmers of the
Prairie Provinces of Saskatchewan, Manitoba, and Alberta
supported the agreement, unlike their Yankee counterparts to
the South, the anti-reciprocity Conservatives defeated the pro-
reciprocity Liberals in the Canadian national election held on
September 21, 1911, thus ruining the chances of the Canadian
Parliament approving reciprocity for the time being. During
the Presidential election of 1912 in the United States, moreover, Theodore Roosevelt reversed his earlier pro-reciprocity
position and assumed the leadership of the anti-reciprocity
forces. To the surprise of no one, President William Howard
Taft came in third to T. R. and Woodrow Wilson in the anti-
reciprocity states of Minnesota and North Dakota; as one
border farmer commented, "we are confronted with a Judas
ready to betray us. "

Another issue of considerable interest to border staters
during this period was the proposed St. Lawrence Seaway.
Between 1912 and 1914 this project was discussed by the prime
minister of Canada and the governor of New York; in 1919,
however, the terminal pier of the New York state barge canal
was opened, a canal designed to divert the large eastward export shipments of western grain from the St. Lawrence route.
At this time the legislatures of Minnesota and North Dakota
transmitted memorials to Congress urging American partici-

pation in the St. Lawrence improvements, but Senator Henry
Cabot Lodge of Massachusetts, who had played a key role in
blocking ratification of the Hay-Bond reciprocity treaty with
Newfoundland between 1902 and 1905, sabotaged for the time
being joint construction of a waterway which the United States
could not unilaterally control.

Turning to Western Canada, in 1899 a modus vivendi
was reached between Great Britain and the United States which
resulted in the marking of a temporary boundary between
Canada and Alaska. This line, though, ran through rich gold
fields at a number of points, as at Porcupine Creek. When
the miners affected made their displeasure known, the chambers of commerce of Seattle and Portland, both Senators from
Oregon, and Senator Addison Foster of Washington publicly
attacked the modus during the summer of 1900.

Finally, on January 24, 1903 the United States and
Great Britain signed the Hay-Herbert Treaty, which set up a
joint commission of three Americans and three Britons to
arbitrate the disputed boundary. Although the shipping and
trading interests of the state of Washington bitterly opposed
this convention, Henry Cabot Lodge cleverly maneuvered it
through the Senate during the course of a long and boring
speech by Senator John T. Morgan, many members having
absented themselves from the floor. (Unfortunately for the
analyst, individual stands were not recorded.) Instead of
three "impartial jurists of repute," the American members
of the commission turned out to be Lodge himself, Senator
George Turner of Washington, and Secretary of War Elihu
Root, none of whom was likely to take the side of Canada.
The commission eventually upheld the American claims by a
4 to 2 majority, Lord Alverstone casting his vote with the
three Americans.

In contrast to American relations with Canada, which
centered around reciprocity, fishing rights, and the Alaskan
boundary, American relations with Latin America between the
Spanish-American War and World War I involved a number of
countries and a number of issues. Following our acquisition
of Puerto Rico in 1898 and the passage of the Platt Amendment in 1901 establishing an American protectorate over Cuba,
however, the Latin American policy of the United States became less of a sectional football than it had been during the
Nineteenth Century. This was largely because many of the
questions that arose relative to Latin America after 1900 did
not directly affect the American people to the extent that a

number in the previous century had.

One important controversy dating back into the Nineteenth Century that was finally settled at the beginning of this
period was the Central American canal. By 1900 the Panama
route was gaining favor among influential eastern newspapers
and leading American engineers; as the Philadelphia Times
observed, "The preference for the Nicaraguan route is determined by other than purely scientific considerations. . . . " In
1901 Great Britain signed the Second Hay-Paunceforte Treaty
which allowed the United States unilaterally to construct a
canal across Central America, also conceding the right of
this nation to fortify it in a memorandum dated August 3.
(The First Hay-Paunceforte Treaty had not granted the latter
right.) During the following year Congress passed the Spooner
Act, which provided for the construction of a canal through
the Colombian province of Panama, thus rejecting the long-
favored Nicaraguan route.

When Colombia delayed ratifying the Hay-Herran convention of 1903 which granted this nation the right to build a
canal across Panama, however, the latter revolted with the
blessing of President Theodore Roosevelt, offering us this
privilege under the Hay-Bunau Varilla Treaty of the same
year. This rather flamboyant exercise in international diplomacy stirred up a furor in this country, with many liberals
and Democrats attacking T. R. , but there was no clear-cut
division of opinion along sectional lines. Among representative journalistic reactions, the Springfield Republican lamented
Roosevelt's latest diplomatic venture as one of the "most dis-
creditable in our history"; on the other hand, the Hartford
Times remarked that Colombia's plight was "entirely her own
fault, " while the Atlanta Journal observed that she was
"needlessly obstructing the world's commerce. " According
to a survey of seventy American newspapers conducted by the
Literary Digest, fifty-three backed Panama in its revolt
against Colombia. Three years later, in 1906, Congress
passed a measure authorizing the construction of a lock canal
through Panama, and eight years later, in 1914, the first
ships entered the Panama Canal.

Examining the roll-calls on the abovementioned treaties,
the one common denominator was the hostility of the South.
The votes were, First Hay-Paunceforte Treaty, 55 to 18 (9
Southerners); Second Hay-Paunceforte Treaty, 72 to 6 (4
Southerners); Hay-Herran Convention, 73 to 5 (4 Southern-
ers); and Hay-Bunau Varilla Treaty, 66 to 14 (8 Southerners,

including pro-Nicaragua John T. Morgan). When the Senate
barely enacted the Spooner Act 42 to 34, 14 Southerners
voted nay. At this time the South was the bastion of the
Democratic Party, and this balloting doubtless reflects partisan opposition to the "Big Stick" policy of a Republican President. Twelve years later, in 1914, the West furnished 17
of the dissenters when the Senate enacted a measure by a 50
to 35 vote repealing the Panama Canal Tolls Act of 1912,
which had exempted American coastwise shipping from its
provisions. In 1912 there had been a number of examples of
Senators crossing party lines, but with a Democrat now sitting
in the White House, only three Senators from the former Confederacy opposed repeal.

        In the case of the Bryan-Chamorro Treaty with Nica-
ragua (ratified by the Senate in 1916), providing the U. S.
with an option on that canal route, and the treaty with Colombia
(ratified by the Senate in 1921) granting that nation $25 mil-
lion in "conscience money, " northeastern and southern Senators were the least opposed, those from the West and the
Middle West the most hostile. The first measure passed the
Senate 55 to 19, the second 69 to 19. Despite the fact that
the latter treaty was a rebuff to the late Theodore Roosevelt,
it easily cleared the Senate and its Republican majority,
thanks in part to the lure of Colombian oil.

        Elsewhere in the Caribbean, in 1904 the United States
intervened in the Dominican Republic to prevent that country's
take-over by European creditors. This specific action became
abstracted into a general principle: the Roosevelt Corollary
to the Monroe Doctrine. Although most Republicans, as well
as the bulk of public opinion, supported the President relative
to this bold intervention, many Democrats were less enthusiastic; the latter, in fact, controlled enough votes in the Senate
to block passage of a Dominican pact for two years, at which
time four Democrats defected. (Partisan Southerners cast 12
of the 19 votes against the Roosevelt Corollary.) Journalistic
critics from the East included the Springfield Republican, the
Boston Transcript, the Philadelphia Press, the New York Sun,
and the New York World, which proclaimed: "never was there
a more grotesque, preposterous and perilous perversion of
the Monroe Doctrine. "

        More pronounced were the sectional divisions of opinion
relative to Cuba. In the case of the abovementioned Platt
Amendment establishing an American protectorate over that
island, Southerners cast 16 of the 20 nay votes against this

amendment to the Army Appropriation Bill on March 2, 1901
when the Senate adopted it 43 to 20, with 25 abstentions. The
Senators from Louisiana spearheaded the movement against
Cuban reciprocity in deference to the sugar-cane interests of
their state; when such an agreement passed the Senate 50 to
16 on March 18, 1903, 13 Southerners were in opposition.
As the sugar-beet states of the North also would be adversely
affected, Representative Edgar Weeks of Michigan lamented in
the House during the course of a debate the previous year:
"Where, under the broad canopy of the sky, arises our moral
and legal obligation to Cuba?" Yet a 1903 treaty with Cuba
incorporating the Platt Amendment won unanimous approval
from the U. S. Senate on March 22, 1904, and even the Cuban
constitution itself embodied the protectorate concept!

With the inauguration of William Howard Taft as President, "Big Stick" diplomacy gave way to "Dollar Diplomacy,"
the banking interests of Wall Street playing the leading role.
In 1910, for example, Taft persuaded four American houses
to invest in the Haitian National Bank, while in 1911 the New
York bankers approved the appointment of Colonel C. D. Ham
of Iowa as collector general of the customs. (The United
States also intervened militarily in Nicaragua the following
year.) Less successful was an attempt in 1909 to interest
Wall Street bankers in the refinancing of Honduran indebtedness; the Senate failed to act on the treaty which Secretary
of State Philander Chase Knox drew up with Honduras to effect
this objective.

After 1910 Mexico became the focal point of this nation's Latin American diplomacy, an era of instability following the overthrow of the long-lived Diaz regime. According
to Earl Pomeroy, "From time to time, between the revolution
that began in Mexico in 1910-11 and the expropriation of oil
lands in 1938, various Westerners, particularly in California,
urged intervention in Mexican affairs. " Senator Reed Smoot
of Utah, for example, actively sought the protection of fellow
Mormons in Mexico between 1911 and 1914. When a Japanese
syndicate began negotiations in 1911 for the purchase of a
large site near Magdalena Bay in Lower California, a shout
of protest went up on the Pacific Coast; the State Department
then filed a protest, whereupon the Japanese withdrew. During
the following year, in 1912, eternally jingoist Senator Henry
Cabot Lodge of Massachusetts prevailed upon the Senate to
enact by a 51 to 4 margin his corollary to the Monroe Doctrine
which extended the scope of the latter to include an Asiatic
power and a foreign company, although under the circum-

stances this gesture was hardly necessary. The high percentage of abstentions on this vote is of no little significance.

   While the Pacific Coast was concerned with the Japanese threat to Mexico, the inhabitants of Texas, New Mexico,
and Arizona were worried about the Mexican threat to this
country. The bandit Pancho Villa, who wished to involve his
one-time chief, President Venustiano Carranza, in a war with
the United States, attacked the town of Columbus, New Mexico
on March 9, 1916, killing eighteen Americans. After Senator
Henry Ashurst of Arizona had demanded more "grape shot"
and less "grape juice" (an attack on former Secretary of State
William Jennings Bryan), and Senator Albert Fall of New
Mexico (a spokesman for the oil interests) had called for the
occupation of Mexico by an army of half a million men, President Woodrow Wilson authorized General John J. Pershing
to pursue Villa into Mexico. Less bellicose was Senator
Thomas Gore of Oklahoma, who proposed a neutral zone along
the Mexican boundary. The impending American involvement
in World War I, however, forced the withdrawal of the Pershing expedition in February 1917.

   Aside from Mexico, the Wilson Administration also intervened militarily in Haiti in 1915 and in the Dominican Republic in 1916, but these bold actions did not stir up the furor
in this country that some of Theodore Roosevelt's applications
of the "Big Stick" did. (Like the Dominican Republic, Haiti
was chronically plagued by financial problems and an unstable
government.) American troops eventually were withdrawn
from the Dominican Republic in 1924, from Haiti in 1934. As
for the sectional aspects of American intervention in the latter, black scholar Rubin Weston has charged in his recent
book on racism and U. S. imperialism that: "... the navy and
marine corps were staffed for the most part by Southerners,
who were not noted for their love and respect for persons of
color and who were subjecting Haiti to naval control without
the consent of the Haitian people. " In contrast, the NAACP
called attention to the alleged injustices resulting from the
American occupation, but without making much of an impact
on American governmental policy there.

   In 1916 the United States also purchased the Virgin
Islands from Denmark for $25 million, almost exactly a half-
century after Secretary of State William H. Seward had made
an abortive attempt to buy them. Admittedly such Progressive Senators as George Norris of Nebraska, Moses Clapp of
Minnesota, and William Kenyon of Iowa were critical, but as

was the case with the Haitian convention of the same year, there was no roll-call when the Senate placed its stamp of approval on the treaty on September 7. Since there was a real danger in 1916 that Germany might overrun Denmark and seize its West Indian possessions, public opinion in this country was highly favorable to this strategic but defensive purchase. As the war clouds darkened, the eyes of most Americans were riveted on Europe, developments in the Caribbean no longer being of primary importance.

Pacific Affairs

Following the defeat of the anti-imperialists in the election of 1900, the United States settled down to administer its overseas colonial empire in the Pacific. A Philippine government act was passed by Congress in 1902, setting up the Islands as an unorganized territory and making its inhabitants citizens of the Philippines; the Taft Commission was retained for the time being as the governing body, the first Islands assembly not meeting until 1907. Unfortunately, the Philippines remained a problem for the United States even following the crushing of the three-year long revolt led by Emilio Aguinaldo in 1902. Nor was there unanimity in this country as to what policy we should adopt towards the Islands. Representative Henry Cooper of Wisconsin introduced a bill in December 1902 reducing the level of duties on Philippine products to twenty-five per cent of those imposed by the Dingley Tariff of 1897, but thanks to the opposition of Senators from sugar-producing states, the Upper House did not even vote on a tariff reduction bill for the Islands until 1909.

By the time of World War I many southern and western Democrats, unlike the Republicans, had come to favor rapid American withdrawal from the Philippines, and President Woodrow Wilson himself supported eventual independence for the Islands. On the other hand, when the Jones bill came up for a final vote in 1916, a minority of Democrats, mostly Roman Catholics from New York and New England, voted with the Republicans against independence, although supporting the remainder of the measure; at this time the Roman Catholic Church was still opposed to an independent Philippines. Among other things, the Jones Act granted to the Islands a bill of rights, male suffrage, and an elective senate. Investing the supreme executive power in a governor-general to be appointed by the President, this piece of legislation reaffirmed the

American intention to withdraw from the Philippines, but only
following the establishment of a stable government.

Turning next to China, we pointed out in the last chapter, relative to the U. S. proclamation of the Open Door Policy
towards China in 1900, that for once sectional cross-currents
of opinion were submerged in a sea of national unity. Unfortunately, American commerce with China and the remainder
of the Far East did not live up to the expectations of the
1890's; as railroad man James J. Hill observed in 1910, "The
country needs to rid itself of the illusion that its Oriental
trade is to be one of the big elements in its future prosper-
ity--a concept still lingering grotesquely in many minds...."
Nevertheless, about half the foreign trade of San Francisco
from the turn of the century to the outbreak of World War II
was with the Far East, while such eastern ports as New York
City did not have easy access to the Orient until 1914, the
time of the completion of the Panama Canal. Among the
leading exports of the Pacific Northwest to the Far East were
kerosene, cotton, and lumber.

The Wall Street bankers who helped implement President William Howard Taft's program of "Dollar Diplomacy"
by investing in Latin America likewise followed suit in China.
Both railroader Edward H. Harriman, who dreamed of a line
through southern Manchuria, and banker J. P. Morgan were
active in this connection. In 1911 an American group including Morgan; Kuhn, Loeb, and Company; the First National
Bank; and the National City Bank joined a consortium of bankers from France, Germany, and England who sought to build
a railroad in southern and western China. Woodrow Wilson,
however, withdrew his support for "Dollar Diplomacy" in
China in 1913, leading the Wall Street Journal to complain
that: "Dollar Diplomacy was at least better than none at all."
Significantly, there was no clear-cut division of sectional or
even political opinion towards Wilson's bold action. Four
years later, in 1917, Wilson reversed himself and attempted
to persuade the somewhat reluctant Wall Street financiers to
join a four-power bankers' consortium of the United States,
Great Britain, France, and Japan. The agreement establishing this was not signed until 1920, thanks to Japanese pro-
crastination.

Despite the fact that a Chinese Exclusion Act had been
passed as long ago as 1882, one still encounters instances of
anti-Chinese agitation following the turn of the century, not
all of them by any means on the Pacific Coast. It was the

Japanese, though, who were the focal point of anti-Oriental
agitation in this country from 1906 onwards, despite the fact
that most Americans tended to sympathize with Japan against
Russia at the time of the Russo-Japanese War of 1904-1905.
The close friendship between the American eagle and the Russian bear had deteriorated badly since the Civil War; among
the factors responsible for this was American resentment at
Russian expansion into Asia, the imprisonment of political
dissenters, the Russification of Finland, and periodical out-
bursts of anti-Semitism. Curiously, many Americans regarded friendship with Japan at the time of this war as a
safeguard for the Open Door Policy in China, although the
Japanese were as imperialistic as the Russians, if not more
so.

During the course of the Russo-Japanese War, no
section was more pro-Japan than the Pacific Northwest. When
the Russian Baltic fleet, en route to the Far East, accident-
ally fired on British fishing smacks off the Dogger Banks,
the Spokane Spokesman-Review commented that it was doubtful
if history afforded the parallel of a war fleet attacking "everything on the high seas, as Don Quixote made war on wind-
mills, carriers, and flocks of sheep. " According to the
Seattle Post-Intelligencer, which favored Japan, "The fight
now going on in Asia [is] a battle between Christianity and
heathenism; between the white man and the yellow; between
the forces of civilization and those of barbarism. " It is significant that Japan, rather than Russia, was regarded by many
Americans at this time as the defender of Christianity, despite the fact that the latter had been a Christian nation for
a millenium.

At the time of the Portsmouth Peace Conference, van-
quished Russia rarely found an editorial defender among the
major newspapers of this country, the Los Angeles Times being one of the more prominent exceptions. Most of the
American press was firmly lined up behind the Japanese: the
New York Sun, the New York World, the New York American,
the Boston Herald, the Springfield Republican, the Philadelphia Public Ledger, the Cleveland Plain Dealer, the Louisville Courier Journal, the Atlanta Constitution, the New Orleans
Picayune, the St. Paul Pioneer Press, the Denver Rocky
Mountain News, the Salt Lake City Deseret News, the Spokane
Spokesman-Review, and the San Francisco Chronicle. Under
the peace treaty signed on September 5, 1905 Japan strength-
ened her position in both Korea and Manchuria, although she
failed to obtain the entire island of Sakhalin from Russia;

ironically, jingoist President Theodore Roosevelt won the
Nobel Peace Prize in 1906 for playing the role of mediator
in these negotiations.

Despite this pro-Japanese editorial near-unanimity,
there was some apprehension on the part of the American
government relative to mushrooming Japanese imperialism in
the Far East.   In 1907 T. R. sent the American navy on a
world cruise (December 16, 1907-February 22, 1909) designed
to show that this nation ranked ahead of Japan as a world
naval power.   Some Easterners, such as Senator Eugene Hale
of Maine, objected to stripping the Atlantic Coast of its naval
protection, but there was no German attack there, and the
Japanese even extended a most cordial reception to the American fleet.

By 1906, though, the focal point of Japanese-American
relations had become directed, not on China, Korea, or Manchuria, but on California, where anti-Japanese agitation had
reached a peak of frenzy comparable to that of the anti-
Chinese movement of a quarter-century past.   As late as
1880, two years before Congress passed the Chinese Exclusion Act, there were only 92 Japanese in the six states of
the Pacific Coast, but by 1900 the total number had reached
20, 507, this number nearly tripling to 57, 903 in 1910.   It was
around the turn of the century that the first instances of anti-
Japanese agitation were reported; in 1899, to cite an early
example, Japanese employed by the Great Northern Railway
were attacked at Trenton, North Dakota, and Saco, Montana.
The following year, in 1900, the first organized protest in
California against the unrestricted admittance of Japanese immigrants occurred at a public meeting in San Francisco, while
in 1901 (and again in 1905) the California legislature submitted
a memorial to Congress pleading for national restrictions on
Japanese immigration.   Idaho, Montana, and Nevada followed
suit at the time of the Russo-Japanese War.

Anti-Japanese sentiment in California now erupted like
a volcano.   On April 1, 1905 the San Francisco Board of
Education formulated a plan for segregating Japanese school
children; one month later, on May 7, the Japanese and Korean
Exclusion League was born at a mass meeting in the same
city.   President Theodore Roosevelt was not amused by this
display of bigotry, commenting to Henry Cabot Lodge that:
"The feeling on the Pacific slope, taking it from several different standpoints, is as foolish as if conceived by the mind
of a Hottentot. "   Following the great earthquake and fire of

April 1906, though, San Franciscans stepped up their program
of discrimination, despite the fact that the Japanese Red Cross
contributed generously to the victims of the disaster. On
October 11, 1906 the Board of Education passed a resolution
segregating all oriental students in a separate building. Actually there were only 93 Japanese students attending the public
schools of the city, and few, if any, were undesirables, so
that it is difficult to justify the school board's action on ra-
tional grounds. Even worse, this episode caused a monu-
mental furor in Japan. On the other hand, in the twelve
months' span ending November 30, 1906 over seventeen thousand Japanese entered this country, two-thirds of them via
Hawaii, a statistic which naturally proved upsetting to many
Americans.

Hoping to check this yellow tide via some sort of
agreement with the Japanese government, T. R. nevertheless
felt it necessary first of all to chastize San Francisco publicly
for its bigotry. This he did in his message to Congress on
December 4, in which he praised Japan for its remarkable
achievements, labeled the action of the school board a "wicked
absurdity, " and recommended that Congress enact a law permitting the naturalization of Japanese. Generally speaking,
Japan was pleased, San Francisco was not. As the Examiner
of that city observed, the 93 Japanese would be forgotten "as
soon as President Roosevelt lays aside his pewter sword,
sheathes his fire-belching tongue and ceases his tin-soldier
yawp about leading the army and navy against our school-
houses. "

Nor was criticism of the chief executive confined to
California. T. R. was also attacked by Governor Albert E.
Mead of Washington, Senator John M. Gearin of Oregon,
Senator Francis G. Newlands of Nevada, Senator Thomas M.
Patterson of Colorado, and by a number of southern members
of Congress as concerned with states' rights as they were
with white supremacy. Among the latter were Representatives
John Sharp Williams of Mississippi, Leonidas Livingston of
Georgia, and Finis Garrett of Tennessee. On December 4,
moreover, a mob of whites assaulted a dozen Japanese laborers in Tacoma, Washington, while in neighboring Seattle ten
thousand individuals signed an anti-Japanese petition around
this time. This demonstrates that anti-Japanese sentiment in
the West reached fever proportions in states other than California.

Journalistic reactions to the San Francisco school seg-

regation episode, like public opinion throughout the country in
general towards the Japanese, tended in the East to be most
favorable to T. R. and most hostile to the racists. The
Cleveland Plain Dealer, for example, complained that "California is beyond reach of the paternal slipper of the national
administration"; the New York correspondent of the London
Times observed that: "There is absolutely no sympathy in the
Eastern States with the anti-Japanese agitation in California."
Whatever criticism there was of the President in the East
concerning his handling of this controversy generally centered
around the question of states' rights and the growing power
of the national government. Conversely, journalistic reactions
in the West, like public opinion there, almost unanimously
supported the anti-Japanese agitators and attacked T. R.
Three exceptions that one might cite were the Seattle News,
the Tacoma Daily News, and the Los Angeles Times, all of
which displayed a marked sympathy for the Japanese cause.

By the beginning of 1907 President Theodore Roosevelt
had come to realize that feeling against the Japanese on the
Pacific Coast was so strong that he would have to support
Japanese exclusion, regardless of whether he personally approved of the latter course or not. He so informed Governor
Gillett in a letter dated March 14. The previous month T. R.
had confided to George Kennan that the basic trouble in San
Francisco was not segregation in the public schools, but
rather the general anti-Japanese climate of opinion, "partly
labor, and partly a deep-rooted racial antipathy, the extent of
which fairly astounds me." After inviting the San Francisco
School Board to Washington for a conference in February, the
President reached an understanding with that group that they
would rescind the segregation order, in return for which the
federal government would restrict Japanese immigration. The
latter objective was effected by an amendment to the Immigration Act of 1907, and by the so-called "Gentlemen's Agreement" with Japan; under the latter Japan promised to withhold
passports from laborers intending to migrate to this country.

Just prior to leaving office in 1909, Theodore Roosevelt managed to persuade the governor of California and the
speaker of the assembly to block enactment of an anti-Japanese
school bill and another measure limiting Japanese ownership
of land to five years. When the Nevada assembly passed a
resolution directed to its California counterpart, in support
of the anti-Japanese measures before it, the President had
the United States Senators from Nevada persuade their state
senate to table the measure. (It was at this time that T. R.

observed to his cabinet that California "was too small to become a nation, and too large to put into a lunatic asylum.")
The following year, after William Howard Taft became President, the California legislature ordered the state commissioner of labor to make a thorough investigation of the Japanese in the state; the commissioner, though, had the courage
to describe the latter as "land owners ... of the best class,"
with the result that the state senate censured him and dis-
approved his report.   The state senate likewise adopted a resolution on February 22, 1911 attacking a new treaty between
the United States and Japan, the day after it was signed, on
the grounds that it omitted the right contained in the treaty of
1894 with China to legislate on immigration restriction.

In 1913 California again attracted national attention
when its legislature passed the Webb Act, an alien land law
primarily directed against the Japanese, which withheld the
privilege of land ownership from aliens and permitted them
to lease land for a period of no more than three years. The
President at this time, Woodrow Wilson, who sent Secretary
of State William Jennings Bryan on a mission to Sacramento
in an attempt to influence the legislature, fared less well in
his attempt to block enactment of this legislation than had
T. R. and Taft relative to its earlier counterparts.

According to Eleanor Tupper, the East generally opposed the Webb Act, the South generally supported it, and the
Middle West was divided; on the Pacific Coast laborers,
farmers, and politicians tended to be favorable, merchants,
educators, and clergymen, unfavorable. (To the surprise of
everyone, the anti-Japanese San Francisco Chronicle opposed
this law.) In this connection Roger Daniels has observed
that: "... the generators of much of California's antidemo-
cratic energy were those very groups supposedly dedicated to
democracy.... Conversely, conservative forces ... were
often on the democratic side. " Elsewhere in the West, alien
land bills later failed to pass in Idaho and Oregon in 1917
after the State Department had raised its voice in protest, but
Oregon and Washington did discriminate against aliens in their
fishing laws of 1913 and 1915.

During World War I Japan was this nation's ally, but
following the termination of that conflict anti-Japanese agitation
resumed on the Pacific Coast. In 1919 the California Oriental
Exclusion League was set up with the stated objective of terminating the Gentlemen's Agreement and barring Asiatics for-
ever from American citizenship. Valentine S. McClatchy also

resigned as the publisher of the Bee newspapers of Sacramento, Modesto, and Fresno at this time and established the
California Joint Immigration Committee. The following year,
in 1920, the California voters approved an initiated measure
at the polls by a margin of 668,483 to 22,086 which provided
that the right to own or lease land must conform with existing
treaty rights, thus further restricting the Japanese. But alien
land legislation was by no means a strictly California phenomenon in the years following World War I; between 1921 and
1925 such states as Arizona, Arkansas, Delaware, Idaho,
Kansas, Louisiana, Missouri, Montana, Nebraska, Nevada,
New Mexico, Oregon, Texas, and Washington all adopted similar measures.

Despite the Gentlemen's Agreement, the number of
Japanese immigrants entering this country doubled from 5,803
in 1908 to 10,064 in 1919, after reaching a peak of 30,226 in
1907. Between 1893 and 1919 a total of 219,048 Japanese
touched foot on American soil, enough to populate a moderately large city. Congress, which during the early 1920's
passed legislation restricting immigration from southeastern
Europe, also looked with extreme disfavor upon oriental immigration. As a result, it enacted a measure on May 26,
1924 which totally excluded the Japanese from this country.
The spirit of San Francisco had triumphed.

World War I and American Intervention

During the summer of 1914 war broke out in Europe.
According to Maynard W. Brown, who has made a study of
editorial opinion at the time, "The news and interpretations
in the American press in the thirty months preceding June,
1914, did little towards developing public opinion in America
as to what was maturing on the European continent." Even
such prominent eastern newspapers as the New York Times
and the New York Tribune offered little truly penetrating editorial comment; the Milwaukee Journal, too, commented only
rarely on European political affairs, despite the fact that it
had many German readers. Of the nine newspapers studied
by Brown, the Portland Oregonian showed more interest edi-
torially in European affairs than any of the others, with the
possible exception of the New York Times. Once the serious
nature of the European crisis was realized, though, editorial
sentiment throughout this country strongly backed Serbia
against Austria, and eventually shifted the blame to Germany

once war had actually broken out.

Most historians today interpret public opinion in this country during the first year of World War I as being most favorable to American aid to the Allies in the Northeast, which section had forged innumerable commercial and financial ties with Great Britain over the years, and least favorable in the Middle West, a section geographically isolated by the Appalachian Mountains and boasting a large German-American population. This interpretation is based largely on a nation-wide poll of editorial opinion which appeared in the Literary Digest on November 14, 1914. According to the latter, the ratio by section of neutral or pro-German editors to pro-Allied ones was 44 to 34 in the East, 56 to 47 in the South, and 122 to 13 in the Middle West. Yet while Alexander de Conde points out that a higher percentage of southern editors favored neutrality than was the case with any other section, George B. Tindall notes that the poll revealed a stronger trend towards the Allies in the South than in any other region. Thus the results of this poll have been interpreted variously.

Andrew Cogswell, who has studied the Montana press for the years 1914 through 1917, goes even further and labels the Literary Digest poll as of doubtful authority. Cogswell, for example, challenges the thesis that the Atlantic Seaboard press was "admittedly a more truculent group than those of the Middle West and the Far West, " taking the position that "The similarities of newspaper attitudes towards the European war from 1914 to 1917 in the newspapers of Montana and Maine are inescapable. " It should be added, however, that a rather atypical situation existed in Montana, in that the copper industry of the state was undergoing a depression, and the decline in exports of this metal as a result of the war further worsened the situation. But, as Cogswell emphasizes, this economic crisis did not alter the general pro-Allied bias of the Montana press.

Examining sectional attitudes towards World War I at greater length, one might begin by referring to the agrarian tradition common to the South, the Middle West, and the Great Plains which had supported war with Spain twenty years previously, and long had been hostile to Great Britain, the world's leading defender of the gold standard. In the opinion of John Clark Crighton, who has made a study of Missouri attitudes during World War I, agrarian opposition to American intervention first began to manifest itself strongly towards the end of 1915. Criticism of rearmament was especially vig-

orous west of the Mississippi, which apparently was much
more fearful of the dangers of militarism than the Middle
West; many of the petitions received by Congress opposing
an increased army and navy came from the former section,
while Governor Arthur Capper of Kansas led a movement to
nationalize the munitions industry. In addition, socialist ideology and a heavy German population were added factors of
consequence in the development of isolationism in North Dakota.
Opponents of the radical Non-Partisan League there attempted
to discredit this organization by accusing it of disloyalty, and
it is true that Non-Partisan Leaguers and German-Americans
were united in their opposition to American involvement in
World War I.

East of the Mississippi and west of the Appalachians,
too, a neutral stance was common. During July 1915, for
example, officers of the First National Bank of Chicago informed Thomas W. Lamont of the House of Morgan that there
was little enthusiasm for a British loan in the upper Mississippi Valley. But it was not only the bankers who opposed
further American involvement; Victor Berger declared that
"if democracy were the object of the war, it would have a
different set of enthusiasts. " Apparently there were some
midwestern states, such as Missouri, which were less pacifistic and isolationistic than others, but even if John Clark
Crighton is correct in his assessment that the pacifism and
isolationism of this section may have been overestimated, they
remain significant phenomena even on a reduced scale. One
must not disregard, moreover, the presence of a large number of evangelical religious sects avowedly pacifistic in ideology throughout the Middle West. Another factor of importance contributing to middle western isolation was that English
ships carried many of the exports of this section, and those
benefitting from this commerce quite naturally opposed any
steps (such as involvement in the war) which might endanger
this arrangement.

Commercial considerations were even more important
to the South, whose cotton exports had been seriously threatened by the outbreak of war between Great Britain and Germany. When the British imposed a blockade that hindered the
exporting of this product to its normal European markets,
Senator John Sharp Williams of Mississippi observed to President Woodrow Wilson that southern politicians had been
forced to adopt an anti-British stance as a result; in August
1915 Great Britain incensed this nation even further by adding cotton to its absolute contraband list. Germany, it must

be remembered, was at this time the second largest importer of American cotton.   It was also of consequence that the chairman of the Senate Foreign Relations Committee, William J. Stone of Missouri, represented a state that both produced cotton and had a considerable German population.   Fortunately for the South, the British government had agreed to maintain the price of cotton at ten cents a pound after placing it on the absolute contraband list, and English purchases and a short crop further elevated the price for middling cotton on the New York Exchange to 12. 30 cents a pound on October 29. Cotton prices continued to rise until 1920, a factor which made it much easier for the South to back the English against the Germans during World War I.

Nevertheless, Virginia-born Woodrow Wilson enjoyed considerable support in the South for his pro-British foreign policy, being the section's "first President since Jefferson Davis. " Thus on September 3, 1914 Henry Watterson of the influential Louisville Courier-Journal affixed to the masthead of his newspaper "To Hell with the Hohenzollerns and Hapsburgs, " keeping this motto there throughout the war. Wilson also appointed a number of Southerners to high positions in his administration, including Colonel Edward House and Ambassador to Great Britain Walter Hines Page.   Since the Civil War, there had been only one Democrat in the White House--Grover Cleveland--and the solidly Democratic South was enraptured with the prospect of no longer having to contend with the foreign policy of a representative of that party which had imposed Reconstruction upon the South.   Local factors, though, were also responsible for the flowering of southern internationalism; following the lynching of Leo Frank on August 16, 1915, many Georgians embraced preparedness so as to disassociate themselves from the anti-Wilson bigot, Tom Watson.

Aside from Watson, several prominent southern members of Congress failed to support the President on his policy towards Europe.   Among these was the Democratic Majority Leader in the House, Claude Kitchen of North Carolina, who opposed the "big Navy and big Army program of the jingoes and war traffickers. "   Then there was Senator James K. Vardaman of Mississippi, who wrote Kitchen that he hoped that others "may be constrained to follow you and save the farmers and wealth producers of this Republic from being plundered in the interest of the manufacturers of munitions of war. "   Vardaman was to go down to defeat in his bid for re-election to the Senate in 1918, having earned the "Kaiser's

Iron Cross" in the opinion of hostile Mississippi editorialists,
but Tom Watson won election to the United States Senate in
1920, running on an Anglophobic, anti-Wilson, and anti-League
platform. (Significantly, the former Populist leader favored
the early recognition of the Soviet Union.)

During January 1915 a large portion of the press of
the smaller cities of this nation initiated a large-scale attack
upon the shipment of war materials to any of the belligerent
powers. According to a poll which the Literary Digest published on February 6, 1915, the most bitter opposition to an
embargo on exports was to be found in the large cities of the
industrial East; there was much more enthusiasm for restrictive legislation in the Middle West and on the Pacific Coast.
Despite the strenuous efforts of the pacifists, this campaign
produced no concrete results.

Of all those groups in the United States that were favorable to the Allied cause, none was more active than the banking interests of New York. On November 4, 1914 the National City Bank of New York City had advanced ten million
dollars to the French government, a loan which was the forerunner of a number of later transactions involving much larger
sums. The following year, in 1915, New York bankers floated
a five hundred million dollar Anglo-French issue by popular
subscription; Thomas W. Lamont of the House of Morgan observed in this connection: "From the very start we did
everything that we could to contribute to the cause of the
Allies." To many opponents of American intervention in
World War I the banking interests of Wall Street were as
great a menace as the "munition makers."

On May 7, 1915 German submarines sank the British
transatlantic steamer Lusitania off the coast of Ireland without
giving the latter warning. (Admittedly the German embassy
did place ads in New York City newspapers the day the Lusitania sailed, warning American travellers to stay off British
ships entering the war zone.) Of the 1,198 who lost their
lives, 128 were Americans. Quite naturally this incident
generated a gigantic wave of anti-German sentiment across
this country, which was heightened by the release around the
same time of the Bryce Commission's report on alleged German atrocities in Belgium and northern France. Nevertheless, there was little editorial sentiment throughout the country
in favor of war with Germany, although David Lawrence was
of the opinion that "a few people on the Eastern seaboard were
clamoring for war." Secretary of Agriculture David Houston,

in fact, discovered most Californians to be more interested in the citrus fruit crop and an improved highway system than in fighting. In the words of the Atlanta Constitution, "the people of the United States do not want war. "

Disturbed by the drift of the nation towards greater involvement in European affairs, William Jennings Bryan refused to sign President Woodrow Wilson's second Lusitania note to Germany, resigning as Secretary of State on June 7, 1915. The much more hawkish Robert Lansing now took over as Secretary of State; while Bryan was more dovish than Wilson, though, Wilson was more dovish than Lansing. Despite Bryan's strong backing in the agrarian South, Middle West, and Great Plains during his three Presidential bids, most editorialists across the country were of the opinion that pacifist Bryan was not fitted to be Secretary of State during a time of world crisis, and that his resignation was probably a good thing for the country. Especially vitriolic was the Louisville Courier-Journal, which proclaimed: "Men have been shot and beheaded, even hanged, drawn and quartered for treason less heinous. "

The following year, on February 17, 1916, Jeff Mc-Lemore of Texas had introduced a resolution in the House of Representatives requesting the President to warn Americans not to travel on armed vessels. This was after Germany had declared that following March 1 she would sink all armed enemy merchant vessels without warning. On February 25, moreover, Senator Thomas P. Gore of Oklahoma introduced a similar resolution in the Senate denying passports to Americans seeking passage on armed belligerent vessels. Strongly opposed by President Woodrow Wilson, who vigorously championed the rights of neutrals, the McLemore Resolution was tabled by the House on March 7, 276 to 142, while the Gore Resolution met a similar fate in the Senate on March 3, 68 to 14. A sectional breakdown of this vote is most enlightening. In the House, for example, New England cast only three votes against the resolution to table, the President enjoying his strongest support among the delegations of the Atlantic Seaboard States; on the other hand, the delegations from Iowa, Nebraska, Minnesota, and Wisconsin lined themselves up solidly behind McLemore, as did a majority of midwestern Representatives. In the Senate, twelve of the fourteen votes supporting the Gore Resolution came from the Middle West, the Great Plains, and the Pacific Coast.

The strong support that the McLemore and Gore reso-

lutions enjoyed among members of Congress from the Middle
West takes on added significance in light of the speaking tour
that President Woodrow Wilson scheduled through this section
in late January and early February. Apparently Wilson made
few converts, at least in Congress. Later that spring, war
opponent Henry Ford won sweeping victories in the Republican
Presidential primaries in Michigan and Nebraska, despite the
fact that he was not even a candidate and tried to take his
name off the ballot. Many pacifists and German-Americans
later backed the selection of Charles Evans Hughes as the
Republican Presidential nominee. Nevertheless, Woodrow
Wilson captured the heavily Scandinavian counties of the Middle West that fall because "he kept us out of the war"; for
the first time in a straight two-party fight, a Democratic
Presidential nominee triumphed in North Dakota. But the key
to the Democratic triumph here was not Wilson, but rather
former Secretary of State William Jennings Bryan, who engaged in a lengthy speaking tour throughout the Mississippi
Valley during the Summer of 1916. Only one state in which
Bryan spoke, in fact, voted for Hughes over Wilson; twenty
years had passed since "The Great Commoner" had made his
first Presidential run, yet his oft-repeated message remained
gospel truth in the eyes of many Middle Westerners.

    The re-elected President, though, no more kept us out
of war during his second term than Franklin Roosevelt or
Lyndon Johnson did following their victories at the polls in
1940 and 1964, respectively. Germany renewed unrestricted
submarine warfare on February 1, and two days later America broke off diplomatic relations with Germany; the Senate
passed a resolution on February 7, by a 78 to 5 margin, endorsing Wilson's action. On February 26 Woodrow Wilson
asked Congress for the authority to arm American merchant-
men. Although the House passed the Armed Ship Bill on
March 1 by the overwhelming majority of 403 to 14 (mostly
Midwestern Republicans), a group of a dozen Senators led by
Robert La Follette of Wisconsin filibustered the bill to death.
Wilson, however, was informed by Secretary of State Robert
Lansing that he could arm merchant vessels without the specific approval of Congress, and this step was taken on March
12, the same day that a German submarine sank the S. S. Al-
gonquin without warning.

    Relations between America and Germany were further
aggravated by the interception and publication in this country
of a coded message sent to the German Minister to Mexico
by Alfred Zimmermann, the German Foreign Secretary. Were

war to break out between Germany and the United States, the former was to propose an alliance with Mexico on the following basis: "That we shall make war together and together make peace. We shall give generous financial support, and it is understood that Mexico is to reconquer the lost territory in New Mexico, Texas, and Arizona." This preposterous scheme also involved Japan abandoning the Allies and joining the Central Powers; Zimmermann was of the opinion that the West and the Middle West would block a declaration of war by Congress in fear that the Japanese might attack the Pacific Coast.

Eastern jingoes were overjoyed by the release of this telegram, being well aware that it increased the likelihood of American intervention, and the House of Representatives did pass the Armed Ship Bill by a nearly unanimous vote the very same day. On the Pacific Coast, too, tempers flared, although the inhabitants of that section felt 'less threatened by a German-backed invasion from Mexico than by a possible German-Japanese alliance. The hostile reaction was particularly strong in the Southwest, previously rather indifferent to the war and only mildly anti-German; the Southeast and the Gulf Coast also were incensed by the revelation of this fantastic plot. After touring the South and the Southwest, former President William Howard Taft reported that the release of the Zimmermann note had turned the weathervane of public opinion in these two sections in the direction of war. (Missouri apparently was an exception to this growth of militancy.) In this connection one might quote an editorial from the Santa Fe New Mexican as representative:

> Sooner or later we are going to have to face this
> international desperado and criminal. Half way
> measures, further listening to the 'pacifists' who
> have labored so long for the ruin of their country,
> will be suicidal. Every iota of energy in the
> country should be devoted to placing America in a
> position to defend her rights, her ships, her citi-
> zens and her territory.

A month later, on April 2, President Woodrow Wilson, thwarted in his attempt to negotiate a "peace without victory," asked that Congress declare war against Germany. "The world," affirmed Wilson, "must be made safe for democracy." The Congressional decision for war, though, was not unanimous; the Senate adopted the war resolution by a vote of 82 to 6 on April 4, the House of Representatives by 372 to 50

two days later.   The six Senators who opposed the declaration
included four from the Middle West-Great Plains area, and
Middle Westerners also cast the bulk of the anti-war ballots
in the House of Representatives.   Yet this protest vote was
by no means spread uniformly across these two sections; the
bulk of it was concentrated in Wisconsin, South Dakota, Illinois, Missouri, Nebraska, and Minnesota, with the anti-war
forces having a majority in only the first two of these states.
In fact, Ohio and Michigan cast only a single ballot against
the war resolution, and Indiana none.

    As for the South, only five Representatives and Senator
James K.   Vardaman of Mississippi voted against the declaration.   Five Pacific Coast members of the House also opposed
the war resolution, while further inland the one-man Nevada
delegation was the only one against it.   The one Northeasterner
to cast a negative ballot was Meyer London, the Socialist
from New York.

    One of the most curious aspects of American partici-
pation in World War I was the strong support given by the
South to intervention, despite the fact that the war centralized
additional power in Washington and thus openly conflicted with
the states' rights philosophy prevelant in that section.   Just
prior to the declaration of war the Arkansas, Oklahoma, and
Tennessee legislatures and the Kentucky senate adopted resolutions in support of Woodrow Wilson's foreign policy.   On
the other hand, southern members of both houses of Congress
almost solidly united to help pass an immigration bill with a
literacy test provision, over Wilson's veto on May 1, 1917,
a month after the declaration of war.   Some Southerners even
urged the exclusion of Negro immigrants, although there was
not much immigration from Africa at this time.

    Aside from American intervention in World War I dur-
ing this year, the overthrow of the monarchy in Russia occurred in March, while the Communist takeover there followed in November.   Over the past quarter century humani-
tarians in this country had protested on several occasions
when episodes of anti-Semitism had occurred in Russia, including the anti-Jewish riots in Kishinev on Easter Sunday
1903, a mere year before the outbreak of the war.   In 1909
Representative Henry M. Goldfogle of New York introduced a
resolution in the House calling for a renegotiation of the
Treaty of 1832 with Russia, while in 1911 there were before
Congress at least a dozen resolutions providing for the outright abrogation of this treaty that had won unanimous Sena-

torial approval nearly a century before. Petitions in behalf
of the latter were received from such states as Massachusetts,
Connecticut, Rhode Island, Virginia, Minnesota, and Wisconsin.

Thus, it is not surprising that a nation whose President desired to make the world safe for democracy would look
with general satisfaction upon the fall of the Romanovs in
March 1917. The Boston Transcript observed that "a night-
mare had been taken from the breast of the whole liberal
world, " while the New Orleans Item rejoiced that the United
States would now not have to align itself with "the most cruel
and despotic government in the world. " Dissenting voices in
this chorus of approval were few and far between. But the
Communist overthrow of the short-lived liberal regime in
November was an entirely different matter; the United States
government did not recognize the new Communist regime until
1933. When the Japanese invaded Siberia in April 1918,
moreover, the editorial response of American newspapers,
regardless of section, was overwhelmingly favorable. President Woodrow Wilson did dispatch 5000 men to Archangel (on
the coast of northwestern Russia) and 9000 to Siberia without
the consent of Congress; the combined forces of the United
States, the Allies, and Japan, though, proved unable to dis-
lodge the Communists from power, and the joint endeavor had
an adverse effect on Japanese-American relations. In 1920
the last contingent of American troops withdrew from Siberia.

The Versailles Treaty and the League of Nations

On November 11, 1918 an armistice was proclaimed,
bringing World War I to a halt. Only six days before, in the
mid-term Congressional elections, the Republicans had won
control of both houses of Congress (the Senate by a narrow
two-vote majority), despite President Woodrow Wilson's pre-
election plea that the voters cast their ballots for Democratic
candidates. Midwestern wheat farmers in particular were
resentful over the imposition of a price ceiling by the administration. According to Seward W. Livermore, twenty Congressional isolationists from both parties, mainly southern
and western based, had been purged earlier that year in the
primary elections; a few more went down to defeat on November 5. Exactly one week after the signing of the armistice,
on November 18, Wilson announced that he would break tradition by attending the peace conference at Paris in person,

accompanied by a commission composed of Colonel Edward
House, Secretary of State Robert Lansing, General Tasker
Bliss, and Henry White.   No member of the Senate was included, while White was the only Republican member; con-
spicuous in their absence were such powerful Republican Senatorial leaders as Henry Cabot Lodge.

        The President sailed for Europe on December 4 on
the George Washington. According to James D. Startt, who
examined the reaction of 168 American newspapers to the
President's trip, 48 per cent supported it, 25 per cent opposed it, and 27 percent remained uncommitted.   No less
than 64 per cent of the large dailies were favorable, although
the Hearst chain failed to editorialize directly on the issue.
As one might expect, several midwestern dailies were hostile,
but even the New York Times, his erstwhile ally, apparently
had serious misgivings: "The greatness of the occasion might
warrant even his astonishing departure from custom, but does
the potential difference in the result warrant it?"   On the
other hand, the Louisville Courier-Journal, which had bitterly
attacked the Hohenzollerns, the Hapsburgs, and William Jennings Bryan, proclaimed that: "Mr. Wilson has very sensibly
decided to go to France" because that is the place where
"the most important business the United States has ever had
will be transacted. "

        The terms of the Treaty of Versailles, which were
presented to the protesting Germans on May 7, 1919, are too
well-known to require detailed analysis.   Among other things,
Germany was required to admit her war guilt under Article
231, to surrender her colonies, Alsace-Lorraine, and the
Saar Basin, and to pay reparations, later fixed at 56 billion
dollars, to those countries she invaded.   Had the Treaty of
Versailles contained no other provisions, doubtless the United
States would have approved it.   Yet attached to the treaty was
the Covenant of the League of Nations, and the latter was
anathema to that large body of Americans who preferred to
follow the non-entangling alliance tradition of George Washington's Farewell Address; aside from those isolationists who
thus opposed the peace settlement on ideological grounds,
there were Republicans who attacked it on partisan ones.

        Let us next examine the early press reaction to Wood-
row Wilson's League proposal.   When the President was on
his way home from Paris in February, the once-skeptical
New York Times commented that the "President's opponents,
the opponents of the League, at Washington and elsewhere, will

contend in vain against an overwhelming public opinion. "
Much to the displeasure of Henry Cabot Lodge, Wilson landed
at Boston, where he was greeted by Republican Governor Calvin Coolidge. Despite his warm reception there, a number
of New England newspapers, including the Manchester Union,
the Providence Journal, the Boston Transcript, and the Rutland Daily Herald, either had serious reservations about the
covenant or refused to accept it as it presently stood. The
Rutland Daily Herald, for example, was of the opinion that:

> Dual, triple, and quadruple alliances have failed
> and always for the same reason--that some nation
> has made itself sufficiently powerful to dominate
> the alliance for its own ends.... Can we hope that
> the President's idealistic League of Nations will ac-
> complish more? Is it not more probable that in
> the end a powerful combination of nations would be
> effected within the League, representing a military
> autocracy that would be just as dangerous... as that
> of Germany?

Generally speaking, eastern editorial opinion was divided, with
both the bulwark of Wilson's support and the core of the resistance located in New York City. Hearst newspapers, both
here and elsewhere, looked with disfavor upon the League.

In contrast, Wilson enjoyed almost unanimous journalistic backing throughout the South, the Nashville Tennessean
hoping that the League would "exterminate the Hun and Hun-
nism for all time, " and the Dallas Morning News commenting
that the arguments of the opposition would "leave the public
mind as little impressed as would a snowflake falling upon a
block of granite. " Editorial opinion was much more critical
in the Middle West, but even here the President enjoyed the
support of such important newspapers as the St. Louis Globe-
Democrat and the Des Moines Register. According to Ray
Billington, there was no concerted attack against the League
by midwestern editorialists until the Summer of 1919.
Throughout the Far West, journalistic support for Wilson was
widespread; newspapers backing the President included the Albuquerque Morning Journal, the Arizona Republican, the Helena
Independent, the Denver Rocky Mountain News, the Los Angeles Times, the Seattle Times, and the Portland Oregonian.
Both the San Francisco Chronicle and the San Francisco Examiner, though, were unsympathetic, as was the Reno Gazette.

On April 5, 1919 the Literary Digest published the

results of a poll of 1,377 editors across the country as to
whether they favored the proposed League of Nations. No
less than 718 announced their support, while still another 478
accepted it conditionally; only 181, or less than one in seven,
registered firm opposition. By section the breakdown of responses was as follows:

Section	Yes	No	Conditional
New England	40	14	41
Middle Atlantic	122	37	104
East North Central	166	48	132
West North Central	85	29	70
South Atlantic	75	13	24
East South Central	45	4	7
West South Central	88	8	21
Mountain	33	8	30
Pacific	64	20	49
Total	718	181	478

        In the United States Senate, no more than a dozen or
so of its members were irrevocably opposed to the League,
a percentage almost identical with the above editorial results.
But these so-called "irreconcilables" included with their ranks
such prominent figures as Hiram W. Johnson of California,
William E. Borah of Idaho, and Robert M. La Follette, Sr.
of Wisconsin; six of the ten seats on the Foreign Relations
Committee were held by "irreconcilables." The Republicans,
it must be remembered, had won paper-thin control of the
Senate in the 1918 Congressional elections, thus allowing that
party to organize this and other committees. In contrast,
the much larger group favoring immediate ratification without
reservations, mostly Democrats, were commanded by the less
well-known Gilbert Hitchcock of Nebraska. The destiny of
the League, however, lay in the hands of a third faction, the
moderates or "reservationists," who perhaps constituted one-
third of the Senate membership. To this day there is no
conclusive evidence as to whether its strategist, Wilson-hating
Senator Henry Cabot Lodge of Massachusetts, sincerely desired a League with modifications, or whether he saw that
the only way to defeat the treaty was to amend it to death.
In any event, on March 4, 1919 Lodge made public a Republican "Round Robin" signed by 39 Senators or Senators-elect
which affirmed that "... the constitution of the league of nations in the form now proposed to the peace conference should
not be accepted by the United States...." Should this bloc

hold firm, it would be impossible for the Wilson Administration to obtain the necessary two-thirds majority for the Versailles Treaty.

On September 10 the Senate Foreign Relations Committee and its "irreconcilable" majority reported out the treaty with 45 amendments and 4 reservations. One week earlier, on September 3, the President had begun a 9,500-mile tour on behalf of the League, during the course of which he delivered 37 speeches in 29 cities. Ohio and Indiana were lukewarm in their reception, while Wilson did not even bother to visit highly isolationistic Illinois; further west the crowds in Missouri, Iowa, Nebraska, and Minnesota were somewhat more enthusiastic, but there still was considerable opposition on the Great Plains. It was on the Pacific Coast and in the Rocky Mountains that Wilson received the heartiest welcome. Denna F. Fleming has written of the President's greeting in Seattle that: "It was doubtful in the history even of recent political campaigns a more remarkable demonstration had been witnessed." At San Francisco, Oakland, Los Angeles, and San Diego the reception was similarly enthusiastic; California, it must be remembered, had been the key state in Wilson's successful re-election campaign of 1916. Undaunted by this overwhelming chorus of approval, isolationist Senators Hiram W. Johnson and William E. Borah conducted their own speaking tour in opposition to the League, occasionally speaking in the same halls as the President a day or so later.

Wilson continued his triumphal tour eastward through Reno, Salt Lake City, Cheyenne, Denver, and Pueblo, with huge crowds extending him a frenzied greeting at each of these stops. There even was talk of the President invading Henry Cabot Lodge's New England. But at Pueblo the end came. Following his unforgettable speech there on September 25 Wilson experienced a physical collapse, suffering a stroke in Washington on October 2 upon his forced return. If the League was to win out now, it would have to be without the active support of the President; nevertheless, the array of forces backing it remained formidable. Aside from the examples of editorial and public support thus far cited, the legislatures of 32 states--two-thirds of the then 48--passed concurrent resolutions endorsing the League, while 33 governors also favored it.

The genius of American politics, it has been observed, lies in the art of compromise. Six years earlier Woodrow Wilson had been willing to alter his program of domestic re-

form, the New Freedom, to guarantee its passage through
Congress; now an older and more experienced but also ailing
Wilson refused to do so relative to the League. Whether his
reaction would have been different had the proposed modifications come from someone other than his bitter enemy Henry
Cabot Lodge is questionable. In any event, Lodge proposed a
resolution of ratification on November 6 that included 14 reservations. When the President urged his supporters on November 18 to defeat the Lodge package on the grounds that it
"does not provide for ratification, but, rather for the nullification of the treaty, " 42 loyal Democrats joined forces with
13 "irreconcilable" Republicans the following day to reject it,
39 to 55. Only four Democrats bolted Wilson. After a second
vote the same day had narrowed the margin to 41 to 51, a
Democratic attempt to win approval without reservations went
down to defeat, 38 to 53. To Senator William Borah of Idaho
it was "the greatest victory since Appomatox"; conversely,
Senator Carter Glass of Virginia lamented the lack of response
"when the greatest Christian statesman of all time summoned
the nations of the earth to enter into a Covenant which contained the very essence of the Sermon on the Mount and was
the consummation, as far as Christian nations would contrive,
of the sacrifice on Calvary. "

     Support for the League, nevertheless, remained strong
enough to force Senator Lodge to bring the treaty up after he
had been approached by representatives of twenty-six national
organizations with a total membership of twenty million. Lodge,
in fact, had entered into negotiations with the Democrats when
a group of Republican "irreconcilables" headed by Borah confronted him with the ultimatum that either he abandon further
attempts at compromise or they would depose him as Republican majority leader. Consequently, the version of the treaty
that Lodge presented to the Senate the second time around was
quite similar to the first; there were now fifteen reservations
instead of fourteen, one having been added in support of Irish
independence. President Wilson remained adamant in his opposition as before, and 12 "irreconcilables" combined forces
with 23 loyal Democrats on March 19 to deny the treaty approval, despite the fact that a clear-cut majority of the Senators voting (49 to 35) favored the latest version.

     Examining the vote on the treaty from a sectional
rather than a partisan standpoint, it should be pointed out
that Henry Cabot Lodge dared not alienate the Irish of Boston
and the Italians of Massachusetts by too strongly endorsing
the treaty. Both the Italians and the Irish were political fac-

tors to contend with throughout the Northeast, especially in New York and Massachusetts. As for the "irreconcilables, " they were by no means geographically limited to the Middle West; William G. Carleton, whose count of 19 is higher than most authorities, includes 6 from the Middle West, 5 from the Far West, 6 from the Eastern Seaboard, and 2 from the South. Yet Ray Allen Billington, commenting on the November defeat of the treaty, declares that "Partisan politics, centered in the Republican Middle West, had struck a death blow at Wilson's idealistic internationalism, " and his interpretation generally is the accepted one.

Equally striking was southern support for Wilson. In November only three southern Democrats, one of them Thomas Gore of Oklahoma, refused to support Wilson and reject the first set of Lodge reservations; in March, 20 of the 23 Democrats who remained loyal to Wilson and helped defeat the second set of Lodge reservations came from the South, only four Southerners backing the Massachusetts Senator. This voting pattern is in harmony with the finding of Dewey W. Grantham that 40 per cent of the resolutions passed by state legislatures between 1917 and 1919 endorsing the League were adopted by southern states. In addition, the South was particularly bitter towards Lodge, pro-League Senator John Sharp Williams of Mississippi attacking both the New England Senator and the Irish-Americans on the floor of the Senate; Lodge had introduced the Force Bill into the House as a Representative in 1890. Had Republican Charles Evans Hughes been elected President instead of Wilson in 1916, however, one may speculate as to whether the heavily Democratic South would have been as vocal in its support of a Hughes League.

Vigorous southern backing for the Wilson League, in fact, far from helping its cause, may well have contributed to its defeat. In this connection Grantham has suggested that:

> Sectionalism was also a factor in the League failure. The Republicans distrusted Wilson because he was a southerner, because southerners were in his cabinet, and because southern Democrats were in control of Congress. They believed Wilson was conspiring to aid the South.

In the Presidential campaign of 1920 the Republicans nominated a party regular, Senator Warren C. Harding of Ohio, while the Democrats selected Governor James Cox of the same state. Assistant Secretary of the Navy Franklin D.

Roosevelt was Cox's running mate, Governor Calvin Coolidge
of Massachusetts, Harding's; Cox firmly endorsed the League,
while Harding straddled the issue. Weary of wars to make
the world safe for democracy, the voters, with women casting ballots for the first time, catapulted Harding into office
over Cox by the smashing majority of seven million votes.
With Cox's defeat the last hopes of the pro-League forces
evaporated. So pronounced was the Republican landslide in
the Middle West that the Democrats held only three of the 24
Senate seats and five of the 138 House seats after the election. In Ohio the German newspapers strongly backed Harding; according to one representative editorial, "Every vote
for Harding is a protest against the persecution of Americans
of German origin during the last years." But Harding also
ran well in the East and the West, faring poorly only in the
pro-Wilson, pro-League, heavily Democratic South. Outside
of "Dixie" the overwhelming bulk of the American people were
in a mood for "Normalcy."

FOR FURTHER READING

    Unfortunately, relatively little is available at the
secondary level dealing with sectional attitudes towards hemispheric affairs during the first two decades of the Twentieth
Century. The situation relative to Canada leaves much to be
desired; in the case of Latin America, it is even worse. For
the reciprocity controversy involving Canada and Newfoundland
of 1898-1902, see Charles S. Campbell, Jr. , Anglo-American
Understanding 1898-1903 and W. Stull Holt, Treaties Defeated
by the Senate; for the abortive reciprocity agreement of 1911,
consult L. Ethan Ellis, "The Northwest and the Reciprocity
Agreement of 1911" and Reciprocity, 1911: A Study in Canadian-American Relations, as well as D. Jerome Tweton, "The
Border Farmer and the Canadian Reciprocity Issue, 1911-
1912." Campbell is also valuable for his treatment of the
Alaskan boundary controversy. Two works that deal at some
length with sectional attitudes towards Latin America are
Dwight Carroll Miner's The Fight for the Panama Route and
Dexter Perkins' The Monroe Doctrine 1867-1907, which touches
on both the Venezuelan and Dominican crises. A key article
is A. F. Cardon, "Senator Reed Smoot and the Mexican Revolutions"; a book analyzing relations with Haiti, Rubin Weston,
Racism in U. S. Imperialism.

    The most extended discussion of American relations

with the Philippines is to be found in Garel A. Grunder and William E. Livezey, The Philippines and the United States. One in search of detailed information on American attitudes towards the Russo-Japanese War must inevitably turn to Winston B. Thorson, "American Public Opinion and the Portsmouth Peace Conference" and "Pacific Northwest Opinion on the Russo-Japanese War of 1904-1905"; Thorson challenges the widespread belief that public opinion in this country turned sharply in the direction of Russia during this gathering. Practically nothing, however, is available on sectional attitudes towards China following the formulation of the Open Door Policy.

In contrast, there is almost a whole library on the repression of the Japanese in San Francisco, the rest of California, and the Far West. Among the pertinent books that one might cite are Thomas A. Bailey, Theodore Roosevelt and the Japanese-American Crisis; Hector C. Bywater, Sea-Power in the Pacific: A Study of the American-Japanese Naval Problem; Ray Watson Curry, Woodrow Wilson and Far Eastern Policy 1913-1921; Roger Daniels, The Politics of Prejudice; Raymond A. Esthus, Theodore Roosevelt and Japan; A. Whitney Griswold, The Far Eastern Policy of the United States; Charles E. Neu, The Uncertain Friendship: Theodore Roosevelt and Japan, 1906-1909; Payson J. Treat, Diplomatic Relations between the United States and Japan 1895-1905 and Japan and the United States 1853-1921; and Eleanor Tupper, Japan in American Public Opinion. Tupper plays down the sympathy for Japanese repression in Washington, Oregon, and California outside of San Francisco, while Bailey presents an extended analysis of eastern and southern reactions to the segregation of Japanese in the San Francisco schools. Bailey, Curry, Esthus, Griswold, Treat, and Earl Pomeroy in his Pacific Slope also discuss examples of anti-Japanese activity in states other than California.

Shifting to Europe, background information on the rapidly deteriorating European situation is to be found in Maynard W. Brown, "American Public Opinion and Events Leading to the World War, 1912-1914." The leading book-length treatments of World War I include Thomas A. Bailey, The Policy of the United States toward the Neutrals, 1917-1918; Warren I. Cohen, The American Revisionists: The Lessons of Intervention in World War I; Ernest R. May, The World War and American Isolation 1914-1917; Daniel Smith, American Intervention, 1917: Sentiment, Self-Interest, or Ideals?; and Charles Callen Tansill, America Goes to War.

Two journalistic surveys of value are Russell Buchanan's
"American Editors Examine War Aims and Plans in April
1917" and Lamar W. Bridges' "Zimmermann Telegram: Reaction of Southern, Southwestern Newspapers. " One might
cite a number of studies of particular states, among which
are Milton L. Ready, "Georgia's Entry into World War I";
Cedric C. Cummins, Indiana Public Opinion and the World
War 1914-1917; Edwin Costrell, How Maine Viewed the War,
1914-1917 and "Newspaper Attitudes toward War in Maine
1914-1917"; John Clark Crighton, Missouri and the World War
1914-1917: A Study in Public Opinion; and Karen Falk, "Public Opinion in Wisconsin During World War I. " Sectional
analyses of interest are Arthur S. Link, "The Middle West
and the Coming of World War I"; I. A. Newby, "States' Rights
and Southern Congressmen During World War I"; the chapter
on World War I by George Brown Tindall in his The Emergence of the New South 1913-1945; and the essay by Link,
"The Cotton Crisis, the South, and Anglo-American Diplomacy, 1914-1915, " in J. Carlyle Sitterson, Studies in Southern History. Developments in Russia from 1917 onwards are
treated by Foster Rhea Dulles in The Road to Teheran: The
Story of Russia and America, 1781-1943 and Peter G. Filene,
Americans and the Soviet Experiment, 1917-1933.

Many works touch upon the League of Nations controversy to a greater or lesser extent. The more significant
articles include two by James D. Startt, "Early Press Reaction to Wilson's League Proposal" and "Wilson's Trip to
Paris: Profile of Press Response"; among the more pertinent
books are Thomas A. Bailey, Woodrow Wilson and the Great
Betrayal and Denna F. Fleming, The United States and the
League of Nations 1918-1920. A work which breaks with traditional interpretations is William G. Carleton's "Isolationism
and the Middle West, " an article which lists no less than 19
"irreconcilables"; for the other extreme, see Dewey W. Grantham, Jr. , "The Southern Senators and the League of Nations,
1918-1920. " Samuel Lubell presents a treatment of the elections of 1916, 1918, and 1920 in his "Who Votes Isolationist
and Why, " stressing the geographical distribution of ethnic
groups in Minnesota and North Dakota, while Seward W.
Livermore limits himself to "The Sectional Issue in the 1918
Congressional Elections. "

CHAPTER 6

FROM WORLD WAR I TO WORLD WAR II

Introduction

Most scholars are in agreement that there was a sectional division of opinion in this country prior to World War II over the twin issues of isolationism and internationalism or intervention. (One, of course, might differentiate between the last two terms, but they are frequently used interchangeably.) The traditional interpretation, as set forth by Wayne S. Cole, affirms that: "There were isolationists in all parts of the country, but they were most powerful in the Middle West and least so in the South." Cole opines that certain ethnic groups, such as the German-Americans, tended to embrace isolationism regardless of section, while Finis Capps makes this point relative to the Swedes; Samuel Lubell carries this argument even further by asserting that: "The hard core of isolationism in the United States has been ethnic and emotional, not geographical." Cole also adds that isolationism tended to be more prevalent in rural and small-town America than in the cities, although the presence in the latter of such ethnic groups as the Irish and Italians (especially in the Northeast) forces us to qualify this generalization.

As for the other side of the coin, Cole points out that "Support for the internationalist view came from all parts of the country, but the Northeast was the most consistently internationalist section and the South the most vehemently interventionist section." It must be added, however, that partisan considerations were also a factor, since the South had long been Democratic, while the Democrats had begun to loosen the Republican hold on the big cities of the Northeast from 1928 on; on the other hand, the traditionally isolationistic Middle West was the bastion of Republicanism during this period. (Lubell's investigations throw considerable light on the latter phenomenon.) There also was a waning of internationalism in the South between 1921 and 1933, during which years the Republicans occupied the White House. But

political ideology was not always correlated with foreign
policy, as there are numerous instances of conservative internationalists as well as liberal ones, of liberal isolationists
as well as conservative ones.

Next let us examine three studies of Congressional
voting that we have not previously cited because their broad
time-span exceeds the chronological bounds of the three main
sections of this chapter. The first of these, by George L.
Grassmuck, encompasses the two decades from 1921 to 1941.
Grassmuck qualifies the image of southern internationalism by
asserting that: "Foreign loan and aid measures did not receive
strong support from the Dixie congressmen at any time between the wars"; on the other hand, the isolationist Great
Plains showed a degree of enthusiasm for participation in
world organization inconsistent with its stands on other foreign
policy issues. As for the border states of Maryland, West
Virginia, Kentucky, Missouri, and Oklahoma, a section rarely
emphasized by analysts, Grassmuck claims that the Congressional representatives of this "geographic no-man's land" generally followed party voting patterns. Even more significant
is his detection of a North/South split in the Rocky Mountain
States, with Arizona being far more internationalist than Montana.

Julius Turner, whose study encompasses the slightly
broader period from 1921 to 1944, finds that metropolitan
groups in both parties, as contrasted with their rural counterparts, showed a greater enthusiasm for increased military,
naval, air, and State Department appropriations, and for international action on the part of the United States. Turner
also challenges the "myth" of southern internationalism in his
discussion of sectional tendencies in the Democratic Party:
"Actually, the South was often opposed to the policy of 'preparedness' in the sessions studied. This attitude was most
apparent in votes on naval appropriations in 1921 and 1937,
but was found as well in roll calls on State Department expenditures and the use of the Marines in Nicaragua, both in
1931. " In contrast, Turner postulates a coast/interior dicho-
tomy splitting the Republican Party in Congress during this
period, singling out the West Central States as being the most
violently opposed to internationalist or interventionist action.
He also dismisses the occasional alliance between the Southern
Democrats and the West Central States Republicans as being
of minor importance, although a majority of the roll calls on
which these two sections joined hands did concern foreign
affairs: navy appropriations (twice); State Department expenses

(twice), and the Nicaragua Marine force (once).

Lastly, in a study dealing specifically with southern politics, V. O. Key, Jr. isolates 34 roll calls for the years 1933-1945 involving foreign policy in which 90 per cent or more of southern Senators combined forces with a majority of non-southern Democrats in opposition to a majority of Republicans. Further dividing these 34 roll calls into four large sub-groupings, Key demonstrates that in each case the Southern Democrats had a higher index of cohesion than did their non-Southern counterparts or the Republicans. We here see these indices of cohesion converted into percentages:

Sub-groupings

	S. D.	n-S. D.	Rep.
9 reciprocal trade program votes	94. 8	84. 1	84. 6
9 preparation for war votes	97. 6	81. 0	81. 5
12 lend-lease votes (1941)	95. 8	76. 8	78. 9
4 U. N. amendment votes (1945)	99. 1	86. 4	70. 0

Unlike the racial question, though, this relative unanimity of the South on foreign policy issues did not set this section against the rest of the country; it rather signified the absence of dissent to an unusual degree. Key also opines that a somewhat different picture might emerge were northeastern Republicans and midwestern Republicans to be treated as separate groups.

Such are the findings of some of the leading scholars who have examined the period between the two world wars. Now let us continue the practice adopted in the introductions to the earlier chapters and isolate some of the key diplomatic votes, to substantiate or challenge the general thrust of these interpretations. Although the Republicans had won control of Congress at the mid-term Congressional election of 1918, they increased their margins two years later when Warren G. Harding captured the Presidency, maintaining their control down to the mid-term Congressional election of 1930. Following this, the Republicans still held a one-vote margin over the Democrats in the Senate, 48 to 47, but the Democrats recaptured the House 220 to 214, in a realignment that reflected the impact of the great depression. Despite the decisive victories of the Republican candidates for President (Harding, Coolidge, and Hoover) over their Democratic rivals in the three Presidential elections held during the 1920's, the

Republicans never obtained a two-thirds majority in the Senate, and only once did so in the House (1921-23).

Southern Democratic bloc voting, which had been in evidence among those Senators opposing Theodore Roosevelt's Latin American policy and supporting Woodrow Wilson's global diplomacy, again manifested itself on October 18, 1921 when the Senate approved the treaties of peace with Germany, Austria and Hungary. On the first two of these, Democrats supplied 12 of the 20 nay votes, with 12 coming from the South; on the third, they cast 16 of the 17 anti-treaty votes, the South providing 11 of them. In contrast, only one Senator voted against the Washington Disarmament Conference agreement of 1922 and the Nine Power Treaty of the same year, but 27 Senators opposed the Four Power Treaty of 1922, 23 of them Democrats, 14 of them from the former Confederacy.

A different pattern emerged when the Panama Canal rather than the Far East was the issue at stake, since it was the Republicans who supplied no less than three-fourths of the anti-treaty votes when the treaty with Colombia came up for final Senatorial approval in 1921. Here it was the West and the Middle West that were the most hostile to a treaty which many Republicans regarded as an insult to the memory of Theodore Roosevelt. Republicans also led the attacking forces five years later when the Senate approved American participation in the World Court with reservations, casting 14 of the 17 nay votes in a roll-call that also featured middle western and western opposition. In the Senatorial votes on legislation restricting immigration and excluding the Japanese in 1924, the handful of foes included members of both parties, but here it was New England that was the least enthusiastic, with the South and West most favorable.

When Herbert Hoover replaced Calvin Coolidge as President in 1929, he continued the generally isolationist foreign policy that had characterized the 1920's, but also took steps towards improving relations with Latin America that foreshadowed Franklin Roosevelt's Good Neighbor Policy. Examining the key diplomatic votes during the Hoover Administration, one discovers that the Kellogg-Briand Peace Pact won Senatorial approval in 1929 by a vote of 85 to 1, while the Five Power Naval Pact obtained a similar endorsement the following year by a 58 to 9 margin that saw Republicans and New Englanders leading the scattered opposition. On the other hand, when Herbert Hoover's war debt moratorium came up for Congressional approval at the end of 1931, a bloc of

Southern Democrats in the House was quite hostile; in the
Senate there was no sharp partisan division.   Here it was the
Great Plains and not the South that furnished half of the dozen
nay votes.

With the election of F. D. R. as chief executive in 1932,
the Democrats gained control of Congress through the end of
World War II, maintaining a two-thirds majority in the Senate
from 1935 to 1943, and in the House from 1933 to 1939. The
outbreak of World War II in Europe saw the Democratic hold
over the lower house of Congress weaken, and by the last two
years of that conflict they were clinging to a mere ten-vote
majority over the Republicans.   Although from 1936 on the
American government was primarily concerned with the role
that America should play relative to the deteriorating situation
in Europe and the Far East, prior to that time, during the
first Roosevelt Administration, several diplomatic issues arose
independent of this general question.   The Tydings-McDuffie
Act of 1934 providing for eventual Philippine independence
cleared the Senate in 1934 by a vote of 68 to 8 (all Republicans), but the St. Lawrence Seaway Treaty with Canada went
down to defeat the same year on a 46 to 42 vote.   A breakdown of the latter roll-call reveals an almost equal degree of
Republican and Democratic hostility in an overwhelmingly
Democratic Senate; New England and Middle Atlantic States
Senators cast 10 nay votes apiece, but Southerners also
supplied 9 in a highly complex vote that saw the Middle West,
Great Plains, and Pacific Coast the most favorable.   The
Reciprocal Trade Agreements program of 1934 also aroused
considerable hostility among Senators, but it still passed by
a decisive 57 to 33 margin, with 28 Republicans opposed and
the South leading the aye forces.   Less fortunate was a new
World Court proposal, which only commanded an inadequate
52 to 36 majority in the Senate when it came up for a vote
the following year; 20 of the nay votes were Democratic, the
Great Plains leading the opposition.   On the other hand,
clear-cut partisan opposition was in evidence when the Senate
voted belatedly after three years to ratify the 1936 treaty with
Panama, as Republicans cast all 15 votes against this treaty,
with New England furnishing six of these.   The earlier Montevideo Treaty of 1933 reflecting F. D. R. 's Good Neighbor
Policy had won unanimous Senatorial approval.

If the common portrayal of Southern Democratic inter-
nationalists backing the President on foreign policy and Middle
Western Republican isolationists opposing him as World War
II approached is not apparent from the above roll-calls, one

finds evidence more in line with this widespread stereotype in
an analysis of the votes dealing with such topics as neutrality
legislation, the draft, and foreign aid.   Yet even here it
should be noted that the Neutrality Act of 1936 was decisively
approved by the House (353 to 27) and by the Senate without
a roll-call, while the embargo on the shipment of munitions
to Spain was overwhelmingly enacted by the House, 411 to 1,
and the Senate, 81 to 0, the following year.   Thus there was
general partisan and sectional agreement on both measures.
Admittedly more opposition was registered when the Neutrality
Act of 1937 won the blessing of the House by a vote of 376 to
13 and the Senate by votes of 63 to 6 and 41 to 15; in the
case of the two Senatorial roll-calls, the nay votes on both
occasions were predominantly Republican, but more were supplied by New England than by the Middle West.

A more typical pattern emerged in the 1938 House vote
on the abortive Ludlow Resolution advocating a national referendum on the declaration of war; this saw most Democrats
and Southerners opposed, Republicans and most Democrats
from west of the Mississippi in favor.   Similarly, when the
Burke-Wadsworth Selective Service Act was approved by Congress in 1940, Southern Democrats played a key role in its
passage, while Midwestern Republicans generally were unfavorable.   On the other hand, the Brown bill calling for aid
to Finland cleared the Senate in 1940 on a 49 to 27 roll-call
that witnessed more Democrats than Republicans voting nay,
with the South in a rather curious alignment with the Great
Plains and the Middle West opposing it.   But when a more
comprehensive bill providing for lend-lease to the Allies won
Senatorial endorsement the following year, 60 to 31, the South
and the Middle Atlantic States were the most favorable, the
Middle West, the Great Plains, and the Pacific Coast the
most hostile in a vote that saw Republican nay votes outnum-
ber Democratic ones by a three-to-two margin.   A similar
breakdown occurred when the Senate voted 50 to 37 later that
year to repeal Section VI of the Neutrality Act.   It is patterns such as these that have contributed to the widespread
portrayal or common stereotype of southern internationalism
v. middle western isolationism.

During World War II both the Republican Party and the
Middle West moved away from isolationism, although a few
die-hards and irreconcilables refused to modify their position.
After the internationalist Fulbright resolution had been approved
by the House in 1943 by a 360 to 29 margin, the similarly
oriented Connally Resolution was passed by the Senate later

that year by an 85 to 5 vote. Here the last-ditch nays were
Democrats Robert Reynolds of North Carolina and Burton
Wheeler of Montana, and Republicans Hiram Johnson of California, William Langer of North Dakota, and Henrik Shipstead
of Minnesota. During the same year measures ending Chinese
exclusion and terminating American extraterritorial rights in
China won the endorsement of the Senate without a roll-call
and by a unanimous vote, despite the fact that Southerners
and Westerners had once been highly favorable to the former.
The Bretton Woods Act establishing the International Bank for
Reconstruction and Development generated somewhat more
opposition, however; when this measure cleared the Senate in
July 1945 by a 61 to 16 vote, 14 Republicans and 2 Democrats
voted nay, 9 of the 16 representing the Great Plains. Nevertheless, the Senate passed the United Nations charter nine
days later by an overwhelming 89 to 2 margin, with only bit-
ter-enders William Langer and Henrik Shipstead openly voting
nay. (Hiram Johnson was in the hospital.) This roll-call
was a far cry from the votes a quarter of a century earlier
on the Treaty of Versailles, and seemingly marked the official arrival of what appeared to be a new era of global involvement in American foreign relations.

The Diplomacy of Normalcy

        The inauguration of Warren G. Harding as President
ushered in what often is referred to as an era of "normalcy."
In the domestic field this period was marked by a suspension
of progressive reforms, in foreign affairs by a retreat from
global idealism. On October 18, 1921 the U. S. Senate finally
ratified separate peace treaties with Hungary, Austria, and
Germany. The last two of these were endorsed by the identical vote of 66 to 20, with 9 abstentions, while the first was
approved 66 to 17, with 12 abstentions. A breakdown of those
roll-calls demonstrates that not a single Senator from states
north of the Mason-Dixon Line and east of the Mississippi
River voted nay; conversely, the eleven former Confederate
states led the opposition in each instance, twice casting 12 of
the 20 nay votes, and 11 of the 17 nay votes. Dixie Democrats, still strong in their allegiance to the foreign policy of
Woodrow Wilson, remained faithful to the lost cause of their
departed leader.

        Ten years later, on June 20, 1931, President Herbert
Hoover suggested a one-year moratorium on both German

reparations and Allied war debts. According to Thomas A.
Bailey, editorial opinion here favored this bold step by a ten
to one margin, although the Wichita Eagle feared that "Europe
may want to place the accent on that more in moratorium. "
When the House ratified Hoover's proposal by a 318 to 100
margin on December 18, those states casting the most votes
against the moratorium were Alabama, Georgia, Indiana, Kentucky, Mississippi, Missouri, Oklahoma, Tennessee, Texas,
and Virginia. As this list demonstrates, the opposition to it
was centered in the South, where Jeffersonian Democrats long
had preached economy, despite the fact that this section had
spearheaded the movement for Woodrow Wilson's League of
Nations. Southern fiscal generosity, it would seem, did not
match its enthusiasm for the League, especially with a Republican occupying the White House. Sectional divisions were
less apparent in the Senate, where Hoover's proposal was enacted by a 69 to 12 margin on December 22, both Senators
from North and South Dakota voting in the negative.

During the 1920's American membership in the League
of Nations remained at most a rather remote possibility, but
there nevertheless was serious talk of our joining the World
Court. George L. Grassmuck, who has studied sectional
biases in Congress on foreign policy issues between the two
world wars, has detected a greater variance in the Senate
among the Democrats than among Republicans in their support
of American participation in permanent international organizations between 1921 and 1932:

Sections - Rep. -	% Favorable	Sections - Dem. -	% Favorable
New England and		Great Plains States	90. 0
North Atlantic	72. 6	Lake States	88. 9
Rocky Mountain	72. 1	The South	83. 7
Lake States	70. 7	New England and	
Pacific Coast	67. 7	North Atlantic	75. 8
Great Plains	63. 4	Border States	69. 0
Border States	62. 4	Rocky Mountain	67. 2
		Pacific Coast	40. 0

Most historians, though, part company with Grassmuck when
he takes the position that "None of the regions sent Senators
to Washington who voted according to a strong sectional attitude regardless of party. " Southern internationalism and
midwestern isolationism were both obviously manifest at the
time of the debate on the Versailles Treaty following World

War I and on neutrality legislation prior to World War II; to assume that they disappeared during the intervening years is a proposition most difficult to accept.

In February 1923 President Warren Harding proposed that the Senate should approve the World Court Statute subject to the four Harding-Hughes reservations, which affirmed the independence of the United States from the League of Nations. Thanks to the opposition of the six senior Republican members (Henry Cabot Lodge of Massachusetts, William E. Borah of Idaho, Frank Brandagee of Connecticut, Hiram Johnson of California, George Moses of New Hampshire, and Medill Mc-Cormick of Illinois), the Senate Foreign Relations Committee bottled up this scheme for over a year until public pressure and House approval by a 303 to 28 margin forced it to take action. It was not until December 17, 1925 that the Senate finally began debate, and this was only after a fifth reservation had been added to the effect that the court should not "without the consent of the United States, entertain any request for an advisory opinion touching any dispute or question in which the United States has or claims an interest. " After cloture had choked off a filibuster, the Senate adopted the World Court proposal by a 76 to 27 margin on January 17, 1926, with the only two negative Democratic votes coming from Cole Blease of South Carolina and James Reed of Missouri.

In terms of a sectional breakdown, the Middle West and the Great Plains led the opposition with a combined total of ten nay votes. When the World Court failed to approve these reservations, the Cincinnati Enquirer sneered on February 11, 1927 that: "The reds, pinks and yellows may rave and try to change the situation, but they will find ... that the color combination loved by the citizenship of America is red, white and blue. " Another indication of the potency of this issue in the Middle West was that former Senator Albert J. Beveridge of Indiana, a court opponent, was able to pressure both of the Senators currently representing his state into voting nay by threatening to run against one of them in the next election.

Following this setback, in 1929 proponents of American membership in the World Court developed the Root Plan, a series of amendments that were acceptable to both the League of Nations and President Herbert Hoover, who submitted the new scheme to the Senate on December 10, 1930 with his endorsement. According to Ray Billington, at this time 66 per cent of the American people favored the World Court, with only 26 per cent opposed; no less than 41 per cent of the nay

votes came from the Middle West.   Despite this widespread
public support, the Senate Foreign Relations Committee took
no action on this proposal until January 1935, with Senator
William E. Borah of Idaho leading the obstructionists.

While the isolationist bloc had its headquarters in the
Middle West, the internationalists had theirs in the Northeast.
As Robert Divine points out, 26 of the 27 directors of the
League of Nations Association in 1929 lived within three hundred miles of New York City.   This organization had branch
offices in three of the six New England States, but only one
(in Chicago) in the eleven-state Middle West.   Most members
of this organization, as well as of the east coast-oriented
Council on Foreign Relations and the Foreign Policy Association, were old-stock Protestants, Anglophilic in outlook; many
were bankers, lawyers, editors, professors, or ministers,
the leading internationalists including Thomas J. Watson, John
Foster Dulles, and Thomas W. Lamont.   Outside of the Northeast, one did encounter occasional pockets of support in such
cosmopolitan and mercantile cities as San Francisco and New
Orleans, but these were decidedly the exception rather than
the rule.

Still another issue with international implications that
was constantly before the American people during the 1920's
was the question of naval disarmament.   At this point in the
narrative it is desirable to review the evolution of sectional
attitudes towards a big navy from the time of the Spanish-
American War.   Generally speaking, the states bordering on
the Atlantic Coast, the Pacific Coast, the Gulf of Mexico, the
Great Lakes, and the Mississippi River were more concerned
about naval matters than other states; the Northeast and the
Atlantic Seaboard dominated both the House and Senate Naval
Committees between 1900 and 1923.   Leading "big navy"
newspapers of this period included the Boston Transcript, the
Providence Journal, the New York Herald, the New York
Tribune, the Philadelphia Bulletin, the Los Angeles Times,
the Portland Oregonian, the Montgomery Advertiser, the Milwaukee Journal and Detroit Free Press, the Kansas City Star,
and the Memphis Commercial Appeal.

In 1921 the outgoing Wilson Administration presented
a Naval Appropriation Bill to Congress providing for a three-
year building program.   At this time Secretary of the Navy
Josephus Daniels offered the nation the alternatives of joining the League of Nations or of building a large navy.   Although this country was far more concerned about the League

than about the navy, Daniels' mandate did receive serious consideration on both the Atlantic and Pacific Coasts, with the New York Times and the San Francisco Chronicle accepting competitive naval building as the only alternative to the League. Nevertheless, Congress refused both to join the League and to build a large navy. The House voted only to complete the 1916 program, eliminating a proposed three-year extension, and the Senate followed suit with little debate, endorsing the appropriation of $464, 891, 000.

While the United States was attempting to disengage itself diplomatically from the rest of the world following World War I, it was also erecting barriers to keep out foreigners. It will be recalled that the Chinese had been excluded in 1882 and the Japanese partially banned in 1907; the growing revulsion against the stream of southeastern Europeans that entered this nation in large numbers from the 1880's on led Congress to pass further regulatory legislation in 1921 and 1924. The first of these quota laws restricted the annual immigration from each country to three per cent of the number of its nationals residing in the United States as of 1910; the more stringent second measure, which halved the 1921 quota and totally excluded the Japanese, reduced the percentage to two and changed the base year to 1890. In addition, it provided for a "national origins" system after 1927 (actually 1929) which further cut back the total annual immigration to 150, 000, again employing a percentage system with 1920 as the base year. One might easily make a strong case for the argument that this legislation was inspired by bigotry, but the fact remains that on no less than six occasions between 1905 and 1914 over a million newcomers arrived within a twelve months' span.

Let us now examine two sets of statistics, one of the percentage distribution of foreign-born white population by geographical divisions, 1850-1930 (Chart A), and the other of the percentage of foreign-born whites in the total population by geographical divisions, 1900-1930 (Chart B). It will be noted that the combined total for New England and the Middle Atlantic States in Chart A is 59 per cent, while in the case of Chart B it is 47 per cent; it is little wonder, therefore, that these two sections were often highly sensitive to foreign policy issues. (Most of the immigrants were concentrated in the large cities.) On the other hand, the South, which ranks near the bottom of Chart A and at the bottom of Chart B, nevertheless adopted an internationalist stance following World War I and prior to World War II, despite the small number of foreign-born there. Then there are the highly rural North

Section	Chart A						Chart B		
	1850	1870	1890	1900	1910	1920	1900	1910	1920
New England	13.6	11.8	12.6	14.1	13.6	13.6	25.7	27.7	25.3
Middle Atlantic	45.4	34.1	30.0	32.3	36.1	35.8	21.4	25.0	22.1
East North Central	24.6	30.2	27.4	25.7	23.0	23.5	16.4	16.8	15.0
West North Central	4.5	12.2	17.0	15.0	12.1	10.0	14.8	13.8	10.8
South Atlantic	4.6	3.0	2.1	2.0	2.2	2.3	2.0	2.4	2.3
East South Central	2.2	1.9	1.1	0.9	0.6	0.5	1.2	1.0	0.8
West South Central	3.9	2.3	2.4	2.6	2.6	2.3	4.0	2.6	2.0
Mountain	0.2	1.4	2.7	2.8	3.3	3.3	17.2	14.9	10.8
Pacific	1.0	3.1	4.6	4.6	6.5	7.5	19.6	19.8	17.1

Central States, where a decline in immigrant stock after 1890
was accompanied by an embracing of isolationism.   Finally,
in the case of the relatively lightly populated Rocky Mountains
and Pacific Coast, one encounters low percentages on Chart A,
yet high ones on Chart B.   As these sections were the most
concerned about Asiatic immigration, they also were the most
concerned about Asiatic diplomacy.

In October 1920 Senators from the Pacific Coast and
the Far West strongly backed a reservation that the League
of Nations was not to concern itself with the domestic affairs
of the United States, in particular immigration.   Outside of
Congress, the Ku Klux Klan mushroomed during the early
1920's in the states of the South, the Middle West, and the
Mississippi Valley.   When the immigration bill of 1924 came
up for a final vote in the House on April 12, only three Representatives from west of the Mississippi and south of the
Mason-Dixon line cast their ballots against it.   Perhaps the
leading critic of the measure in the Senate was Le Baron Colt
of Rhode Island, who observed that the bill was "based upon
racial discrimination, which is the most dangerous and un-
American principle ever propounded in the American Senate";
in rebuttal Morris Sheppard of Texas complained about that
"large element" among the foreign-born "which forms the main
source and breeding ground of revolutionary and anarchistic
propaganda in this country, such as Bolshevism, I.W.W.-ism,
communism, and similar movements countenancing violence
and disorder."   The two Senatorial votes saw the South and
the West almost unanimously favorable, with the Middle West
leading the scattered opposition.

Relative to Japanese exclusion, Eleanor Tupper is of
the opinion that this measure generally had the backing of the
South and the West, with the Middle West divided, and the
East opposed; on the other hand, Richard O'Connor maintains
that newspapers all over the country supported the proposed
legislation, with the Springfield Republican being one of its
rare critics.   There was a temporary breakdown in the alliance between the West and the South in the Senate on this
issue, thanks to Senator Samuel Shortridge of California supporting an anti-lynching bill in 1922 and 1923; the two embittered Tennessee Senators, Kenneth McKellar and John
Shields, eventually did close ranks and endorse the restrictive
legislation.   Japanese exclusion became law shortly thereafter, in 1924, as a part of the abovementioned immigration
bill enacted during that year.

Aside from Japanese immigration into this country,
Japanese expansion throughout the Orient was a matter of deep
concern to this nation during the era of Normalcy. The Washington Conference of 1921-1922, as we have noted, dealt with
the Pacific and the Far East as well as with naval disarmament. In fact, the only one of the nine treaties drawn up at
this gathering which encountered stiff Senate opposition was
the Four Power Treaty that provided for consultation in the event
of "aggressive action" in the Pacific, thus terminating the
Anglo-Japanese Alliance. This passed by the relatively small
margin of 67 to 27. Despite their commitment to the League
of Nations, the presence of Oscar W. Underwood of Alabama
as a delegate to the Washington Conference, and their aver-
sion to Japanese immigration, Southern Democrats divided
sharply in their votes on this Four Power Treaty and its amendments. In fact, only 8 out of 22 supported ratification on the
final roll call; 14 voted nay, as did one Kentucky Senator.
Here is still another indication that southern internationalism
was highly partisan in nature, declining when the Republicans
occupied the White House.

In 1927 the South Manchurian Railway, a Japanese en-
terprise, sought a loan of $40, 000, 000 from the House of
Morgan. Some American newspapers, among them the New
York Times and the San Francisco Chronicle, supported this
project, but Chinese opposition blocked its execution. The
following year, in 1928, there was a clash between Japanese
troops and Chinese Nationalist soldiers when the latter began
widespread looting in the Shantung peninsula city of Tsinan.
Significantly, the attitude of a large section of the American
press was pro-Japanese; in the words of the San Francisco
Chronicle, "Japan was forced to protect her people and pro-
perty in Shantung. " American editorial opinion, however, began to turn against Japan when that nation took over South
Manchuria by force in 1931-32, setting up the puppet state of
Manchukuo. Our official response was the so-called Stimson
Doctrine of Secretary of State Henry Stimson, contained in a
note addressed to both Japan and China: "(The United States
does not) intend to recognize any treaty or agreement ... which
may impair ... the sovereignty, the independence, or the territorial and administrative integrity of the Republic of China
... or the Open Door Policy. " Despite British unenthusiasm,
Stimson's proposal won League backing, but talk of economic
sanctions rapidly cooled off American journalistic enthusiasm.

Concluding this discussion of sectional attitudes towards
foreign policy between 1920 and 1932, Selig Adler singles out

the Chicago Tribune and the Kansas City Star as representative
isolationist papers between the two world wars, and the New
York Times, the New York Herald Tribune, and the Chicago
Daily News as typical internationalist ones.   Yet James T.
Russell and Quincy Wright, who have examined in depth the
attitudes of the New York Times, the Chicago Daily News, and
the Chicago Tribune towards France and Germany between 1910
and 1929 have uncovered similarities too pronounced to disregard.   In each case anti-German sentiment reached its peak
in 1918, pro-German feeling standing at approximately the
same level in 1916 and 1920; in each case pro-French sentiment attained its zenith in 1918, with anti-French feeling
steadily gaining thereafter.   This study, whatever its national
implications may be, gains in importance when one considers
that Chicago was the home of many Germans as well as many
isolationists.

        A study of 40 newspapers made by Julian Woodward in
1930, moreover, revealed that seven of the ten newspapers
that devoted the most space to foreign news were of New England or Middle Atlantic origin.   In contrast, the highest rank-
ing southern newspaper, the Memphis Commercial Appeal,
stood no higher than sixteenth.   If the South was an internationalist as the Northeast at this time, it was not because it
was thoroughly saturated with foreign news.   Even the isolationist Middle West placed four of its newspapers in the first
fifteen, with the isolationist Chicago Tribune leading the way.
The Pacific Coast and the Rocky Mountains enjoyed no representation outside of four California newspapers, with the single
exception of the Portland Oregonian.   It is, of course, difficult to generalize on the basis of this list, but there does
seem to be considerable evidence that there is no direct relationship between exposure to foreign news and the spectrum
of isolationist/internationalist attitudes.

The Diplomacy of F. D. R. , 1933-1939

        In November 1932 the Democratic nominee for Presi-
dent, Governor Franklin D. Roosevelt of New York, triumphed
at the polls over the incumbent Republican, Herbert Hoover.
It will be recalled that the 38-year-old F. D. R. , running as
the unsuccessful Democratic Vice Presidential nominee in 1920,
had endorsed the League of Nations; twelve years later, however, Roosevelt totally reversed his field in a successful bid
for the support of the isolationist newspaper publisher William

Randolph Hearst.   The pivotal issue during this campaign was
the slow recovery of this nation from the great depression,
and neither party paid much attention to foreign policy.   In
this connection F. D. R. 's one-time advisor, Raymond Moley,
has written in <u>After Seven Years</u> that:

> A declaration of what I understood to be Roosevelt's
> views on the subject was likely to cost him more
> undecided votes than it would make for him.   He
> was already sure of the West and Middle West, where
> his views on foreign affairs would be immensely
> popular.   There was no advantage in alienating those
> Eastern elements which would shy at his policies.

During the course of the campaign F. D. R. did pay tribute to
President Woodrow Wilson on several occasions, but it was
invariably to praise his domestic achievements rather than the
League of Nations.

As chief executive one of Roosevelt's first actions in
the foreign relations field was to recognize Communist Russia,
which American troops had invaded in collaboration with Allied
forces during 1918 in an attempt to aid the anti-Bolsheviks
and prevent a Japanese take-over of Siberia.   A number of
developments during the 1920's, though, had gradually altered
our originally hostile stance to the new Marxist government of
Russia.   In the first place, the Five Year Plan favorably impressed a number of Americans; secondly, the United States
was beginning to become concerned about Japanese imperialistic designs on the Far East, and the Soviet Union came to
be looked upon as the most likely check to this threat.   A
group of American Congressmen, moreover, visited Russia in
the Summer of 1923 and, although disturbed by the lack of
freedom there, were generally favorable to the resumption of
economic relations.   Among those who were impressed by the
Soviet experiment were Senators Burton K. Wheeler of Montana, Smith W. Brookhart of Iowa, Robert M. La Follette, Sr.
of Wisconsin, and William H. King of Utah, the first three of
whom had been actively involved in the Progressive movement.
King had been extremely critical of the Communist regime
several years previously, but changed his views following his
trip.

During the 1920's a modest but significant trade grew
up between the Soviet Union and the United States.   According
to Saul G. Bron, this extended to practically every section of
this country; the Russians were particularly interested in

southern cotton and eastern and middle western industrial
equipment.   That some of these purchases were of more than
token importance is evidenced by the observation in the Cleveland Plain Dealer of January 2, 1930: "Had it not been for
these Russian orders, many Cleveland factories would have
faced a shutdown when automobile orders temporarily stopped."
Among those West Coast factories that benefitted from Soviet
orders was the Stockton plant of the Caterpillar Tractor Company, which a Soviet contract kept working at full capacity
during an entire summer.   Despite the observation of the Grand
Rapids Herald that: "We have not yet reached the stage where
it is necessary for us to sacrifice our national honor in favor
of business, " few Americans seemed willing to forego commerce with the Soviet Union on the grounds of principle.

At the time of American recognition of Russia, in 1933,
the Committee on Russian-American Relations of the American
Foundation sent a questionnaire to more than 1, 100 newspapers
inquiring as to whether they favored the recognition of Russia.
No less than 63 per cent of these advocated recognition, with
26. 9 per cent opposed.   A sectional breakdown of results revealed that the proportionate order of support by section was:
South Atlantic States, West South Central States, East South
Central States, Middle Atlantic States, West North Central
States, Mountain States, Pacific States, East North Central
States, New England States.   Here is another indication that
the South from the time of Woodrow Wilson generally pursued
a more internationalist policy than did the other sections; the
hostility of New England is more difficult to explain, but the
relative enthusiasm of the Middle Atlantic States is in line
with that section's commercial orientation.

An entirely different question which confronted the Roosevelt Administration was whether or not to grant the Philippines their independence.   In the last chapter we pointed out
that when the Jones bill came up for a final vote in 1916, a
minority of Democrats, mostly Roman Catholics from New
York and New England, voted with the Republicans against independence, although supporting the remainder of the measure.
By the early 1930's, the pro-independence forces, spearheaded
by the sugar cane Senators from Louisiana and their colleagues
from the beet sugar western states, had lined up enough support to implement their desires.

Early in 1933 Congress passed the Hawes-Cutting Act
over President Herbert Hoover's veto.   This measure, which
provided for independence after 12 years, also reserved to

this nation the right to maintain army and navy bases there.
When the House had enacted its own version of this act by an
overwhelming 306 to 47 margin in April 1932, no less than
thirty of the nay votes came from New England and the North
Atlantic States; an additional nine were cast by representatives from such industrial cities as Chicago, Cincinnati, Detroit, Louisville, and Milwaukee. (There was no record vote
in the Senate.) That fall President Herbert Hoover, making
an unsuccessful bid for the support of the beet sugar states,
told an audience at Denver that the then pending bill would
prove a liability both to the American farmer and the Philippines. Still another aspect of this question was Filipino immigration; residents of the West Coast, who had successfully
engaged in vendettas against the Chinese and the Japanese,
were no more favorably disposed to an influx of Orientals from
the newly independent island nation.

    Filipino independence was likewise an object of contro-
versy in the Philippines, as the terms of separation had to be
acceptable to the latter as well as to the United States.   In
rejecting the Hawes-Cutting Act in October 1933, the island
legislature asserted (with considerable justification) that its
basic purpose was to bar exports and immigrants from the
Philippines.   Nevertheless, the new Tydings-McDuffie Act,
which Congress enacted on March 24, 1934, was largely a
verbatim transcript of the Hawes-Cutting Act, although it did
provide for the relinquishment of the military bases and for
negotiations relative to the naval ones.   After passing the
Senate by a 68 to 8 (all Republicans) vote, the Tydings-Mc-
Duffie Act won the unanimous approval of the Filipino legislature on May 1.

    If a desire to block trade was one of the basic motives
behind the granting of Filipino independence, the wish to facilitate commerce underlay the passage of reciprocal trade
agreements legislation in 1934.   The individual most responsible for this program, Secretary of State Cordell Hull of
Tennessee, was both a Southerner and a Democrat; four years
earlier the Republican Hoover Administration had passed the
highly protective Hawley-Smoot Tariff, which had dealt a
severe blow to southern commerce.   In Congress no less than
95 per cent of the southern membership voted for reciprocal
trade, while a Gallup poll taken four years later revealed that
92 per cent of its southern sample favored the general principles underlying the Hull program.   Admittedly some southern
industrialists, including the textile manufacturers, did support
protection, but cotton and tobacco growers and exporters quite

naturally backed Hull vigorously. Traditionally, of course,
most Southerners--as well as most Democrats--long favored
a low tariff.

Another issue dating back earlier in the century which
was not resolved at this time was that of the proposed St.
Lawrence Seaway. We noted in the last chapter that Senator
Henry Cabot Lodge of Massachusetts spearheaded the move-
ment against this scheme around the time of World War I.
When the St. Lawrence Seaway came up for consideration again
in 1934, Senator Robert La Follette of Wisconsin was one of
its leading proponents; Senators William Dietrich of Illinois,
Bennett (Champ) Clark of Missouri, and John Overton of
Louisiana were among the more prominent speakers in oppo-
sition. The arguments employed against the St. Lawrence
Seaway included complaints that it would be injurious to the
United States, usurp the power of Congress, and relinquish
American sovereignty over Lake Michigan. The treaty did
secure a majority in the Senate, but the 46 to 42 vote fell
short of the necessary two-thirds margin, with western New
York and Pennsylvania and the state of Illinois exerting the
greatest pressure on that body to reject it. A sectional breakdown, moreover, reveals that the proposed scheme was opposed by all the Atlantic Seaboard States except South Carolina
and by all the Gulf States except Alabama, although the Pacific
Coast was favorable, as was every Canadian border state west
of Pennsylvania and New York aside from Illinois. Especially
disappointed in the outcome were the port of Duluth and the
wheat-growing farm areas to the west of the Great Lakes,
whose economic health was highly precarious following several
years of the great depression.

North Dakota in particular was in a mood of revolt
against the Eastern establishment. Its state senate, for example, adopted a resolution in 1933 which recommended that
North Dakota and certain other western states secede from the
Union; this resolution also attacked Wall Street, charging that
it had pressured the American government into dispatching
American troops abroad to protect its loans. Most of the
state's leading daily newspapers constantly adhered to an isolationist line, with the Republican Grand Forks Herald being
a notable exception. From this provincial atmosphere had
emerged Senator Gerald Nye, the chairman of the newly created Senate Munitions Investigating Committee. This one-time
editor of a county-seat weekly, observed Jeannette P. Nichols,
had jumped "from the narrow confines of an every-Thursday
deadline to the broad arena of the world's most powerful

legislative body. " In his youth Nye had defended Woodrow
Wilson and the League of Nations, but he soon had to come
to grips with the fact that this heavily Scandinavian and German state was a hotbed of pacifism and isolationism, only
occasionally abandoning the latter as in his concern for the
Spanish Loyalists. Nye, moreover, was by no means out of
step with the remainder of his committee, as only Senator
James P. Pope of Idaho was an ardent non-isolationist.

Although North Dakota was and is a highly agrarian
state, it is not without significance that a number of midwestern businessmen were also opposed to intervention prior
to Pearl Harbor. These included meatpackers Jay C. Hormel,
Philip T. Swift, and John Cuhady, George N. Peek of the
Moline Plow Company, and General Robert E. Wood of Sears
Roebuck and Company, which enjoyed heavy sales among
farmers. Nye, in fact, was even friendly to automobile maker
Henry Ford, an individual with a rural background and a
World War I pacifist. Nevertheless, Nye's community of interest with these businessmen as a result of their similar outlook on foreign policy did not prevent the North Dakota Senator
from attacking the financial and business leaders of Minneapolis and St. Paul, who were heavily involved in his state,
and those of Wall Street and the urban Northeast.

When Nye investigated the munitions makers allegedly
responsible for American involvement in World War I, therefore, he was engaging in an anti-business and well as an anti-
war vendetta, with the executive branch of the federal government also an eventual target. No less than four members of
his committee (Nye, Pope, Bennett Clark of Missouri, and
Homer Bone of Washington) favored governmental ownership
of munitions industries; all four Senators were liberals from
states west of the Mississippi. On the other hand, opposed
to governmental ownership were the three conservatives from
east of that river: Walter George of Georgia, Arthur Vandenberg of Michigan, and William Barbour of New Jersey. Thanks
in part to Nye's crusade, highly agrarian North Dakota was
to rank last among the 48 states in the value of defense con-
tracts awarded from June 1940 to March 1941. Nye, however
was unquestionably instrumental in strengthening isolationist
sentiment in this country and laying the groundwork for the
neutrality legislation of 1935-1939.

It was against this background that President Franklin
D. Roosevelt attempted to resurrect the World Court scheme.
After he had urged ratification of this proposal on January 16,

1935, the Senate rejected the treaty by a margin of 52 to 36 on January 29, seven votes short of the necessary two-thirds majority, with 17 Senators from the Middle West and the Great Plains predictably opposing it. Both Senators from North Dakota, South Dakota, Minnesota, and Iowa cast nay ballots. Lest one blame its defeat entirely on the efforts of these two sections, it should be added that there were eight no votes from the Northeast, five from the Far West, and five from the South as well; nevertheless, every section outside the Middle West-Great Plains area was favorable to the treaty by at least a two-to-one margin. Among the more prominent southern foes of the court were Robert Reynolds of North Carolina, Richard Russell of Georgia, and Huey Long of Louisiana. Although editorial opinion across the nation had endorsed this proposal by a three to one margin, no less than 20 Democrats failed to support F. D. R.

There was no serious attempt to bring about American involvement in the League of Nations during the New Deal, but two referendums conducted in Massachusetts in 1932 and 1934 substantiate the image of the Northeast as being internationalist in outlook. The first of these gave the League a 63. 2 per cent to 36. 8 majority, the second a 62. 31 to 37. 69 per cent one. Yet both Senators from Massachusetts still voted against American membership in the World Court in January 1935, thanks to the vocal opposition of this isolationist minority. That partisan considerations frequently entered into sectional attitudes towards American participation in international organizations is evidenced by the following breakdown by George Grassmuck, of roll call votes in the Senate between 1933 and 1941, showing the percent favorable of the total votes cast:

Republican		Democrat	
Lake States	28. 6	New England and	
New England and		North Atlantic	86. 8
North Atlantic	22. 1	Lake States	80. 4
Pacific Coast	17. 4	Rocky Mountains	79. 2
Rocky Mountains	13. 0	The South	75. 8
Great Plains	07. 4	Border States	74. 6
		Great Plains	61. 5
		Pacific Coast	57. 1

Still another development during this period which had international implications was the passage of the Silver Purchase Act in June 1934, a measure designed to benefit Amer-

ican silver producers.   Among other things, it empowered the
President to increase the monetary value of the Treasury's
silver holdings to the point where they were equal to one-third
the value of its gold stocks.   According to Thomas A.
Bailey, the silver bloc from the Rocky Mountains thereby "forced
upon the Washington government a silver purchase plan which
further undermined the shaky Chinese currency, and in this
way contributed to the demoralization of a friendly power
which we were hoping to bolster as a counterweight to Japanese imperialism. " Opposition was strongest in the North-
east--New England and the Middle Atlantic States--where the
gold forces had their headquarters.

     Two years later the Spanish Civil War broke out, pit-
ting the republican government, which was backed by the Communists, against the Franco-led insurgents, who were supported by Germany and Italy.   Looking at sectional variations
in opinion, there was slightly more pro-Franco feeling in New
England and the Middle Atlantic States, where Catholics were
proportionately greatest; in contrast, Loyalist sentiment was
at its peak in the Rocky Mountain area and on the Pacific
Coast.   On August 14 F. D. R. made a speech affirming that:
"I can make certain that no act of the United States helps to
produce or to promote war. " Shortly thereafter Senator Nye
attacked a resolution introduced by Key Pittman of Nevada,
specifically imposing an embargo on the shipment of munitions
to Spain, on the grounds that it placed a greater hardship on
the republicans than on the insurgents.   This resolution, however, passed the Senate by a 81 to 0 vote and the House by
411 to 1 on January 6, 1937, the United States remaining officially neutral.

     When General Francisco Franco finally emerged vic-
torious early in 1939, following the capture of Barcelona, the
strongest voices in Congress for immediate recognition included Senator Dennis Chavez of New Mexico and Representative John W. McCormack of Massachusetts, both of whom were
Catholics.   The House of Representatives of heavily Catholic
New Mexico also adopted a resolution favoring the recognition
of the Franco regime by our government.   Another advocate
of immediate recognition was isolationistic Senator Robert
Reynolds of North Carolina, who not only was pleased at the
defeat of the "communists, anarchists, and syndicalists, " but
also was conscious of the commercial advantages that would
accrue to the South as a result, including an extra market for
its cotton.

A far greater menace to the peace of Europe than the Spanish Civil War arose when Nazi leader Adolf Hitler came to power in Germany as Chancellor early in 1933. Due to the non-existence of the Gallup poll and of any pertinent votes in Congress during his early years in office, one must rely on a sampling of editorial opinion to determine sectional attitudes, if any, towards Hitler. Theoretically one might expect the press of the heavily German Middle West to be more sympathetic towards him than that of other sections, but an examination of middle western newspapers during the mid-1930's reveals them to be isolationist, not Hitlerian, in orientation. It was not until 1936 that editorial opinion in this country seemingly began to turn against Hitler, following such developments as the German occupation of the Rhineland and the German-Japanese Anti-Comintern Pact. Yet when Mayor Fiorello La Guardia of New York City made a vicious attack on the German dictator on March 3, 1937, a majority of American newspapers criticized La Guardia's address as an example of bad taste on the part of an important municipal official.

The Munich Agreement of 1938, transferring the Sudetenland from Czechoslovakia to Germany, moreover, received no worse than a mixed reception in this country's press, despite the fact that it was an obvious attempt to appease Hitler; many American newspapers, in fact, even had words of praise for the British Prime Minister, Neville Chamberlain. The New York Daily News went so far as to comment: "Now is the time for haters of Hitler to hold their harsh words. He has made a significant gesture towards world peace, one that nobody but himself could have made at this time." A study of the coverage by American newspapers of a Hitler speech to the Reichstag the following year reveals that the complete text was carried by several midwestern papers as well as by ones on the Atlantic and Pacific Coast, thus negating the theory that there was a correlation between isolationism and ignorance.

Sectional differences in opinion towards Hitler were slightly more apparent in a poll taken by Fortune in January 1936, in response to the question: "Do you believe that in the long run Germany will be better or worse off if it drives out the Jews?" Here the heavily German Middle West showed the greatest tolerance of Hitlerian persecution, but only by a small margin:

Region	Better, Approve	Worse, Disapprove	Don't Know, No Answer
Northeast	14. 0%	54. 6%	31. 4%
Midwest	16. 1	55. 1	28. 8
Southeast	7. 5	60. 0	32. 5
Southwest	14. 7	52. 4	32. 9
Mountain States	9. 8	41. 0	49. 2
Pacific Coast	14. 3	61. 1	24. 6

In the case of Japan, one would expect the Pacific
Coast to be less sympathetic than any other section towards
Japanese imperialistic ambitions in the Far East. Again, for
the first Roosevelt Administration we must rely largely on
editorial opinion, and again sectional attitudes do not vary
widely. Following the gradual ebbing of the Manchurian crisis
in 1934 after both the League of Nations and the United States
had failed to chastize the Japanese, there was a marked decline in enthusiasm on the part of the internationalist press
for several years relative to American involvement in the Far
Eastern imbroglio. Curiously, the Chinese did find a supporter in the abovementioned Chairman of the Senate Foreign
Relations Committee, Key Pittman of Nevada, who delivered
a violently anti-Japanese speech on the floor of the Senate in
February 1936. One of the few newspapers that supported
Pittman was the San Francisco Chronicle, which advocated our
taking a firm stand on behalf of American rights in the Orient
even if it led to war between the United States and Japan.

A generally restrained attitude persisted even after the
sinking of the Panay, an American gunboat, by the Japanese
above Nanking on December 12, 1937. (War had broken out
between China and Japan on July 7.) According to Dorothy
Borg, State Department surveys of editorial opinion made at
the beginning and the height of the crisis failed to reveal any
highly bellicose attitudes towards Japan, aside from such rare
exceptions as the New York Times. Fifty years previously,
in contrast, the sinking of the Maine had triggered off the
Spanish-American War. Some American newspapers, in fact,
even displayed a slightly unfriendly attitude towards China
during this period, of which the Chicago Tribune was a prominent example.

The key weapon in the isolationists' arsenal in the years
prior to World War II, of course, were the different pieces
of neutrality legislation designed to forestall our involvement
in another European war. Thus the 1935 measure not only

prohibited all arms shipments, but also forbade American citizens to travel on belligerent vessels except at their own risk, while its 1936 counterpart outlawed the extension of loans or credits to belligerents.   Aside from the previously mentioned joint resolution of January, 1937 that forbade the export of munitions for use in the Spanish Civil War, another act passed on May 1 authorized the President to list commodities other than munitions which were to be paid for on a cash-and-carry basis, and prohibited travel on belligerent vessels.   Two years later, following the outbreak of war in Europe, Congress enacted still another neutrality law, repealing the arms embargo and permitting cash-and-carry exports of arms and munitions to belligerent powers, a measure which had been before that body prior to this event.

Next let us examine the sectional aspects of the votes in Congress on some of these pieces of neutrality legislation. When the Neutrality Act of 1936 passed the House by a 353 to 27 margin, the Middle West cast 17 of the nay votes in protest against its lack of severity; in the Senate, where there was no roll call on the final passage, ten Midwesterners led the movement for broader trade restrictions.   On the other hand, Key Pittman's cash-and-carry resolution of 1937 cleared the Senate in its final form by a 63 to 6 margin; here the maritime states of New England spearheaded the opposition with 4 votes.   This vote demonstrates that sections other than the Middle West adopted isolationist postures at times.   Still another vote of interest was that on the unsuccessful attempt in the House on June 30, 1939 to delete the Vorys Amendment from the Bloom Bill; this amendment provided for a limited embargo covering arms and ammunition, but excluded implements of war.   Unquestionably the most important feature of the sectional breakdown on this vote was the hostility of the South, long the most military-minded region of the nation. Here the totals were: for passage 214, against passage 173; Middle West, for 97, against 32; Northeast, for 74, against 42; West, for 23, against 16; South, for 20, against 83. When the Vorys proposal was presented again to the House on November 2 after having been deleted by a joint House-Senate committee, the House reversed its original stand and rejected it, 245 to 179, with the South again opposing it by an overwhelming majority.   This, of course, was following the outbreak of the war in Europe.

George S. Grassmuck, who has analyzed the entire spectrum of Congressional votes on neutrality legislation between 1935 and 1941, has concluded that these were highly partisan as well as frequently sectional in nature. For House Democrats the favorable percentage of total votes cast on neutrality relaxation was 74. 9, for Senate Democrats, 70. 3; in contrast, the figure for Senate Republicans was 31. 8, for House Republicans a mere 13. 0. In this connection Democratic Senators from the states of Idaho, South Dakota, Ohio, and Massachusetts showed a far greater unwillingness to relax neutrality legislation than did their colleagues from other states, while such Republican Senators as Joseph Ball of Minnesota, George W. Norris of Nebraska, and Chan Gurney of South Dakota were atypical in their support of measures of this type. In the House, Great Plains Democrats were the least amenable to relaxation, Republicans from the South, New England, the North Atlantic States, and the Pacific Coast the most favorable. There was also apparently a direct relationship in both parties between representing a metropolitan district and supporting the relaxation of neutrality legislation.

Still another index of isolationist/internationalist attitudes was the Congressional vote on the Ludlow Resolution. This measure, originally introduced in 1935 by Representative Louis Ludlow of Indiana, provided for a national referendum on a declaration of war. Although one national poll taken in 1937 revealed that 73 per cent of those interviewed supported a constitutional amendment of this type, President Franklin D. Roosevelt and Secretary of State Cordell Hull opposed it, and the House voted by a 209 to 188 margin on January 10, 1938 to return it to committee. While the Ludlow Resolution was supported by most Republicans and by most Democrats from the west of the Mississippi, it was generally opposed by Representatives from the South and the Northeast. Perhaps Ludlow would have enjoyed more success had he not antagonized the South by unsuccessfully sponsoring an anti-lynching bill that Senators from that section filibustered to death. On the other hand, the entire House delegation from Kansas voted in the affirmative, despite the opposition of former governor and Republican Presidential nominee Alfred Landon.

As of 1937 the majority of Americans not only were still opposed to American involvement in the League of Nations, but also regarded American intervention in World War I as a mistake, if two national AIPO polls are to be accepted as representative. Here a comparative analysis of the sectional breakdowns of the votes in each poll is enlightening, as it provides further evidence of southern internationalism:

Join League of Nations			W. W. I Role a Mistake		
Section	Yes	No	Section	Yes	No
New England and			New England	67%	33%
Middle Atlantic	33%	67%	Middle Atlantic	71	29
East Central	33	67	East Central	74	26
West Central	31	69	West Central	68	32
South	44	56	South	61	39
Far West	27	73	Rocky Mountain	72	28
			Pacific Coast	76	24

These figures represent percentages of decided interviewees only, as those with no opinion have been eliminated from the computations.

While one obviously found internationalists in sections other than the South, by no means did every isolationist hail from the Middle West. As Manfred Jonas points out, isolationism "was a general American sentiment, not, as sometimes pictured, simply a Midwestern phenomenon born of the insularity of the American interior." There were also Republican isolationists and Democratic isolationists, liberal isolationists and conservative isolationists. Among the prominent non-midwestern isolationists in Congress that one might single out are Senators William E. Borah of Idaho, Hiram Johnson of California, and Robert Reynolds of North Carolina, and Representatives Maury Maverick of Texas, Hamilton Fish, Jr. of New York, and George Tinkham of Massachusetts. According to Ray Billington, the Congressional delegation from the Middle West may have been more isolationist than the public opinion of that section, instead of faithfully mirroring it.

On October 5, 1937 President Franklin Roosevelt delivered his famous Quarantine Speech in Chicago. This marked the high point of American interventionism prior to the outbreak of World War II; as one might expect from the two 1937 polls that we have just cited, the American people were not yet in a mood to quarantine the aggressors, so that F. D. R. regarded it a wise course to play down his remarks afterwards. There being no Congressional vote of approval or disapproval on the Quarantine Speech, we must rely on editorial opinion for our analysis. As one might expect, the highly isolationistic, strongly Republican Chicago Tribune was quite displeased at a Democratic President choosing its own backyard to suggest intervention:

Those Chicagoans who went yesterday to see a bridge dedicated, those who gathered at the curbstones to see a President pass in a shower of ticker tape, and those who sat at their radios to hear some words of peace, these and many more found themselves last night the center of a world-hurricane of war fright. President Roosevelt came to Chicago to bless the bridge that spans two delightful and peaceful park systems.

He talked war.

Despite the chorus of disapproval generated by the Chicago Tribune and the equally isolationistic Hearst press, the vast majority of newspapers throughout the country by no means subjected the Quarantine Speech to vituperative attacks. In fact, a number were quite disappointed that the President did not follow through and implement the program that he had alluded to at Chicago; among these were the San Francisco Chronicle and the Los Angeles Times, two Pacific Coast newspapers that were quite naturally concerned about the Japanese menace, and the Milwaukee Journal and the Christian Science Monitor of Boston. But the admonition of the Wall Street Journal to "Stop Foreign Meddling: America Wants Peace" triumphed for the time being, and the proposed economic boycott and naval blockade of Japan failed to become a reality.

Although Franklin Roosevelt was obviously attempting to move this nation away from isolationism in the direction of interventionism before it was ready to take this bold step, a FOR poll taken in 1938 revealed that every section of the country approved of his foreign policy. The percentages were as follows, excluding the undecided and uninformed: Pacific Coast, 89. 9; Southwest, 87. 3; Southeast, 87. 1; Mountain States, 71. 5; Northern Plains, 71. 3; Middle West, 70. 0; and Northeast, 70. 0. This sectional unanimity of approval for F. D. R. 's foreign policy also ran counter to the fact that different sections had different interests, some highly incompatible; a Gallup poll of the most interesting news stories of 1938, for example, broke down by section as follows:

New England	South	Middle West	West
1. Hurricane	1. Munich	1. Munich	1. Munich
2. Munich	2. Nazi persecutions	2. Republican gains	2. Nazi persecutions
3. Republican gains	3. Wages and hours bill	3. Nazi persecutions	3. Sino-Japanese War

Still another Gallup poll, this one conducted in April 1939, revealed that there was a general preoccupation with the war question throughout most of the country. The Northwest Coast in particular was sensitive to the imminence of hostilities abroad, while the Eastern Seaboard also was quite agitated over the likelihood of open conflict. Yet as he moved into the interior, Gallup found more skepticism as to the inevitability of war in such cities as Denver and Chicago, and discovered isolationism on the rampage in Minneapolis. The Solid South expressed its contempt for Hitler and Mussolini, with an occasional outburst of anti-Semitism, but Senator William E. Borah's Idaho took an isolationist stance, viewing with alarm the direction in which events were drifting.

As World War II approached, President Roosevelt was confronted with a dilemma: western Democrats were often progressives on domestic issues and isolationists towards foreign policy, while southern Democrats frequently were conservatives as to domestic reform but internationalists as to foreign affairs. It was only the eastern Democrats who generally supported him on both domestic and foreign policy. Thus, to implement the former F. D. R. had to forge an alliance of West and East, to implement the latter one of East and South. During the 1938 primaries Roosevelt attempted (with little success) to purge southern conservatives such as Walter George of Georgia; during 1938, too, Congress passed the last major piece of New Deal domestic legislation, the Wages and Hours Act. After this a coalition of Republicans and Southern Democrats prevented the enactment of further measures of this type. But war in Europe was only a year away, and it was only natural that the attention of the nation would turn more and more towards foreign affairs and away from domestic reforms, so that F. D. R. could now afford to sacrifice western support for the latter.

The Diplomacy of F. D. R., 1939-1945

On August 23, 1939 Nazi Germany and Communist Russia signed an agreement at Moscow which stipulated that not only would each party abstain from attacking the other, but also that either party would remain neutral in the event that the other was attacked by a third party. This pact, which freed Hitler's hands relative to Poland, aroused confused and contradictory editorial comments in this country; despite growing apprehension, some journalists nevertheless hoped that

actual hostilities would not ensue in the near future. This
bit of wishful thinking was rudely shattered one week later,
when Hitler invaded Poland. After Great Britain and France
had declared war on Germany, the United States affirmed its
neutrality, although President Franklin Roosevelt felt com-
pelled to observe that: "This nation will remain a neutral
nation, but I cannot ask that every American remain neutral
in thought as well."

For the moment Hitler was the arch-villain to most
Americans, but the eroding Russian image also struck rock
bottom here following the Communist invasion of Finland on
October 14. It will be recalled that Finland had been the only
European nation not to default on its World War I debt. The
Dallas Morning News, for example, lambasted the "murderous
and unprovoked attack, " while the Washington Evening Star
was horrified at the "peculiarly revolting lust of Stalin"; the
Cleveland Plain Dealer likewise was nauseated at the "sheer
brutality of the Soviet action. " Ironically, some of the most
vocal criticisms emanated from such northeastern states as
Pennsylvania, Ohio, and New York, yet each of these states
had averaged in excess of one million dollars' worth of business with Soviet trade representatives during 1939. Forced
to make a choice between Mammon and Finland, most American businessmen chose Mammon, with the copper trade being
a case in point.

Despite a vigorous display of resistance, Finland
eventually capitulated to the Russians on March 12, 1940,
shortly after F. D. R. had signed a Congressional act on
March 2 authorizing a non-military loan to Finland under the
auspices of the Reconstruction Finance Corporation. Not only
was this act supported by such eastern internationalists as
Representative Emanuel Celler of New York, but also by such
midwestern isolationists as Senator Prentiss Brown of Michigan, who had authored this bill in an attempt to placate his
loyal Scandinavian constituency. Foes of the measure in the
Senate included Pat Harrison of Mississippi, whom Roosevelt
had deposed as Majority Leader, Walter George of Georgia,
Robert Reynolds of North Carolina, Bennett Clark of Missouri, Rush Holt of West Virginia, Arthur Capper of Kansas,
William E. Borah of Idaho, and Hiram Johnson of California;
among its supporters were Robert La Follette of Wisconsin,
Arthur Vandenberg of Michigan, Henrik Shipstead of Minnesota, Lynn Frazier of North Dakota, and Josiah Bailey of
North Carolina, most if not all of whom generally were to be
found in the isolationist camp. The Brown Bill cleared the

Senate by a 49 to 27 margin, with the Great Plains, the Middle West, and the South most hostile. In the House it passed by 168 to 51, and even arch-isolationist Representative Hamilton Fish of New York jumped on the bandwagon. Admittedly Finland did not receive significant aid as a result of the enactment of this measure, but it nevertheless was an important symbolic gesture.

With the fall of the Netherlands and Belgium in May and June of 1940, public opinion in this country began to shift even further in the direction of intervention. As for the New York business circles, which early had supported the British and French during World War I, many signs indicated that sentiment for aiding the Allies in every way possible was crystallizing; this also was true of the Middle West, but to a lesser extent. The Committee to Defend America by Aiding the Allies was set up in May 1940 with Republican newspaper editor William Allen White of Kansas as its first head, its national membership heavily sprinkled with eastern lawyers and college professors. Yet by the end of June France and Norway also had fallen, as Hitler's juggernaut continued its relentless march.

An even more significant reaction to the Hitlerian threat was the Burke-Wadsworth Act, or Selective Training and Service Act, which Congress approved in September after a heated debate. Again the support of the South was vital, and that military-minded region generously lent its support; the only southern Senator to oppose conscription was "Cotton Ed" Smith of South Carolina, while in the House only three Republicans from Tennessee and Kentucky voted in the negative. (More than half of the training camps were subsequently established south of the Potomac.) In contrast, Middle Westerners (especially Republicans) in both the House and the Senate were generally hostile to selective service, with Michigan, Wisconsin, North Dakota, and South Dakota leading the opposition. Such liberal Senators as George Norris of Nebraska and Robert La Follette of Wisconsin were fearful that the draft might endanger domestic liberties and foster domestic fascism, while Ernest Lundeen of Minnesota offered as a rather impractical alternative the seizure of all French and British possessions in the New World. Despite strong midwestern opposition, the Burke-Wadsworth Bill passed the House by a 263 to 149 vote, and cleared the Senate by a 58 to 31 margin, President Franklin Roosevelt signing it on September 16. By October 29 the first draft number had been selected.

Sectional attitudes were also apparent in the 1940 Presidential election, which saw F. D. R. winning an unprecedented third term by defeating the Republican nominee, former utilities executive and Democrat Wendell Willkie of Indiana. In a FOR poll of American businessmen conducted in September as to which of the two nominees could handle foreign affairs better, 68. 0 of the Midwesterners and 56. 2 per cent of the Southerners chose Willkie, the national average for the latter being 64. 4. As T. R. Fehrenbach has pointed out, for Willkie to have won this election he would have had to play to the baser feelings of midwestern isolationists and big-city Anglophobes; instead, the author-to-be of One World adopted a foreign policy line that in many respects paralleled that of the President, supporting Roosevelt on the destroyer deal and opposing a delay in conscription.

F. D. R. did win re-election in November, amassing 27, 244, 160 popular votes and 449 electoral ones (38 states) to 22, 305, 198 popular votes and 82 electoral ones (10 states) for Willkie. Nevertheless, he lost Great Plains states with a heavy concentration of German-Americans in the population such as Kansas, Iowa, Nebraska, South Dakota, and North Dakota, with the Russians-Germans of the latter state spearheading the defection. Throughout the country his share of the major party vote declined approximately seven per cent from the high water mark of 1936. Roosevelt also lost ground in Richmond County (Staten Island) in New York, where there were few Germans but many Italians who were upset at his "stab-in-the-back" speech following Mussolini's invasion of France. On the other hand, F. D. R. increased his vote seven per cent in Maine, a northeastern state ethnically tied to Great Britain, while Polish-American precincts in cities like Buffalo, Milwaukee, and Detroit went twenty-to-one for Roosevelt.

In his annual message to Congress, delivered January 6, 1941, Franklin Roosevelt recommended a program of lend-lease to the Allies, as well as enunciating the famous "Four Freedoms. " On March 8 lend lease legislation passed the Senate 60 to 31, while on March 11 it cleared the House 317 to 71; the initial appropriation was for seven billion dollars, but by the end of the war the amount had reached the fifty billion dollar mark. An AIPO poll taken while the bill was pending revealed that 77 per cent of the Southerners polled favored lend lease, and the only Southerners to oppose it in Congress were Robert Reynolds of North Carolina in the Senate and Hugh Peterson of Georgia in the House. As usually was

the case with votes in the foreign relations area, most Senators and Representatives from the Middle West were strongly
opposed to lend lease, and the Chicago Tribune greeted the
enactment of this measure with the headline: "Senate Passes
Dictator Bill. " Yet even the Far West was sharply divided
on this question.

On June 22 Hitler invaded Russia, thus abruptly terminating the two-year pact between that country and Germany.
A survey taken by the New York Times of public sentiment in
Boston, Atlanta, Chicago, Omaha, St. Paul, Dallas, San Francisco, and Portland revealed that the attitude of New England
and the Pacific Coast with respect to the war in general remained unchanged. On the other hand, the citizens of Atlanta,
Chicago, St. Paul, Omaha, and Dallas looked upon both Communist Russia and Nazi Germany as undesirables, but tended
to fear the latter more; significantly, most of those favoring
increased aid suggested that it be directed toward Great Britain
rather than Russia.

Despite the German attack on the latter, the House
barely approved an eighteen months' extension of the draft on
August 12 by a paper-thin 203 to 202 margin. The South and
the Southwest cast an overwhelming vote of 120 to 10 on behalf of this administration measure, but the belt of states
stretching from New England, New Jersey, and Pennsylvania
across the Middle West to the Pacific Northwest voted by a
two-to-one margin or more against extending conscription,
with Montana, Rhode Island, and Connecticut splitting evenly.
In the Senate the margin was somewhat more decisive, 45 to
30; here the only southern Senators to vote in opposition were
"Cotton Ed" Smith of South Carolina, W. Lee O'Daniel of
Texas, and Robert Reynolds of North Carolina.

Two months later, on October 17, the House voted to
repeal Section VI of the Neutrality Act of 1939 by a 259 to
138 margin. After the Senate passed a more comprehensive
measure, 50 to 37, on November 7, the House had second
thoughts, and only adopted by a 212 to 194 margin on November 13 a bill that was more drastic than the one it had originally enacted. In this connection the vote-split in some of
the supposedly internationalist northeastern states is most
surprising: Massachusetts, 7 to 6; New York, 25 to 20; New
Jersey, 5 to 9; Pennsylvania, 10 to 20. As for the other
sections, the South was favorable, the Middle West opposed,
and the Far West divided. Leading the Republican attack outside of Congress was Wendell Willkie, who appealed for an

end to "the shame and deception of the hypocritical Neutrality Laws. "

Let us next examine various public opinion polls for the period 1939-1941 on such explosive issues as neutrality, to see whether they reflect any significant variations from section to section. One poll (AIPO) conducted in October 1939, one month after the outbreak of war in Europe, focused on the question: "If it appears that Germany is defeating England and France, should the United States declare war on Germany and send our army and navy to Europe to fight?" Here the range of favorable responses, by section, was: South, 47; New England, 33; West, 28; Middle Atlantic, 27; West Central, 26; East Central, 25. Likewise, the percentages favorable to helping England, even at the risk of getting into the war ourselves, were: South, 70; West, 54; New England and Middle Atlantic, 52; East Central, 48; and West Central, 43; according to a June 25, 1940 AIPO poll.

On the other hand, Hadley Cantril, Donald Rugg, and Frederick Williams, who made an in-depth study of public opinion from mid-summer to mid-October, 1940 found that "The most significant geographic increase in the desire to help England is to be found in the Rocky Mountain States. " Still another poll (OPOR), taken two months before Pearl Harbor, on September 2, 1941, posed the alternatives: 1) that this country keep out of war; or 2) that Germany be defeated. Again the South led the interventionists, with the range of favorable responses to the second alternative running as follows: South, 88; New England and Middle Atlantic, 70; West, 69; West Central, 64; East Central, 63. Other public opinion polls for this period generally yield similar results, although the sectional differences of opinion are far less pronounced than the voting patterns in Congress might lead one to expect. Gabriel Almond suggests relative to the former that: "The Middle West deviated in the isolationist direction on the average by around 8 to 10 per cent. The South deviated in an interventionist direction on the average by more than 15 per cent. "

Also of interest is the 1940 Gallup poll presented below that focused on the question as to whether it was a mistake for the United States to enter World War I. It should be compared with its 1937 counterpart previously cited:

Section	Yes, Mistake	No	No Opinion
New England and			
Mid-Atlantic	37	44	19
East Central	43	35	22
West Central	45	42	13
South	24	55	21
West	42	38	20

Turning to the historical background underlying these statistics, one may attribute midwestern isolationism to a number of factors: geographical insularity, a large German population, Republican opposition to Franklin Roosevelt, widespread pacifism, and anti-capitalist hostility towards Wall Street. Prior to World War II the highly isolationist America First organization had its headquarters in Chicago. On the other hand, a number of scholars writing during and after World War II have theorized that this phenomenon has been disproportionately emphasized. W. W. Waymack, for example, has proclaimed after studying the public opinion polls (as has Robert J. Blakely) that "the 'die-hard' isolationism attributed to the Middle West is largely an illusion," while William G. Carleton has concluded relative to Congress that "even here the isolationism of the Middle West has been greatly exaggerated." The evidence presented in this volume, although perhaps tarnishing the legend, by no means dismisses it.

As for southern internationalism, again there are at least a half-dozen factors that have contributed to this phenomenon: racial and cultural ties with Great Britain, the search for a cotton, tobacco, and rice market, the memory of Woodrow Wilson's League of Nations, a strong military tradition, proximity to both the Atlantic Ocean and the Gulf of Mexico, and loyalty to a Democratic President. Prior to World War II America First enjoyed less support in the South than in any other section. Conversely, the South led the nation in volunteers; a Representative from Alabama observed in this connection that the draft was necessary "to keep our Southern boys from filling up the army." According to T. R. Fehrenbach, Texas was by far the most belligerent state. Aside from the solid pro-Administration vote that the South generally delivered on foreign policy measures, many Southerners held key committee chairmanships during World War II. Perhaps the most vocal southern interventionist was Senator Claude Pepper of Florida; in May 1940 Pepper proclaimed that: "It is not written in the holy writ of Americanism that

America should be a mere spectator at Armageddon. " Pepper's actions in Congress bolstered this philosophy, although he lost his Senate seat after the war when his opponents accused him of being an extreme leftist.

Despite this overwhelming evidence in support of southern internationalism, Alexander De Conde is of the opinion that scholars have overlooked or even ignored a number of examples of southern isolationism. De Conde, for example, points out that:

> Before 1938 the South did not differ markedly in sentiment from other sections on issues of preparedness and neutrality. In some respects, according to public opinion surveys, it lagged behind the rest of the country. It placed a greater value on neutrality than did other sections, and it favored withdrawing American troops from the Far East lest the United States become too involved with Japan. Southerners in the days before Pearl Harbor were, in comparison to other Americans, less favorable to participation in an international organization for peace than they were for going to war.

One might add that the ranks of the isolationists in Congress between the two world wars did include Senators Tom Watson of Georgia, Huey P. Long of Louisiana, and Robert Reynolds of North Carolina, and Representative Martin Dies of Texas.

Once the United States had entered World War II, the South underwent a transformation of major proportions. During the war years the federal government pumped over ten billion dollars into the South for the construction and operation of defense plants; as a result, the South accelerated its march towards industrialization begun after the Civil War. As for trade, the main shipping lines already had been diverted from Europe to Latin America, with the South exporting such products to the latter as cigars and cigarettes, and cotton and rayon textiles, and importing in return such products as coffee, bananas, chocolate, nitrates, sugar, copper and raw wool. There was also a large-scale movement of southern whites from the rural areas to the metropolitan areas and industrial plants, North and South, and to military service, both here and overseas; the southern Negro likewise broadened his horizons upon encountering social climates other than the segregationist one to which he had become accustomed. Isolationist Senator Robert Reynolds of North Carolina chose to

retire in 1944, but interventionist Senators Claude Pepper of
Florida, Lister Hill of Alabama, J. William Fulbright of
Arkansas, and Tom Connally of Texas continued to exert
strong leadership in Congress. Nevertheless, racism and
bigotry still manifested themselves in the South on occasion;
as late as 1943 a number of southern Congressmen opposed
Chinese immigration on a quota basis.

During World War II the Middle West became less
isolationist and more like the other sections in its attitudes
towards foreign policy. Thomas A. Bailey points out in this
connection that: "In 1943 the Middle West was only slightly
less trustful of Russian cooperation, slightly less enthusiastic
about a new League of Nations, and slightly less favorable
to an international police force." Franklin Roosevelt's internationalist foreign policy, one might add, contributed to the
demise of such prominent midwestern third parties as the La
Follette Progressives in Wisconsin and the Farmer-Laborites
in Minnesota, both of which generally sympathized with the
New Deal but tended to be hostile towards global meddling.
The Progressives eventually joined the Republican Party in
1946, the Farmer-Laborites the Democratic Party in 1944.

As for the Pacific Coast, during the 1930's the Pacific
Northwest had protested when the operators of the Japanese
fishing canneries began to constitute a menace to Alaskan
salmon. With the attack on Pearl Harbor, the federal government relocated a number of Pacific Coast Japanese in the interior. An AIPO poll taken in December, 1942 revealed that
while only 17 per cent of the national total would not allow the
Japanese to return to their homes, for California, Oregon,
Washington, Nevada, and Arizona alone the figure was 31 per
cent. According to Chester H. Rowell, who sampled public
opinion on the West Coast at the time of the outbreak of
World War II, sentiment there had become progressively pro-
China at the same time that it had become progressively anti-
Japan.

Thanks to the national scope of this feeling, the following year (1943) witnessed the Congressional enactment of a
measure terminating Chinese exclusion. Despite the opposition of Senator Hiram Johnson and such McClatchy family
newspapers as the Sacramento Bee, exclusion repeal won the
backing of the chambers of commerce of Seattle, Tacoma,
Portland, San Bernadino, and San Francisco, Representative
Warren Magnuson of Washington and delegate Joseph R. Far-
rington of Hawaii, and the once pro-restriction San Francisco

Chronicle. Among the non-Westerners who favored repeal,
the name of Representative Walter Judd of Minnesota stands
out; Judd had been a medical missionary in China prior to
winning his House seat in 1942. Southern advocates of continued exclusion included the prominent North Carolina isolationist and demagogue, Robert R. Reynolds, who alleged that
the repeal bill had been introduced under the influence of
"war hysteria. " Unfortunately for purposes of analysis, there
was no record vote on this question.

During 1943 the House of Representatives also approved
the Fulbright resolution in June by a resounding 360 to 29
vote; this resolution committed the United States to participate
in "appropriate international machinery, with power adequate
to establish and to maintain a joint and lasting peace, among
nations of the world. " No less than 24 of the 29 nay votes
came from the Middle West. In the Senate, the counterpart
of the Fulbright proposal was the Connally Resolution, which
recommended that "the United States, acting through its constitutional processes, join with free and sovereign nations in
the establishment and maintenance of international authority
with power to prevent aggression and to preserve the peace
of the world. " A little stronger than the briefer House version, the Connally Resolution won the endorsement of the
Senate in November by an overwhelming 85 to 5 vote, with
even Gerald Nye of North Dakota voting in the affirmative.
The five nay votes here were cast by long-time, hardcore
isolationists, three of them Republicans, two of them Democrats: Hiram Johnson of California, William Langer of North
Dakota, Henrik Shipstead of Minnesota, Burton K. Wheeler of
Montana, and Robert Reynolds of North Carolina.

Two years later the Senate approved the Bretton Woods
bill, establishing an International Monetary Fund and the International Bank for Reconstruction and Development, by a 61
to 16 margin on July 19. (This measure had earlier passed
the House 345 to 18.) A leading opponent was Senator Robert
Taft of Ohio, who questioned the economic basis of wars and
feared that America would become a global Santa Claus. No
less than 9 of the nay votes were cast by Senators from the
Great Plains States, traditionally isolationistic in orientation
and hostile to eastern international financiers. Nine days
later, on July 28, the Senate also gave its blessing to American participation in the United Nations by an 89 to 2 vote.
On this occasion only Senators Langer and Shipstead voted in
the negative, the dying Johnson being too ill to cast his ballot
against it. Shipstead asserted that "Perpetual intervention

means perpetual war, " while Langer declared that "The adoption of the Charter ... will mean perpetuating war. " By now
the ranks of the isolationists had dwindled almost to the
vanishing point. It remained for the Vietnam War to generate
a new school of isolationism twenty years later, liberal in
orientation but with a much greater geographical distribution.

In closing, let us trace the evolution of sectional attitudes towards world organization during World War II, placing
special emphasis on the public opinion polls and endorsements
by various states. Among those states that passed resolutions
declaring that "all peoples of the earth should now be united
in a commonwealth of nations to be known as the Federation
of the World" were Alabama, North Carolina, Maryland, and
Rhode Island; in 1942 the Florida legislature also adopted a
memorial requesting the President and Congress "to call at
the earliest possible moment a convention of representatives
of all free peoples to frame a federal government under which
they may unite in a democratic world government subject to
ratification by each people concerned. " In addition, the legislatures of New Jersey, New Hampshire, and Connecticut passed
resolutions calling for a study of the world federation concept, and the New York legislature enacted one urging the
President and Congress to support an international organization embracing every nation whose object was to maintain a
lasting peace. As for referendums, in November 1942 the
voters of Massachusetts approved by a seventy-five per cent
favorable majority a resolution instructing the state legislature "to call at the earliest possible moment a world convention to discuss the formation of an organization of nations. "
Needless to say, most of these expressions of interest came
from the Northeast and the South, the two most internationalist sections of the country.

Once the war had started, of course, sectional differences of opinion with regard to internationalism tended to
evaporate. When the AIPO conducted a poll in July, 1941,
asking whether the United States should have joined the League
of Nations after World War I, the range of favorable responses
was as follows: West, 42; South, 39; New England and Mid-
Atlantic, 39; East Central, 35; and West Central 27. Western
internationalism was again manifest in the fifth Woman's Home
Companion poll, published in April 1943, the West being most
firmly of the opinion (with the spread of responses among
sections again narrow) that Americans should be devoting
thought now to post-war problems, and that there should be
a permanent world congress to act upon international disputes.

Then there is the July, 1945 AIPO poll measuring favorable
responses to the question of whether this country should approve the United Nations Charter for a world organization as
adopted at the San Francisco Conference; this found the South
to be the least enthusiastic section in another very limited
range of favorable responses: East and West Central, 68; Far
West, 65; New England and Middle Atlantic, 64; and South, 62.
If indeed there has been a decline in southern internationalism
following World War II, one may find early evidence of it in
polls such as this one, and in two for the year 1946 that we
will examine in the next chapter.

FOR FURTHER READING

        Looking first at the diplomacy of Normalcy, there is a
state-by-state breakdown of the votes in the Senate and the
House of Representatives on the ratification of the Hoover
Moratorium in Council on Foreign Relations, The United States
in World Affairs 1932. One of the best sources for Congressional votes on the World Court and international organization,
as well as on the Four Power Treaty of 1922, is George L.
Grassmuck, Sectional Biases in Congress on Foreign Policy;
Robert Divine surveys internationalism outside of Congress in
his Second Change: The Triumph of Internationalism in Amer-
ica During World War II. For attitudes towards the navy, see
C. Leonard Hoag's Preface to Preparedness. Books dealing
with immigration in general include Maurice R. Davis, World
Immigration, and George Stephenson, A History of American
Immigration 1820-1924; more specifically with Japanese ex-
clusion, Richard O'Connor, Pacific Destiny: An Informal His-
tory of the U. S. in the Far East, 1776-1968; Eleanor Tupper,
Japan in American Public Opinion; and Rodman W. Paul, The
Abrogation of the Gentlemen's Agreement. Attitudes towards
China and Japan are traced in such books as Dorothy Borg's
The United States and the Far Eastern Crisis of 1935-1938 and
Charles C. Tansill's Back Door to War: The Roosevelt Fore-
ign Policy 1933-1941; the League of Nations' handling of Jap-
anese imperialism circa 1933 is examined by Denna Frank
Fleming in his The United States and World Organization 1920-
1933. One might also consult various comparative studies of
American newspapers and foreign policy; two of the more im-
portant of these are James T. Russell and Quincy Wright,
"National Attitudes on the Far Eastern Controversy" and Julian
L. Woodward, Foreign News in American Morning Newspapers.
Relative to the interpretations set forth in some of the above-

mentioned books, it might be added that Grassmuck and
O'Connor play down sectional differences, while Tupper emphasizes them.

As for the period 1933-1939, Charles A. Beard examines Franklin Roosevelt and the Election of 1932 in his
American Foreign Policy in the Making 1932-1940. American
attitudes towards Russia prior to and at the time of recognition are discussed in Peter Filene, Americans and the Soviet
Experiment, 1917-1933; Saul G. Bron, Soviet Economic Development and American Business; Meno Lovenstein, American
Opinion of Soviet Russia; and Foster Rhea Dulles, The Road
to Teheran: The Story of Russia and America, 1781-1943. By
far the most comprehensive treatment of the granting of Philippine independence is found in Garel A. Grunder and William
E. Livezey, The Philippines and the United States; James
Morton Callahan treats less exhaustively the Congressional
rejection of the St. Lawrence Seaway in his American Foreign
Policy in Canadian Relations. A key study of a leading iso-
lationist is Wayne S. Cole's Senator Gerald P. Nye and
American Foreign Relations. For Congressional votes on the
World Court and international organization, again see the book
by Grassmuck. Studies that dissect American attitudes towards the contemporary Spanish Civil War include Richard
P. Traina, American Diplomacy and the Spanish Civil War;
F. Jay Taylor, The United States and the Spanish Civil War;
and the doctoral dissertation by Hugh Jones Parry, The
Spanish Civil War: A Study in American Public Opinion, Propaganda, and Pressure Groups. Unquestionably the best
coverage of editorial reactions in this country to developments
abroad is the abovementioned book by Tansill, while the best
collection of polls relating to American attitudes towards
foreign policy in general is Hadley Cantril's Public Opinion
1935-1946. Two more technical studies of American journalism worth citing are J. Wymond French and Paul H. Wagner,
"American Reporting of a Hitler Speech, " and Quincy Wright
and Carl J. Nelson, "American Attitudes Towards Japan and
China, 1937-38"; in 1939 the House Foreign Affairs Committee
published a sampling of editorials from newspapers in 23
states for May and June in its American Neutrality Policy.
The abovementioned Borg book is also valuable for its treatment of Congressional as well as editorial reaction to Japanese imperialism. For Congressional votes on neutrality
legislation, again see the book by Grassmuck, and Robert A.
Divine, The Illusion of Neutrality. A highly restricted but
none the less interesting article is Bruce L. Larson, "Kansas and the Panay Incident, 1937. " As for the overall pic-

ture, Basil Rauch examines F. D. R.'s forging of sectional
alliances in support of both his domestic and foreign policies
in The History of the New Deal.

The Russian attack on Finland and the Congressional
reaction to this act of aggression is most comprehensively
discussed in Robert Sobel, The Origins of Interventionism:
The United States and the Russo-Finnish War; American reactions to World War II in general are investigated in William
L. Langer and S. Everett Gleason, The Challenge to Isolation
1937-1940 and The Undeclared War 1940-1941, and in T. R.
Fehrenbach, F. D. R.'s Undeclared War 1939 to 1941. For the
Election of 1940, again consult the books by Gerson, Lubell,
and Fehrenbach, as well as Lubell's article "Who Votes Isolationist and Why." Those retrospective articles concentrating
on a single section and its attitudes towards foreign relations
include Ray Allen Billington's "The Origins of Middle Western
Isolationism"; William G. Carleton's "Isolationism and the
Middle West"; Robert P. Wilkins' "Middle Western Isolationism: A Re-examination"; Chester H. Rowell's "The Pacific
Coast Looks Abroad"; Wayne S. Cole's "America First and
the South, 1940-1941"; Alexander de Conde's "The South and
Isolationism"; and Marian D. Irish's "Foreign Policy and the
South." De Conde challenges the widespread assumption that
the South was far more internationalist than the other sections.
In this connection one also should consult Paul Seabury's brief
monograph The Waning of Southern "Internationalism." Another
work that breaks with traditional interpretations is the master's thesis by Nels Manuel Lillehaugen, A Survey of North
Dakota Newspaper Opinion on Foreign Affairs, 1934-1939;
Lillehaugen points out that North Dakotan isolationism was not
monolithic.

Among those studies treating the impact of World War
II on various sections following Pearl Harbor and related
events are the abovementioned article by Irish; Francis Butler
Simkins, A History of the South; the abovementioned article
by Lubell; and Norris Hundley, "The Politics of Water and
Geography: California and the Mexican-American Treaty of
1944." By far the best treatment of wartime Congressional
developments is that found in Robert A. Divine, Second Chance:
The Triumph of Internationalism in America During World
War II. Sectional attitudes towards a wartime measure are
traced in Fred W. Riggs, Pressures on Congress: A Study
of the Repeal of Chinese Exclusion.

The three broadly gauged investigations of Congres-

sional attitudes noted in the introduction are the abovementioned book by Grassmuck, Julius Turner's Party and Constituency: Pressures on Congress, and V. O. Key Jr.'s Southern
Politics: In State and Nation. The book cited by Wayne S.
Cole is his An Interpretive History of American Foreign Relations, that by Finis Capps his From Isolationism to Involvement: The Swedish Immigrant Press in America 1914-1945.

CHAPTER 7

FROM WORLD WAR II
TO THE VIETNAM WAR

Overview and Analysis

During the quarter-century that has elapsed since the
end of World War II the United States government has been
continuously preoccupied with foreign affairs, thanks to its
commitment to the United Nations, the numerous treaties that
it has signed with foreign nations, the persistence of the
"cold war" with the Soviet Union and Communist China, and
its involvement in the Korean War and the Vietnam War. In
contrast to the isolationism that characterized many epochs,
there is no corner of the globe in which the American government is not vitally interested today: Europe, Africa, the
Near East, the Far East, Latin America, Canada. Nevertheless, especially since the outbreak of the Vietnam War,
there has been a movement in this nation away from leadership in world affairs, particularly among domestic liberals
who fervently wish that our enormous defense budget be spent
instead on such costly projects as rebuilding the cities, and
improving the lot of minorities.

In sectional terms, perhaps the most important development of the post-World War II period has been the waning of southern internationalism. We will examine this and
related phenomena in an overview and analysis of sectional
tendencies and Congressional voting patterns, followed by a
chronological survey of each Presidential administration in
terms of the key issues. It is, of course, impossible to present a detailed history of American foreign policy since 1945
without making this chapter disproportionately long; assuming
a general familiarity with postwar developments on the part
of the reader, we will concentrate on that material which directly relates to our topic.

We need to recognize that the common practice of
viewing foreign policy along isolationist/internationalist lines

230

frequently results in oversimplification.   In fact, one might
single out as many as four conflicting approaches subscribed
to by varying segments of the American public, each involving some degree of active involvement in world affairs. These
are: 1) a primary emphasis on the military, with support
for foreign military aid, a large defense budget, military intervention in the Dominican Republic and South Vietnam, and
pro-U. S. conservative regimes abroad; 2) a preference for
economic and multilateral over military and bilateral aid, a
reliance on the United Nations and other international organizations, and the backing of progressive governments overseas;
3) the utopian left, which favors some type of world government and maintains that foreign aid only retards inevitable
revolution; and 4) the far right, which embraces a policy of
"going it alone" and even preventive war.   It should be added,
too, that many "isolationists" of the late 1940's who opposed
the Truman Administration's involvement in European affairs
several years later favored a unilateral policy of attacking
Communist China when the Korean War deadlocked.

Internationalism, though, has been far more widespread
in the South.   It has been pointed out that Southerners were
among the strongest supporters of Virginia-born President
Woodrow Wilson's League of Nations following World War I,
and that prior to our entry into World War II this section
gave more solid backing to President Franklin Roosevelt's
preparedness policies than any other section.   Thus it is not
surprising that the South would similarly endorse the global
diplomacy of still another Democrat, Border Stater Harry
Truman of Missouri.   Beginning with the mid-1950's opinion
polls and Congressional votes revealed a waning of southern
internationalism, but a Republican President, Texas-born
Dwight Eisenhower, generally enjoyed the co-operation of various influential Congressional Southern Democrats.   Generally
speaking, the South began to lose interest in supporting internationalist policies when these: 1) became focused on Africa
and Asia rather than Europe; 2) became less militaristic and
more economic in emphasis.   As for the most recent decade,
Democratic President John Kennedy of Massachusetts experienced a lessening of southern support in Congress for his
foreign policy at the time of his death, despite an initial burst
of enthusiasm following his inauguration, while his successor,
Lyndon Johnson, fared better, thanks to overwhelming Democratic majorities in both houses of Congress and his consummate
political skill, until the Vietnam War began to undermine his
backing.

The growing industrialization of the South during and
after World War II was also a factor of considerable consequence relative to its shifting stance on foreign policy. At
the time of its inauguration in 1934, the reciprocal trade
agreement program enjoyed greater support there than in any
other section, yet a quarter of a century later the South was
showing less enthusiasm for reciprocal and liberalized trade
than any other. The textile and clothing industries in particular have experienced heavy competition from Japan in recent
years. One reason why foreign aid has become increasingly
unpopular in the South is that the program's geographical emphasis has shifted from Europe to the underdeveloped areas
of the globe that compete agriculturally and industrially with
it; American financed irrigation programs, for example, might
lead to increased cotton production overseas. Although the
tobacco and cotton lobbies both carried on an intensive campaign in 1948 on behalf of the European-oriented Marshall
Plan, in 1956 southern Senators played a key role in sabotaging American financial aid for the construction of the Aswan
Dam in Egypt. One, too, must not lose sight of the consequences of the growing economic interdependence of this section. According to Paul Seabury, "The striking integration
of the South into the national economy subtly exacted the price
of weakening its commitment to an international economic
order. "

As one might expect, racial factors have similarly
colored southern attitudes towards the rest of the world.
Southerners hesitant to let Negroes vote or attend white
schools could hardly view with much enthusiasm the activities
of the United Nations, in whose General Assembly a small
"black" nation such as Liberia possesses voting strength equal
to that of the United States, despite national polls revealing
little divergence in sectional attitudes over the years towards
the world organization. The independence movement throughout the former colonial world is similarly equated by many
Southerners with the civil rights movement in this country.
As a result, it is not surprising that there would be little enthusiasm for foreign aid in such states as Mississippi, South
Carolina, Louisiana, North Carolina, and Georgia. That
Southerners would likewise be hostile to liberalized immigration programs that might flood this nation with non-Anglo-
Saxons goes without saying. Like their white counterparts,
Southern Negroes appear to be less favorably disposed to in-
ternationalist global policies than blacks elsewhere, a phe-
nomenon which merits further study.

Still another explanation for the recent resurgence of southern isolationism might also be offered. The Jeffersonian wing of the Democratic Party has long been economy-minded, and Southerners adhering to this tradition would hardly look with favor on large-scale foreign aid; a 1963 Gallup Poll found this section to be the most opposed. The Jeffersonian wing likewise has been traditionally fearful of an overly strong President, and there was strong support in the South for the Bricker Amendment of the early Eisenhower years, limiting the power of the President to negotiate executive agreements with other nations. It is also possible that southern members of Congress, many of whom had enjoyed a free hand at one time to vote as they pleased on foreign policy issues provided that they cast their ballots in the prescribed manner on such domestic issues as race, are now being increasingly subjected to constituency pressures on the former as well. In this connection Alfred O. Hero, Jr. has pointed out that: "When Southern voters in large numbers have used world affairs as a major criterion for selecting among candidates, the issues have seemed to be concerned with peace or war or economically oriented like trade, tariffs, and foreign aid where direct interests in jobs, income, or taxes were patent." There also appears to be a direct correlation between lack of information about foreign affairs in the South and the opposition there to an internationalist foreign policy, educational levels being lower in this section than in any other, although regional differences in this respect have steadily declined since World War II.

Less analyzed and more elusive are the reasons for the movement of the Middle West away from isolationism. Paul Seabury has suggested that the social revolution brought about by the New Deal helped to dissolve the sectional grievances that many Middle Westerners had against the eastern industrial forces of Wall Street and their international allies. The Middle West, too, is not as overwhelmingly Republican in its Congressional representation as it once was, and there appears to have been a marked correlation between isolationism and Republicanism during the inter-war period, 1918-1941. As for its immediate post-World War II political leaders, Republican Senator Arthur Vandenberg of Michigan dramatically abandoned isolationism following Pearl Harbor, while Republican Senator Robert Taft of Ohio approached internationalism more cautiously. More sympathetic to the reasoning of Taft than Vandenberg was the powerful Chicago Tribune, which interlaced attacks on the Truman Administration with endorsements of General Douglas MacArthur's "no substitute for victory" stance towards the Korean War.

Writing in 1957, Democratic Senator Paul Douglas of
Illinois, a liberal and an internationalist, concluded that " . . .
while isolationism is still strong in the great heartland of
America--and has been recently reinforced by business desires for lower expenditures and a tax cut--it is basically not
as strong as it once was." Another study by Maynard Kniskern that appeared in 1963 likewise opined that "isolationism
is not only dead but unremembered" in the eyes of Midwesterners. An analysis of Congressional roll calls over the past
quarter-century, however, reveals that this midwestern retreat from isolationism is by no means complete; Julius
Turner and Edward V. Schneier, Jr., in fact, trace a "Cen-
tral-Southern Alliance" in recent years against foreign aid.
Despite Wisconsin Senator Joseph McCarthy's anti-Communist
crusade, 1953 and 1955 Gallup Polls found the Middle West
most in favor of trade with Russia and an agricultural exchange.

Among those pockets of traditional isolationism that remain intact today, heavily rural North Dakota is perhaps the
most prominent example. One might debate the point as to
whether North Dakota is actually a midwestern state, as it
probably fits more securely into the Great Plains or West
North Central categories. Nevertheless, there is no question
but that internationalism is a stranger here, Gerald Nye of
munitions investigation fame being the state's most prominent
spokesman on foreign policy prior to World War II. In 1945,
moreover, Senator William Langer cast one of the two votes
against American participation in the United Nations, while
Langer, Senator Milton Young, and Representatives William
Lemke and Usher Burdick all voted against the bill to supply
arms to the NATO powers several years later. Following the
outbreak of the Korean War the North Dakota legislature transmitted a memorial to Congress calling for the withdrawal of
American troops from Korea, while in 1952 Democratic Presidential nominee Adlai Stevenson received only 28.5 per cent
of the vote in this state after his Republican rival, General
Dwight Eisenhower, had promised to go to Korea if elected.
Four years later Eisenhower won another decisive victory over
Stevenson in North Dakota, despite widespread farmer dissatisfaction with the farm policies of "Ike's" Secretary of
Agriculture, Ezra Taft Benson. When Hanno R. E. Hardt
studied the North Dakota press in 1965, he concluded: "The
amount of foreign news in the seven newspapers of the state
compares favorably with previous studies in other states.

However, the coverage of events in terms of editorials, editorial cartoons and pictures was smaller. . . . " Summarizing the period 1921-1964, Julius Turner and Edward V. Schneier, Jr. discovered, after examining roll calls for eight representative Congressional sessions, that Republicans from North Dakota and the West Central States opposed international or interventionist action on every occasion (32 times).

Turning to the Rocky Mountains and the Pacific Coast, the two sections that together form the West, this entire area is frequently looked upon as being more internationalist than the Middle West. A 1953 Gallup Poll found the West most amenable to international cooperation. Still, as Alfred O. Hero, Jr., has pointed out, ". . . social mobility is at least one of the source factors for the apathy towards world affairs and the anti-intellectualism which seem more widespread in the faster growing cities of the Far West than elsewhere except in Texas. " This is especially true of California, where only a quarter of the population is native-born; while perhaps a half of the latter might be characterized as internationalists, a majority of the three-quarters who are not native-born Californians are of the opinion that this nation has assumed too large a role in world affairs. A large percentage of these newcomers are elderly people who go there to retire and "let the rest of the world go by. " An equally important segment consists of younger individuals climbing the social and economic ladder, too busy to concern themselves with international affairs. As one might expect, the rural element throughout the West also tends to be isolationistic in orientation. Generally speaking, the Southwest is perhaps the most internationalist-minded sub-division of this section, while the Rocky Mountain area is not as isolationist as the voting record of its representatives in Congress would indicate.

In contrast, the Northeast has perhaps changed less since World War II than have the other three sections, at least down to the last few years. Consequently, attitudes towards foreign policy here are largely a continuation of past trends; the stereotype persists that this is the most internationalist of all sections, thanks to the numerous financial ties between Wall Street and Great Britain. Nevertheless, there have been occasions on which certain ethnic groups, Catholics and urban dwellers have adopted stances tinged with isolationism, in particular during the years preceding World War I and II. As we noted in the previous chapter, the outward-looking maritime states of New England cast four of the six votes against Senator Key Pittman's cash-and-carry resolution

when it came before the Senate in 1937. Thus it is a mistake
to regard northeastern internationalism as monolithic. Even
in more recent years it was the Northeast that led the opposition to American involvement in the Vietnam War; dovish
Massachusetts was the only state to give its vote to George
McGovern in his landslide Presidential defeat in 1972. Whether
this is indicative of a general trend away from internationalism, or merely constitutes a special case, remains to be seen.

Although it is difficult to measure their political impact with great precision, it remains probable that the existence of pockets of nationality group voters in a single state,
or in groups of states, has influenced the course of American
diplomacy on occasion. (Authorities who have endorsed the
ethnic hypothesis at one time or another to varying degrees
include V. O. Key, Jr., Samuel Lubell, and Seymour M. Lip-
set.) Ohio, for example, boasts a considerable German population, and Senator Robert A. Taft was a leading critic of
the Nuremberg war crimes trials following World War II; there
also is a heavy concentration of Jews in New York City, and
both President Harry Truman and Governor Thomas E. Dewey
adopted strongly pro-Palestine stances as early as 1946, two
years before the Presidential election in which they were
opposing candidates. One might also cite in this connection
the large number of Italians in such states as New York, New
Jersey, Pennsylvania, Massachusetts, and California, who
requested leniency for their homeland following the defeat of
Italy in World War II, and advocated support for the latter's
claims relative to Trieste against those of Yugoslavia. There
also are quite a few Poles in the abovementioned states, and
in Michigan and Wisconsin, who have demanded that the
American government adopt a firm stand towards Soviet Russia.
As for the Pacific Coast and the Rocky Mountains, the Chinese
and the Japanese long have been targets of discrimination
there; and throughout the Southwest many Spanish-Americans
and Mexican-Americans have begun to make their voices heard
politically.

In 1960 Leroy N. Rieselbach published an article entitled "The Basis of Isolationist Behavior" in which he attempted to determine through a study of Congressional roll
calls for the years 1939-1941 and 1949-1952 whether there
was a strong correlation between the indices of isolationism
and ethnic background. Concentrating on the Germans and the
Irish, Rieselbach cast doubt upon the validity of the ethnic
hypothesis: "...representatives of districts populated by
Americans of German and Irish ancestry vote isolationist less

than half the time, and some do not do so at all. '' Rieselbach, who also found the "rural-Midwestern" interpretations
of isolationism to be only moderately accurate, instead
stressed Republicanism and conservatism as factors contributing significantly to isolationist behavior. Despite these findings, however, Rieselbach partially reversed his thinking in
his 1964 article, "The Demography of the Congressional Vote
on Foreign Aid, 1939-1958, " in which he suggested that ". . .
in each Congress since the 80th there was a significant,
though small, positive correlation between ethnicity and internationalism. " Samuel Lubell, on the other hand, questions
the present-day usefulness of the ethnic hypothesis, especially
since the emergence of Russia rather than Germany as the
major threat to American global hegemony, but Lubell is of
the opinion that this concept was applicable prior to World
War II. Thus even authorities are unable to agree on this
topic.

While some commentators have attempted to explain
isolationism on ethnic grounds, others have offered interpretations which pit rural isolationism against urban internationalism. In this connection Alfred O. Hero, Jr., has observed
that ". . . isolated rural and smalltown inhabitants constitute a
major segment of the backbone of remaining American isolationism. " The latter phenomenon, of course, has been urban-
oriented at times, as among German-American and Italian-
American city dwellers prior to World War II. Nevertheless,
the case study of post-World War II North Dakota that we have
presented offers evidence that in terms of a long-term commitment, isolationism is more at home in a rural setting.
According to Samuel Lubell, "Isolationism is ... most per-
sistent in areas of cultural insularity, " as among the Russian-
German farmers of the Dakotas, Nebraska, and Kansas. One
study of voting patterns in the 83rd through 85th Congresses
(1953-1959), moreover, revealed that urban members provided
much more support for foreign aid than did their rural counterparts, while another encompassing the years 1950-1955
demonstrated that 75 of the 86 members of the House who
consistently opposed foreign aid represented agricultural districts, many of them in the Republican Middle West. Alfred
de Grazia similarly found the rural West much more isolationist at the time of the Korean War than the urban West.

Unlike other sections of the country, few immigrants
from abroad are to be found in the South, yet this section
stands alone in the overwhelming ascendancy of the Protestant
faith there, Catholics being numerous only in southern Louis-

iana and a few other places. According to Alfred O. Hero,
Jr. , this southern Protestant community has remained less
well informed than its counterpart outside of the South about
most aspects of world affairs well into the 1960's, in contrast to the southern Catholic community. Outside the South
during the initial post-war decade, though, white Protestants
were better informed on foreign policy questions than white
Catholics, but by the mid-1960's those religious differences
had virtually disappeared. Nevertheless, white Protestants
on the Pacific Coast were probably better informed that their
counterparts in the other sections, while Catholic whites in
the Northeast, many of whom are of immigrant stock and
limited educational background, were probably less well informed than their co-religionists elsewhere.

  With regard to differences in attitudes towards foreign
policy from section to section, they have only partially paralleled the informational differences. Protestant whites in the
South, for example, have become decidedly less internationalist than they were at one time; prior to Pearl Harbor the
relative absence of Catholics from this section acted as a
deterrent to isolationism, but in more recent years it has had
precisely the opposite effect. By the mid-1960's, too, white
Catholics in the Middle West and the West had become more
liberal than their white Protestant neighbors on a number of
foreign policy issues, although this was not true of the Northeast. Unlike three decades ago, Catholic Italy and semi-
Catholic Germany are no longer our foes, their place having
been taken by an officially atheistic Russia, which both
American Catholics and American Protestants may attack with
impunity.

  We shall consider next the question as to whether there
may be in fact a highly isolationistic area whose boundaries
are not coterminous with those of any of the major sections
of this country. Ralph H. Smuckler, who made a study of
roll-call votes in Congress between 1933 and 1950, has concluded that there is such a region of isolationism stretching
across the northern part of the United States, but by no
means geographically identical with the Middle West. In the
words of Smuckler, "The isolationist region extends further
to the west than does the Mid-west. Idaho and Wyoming lie
outside of the midwestern region. Furthermore, the core of
the isolationist region--Nebraska, Kansas, and the Dakotas--
lies on the Western fringe of the Midwest. " As one might
have expected, the voting records of both the House of Representatives and the Senate for this period confirm that North

Dakota was the most isolationist state; one mild surprise was
the presence of Vermont among the top twelve on the House
list. During the five years following the termination of World
War II, moreover, Louisiana and Mississippi adopted an isolationist stance out of line with the general internationalist
philosophy that characterized southern voting. An examination
of the House votes on the Reciprocal Trade Agreements program reveals that four New England states ranked among the
twelve most isolationist, with another belt of isolationism
stretching from Minnesota to the Pacific Coast. It must be
pointed out with regard to this data, however, that isolationistic districts sometimes adjoin internationalist ones within
the same state, and that it is an error to assume that each
state invariably votes as a monolithic unit on foreign policy
matters. One of Smuckler's more controversial findings was
that, regardless of a widespread assumption to the contrary,
isolationism tends to be stronger in the more highly educated
communities.

One might well compare Smuckler's findings with
another set that also terminates in 1950, H. Bradford Westerfield's Foreign Policy and Party Politics: Pearl Harbor to
Korea. (Westerfield's monograph actually begins with 1943.)
With regard to foreign aid, Westerfield discovered that Midwestern Republicans supported this program with much less
enthusiasm than did their coastal counterparts; this Middle
West/coastal split also was in evidence at the 1952 Republican convention, where Senator Robert Taft was the candidate
of the midwestern isolationists and General Dwight Eisenhower
of the coastal internationalists. Whereas Smuckler challenged
the correlation between a high educational level and adherence
to internationalism, Westerfield questioned that between ruralism and isolationism, at least as far as the Republican Party
is concerned: "It will be readily observed that there was no
striking difference in the distribution of administration support on foreign aid between the metropolitan and non-metro-
politan GOP congressmen from any particular region. " In
contrast, between 1943 and 1950 the Democratic Party was
split along Northeastern/Southern lines, with the latter more
isolationist, despite the fact that the Democrats held the
White House down to 1953, a factor which should have tended
to solidify party unity. Midwestern Republicans and Southern
Democrats, in fact, even formed informal alliances on such
issues as the immigration of displaced persons and alien en-
listments in the army. Although Midwestern Republicans often
adopted a strongly anti-Communist stance following World War
II, they nevertheless exhibited a glaring inconsistency in their

failure to support a number of programs designed to counter-
act the Russian threat, such as the 1947 Truman Doctrine of
aid to Greece and Turkey.

A more restricted study by Duncan MacRae, tabulating
roll calls in the House during the 81st Congress (1949-51),
confirms the above findings to a substantial degree. Atlantic
and Pacific Coast Republicans were more favorably disposed
to foreign aid than were their Lake and Great Plains states
counterparts, while urban Northern Democrats supported the
latter more enthusiastically than did their southern and rural
Border State colleagues. (Mississippi ranked at the top of
the extreme anti-aid category.) Nevertheless, MacRae does
break with traditional interpretations in his assertion that
"The representatives from districts having at least 50 per
cent farmers ... are slightly more favorable to foreign aid
than might be expected in view of the general tendencies of
their region and district type." Thus, it would seem, agrarian
radicalism is not necessarily correlated with isolationism.

During the early 1950's two important events occurred,
both of which had a significant impact on Congressional attitudes towards foreign policy: American participation in the
Korean War and the election of a Republican President in
1952. Gerald Marwell, who has analyzed voting patterns in
the House of Representatives between 1949 and 1954, has
pointed out that with the swearing in of Dwight Eisenhower as
chief executive "... the proportion of Coastal Republicans who
were pro-involvement increased markedly, while the proportion of Southern Democrats taking this position declined."
With the 1950 Congressional election there was a marked influx of Midwestern Republicans, with the 1952 Presidential
election, of Coastal Republicans; in contrast, the number of
Northern Democrats dropped 30 per cent between the 81st
Congress and the 83rd. A study by William T. Cozort on
opposition to foreign aid legislation in the House revealed that
during the five-year period from 1950 through 1955 a majority
of the delegations from eleven midwestern states voted against
foreign aid bills 58.18 per cent of the time, with Nebraska,
South Dakota, and Wisconsin leading the opposition.

As for the Eisenhower years, Leroy N. Rieselbach
theorizes in The Roots of Isolationism, that 1) Representatives of both parties from the East in the 83rd (1953-5) and
85th (1957-9) Congresses were more internationalist and less
isolationist than the other regional groupings on foreign aid;
2) Eastern and Midwestern Democrats were more interna-

tionalist than Democrats from the South and West on both
scales in the three most recent Congresses; 3) Midwestern
Republicans were more isolationist than coastal representatives in each Congress on foreign aid and in the 83rd and
84th (1955-7) Congresses on foreign trade; 4) Southern Democrats shifted steadily toward greater isolationism and lesser
internationalism on both aid and trade than legislators from
other regions. Rieselbach, perhaps more so than any other
authority, has demonstrated that the pattern of sectional responses to foreign policy often varies markedly from Congress
to Congress.

    Nevertheless, it must be strongly affirmed, with ref-
erence to foreign aid, that Midwestern Democrats were much
more internationalist during and after World War II than their
Republican colleagues, while prior to the decline in southern
internationalism during the mid-1950's Republican members
of Congress from that section were much more isolationist
than their Democratic neighbors. This has led Leroy N.
Rieselbach to conclude that: "The true significance of region
can be seen only with the introduction of controls for party."
Significantly, Mountain States Congressmen of both parties
were on the average more isolationist than their coastal
counterparts, East and Pacific Coast legislators of both parties
being the most internationalist groups; as we noted previously,
however, the Rocky Mountains section is not as isolationist
as the voting record of its representatives in Congress would
indicate.

    More unexpected are the findings of David N. Farns-
worth, whose book The Senate Committee on Foreign Relations
concludes that during the decade 1947-1956 the hearings on
the proposed St. Lawrence Seaway were the only ones in
which the committee was clearly split along geographical lines.
In 1952, for example, Senator Leverett Saltonstall of Massachusetts keynoted the opposition testimony, while Senator Alexander Wiley of Wisconsin, a member of the committee, spearheaded the pro-Seaway forces. Southern foes of the St. Lawrence project included Tom Connally of Texas, Walter George
of Georgia, and J. William Fulbright of Arkansas. The Wiley-
Dondero Act establishing the St. Lawrence Seaway Development Corporation eventually passed Congress in 1954, and the
St. Lawrence Seaway and St. Lawrence power project was
formally opened in 1959.

    Returning to the House of Representatives, Holbert N.
Carroll has demonstrated in a study covering the period 1948-

1965 that Republican opposition to foreign aid remained centered in the Middle West, reaching a high of 80 per cent in 1965, after this section had returned a slight majority for the Marshall Plan in 1948 and 1949. More surprising was the defection of the Western Republicans, whose level of support for foreign aid dropped from 60 per cent prior to 1962 to a mere 25 per cent for the period 1962-1965; this remarkable metamorphosis is partly attributable to the growing number of conservatives elected to Congress from this section, and partly to the inauguration of a Democratic President in 1961. Since Southern Republicans were almost unanimously opposed to foreign aid, this left only the Northeast as a champion of foreign aid among the Congressional members of this party.

As for the Democrats, Southerners did give strong support to various pieces of defense legislation between 1948 and 1965, yet by the mid-1950's this section had begun to cast majorities against foreign aid, an average of 60 per cent of the Southern Democrats voting in the negative on this type of legislation between 1957 and 1965. W. Wayne Shannon, who has examined the more limited period from 1959 through 1963 relative to both houses of Congress, concludes that: "Though northern Democrats were usually favorable to internationalist policies, southern Democrats dissented from this position and Republicans vacillated considerably." A key figure in the sabotaging of foreign aid between 1959 and 1962 was Representative Otto Passman of Louisiana. In addition, southern members of Congress, who had extended overwhelming support to the Reciprocal Trade Agreements Act in 1934, had begun to give similar legislation much more limited backing during the late 1950's and early 1960's.

The general picture that emerges from the abovementioned studies is one of a South less internationalist after the mid-1950's, a Middle West still manifesting isolationist tendencies at times, and Atlantic and Pacific Coasts both generally internationalist. An analysis of key roll-calls in general substantiates this broad outline, but also reveals that southern internationalism in its heyday was by no means unanimous or monolithic. Even before the mid-1950's the South was more favorably disposed to the white nations of Europe than to the black countries of Africa, while it was also more favorably inclined towards military adventures such as NATO than towards foreign aid. Yet even in recent years, with southern internationalism apparently on the decline, the South has remained more steadfast in its backing for American intervention in South Vietnam than such sections as the Northeast, despite the fact that many white Southerners have long regarded the yellow race to be inferior like the black one. Among the other sections, one also frequently detects from roll-call to roll-call varying degrees of internationalism or isolationism; sometimes it is possible to explain these in political terms, but often one must go outside the halls of Congress to assemble supplementary data in an effort to account for these fluctuations.

One inevitably wonders whether public opinion polls parallel Congressional votes. Alfred O. Hero, Jr., who has made an exhaustive study of the former in his excellent book The Southerner and World Affairs, uses them to demonstrate that the typical Southerner is less internationally oriented than he once was. One serious problem that arises in correlating House and Senate roll-calls with public opinion polls, however, is that the latter frequently measure attitudes towards a foreign country (Russia) or a foreign leader (De Gaulle) or a foreign "hot spot" (Berlin) rather than towards a treaty or a piece of legislation involving foreign affairs. To be truly meaningful, a public opinion poll should be taken at exactly the same time that such a treaty, etc. was either approved or defeated; to complicate matters further, not every public opinion poll dealing with foreign policy measures sectional attitudes. Thus, in the recently published three-volume compilation of Gallup polls for the years 1935-1971, only about 30 are pertinent to this study, and about a quarter of these deal with the Vietnam War; for a period of twenty-five years, this by no means constitutes saturation coverage. In the pages that follow, public opinion polls will be correlated with Congressional roll-calls where appropriate, but there are too few pairings to enable one to generalize meaningfully. Where the polls do diverge from Congressional voting patterns, it is not always easy to analyze why they do so, as the polls may consist only of the raw data with no accompanying explanation.

Since the end of World War II the only foreign policy issue that public opinion polls have continually measured with any regularity is that of American attitudes towards the United Nations and the broader question of international co-operation. Despite the waning of southern internationalism, it is highly significant that backing for the United Nations has remained more or less uniform or constant, regardless of section; this finding is present not only in the public opinion polls of the Gallup office, but also those of other measuring agencies for the past three decades. Those minor variations that have occurred may be traced in the various articles cited in the annotated bibliography at the end of the chapter.

1945-1961: Harry Truman and Dwight Eisenhower

When Harry Truman took over as President following
the death of Franklin Roosevelt in the Spring of 1945, he enjoyed the support of a Congress where the Democrats held a
56 to 38 majority over the Republicans in the Senate and a
242 to 190 majority in the House. Admittedly Southern Democrats had joined forces with the Republicans to block the
passage of further New Deal legislation after 1938, but the
Dixiecrats continued to back the internationalist foreign policies of Harry Truman as they had those of Franklin Roosevelt. Some former Republican isolationists, too, such as
Senator Arthur Vandenberg of Michigan, joined the internationalist camp after World War II, forging an alliance with
their Democrat counterparts on behalf of a bipartisan foreign
policy.   Thus the global diplomacy of H. S. T. did not grind
to a halt when the Republicans won their greatest Congressional victory since the days of Herbert Hoover in November
1946, capturing the Senate by a margin of 51 to 45 and the
House by 246 to 188.   It was during the life of this so-called
"do nothing" 80th Congress (1947-8) that the Italian, Bulgar-
ian, Hungarian, and Rumanian peace treaties, the Truman
Doctrine, and the Marshall Plan won Senatorial approval.

The Democrats did regain control of Congress when
Harry Truman won re-election as President in 1948, but the
Republicans narrowed the Democratic margin of ascendancy
in the Senate to a 49 to 47 split in the Congressional election
of 1950 following the outbreak of the Korean War.   When the
Truman Administration's policy of containment failed to bring
victory in Korea, a number of Republicans abandoned biparti-
sanship and called for total victory there, despite the fact
that some of them had been decidedly cool to earlier attempts
by H. S. T. to halt the Communist advance in Western Europe.
Advocates of a firm stand were perhaps most numerous on
the Pacific Coast.

Truman's successor as President, General Dwight
Eisenhower, was far more popular with the people than H. S. T.
had been, and remained so during his entire eight years in
office.   Under "Ike" the Korean War drew swiftly to a close.
The first six years of the Eisenhower Presidency continued
the razor-thin spread between the two major parties in the

Senate, although technically the Democrats organized the
Senate after Ike's first two years in office. The Republicans
controlled the House in 1953 and 1954 by a narrow 221 to 212
margin, but the Democrats won a clearcut majority in the
Congressional election held during the latter year and have
dominated the lower house ever since. During the last six
years of his Presidency the non-political Eisenhower managed
to obtain Congressional approval of his major foreign policy
schemes, despite the waning of southern internationalism after
1955. This highly successful record was largely attributable
to the efforts of two Texans, Senate Majority Leader Lyndon
Johnson and Speaker of the House Sam Rayburn, as well as
those of the Chairman of the Senate Foreign Relations Committee, Walter George of Georgia. This delicate balance between Democrats and Republicans in the Senate was upset in
the Congressional election of 1958, when the Democrats cap-
italized on a recession to win control of that body by an overwhelming 62 to 34 margin and of the House by 280 to 152.
Even so, Ike still managed to act with a reasonable degree
of effectiveness in the foreign affairs sphere during his last
two years as chief executive.

Returning to the Truman Administration and the immediate post-World War II period, now that the United Nations
was established the Senate was free to turn its attention to
the World Court, an organization which had incurred less
hostility on the part of American isolationists between the two
world wars than the League of Nations. On August 2, 1946
the Senate adopted by a 51 to 12 vote the Connally Amendment instructing the President to declare that this nation accepted compulsory jurisdiction of the International Court of
Justice except in "matters which are essentially within the
domestic jurisdiction of the United States. " On this occasion
Westerners cast half of the negative votes, New Englanders
four, and the Southerners two; while only two Republicans
were opposed, ten Democrats were hostile. Although the
minority suffered an overwhelming defeat, the dozen nay votes
still represented a far larger body of dissent than the two
isolationists who had opposed American entry into the United
Nations.

Yet what had hopefully been looked upon as the dawn
of a new era of peace instead witnessed a growing confrontation between the United States and the Soviet Union, ushering
in the so-called "cold war. " With Russia no longer a close
ally, American relations with Great Britain assumed an even
greater importance than they had during World War II. Earl-

ier that year, on May 10, 1946, the Senate had adopted a joint
resolution authorizing a loan of 3.75 billion dollars to England; the margin of victory was 46 to 34 (19 Republicans and
15 Democrats), and the Great Plains (12 votes), the Middle
West (8 votes), and the South (7 votes) supplied the bulk of
the nay votes. While the opposition of the first two sections
was largely attributable to isolationism and Anglophobia, in
the case of the South a tradition of economy was perhaps the
key factor. Despite this expression of dissent, in the Spring
of 1945 Frederick W. Williams found that the South and the
Southwest were more favorably disposed than any other sections (71 per cent) to a permanent military alliance between
the United States and Great Britain; like Vincent Sheean, Williams also discovered, after sampling public opinion throughout the country, that the Pacific Coast (53 per cent) was the
least favorable to such an agreement. Here again the significance of the particular type of diplomatic issue is strikingly
manifest.

With respect to the peace treaties with Germany and
its European allies, these enjoyed much easier going in the
Senate than their counterparts had a quarter of a century previously. The Northeast played a leading role in the campaign
to soften the Italian peace treaty signed on February 10, 1947;
here former Governor Charles Poletti of New York, ex-Rep-
resentative Claire Booth Luce of Connecticut, and Governor
John Pastore of Rhode Island spearheaded the opposition. The
Senate ratified this on June 25 by the lopsided vote of 79 to
10, with 7 Republicans hostile in a balloting devoid of sectional
trends.   In contrast, the peace pacts with Bulgaria, Hungary,
and Rumania were approved (without enthusiasm, according to
Thomas A. Bailey) by the Senate on February 10 of the latter
year without a roll-call vote, despite the fact that the treaties
were not popular with the American people.

Ethnic considerations, not surprisingly, were a factor
in the 1948 Presidential election, since many Germans who
had deserted F. D. R. because of his belligerency towards Hitler in 1940 and 1944 returned to the Democratic fold in 1948,
being largely responsible for Harry Truman carrying such
states as Ohio.   (The Berlin airlift, one must remember, was
going on at this time.) Aside from the numerous German-
Americans who voted for H. S. T. in such states as Missouri,
Ohio, Minnesota, Wisconsin, and Iowa, many Polish-Ameri-
cans in such large cities as Cleveland, Detroit, Milwaukee,
Pittsburgh, and Chicago supported the incumbent President,
despite Franklin Roosevelt's alleged "betrayal" of Poland. It

will also be recalled that the presence of a large concentration of Jews in New York City and other large northeastern
metropolises led President Harry Truman and Governor
Thomas Dewey of New York to adopt strongly pro-Palestine
stances well in advance of the 1948 Presidential election. Conversely, a 1945 New York Herald Tribune poll revealed that
the South exhibited far less enthusiasm than did any other
section for the establishment of a national Jewish state in
Palestine (67 per cent vs. 83. 2 for the Far West); not only
are there few Jews in the South, but the anti-Semitic tradition
has never been strong there.

One of the milestones of post-World War II foreign
policy was the 1947 Truman Doctrine of aid to Greece and
Turkey, two other Eastern Mediterranean "hot spots, " while
another was the 1948 Marshall Plan for the economic reconstruction of Western Europe.   The first of these was hardly
attributable to political expediency, as there are far fewer
Greeks and Turks in this country than Jews, Italians, Germans, and Poles.   In any event, it was the Northeast which
gave both measures the most solid backing when they came
up for final Senate approval, with the North Central States
providing the most vigorous opposition.   (The Truman Doctrine
passed 67 to 23, the Marshall Plan 54 to 17.)   Yet even the
states regarded as most isolationist by Smuckler (North Dakota, Idaho, Kansas, Nebraska, Wisconsin, and Minnesota)
went only so far as to split (6 votes to 6) on the latter question.   According to a Gallup poll conducted in February 1948,
favorable responses towards the Marshall Plan were less frequent in the East Central and West Central sections than in
any other.   The lack of enthusiasm of the North Central section also is partly attributable to the opposition of the section's most influential newspaper, the Chicago Tribune.   Despite the hostility (on left-wing grounds rather than right-wing
ones) of Florida's Senator Claude Pepper, the South generally
supported both the Truman Doctrine and the Marshall Plan,
the cotton and tobacco lobbies carrying on an extensive campaign on behalf of the latter.   Opposition to both measures
also tended to be partisan, the Republicans casting 16 of the
23 votes against the Truman Doctrine and 14 of the 17 against
the Marshall Plan.

Similarly, when the North Atlantic Treaty pledging the
United States, Canada, and ten European countries to "unite
their efforts for collective defense" came to a vote on the
Senate floor a year later, on July 21, 1949, not a single
southern vote was cast in opposition and only one northeastern

one, although the North Central States as usual were at the
forefront of the isolationist forces. Two Gallup polls conducted earlier that year had revealed that the Far West was
more favorably disposed towards NATO than any other section, a striking rebuff to the geographical propinquity hypothesis. While the NATO treaty passed the Senate by an 82
to 13 margin, with 11 Republicans voting nay, the Mutual Defense Assistance Act of 1949, which authorized $1.3 billion
in military aid to NATO and to other countries, received only
a 55 to 24 favorable vote on September 22. At this time
economy-minded Southerners cast seven nay ballots, yet northeastern support held fast, only three negative votes being registered from that section; Democratic hostility was more
noticeable here, 11 members of that party being opposed.
Two years later, at the time that the Senate confirmed General Dwight Eisenhower's nomination as NATO commander,
Senator John McClellan successfully proposed an amendment,
adopted by a 49 to 43 margin on April 2, 1951, to the effect
that no ground troops beyond the four divisions planned should
be sent to Europe without Congressional approval. The military-minded South was responsible for no less than 14, or
almost one-third, of the nay votes, the Northeast following
suit with 13. Even more significantly, Republicans generally
favored this measure, while Democrats (no less than 36) generally opposed it.

Despite the abovementioned examples of southern internationalism, the Point Four program inaugurated in 1950,
which provided technical assistance to the underdeveloped
countries of the globe, incurred the wrath of the Southerners,
being the only aid bill during the Truman Administration which
was opposed by a majority of southern Senators. Europe, of
course, does not compete with the South agriculturally, but
such nations as Egypt and India do. When Point Four narrowly cleared the Senate by a 37 to 36 margin on May 5, 1950,
the South spearheaded the opposition with 11 votes, the Great
Plains States and the Middle West casting respectively 8 and
7 nay votes; this was a highly partisan vote, with the Democrats being 29 to 11 in favor and the Republicans 25 to 8
against. While this particular measure relating to the so-
called "third world" barely won Senatorial approval, only Republican Eugene Millikin of Colorado voted against the Inter-
American Treaty of Reciprocal Assistance when it passed the
Senate on December 8, 1947. Since the days of Herbert
Hoover and Franklin Roosevelt, with the exception of such
issues as the Panama Canal, Latin America no longer in-
spires the sharp divisions of opinion in Congress that marked

the administrations of Theodore Roosevelt and Woodrow Wilson, and sometimes even an official roll-call is dispensed with, as in the case of the Charter of the Organization of American States which the Senate ratified on August 28, 1950.

Shifting our attention to the Far East, on March 20, 1952 the Senate finally ratified the peace treaty with Japan by a 66 to 10 margin, with every nay vote but one Republican. The South, which in 1924 had joined forces with the West to bring about the exclusion of Japanese immigrants, cast no votes against this treaty, although five Senators from the West did so. The former represented a significant display of Senatorial independence, since in the words of Bernard Cohen, "The South was the repository of the greatest ill-will harbored by any region against the Japanese." A security treaty with Japan was also ratified the same day, 58 to 9; not a single Democrat or a single Southerner opposed this treaty. On this productive March 20 the Senate likewise placed its stamp of approval on a Mutual Defense Treaty with the Philippines and a Security Treaty with Australia and New Zealand, without going through the formality of a roll-call vote.

Despite the fact that, according to a 1952 Gallup Poll, Westerners were more favorably disposed to a mutual defense pact for the Pacific than were the inhabitants of any other section, there was considerable hostility towards the Japanese in the economic sphere. Members of the West Coast fishing industry in particular favored treaty restrictions on the Japanese; in the Spring of 1951 both the Oregon senate and house of representatives endorsed a joint memorial that opposed the use by Japanese nationals of North American fisheries. In this connection a three-power North Pacific Fisheries Convention including Canada won ratification the following year as a compromise acceptable to all parties. When a new trade agreement was signed between this nation and Japan in 1955, though, it was attacked by members of Congress representing several textile producing states, including Senator Olin Johnston of South Carolina, Senator Frederick G. Payne of Maine, and Representative Edith Nourse Rogers of Massachusetts, as well as by a spokesman for the glassware and pottery industries, Representative Cleveland Bailey of West Virginia.

A far more controversial event, which was the focal point of attention for most of the second Truman Administration, was the Korean War, which broke out in the summer of 1950. Although editorial opinion throughout the country regardless of section generally backed American intervention at

first, the Truman Administration's failure to press the war
to a clear-cut victory eventually led to such anti-Truman
organs as the Chicago Tribune blasting H. S. T., while the
more liberal and less isolationist Washington Post continued
to support the chief executive. The Republican New York
Herald Tribune, which had observed of the original American
intervention that President Truman had acted "with magnifi-
cent courage and terse decision, " later criticized General
MacArthur for "one of the greatest military reverses in the
history of American arms" when the Chinese Communists
swarmed down into North Korea. Generally objective were
the New York Times and the Christian Science Monitor, two
respected organs well-known for the incisiveness and accuracy
of their news accounts.

Unfortunately for the purposes of analysis, Congress
never officially declared war on North Korea, so that it is
impossible to subject such a vote to a sectional breakdown.
As for public opinion in general, Samuel Lubell has concluded
relative to a highly isolationist Minnesota county that: "Not
only in Stearns but in other German-American counties I visited in other states, I found this same tendency to see the
Korean War as a vindication of opposition to America's wars
against Germany"; Lubell, however, is of the opinion that the
1950 Congressional election represented at most a moderate
revival of isolationism, despite Senator Robert Taft's overwhelming re-election victory in Ohio with its considerable
German population.

Nevertheless, the enthusiastic receptions that General
Douglas MacArthur received in such cities as Honolulu, San
Francisco, and New York City, and before Congress upon his
return home after his firing by President Harry Truman early
in 1951, manifested, if not an endorsement of Asian unilat-
eralism, at least a marked disagreement with the latter's
handling of the Korean War. Arthur Schlesinger, Jr. has
chronicled some additional, and even more extreme, examples
of pro-MacArthur sentiment in his book The General and the
President; Secretary of State Dean Acheson, for example, was
burned in effigy in Ponca City, Oklahoma, while in Seattle a
critic of MacArthur had his head shoved into a bucket of beer
and held there. Particularly instructive are two sets of Gallup polls conducted in June and November of 1952 (the month
of the Presidential election) as to whether American involvement in the Korean War was a mistake or not:

Section		Yes, Mistake	No, Right Worthwhile	No Opinion
East:	June	34	61	5
	Nov.	56	37	7
Midwest:	June	41	52	7
	Nov.	60	32	8
South:	June	39	53	8
	Nov.	56	33	11
West:	June	34	57	9
	Nov.	60	35	5

In the 1952 Presidential election both major parties nominated internationalists for President: the Republicans, General Dwight Eisenhower, and the Democrats, Governor Adlai E. Stevenson of Illinois. It will be recalled that the Republican convention of this year witnessed a bitter struggle between coastal internationalists backing Eisenhower and mid-western isolationists supporting Senator Robert A. Taft, who also enjoyed considerable strength among the southern "rotten boroughs. " As we have seen from the polls cited above, public opinion between the conventions and the general election moved, if not in an anti-internationalist direction, at least in an anti-interventionist one relative to Korea. According to Alfred de Grazia, "The entrance of the United States into the war in Korea ultimately defeated the Democratic Party in the West, in November 1952, " although the voters in this section apparently were somewhat more reluctant to blame the Truman Administration for the Communist take-over in China in 1949, an event which made possible the Korean War. The West also was more militant than any other section relative to the latter, as 45 per cent of de Grazia's interviewees from that section favored a stronger stand (bombing China, etc.), as compared with 40 from the Midwest, 36 from the Northeast, and 34 from the South. Those statistics should be compared with those for the Vietnam War two decades later.

The inauguration of Dwight Eisenhower as President in 1953 marked a new era in which there was greater parity between the White House and Capitol Hill, as Ike did not favor the tradition of a strong President to the extent that F. D. R. and H. S. T. had. Nevertheless, the Senate rejected by a one-

vote margin (60 to 31) on February 26, 1954 a Constitutional
amendment which, among other things, required Congressional
approval of executive agreements; originally proposed by isolationist John Bricker of Ohio, the "Bricker Amendment"
came up for a final vote in the form of a watered-down substitute offered by internationalist Walter George of Georgia.
No less than 14 of the 31 nay votes came from the Northeast,
with the South (3), Great Plains (1), and Far West (4) offering the least opposition. While Northern Democrats rejected
the Bricker Amendment narrowly, their southern counterparts
favored it overwhelmingly, the latter vote in all likelihood reflecting the states' rights tradition of the region rather than
an upsurge in isolationist sentiment. No less than 14 Republicans opposed this measure, along with maverick former
Republican Wayne Morse of Oregon.

We have previously noted in our discussion of the Senate
Foreign Relations Committee during the years 1947-1956 that
the hearings on the St. Lawrence Seaway were the only ones
in which the committee was clearly split along geographical
lines, with the Great Lakes states generally favorable and the
Northeast and the South usually opposed. When the Senate
recommitted this project on June 18, 1952 by a 43 to 40 vote
the North Central States led the movement against this motion;
two years later, when the Senate finally approved the scheme
on January 20, 1954 by a 51 to 33 margin, the South spearheaded the opposition with 12 votes. Neither vote revealed a
sharp partisan division. As for another hemispheric waterway
project, long in existence, on July 29, 1955 the Senate approved a new Panama Canal treaty that raised the annuity,
returned certain lands, surrendered a number of sanitary controls, and provided for the more equitable sharing of economic
benefits. This perhaps overly generous agreement also incurred the wrath of the South, that section casting 9 of the 14
nay votes (13 of them Democratic), while a total of 72 Senators voted in favor. Traditionally the South has been highly
sensitive on the canal question, and today it still remains so.

Far more explosive was the Formosa issue. Although
Chiang Kai-shek did not take advantage of President Dwight
Eisenhower's lifting of the U.S. 7th Fleet's blockade of Formosa and attack the Communist-controlled mainland, Red
Chinese leader Chou En-Lai announced on August 11, 1954
that the Nationalist government on Formosa must be liquidated,
a declaration that our President countered on August 17 with
the statement that "any invasion of Formosa would have to
run over the 7th fleet. " On September 3 the Communists be-

gan bombarding the Nationalist-held offshore island of Quemoy,
the Nationalists the nearby Communist-held island of Amoy.
After the United States and the Chiang Kai-shek regime had
signed on December 2 a mutual defense treaty that did not
apply to the offshore islands, President Dwight Eisenhower
asked Congress on January 24, 1955 for authority to raise an
armed force to "assure the security of Formosa and the Pes-
cadores." Although this resolution was passed overwhelmingly
by both houses of Congress, clearing the House 410 to 3 and
the Senate 85 to 3, four days later Democratic Senator Herbert Lehman of New York proposed an amendment to eliminate
Presidential authority for the security of related positions and
territories of the area or to take other measures he deemed
appropriate. (Lehman, Wayne Morse, and William Langer
had opposed the original resolution.) This was rejected by a
lopsided 74 to 13 margin, with the South spearheading the
pro-Eisenhower forces and isolationist Langer the only Republican opposed.

　　　　Another "hot spot" during this period was the Middle
East. On December 17 both the United States and England
offered financial assistance to Egypt for the construction of
the Aswan Dam, an offer which the Egyptian government accepted on July 17 of the following year. Two days later,
however, Secretary of State John Foster Dulles withdrew the
American offer, and a week later General Gamal Abdel Nasser
reciprocated by nationalizing the Suez Canal. Southern Senators in particular were opposed to this project, being fearful
of Egyptian cotton competition; the Senate Appropriations Committee wrote into its report on the foreign aid bill a require-
ment that no funds be spent on the Aswan Dam without advance
approval by the committee, while Walter George of Georgia,
the Chairman of the Senate Foreign Relations Committee, also
attacked this scheme. Significantly, George chose not to run
for re-election in 1956 rather than face a challenge from isolationist Herman Talmadge, the son of the notorious demagogue
Eugene, who proved to be the first Southerner to win election
to the Senate since the end of World War II on a platform
hostile to internationalism.

　　　　In the Fall of 1956, on October 29, Israel invaded the
Gaza Strip and the Sinai Peninsula, while two days later the
British and the French launched an attack on Egypt; a week
later American pressure and Russian threats of intervention
led to a cease-fire. The public reaction here to this skirmish
unquestionably widened the margin of victory of Dwight Eisenhower over Adlai Stevenson in the Presidential election of 1956.

Considering the large number of Jews in New York City and
elsewhere in the urban Northeast, which led Mayor Robert
Wagner to block a parade for Saudi Arabia's King Saud in January 1957, it is not surprising that an editorialist for Africa
Today has concluded that "... the only times African issues
seriously stirred America were the Suez Crisis of 1956 and
the Congo Crisis of 1960."

Two months after his re-election, on January 5, President Dwight Eisenhower proposed the so-called Eisenhower
Doctrine, by means of which the chief executive placed the
Communist world on notice that the United States would per-
mit no further Communist conquests in the Middle East.   To
the isolationist Chicago Tribune, this was "a goofy design for
foreign meddling."   Presented as a resolution, this doctrine
passed the Senate exactly two months later by a 72 to 19 margin, with the South casting 11 nay votes and 16 Democrats
opposed.   According to Malcolm E. Jewell, "A significant
shift in southern voting away from the support of the collective security measures did not become evident until 1957 when
the Middle East Resolution was passed."   But when Ike sent
troops into rebellion-torn Lebanon in 1958, according to
Newsweek, only in Michigan were critics more numerous than
proponents of this action, with Pennsylvania split; "no comment" responses were most common in Texas and Illinois,
the home of the Chicago Tribune.   The following year, in
1959, 66 members of the House of Representatives sent telegrams to Eugene Black, President of the International Bank
for Reconstruction and Development, attacking a proposed 56
million dollar loan to the United Arab Republic for the purpose of developing the Suez Canal.   To the surprise of no
one, nearly half of these telegrams came from New York and
New Jersey, two states with a high concentration of Jews.

As for other parts of Africa, Senator John Kennedy of
Massachusetts emerged as the foremost Senate champion of
Algerian independence, introducing a resolution in 1957 favoring this step.   Among the leading critics of Kennedy was
another Democrat, Representative Emanuel Celler of New
York, who described the resolution as "immature" and "un-
fair."   In contrast, when South African police fired upon a
group of Africans demonstrating against the Pass Laws at
Sharpeville in March 1960, the Mississippi legislature voted
to congratulate the Union government on its handling of the
affair.   With regard to the Congo, whose independence birth
pangs in 1960 had precipitated an international crisis, there
was a particularly sharp division of opinion in Congress.

Midwestern Republican Representative H. R. Gross of Iowa
emerged during the 1961-2 sessions of Congress as the major
proponent of reduced U. S. contributions to the U. N. 's Congo
operation; while a majority of Southern Democrats (47 to 41)
supported the recommital motion during the 1962 session, only
one Northern Democrat did so.

Still another question which came up for consideration
before the Senate near the end of the Eisenhower Administration was the Antarctic Treaty. This was an agreement involving eleven nations other than the United States which was
designed to ensure the permanent use of Antarctica for peaceful purposes; needless to say, Congress had no extended voting record vis-à-vis this icy continent to which one might
refer for purposes of comparison. When the Antarctic Treaty
easily won Senate approval on August 10, 1960 by a 66 to 21
margin, Southerners led the opposition, casting no less than
15--approximately three-fourths--of the nay votes, of which 17
were Democratic. Although the Senate Foreign Relations Committee had endorsed this agreement by a unanimous vote, such
Democratic Senators as Clair Engle (California), Strom Thurmond (South Carolina), Thomas Dodd (Connecticut), and Richard Russell (Georgia) attacked it on the grounds that the Russians (who also signed the treaty) were not to be trusted.

Two other treaties dating from the last years of the
Eisenhower Presidency that encountered Senatorial opposition
in the double figures were the Atoms for Peace Treaty, which
the Senate ratified by a 67 to 19 vote on June 18, 1957, and
the fourteen nation convention establishing the Organization for
Economic Cooperation and Development, on which the Senate
did not actually place its stamp of approval by a 72 to 18 vote
until March 16, 1961, after John F. Kennedy had taken office
as chief executive. In the case of the former, nays were almost equally divided between the Democrats and Republicans
in a vote lacking marked sectional trends. On the OECD
treaty, nine of the eighteen nay votes were cast by Southerners during a balloting that saw 11 Democrats opposed; in
ratifying it the Senate demanded a guarantee that the pact did
not reduce the power of the President or Congress. Aside
from these, no treaty signed during Ike's two terms experienced significant opposition in the Senate.

1961-1973: Kennedy, Johnson, and Nixon

In the hotly contested Presidential election of 1960

Democrat John Kennedy barely managed to eke out a narrow
victory over Republican Richard Nixon.   Nevertheless, the
Democrats increased their margin over the Republicans to 65
to 35 in the Senate, while suffering a loss of approximately
twenty seats in the House.   Two years later, at the time of
the Congressional election of 1962, the balance of power in
the House remained the same, but the Democrats succeeded
in winning control of the Senate by a two to one majority (67
to 33), the most complete dominance of this body they had
enjoyed since the days of the New Deal.   Unfortunately for
Kennedy, though, Southern Democrats not only joined forces
with the Republicans to block passage of most of JFK's domestic New Frontier program; they also unsuccessfully attempted to defeat such key items on Kennedy's foreign policy
agenda as the U. N. Bonds purchase and the Limited Nuclear
Test Ban Treaty.   This was in marked contrast to the days
of Franklin Roosevelt and Harry Truman, when Southern Democratic opposition to administration policies generally stopped
at the water's edge.

John Kennedy's tragic assassination brought to power
that master Congressional manipulator, Lyndon Johnson. Under L. B. J. Congress enacted a huge corpus of domestic legislation implementing the Great Society concept, especially
after Johnson won an overwhelming victory at the polls over
right-wing Republican nominee Barry Goldwater in the Presidential election of 1964.   As a result of this election, Democratic Senatorial strength crested at a flood peak of 68 seats
to 32 for the Republicans, while in the House the Democrats
reached a greater than two to one ascendancy over the Republicans, 295 to 140.   Even so, the continuing rift between
Northern Democrats and Southern Democrats manifested itself
on such issues as American intervention in the Dominican Republic and the U. S. -Soviet Consular Treaty.   By the time of
the 1966 Congressional election, too, the American public's
growing disillusionment towards the Johnson Administration
as a result of its handling of the U. S. involvement in South
Vietnam had begun to have a marked impact.   The Democratic
margin over the Republicans in the Senate declined to a 64/36
ratio, in the House to a 248/187 one.

Thanks to the continuing agitation over the Vietnam War
and increasing riots in the cities and on the campuses, Richard
Nixon was able to engineer one of the most remarkable come-
backs in American political history by narrowly winning the
Presidency in 1968 over his Democratic opponent, Hubert
Humphrey.   The Democrats, though, still maintained control

of the Senate, 57 to 43, and of the House, 243 to 192; this
marked the first time that a newly-elected President was confronted with a Congress both houses of which were dominated
by the other major party. Two years later, in the Congressional election of 1970, the Republicans made slight gains in
the House, but suffered slight losses in the Senate. Although
in the upper house the Northern Democrats sided with the Republicans and against the Southern Democrats on such issues
as the Nuclear Proliferation Treaty and the authorization for
the International Development Association, a Republican-
Southern Democratic coalition emerged on such votes related
to the Vietnam War as the Cooper-Church Amendment and the
McGovern-Hatfield Amendment. "Doves" were to be found in
every part of the country, like "hawks, " but opposition to this
conflict was probably greatest in the Northeast. Thus it came
as no surprise that Massachusetts was the only state that war
critic George McGovern carried in his landslide defeat at the
hands of Richard Nixon in the Presidential election of 1972.

To return to a more successful Democratic candidate,
the swearing-in of John Kennedy as President led to an early
testing of our youngest elected chief executive by the international Communist hierarchy. After J. F. K. had met with
Nikita Khrushchev in Vienna in June, 1961 the Soviets erected
a wall or barricade between East and West Berlin in August.
According to an AIPO poll conducted between July 30 and
August 3, the percentage of favorable responses by section
to the question: "Do you think we should keep American forces
in Berlin--along with British and French forces--even at the
risk of war" was: Far West, 85; East, 82; Midwest, 82; and
South, 81. A "fight our way into Berlin if necessary" inquiry aroused the greatest enthusiasm in the Midwest (77 per
cent), the least in the South (65 per cent), although a Newsweek poll found the Middle West apathetic, Alaska bellicose.
Fortunately for all parties concerned, the Communist-built
wall failed to precipitate open hostilities, just as the Berlin
blockade of 1948-9 did not lead to an armed showdown. On
July 31, just prior to the actual construction of the wall,
Congress overwhelmingly approved J. F. K's request for a call-
up of 250, 000 reservists, with only two Representatives and
no Senators voting nay.

Partisanship had been more in evidence two months
previously when Congress authorized the initial grant of
$500, 000, 000 for the Alliance for Progress with the Inter-
American appropriation bill. After the House had passed this
measure by an initial vote of 329 to 83, the Senate placed its

final stamp of approval on it by a much closer 41 to 26 margin, with 33 abstentions, on May 25. No less than 20 Republicans voted nay, although their sectional distribution was not of consequence. The following year, in 1962, traditional alignments on tariff issues broke down when the Trade Expansion Act was before Congress; the final Senate vote on September 19 saw seven Republicans and Southern Democrat Strom Thurmond of South Carolina combine forces against a majority of 78. According to Alexander De Conde, in the House "formerly protectionist business groups in the North and on the West Coast had supported the bill, and some of the new industrialists from the historically free trade South had opposed it."

As the Kennedy Administration progressed, it became apparent that the initial flurry of cooperation from Southern Democrats was only temporary, and that the party's representatives in Congress were dividing along North/South lines on foreign policy issues as well as on such domestic questions as civil rights. When the House on September 14, 1962, by a 257 to 134 vote, authorized the President to match up to 100 million dollars in purchase of United Nations bonds by other U. N. members, Northern Democrats approved this measure by an overwhelming 133 to 2 margin, while Southern Democrats more narrowly favored it, 58 to 44, and Republicans opposed it, 88 to 66. In the Senate the South cast 11 of the 22 nay votes, 70 Senators voting aye. It already has been pointed out that Northern Democrats were far more sympathetic at this time than their southern counterparts towards generous American contributions to help finance the U. N. 's Congo operation. Although an August Gallup Poll had detected 73 per cent approval in the East, 10 Southern Democrats opposed the Limited Nuclear Test Ban Treaty when it came up for ratification on September 24, 1963. Here the official tally was 80 to 19, with 25 Republicans and 41 Northern Democrats voting for it.

It was also a Southerner, Republican John Tower of Texas, who cast the only vote against the Chamizal Boundary Treaty with Mexico on December 17 after the Senate had rejected Tower's reservation to require approval by the Texas legislature. One might refer in this connection to the observation of Dwight Wood, that the only cities and states which have a vital interest in Latin America now are Miami, New Orleans, Texas, New Mexico, and southern California; U. S. policy towards our neighbors to the South is no longer a sectional football. Yet the events that took place in Cuba after

January 1, 1959, at which time Fidel Castro deposed the long entrenched dictator, Fulgencio Batista, focused the eyes of the entire nation on this nearby Caribbean island.

At first public opinion towards Castro ranged across a wide spectrum, and the same generalization holds true of editorial opinion. A survey of 17 leading American dailies between that date and April 1961 reveals that those most critical of the Cuban dictator included the New York Mirror, the San Francisco Examiner, the New York Daily News, the Chicago Tribune, and the Los Angeles Times; those least critical were the New York Post, the St. Louis Post-Dispatch, the New York Times, the Denver Post, and the Washington Post. Of these, the San Francisco Examiner and the New York Mirror were the only two to openly demand the use of U. S. troops during the ill-fated Bay of Pigs invasion in April 1961. No marked sectional pattern emerges from this analysis of editorial stances, however.

A Newsweek poll published two weeks before the midterm Congressional elections on October 22, 1962 revealed that approximately 90 per cent of the American public opposed an invasion of Cuba in the near future. This was the same day that President John Kennedy announced, in the aftermath of his discovery that the Soviets were constructing missile launching-pads there, that this nation would impose a quarantine on all ships carrying offensive weapons to Cuba. In September Congress had overwhelmingly passed an all-necessary steps resolution. Even before the missile crisis the Republicans attempted to make Cuba an issue in a half-dozen or so of the most conservative states in the Union; located in the Middle West, the Southwest, and the South, these included Indiana, Illinois, Texas, Oklahoma, Arkansas, and Florida. According to Newsweek, "In most of the West and in the Northeast, Cuba [had] not developed into a major issue." Unfortunately for the Republicans, though, the missile crisis consolidated public opinion throughout the country behind the Kennedy Administration's policy of standing up to the Soviets. The election results, though, were inconclusive. Hawkish Republican Senator Homer Capehart of Indiana lost to Birch Bayh, yet Republican Senator Everett Dirksen, a critic of Kennedy on Cuba, won re-election in neighboring Illinois; in Arkansas J. William Fulbright, who opposed the Bay of Pigs invasion, emerged victorious, while Democrat John Connally, Secretary of the Navy at the time of the latter, was elected governor of Texas. In 1963 a Gallup Poll revealed that the Midwest was the most satisfied with JFK's Cuban policy, the South the least.

Within a year, however, John Kennedy was dead and
Lyndon Johnson President. Whereas J. F. K. was concerned
about Cuba, L. B. J. feared a Communist take-over in the Dominican Republic, dispatching American troops there on April
28, 1965 in an attempt to protect U. S. citizens and prevent a
Communist revolution. When the House voted by a 312 to 52
margin on September 20 in effect to endorse the unilateral use
of force to prevent a Communist coup anywhere in the Western
Hemisphere, 49 Northern Democrats and 3 Republicans cast
the only nay votes. On this occasion L. B. J. 's most enthusiastic supporters were military-minded Southern Democrats.

Conversely, the race conscious South fought the repeal
of the national origins quota system, casting two-thirds of the
nay votes in the House and three-fourths in the Senate. Along
with the West, this section had played a key role in passing
the legislation establishing this system four decades previously.
During the following year Southern Democrats in the House
joined forces with the Republicans to so modify the Export-
Import Bank bill as to prohibit it from guaranteeing the credit
of any Communist nation; in 1967, though, an unsuccessful
attempt in the Senate to prevent the Export-Import Bank from
financing arms purchases by less developed countries saw only
the Southern Democrats supporting this move, with both Republicans and Northern Democrats opposed. Similarly, on
March 16 of the latter year a dozen Southern Democrats led
the attack on the U. S. -Soviet Consular Treaty, which the upper
chamber ratified by a margin of 66 to 28. Northern Democrats strongly backed this agreement, while 13 of the minority
bloc of 35 Republicans balloted in the negative. A Southern
Democratic-Republican attempt to withhold the most-favored-
nation tariff privilege from Poland until it was determined
whether Poland was supplying war material to North Vietnam
narrowly lost in the House that autumn, thanks to the opposition of 137 out of 146 Northern Democrats.

As for Africa, Kenneth W. Grundy pointed out in the
December 1966 issue of Africa Today, relative to Congressional attitudes during the past two years, that: "... over
90% of the critical Democratic references are by Southern or
border state members of Congress. Almost 69% of sympathetic Republican references come from the Northeast states.
Republican criticism is centered in the Mid-West, representing almost 70% of such references. " As one might expect,
an independent Southern Rhodesia enjoyed wide support among
southern members of Congress; in contrast, one of Southern
Rhodesia's most severe critics in the House has been a liberal

Northern Democrat, Donald Fraser of Minnesota.   A study
published by the African-American Institute two years later
similarly concluded that: "Whites in the South have been less
inclined to favor aid to Africa than their non-Southern counterparts, but, outside the South, there are not great differences,
with Northeasterners being only slightly more 'liberal in their
views' than persons in the Midwest, Plains, Rocky Mountain
region, and Far West."

        Turning to Egypt and its 1967 conflict with Israel, dur-
ing which the United States remained officially neutral and
Congress failed to act, a Gallup poll taken after this Six-Day
War asked: "... are your sympathies more with Israel or
more with the Arab states?" This revealed that the South,
where there are few Jews, registered 65 per cent support for
Israel, while the East, where there are a large number,
lagged far behind with only 50 per cent. (The Arabs did
poorly in every section, reaching their high in the West with
a 5 per cent backing.) A series of other Gallup polls taken
during the second Johnson Administration, as to whether this
nation should send troops into the Dominican Republic, the
Middle East and Czechoslovakia, similarly uncovered the
greatest enthusiasm in the South.   On the other hand, the
proposed admission of Communist China into the United Nations received considerably less support in the South than in
any other section.   Writing in 1966, A. T. Steele observed
that: "In general, I found the west coast more flexible on
China policy than the east coast, the east coast more elastic
than the Midwest, and the Midwest less conservative than the
Southern and Mountain states." One might also cite two 1968
polls, one dealing with President Johnson's handling of the
Pueblo crisis, the other with keeping our troops in West Germany.   On the first of these, the East was the most lauda-
tory and the South most censorious; for the second, the West
showed the greatest enthusiasm.

        There remains for consideration the Vietnam War, an
issue which grew to the point where it divided the American
people to a degree that has had few, if any parallels, in
memory.   Writing in 1967, Arthur Schlesinger, Jr. pointed
out in his book, The Bitter Heritage: Vietnam and American
Democracy 1941-1966, examples of the stifling of anti-Vietnam dissent from every section: a man twice duly elected to
the Georgia legislature denied his seat because of his views
on Vietnam, a ninth-grade teacher in Las Vegas, Nevada expelled from the American Federation of Teachers for not
saluting the flag at a school assembly out of disagreement

with governmental Vietnam policy, students suspended from
high school in Cleveland and Pittsburgh for wearing black arm-
bands in mourning for Vietnam dead. In more recent years,
of course, political leaders from both major parties have
questioned our Vietnam policy, more often than not to their
political advantage rather than to their political detriment; to
cite a half-dozen examples from the Senate, one might single
out as representative Charles Goodell of New York (who did
go down to defeat in the 1970 general election), John Sherman
Cooper of Kentucky, J. William Fulbright of Arkansas, George
McGovern of South Dakota (an unsuccessful entry in the Democratic Presidential sweepstakes of 1968), Frank Church of
Idaho, and Mark Hatfield of Oregon. These men represent
every section of the country.

Nevertheless, Gallup polls for the period 1966-1969 reveal some variation in attitude from section to section. An
averaging of 14 polls for this three-year time-span demonstrates that the East more so than any other section felt that
the Vietnam War was a mistake, the West less so. A series
of polls on the Vietnam question by Louis Harris published in
Time on October 31, 1969, after Richard Nixon had taken
office, similarly found the East most in favor of the immediate withdrawal of all American troops from Vietnam and a
unilateral cease-fire, with the Middle West least amenable to
the former alternative and the South to the latter. Further
evidence of white southern bellicosity is to be found in polls
conducted in 1964 and 1968 by the Survey Research Center of
the University of Michigan. On the other hand, a series of
local polls taken in 1967 by such widely scattered newspapers
as the Cleveland Plain Dealer, the Charleston (W. Va.) Gazette-
Mail, the Croton-Cortland News and the Hastings News of New
York State, and the Clarke Press, a shopping paper in the
Greater Portland, Oregon area, all revealed a degree of
dovishness far out of line with the findings of Gallup and Harris. Relative to these local polls, it might be suggested that
Vietnam war critics perhaps felt more strongly about the war
than its proponents, and thus voted more heavily than did the
latter.

Turning to recent elections and the Vietnam War, it
will be recalled that Senator Barry Goldwater's capturing of
the Republican Presidential nomination represented something
of a revolt on the part of the South and the West against the
Northeast. Picturing Goldwater as a nuclear maniac, Lyndon
Johnson easily won election on a peace and prosperity plank,
the Republican nominee carrying only five southern states and

his native Arizona. But as was the case with Wilson in 1916
and with F. D. R. in 1936, who also campaigned as peace candidates, the post-election period witnessed escalation rather
than disengagement in Vietnam. When the Western Governors'
Conference met in Las Vegas in the Spring of 1966, Time reported that: "While most of the twelve Governors present...
endorsed the Administration's basic policy, many of them expressed misgivings over the conduct of the war and the future
of the Saigon government. " This, it will be recalled, was
the section which according to the abovementioned Gallup polls
was less inclined than any other to the belief that the Vietnam
War was a mistake.

Editorial reactions, although more difficult to measure
quantitatively, threw additional light on public opinion towards
the Vietnam War. According to David S. Myers' study of
"Editorials and Foreign Affairs in the 1964 Presidential Campaign, " "... matters of foreign affairs were the prime factors
in Lyndon Johnson's victory.... " Of the editorials catalogued,
13. 3 per cent dealt with the Vietnam War, 17. 7 concerned
nuclear weapons control, and 38. 6 foreign policy in general.
While the Atlanta Constitution stressed the need for a President who "does not shoot from the hip, " the Baltimore Sun
described Senator Goldwater's world view as "incredibly
naive, almost childlike"; to the Washington Post, Goldwater
was naive and dangerous, " to the New York Times, "ill-
fitted" to lead the United States in its international relations.
Among the leading newspapers to endorse the Republican
nominee were the Chicago Tribune and the Los Angeles Times.
Curiously, though, most Vietnam editorials were anti-adminis-
tration, with even the Christian Science Monitor of Boston
taking a rare partisan stand in its attack on L. B. J. As was
the case with the Korean War, political rather than sectional
factors were apparently more decisive in the shaping of editorial positions.

By the Spring of 1968, four years later, the number of
hawkish newspapers had noticeably dwindled: the New York
Daily News, the Chicago Tribune, the St. Louis Globe Democrat, the San Diego Union, the Atlanta Constitution, the Philadelphia Inquirer, and the San Francisco Examiner. Among
the doves were the New York Post, the New York Times, the
Milwaukee Journal, the St. Louis Post-Dispatch, the Boston
Globe, the San Francisco Chronicle, the Miami Herald, and
the Minneapolis Tribune. In a study of ten of the nation's
prestige newspapers, "Editorials and Foreign Affairs in the
1968 Presidential Campaign, " David S. Myers concluded that

voters ". . . were motivated primarily by matters of foreign
affairs, especially the issue of Vietnam. " The Los Angeles
Times editorialized more on foreign affairs than any of the
other nine; no less than 49. 6 per cent of all foreign affairs
and multi-topical editorials in these ten newspapers dealt
with Vietnam. To the Atlanta Constitution, the latter conflict
was a "tragic war, " to the Baltimore Sun it was the "most
miserable of conflicts. " On the other hand, the Chicago
Tribune referred to Vietnam as "the testing ground for the
communist theory that 'wars of national liberation' can bring
the United States and the west to their knees, " it being the
only newspaper on Myers' list to attack President Lyndon
Johnson's announcement on October 31 that all bombing of
North Vietnam would cease the following day ("a unilateral
sellout").

Finally, let us examine key roll-calls in Congress
relative to sectional attitudes on the Vietnam question during
the L. B. J. years. Technically, Congress has never declared
war on North Vietnam, as technically it never declared war
on North Korea. After the Communists had attacked U. S.
destroyers patrolling the Gulf of Tonkin early in August 1964,
however, the House and the Senate voted on the 7th, the
former 414 to 0 and the latter 88 to 2, to pass a resolution
declaring support for "the determination of the President, as
Commander-in-Chief, to take all necessary measures to repel
any armed attack against the forces of the United States and
to prevent further aggression. " Only Democratic Senators
Wayne Morse of Oregon and Ernest Gruening of Alaska voted
against the Gulf of Tonkin Resolution; as we have noted, both
lost their seats in the 1968 elections. A list of some of the
votes on Vietnam in Congress during Lyndon Johnson's last
four years as chief executive (see page 265), demonstrates
that Congress had yet to embrace the dovish philosophy on a
wholesale basis. In the first three roll-calls an aye vote is
a vote for the Johnson Administration, while in the fourth it
is the nay votes that register support for L. B. J.

After Richard Nixon took office as President, though,
the anti-Vietnam votes began to snowball in both houses of
Congress. While liberal Northern Democrats had become
increasingly desirous that the war be terminated so that this
nation might wholeheartedly devote its attention to assorted
domestic reforms, conservative Southern Democrats were confronted with a Republican Administration with which they often
agreed on domestic policy, regardless of whether the President
was following an overt "Southern Strategy" or not. What the

Body	Date	Item	Rep.	N.D.	S.D.	Total
Senate	3/1/66	Motion to Table Morse Amendment Repealing Gulf of Tonkin Resolution	32-0	39-4	21-1	92-5
House	3/15/66	Defense Department $13 Billion Supplemental Appropriation for Southeast Asia	122-0	178-3	89-0	267-3
Senate	3/1/67	Clark Amendment Supporting Honorable Settlement of War and Convening of an International Meeting	24-10	37-1	11-8	72-19
House	3/2/67	Brown Amendment that Fiscal 1967 Supplemental Defense Appropriation not be Used for Military Operations in or over North Vietnam	0-173	18-115	0-84	18-372

long-range consequences of this frequent collaboration will be
is impossible to determine at this time, but there is little
evidence at hand currently that Mr. Nixon planned to abandon
it. If anything, the chief executive apparently had expectations
that the Democratic Party would be eventually taken over by
Northern "doves" and "radlibs, " leaving the Republican Party
as the spokesman for the majority both on foreign policy and
its domestic counterpart.

Nevertheless, a breakdown of Congressional roll-calls
on some key foreign policy issues during the first year that
Richard Nixon was President reveals that on the Nuclear Proliferation Treaty, which passed the Senate on March 13 by an
83 to 15 vote, eight Republicans and seven Southern Democrats provided the opposition. In contrast, not a single
Northern Democrat cast his ballot against it. This treaty
actually was a hold-over from the Johnson Administration,
the Soviet invasion of Czechoslovakia in August 1968 having
temporarily halted American action on it. The following year,
on April 19, 1970, the Senate approved a Nuclear Arms
Freeze Resolution 72 to 6, with four Democrats and two
Southerners opposed; this was a resolution on which President
Nixon failed to take a public stand.

Another measure dating from the L. B. J. era was the
authorization of a $480 million American share of a $1. 2
billion replenishment of the loan fund of the International Development Association, an organization which has been described as the soft-loan window of the World Bank group.
When this administration-backed proposal cleared the House
by a 247 to 150 margin on May 12, its victory was attributable to the strong support of the Northern Democrats, who
overwhelmingly favored it 131 to 10; on the other hand, a
majority of Republicans (94 to 85) and Southern Democrats
(46 to 31) failed to back the authorization. In the Senate, both
the Republicans (20 to 15) and the Northern Democrats (23 to
6) returned majorities for it when it came up for a final vote
(49 to 34) on May 14, with the Southern Democrats two-thirds
unfavorable (13 to 6). On June 25, moreover, the Senate
finally enacted the two-year-old "National Commitments Resolution" designed to reassert a Congressional voice in decisions
committing this country to the defense of foreign nations, 70
to 16; Southern Democrats, who traditionally have been fearful of an overly strong executive, were unanimously in favor
of this resolution, while only two-thirds of the Republicans
backed it. (Nixon himself was rather lukewarm.)

Finally, on December 2, the House adopted a resolution backing the Nixon Administration's attempt to achieve
"peace with justice in Vietnam. " On this occasion it was the
Northern Democrats who dissented the most strongly, that
faction providing 54 of the 55 nay votes.   (334 Representatives voted for the measure.) Here we see another example
of the old Republican-Southern Democratic coalition that was
noticeably absent on the other three votes, which, however,
were not directly concerned with the Vietnam issue.

During 1970 the Indochina question largely monopolized
the attention of Congress to the exclusion of other foreign
policy topics.   Especially controversial was Nixon's dispatching of American troops into Cambodia on April 30 to execute
a two-month offensive designed to clean out the Communists
from the border area adjoining South Vietnam.   On June 30
the Senate adopted by a decisive 58 to 37 margin a resolution
sponsored by Republican John Sherman Cooper of Kentucky
and Frank Church of Idaho barring the further expenditure of
funds for U. S. military operations in Cambodia; despite the
opposition of the Republicans (26 to 16) and the Southern
Democrats (10 to 7), a unified Northern Democratic bloc (35
to 1) spearheaded the victorious Cooper-Church forces.
Nevertheless, in another key vote on September 1 the Senate
rejected an "End the War Amendment" identified with Democrat George McGovern of South Dakota and Republican Mark
Hatfield of Oregon that set a December 31, 1971 deadline for
the complete withdrawal of U. S. troops from Vietnam.   Here
the roll-call was 55 to 39, with strong Northern Democratic
backing (29 to 6) being insufficient to offset equally strong
Republican (34 to 7) and Southern Democratic (15 to 3) hostility.   The Senate also voted on two occasions to repeal the
Gulf of Tonkin Resolution; on the second of these roll-calls,
the first being a political maneuver and thus not a totally reliable barometer, five Southern Democrats cast the only nay
votes.

As the Vietnam War was winding down during the last
two years of the first Nixon Administration, our President
was simultaneously attempting to improve relations with Communist China and the Soviet Union.   These efforts culminated
in trips by him to both of the latter countries in 1972, and
apparently helped to strengthen his hold on the American
electorate.   A Gallup Poll taken a year previously in May
1971, however, revealed that the South (33 per cent) was far
less favorably inclined than the West (51 per cent) toward
allowing Communist China into the United Nations.   Another

Gallup Poll taken in October 1971, moreover, demonstrated
that most Americans, regardless of section, regarded Communist China as a greater threat to world peace than the
Soviet Union; here the West (33 per cent) was the most suspicious of the latter, while the Middle West (60 per cent) was
the most skeptical of the former. The following year, on
August 3, 1972, the Senate approved by an overwhelming 88
to 2 margin a treaty with Russia which would limit both that
nation and the United States to two antiballistic missile in-
stallations. The only nay votes on this occasion were those
of Democrat James Allen of Alabama and Conservative James
Buckley of New York. A month later the SALT Agreement
with the Soviet Union, restricting the deployment of offensive
missiles, passed the Senate by an identical 88 to 2 vote; earlier, Republicans and Southern Democrats had joined forces to
push through the Senate, on a 56 to 35 roll call, the Jackson
Amendment urging that this nation take a hard line in future
negotiations vis-à-vis a permanent agreement.

In other actions relative to foreign policy matters not
pertaining to the Vietnam War, both Houses of Congress in
1971 defeated a move to restrict the extension of the draft to
one year instead of two, as President Nixon had requested.
Generally speaking, Republicans and Southern Democrats voted
for the longer extension, Northern Democrats for the shorter.
In October of this year, however, the Senate rejected by a 27
to 41 vote a foreign aid authorization bill which had earlier
passed the House; this marked the first time since the inception of the foreign aid program that either house of Congress
had ever defeated such a measure. While Senatorial Republicans narrowly supported the bill 19 to 15, Northern Democrats opposed it 7 to 14 and Southern Democrats repudiated
it by an overwhelming 1 to 12 margin. A year later, in July
1972, the Senate defeated on a 42 to 48 roll-call a $1.72
billion foreign military aid authorization bill which included
funds for Bangladesh relief after "doves" had added the
Brooke Amendment cutting off funds for American involvement
in Indochina. This time Northern Democrats were cast as
the main supporters of foreign aid in a deceptive vote. On
the other hand, a proposal limiting the number of American
troops stationed in Europe to 250,000 after June 15, 1972 was
defeated by the Senate in November 1971 by a 39 to 54 margin; here Republicans were generally opposed (5 to 37),
Northern Democrats generally favorable (26 to 7), and Southern Democrats split (8 to 10). Southern Democrats also
joined forces with Republicans in May 1972 to block a resto-
ration by the House of United Nations funds that had been de-

leted from an appropriations bill by committee, although their victory proved to be short-lived.

Congressional votes on the Vietnam War during 1971 and 1972 continued to follow the established pattern of a Republican-Southern Democratic "hawkish" alliance against Northern Democratic "doves," with some degree of variation from roll-call to roll-call. On June 22, 1971 the Senate adopted by a 57 to 42 vote the Mansfield Amendment setting a nine-month deadline for the complete withdrawal of U.S. troops from Indochina, pending the release of all American prisoners of war; this marked the first time that a majority in either house of Congress had supported such a measure. Here Republicans, who were following the lead of their President, were largely opposed (12 to 32), but Northern Democrats were almost unanimously favorable (35 to 2), and Southern Democrats split (10 to 8). Later that year in October, however, the Senate rejected on a 44 to 47 roll-call the Cooper-Church Amendment requiring that Indochinese funds be used only to effect troop withdrawals. On this occasion Southern Democratic hostility (3 to 13) was a key factor in the defeat.

Turning to the more "hawkish" House, on several occasions in 1971 it defeated proposals embodying either directly or indirectly the principle underlying the Mansfield Amendment, with the abovementioned coalition noticeably in evidence. The following year, in 1972, the House Foreign Affairs Committee did vote 18 to 17 to add an end-the-war amendment to a military authorization bill, the first time a House committee had ever done so, but the House itself eventually deleted this provision in August by a 229 to 177 vote, even though a caucus of House Democrats had overwhelmingly come out in April for the establishment of a withdrawal date. Two months later, in October, the House failed to pass by the necessary two-thirds majority a bill which would have restricted American travel to nations with which the United States was at war --i.e., North Vietnam. This 230 to 140 vote, like the August one, pitted an overwhelming majority of Northern Democratic "doves" against an overwhelming majority of Southern Democratic and Republican "hawks." Unlike the Senate the House more or less backed Nixon's Vietnam policy up to the end of that conflict early in 1973.

FOR FURTHER READING

Two works which are absolutely essential to an understanding of this period are Congressional Quarterly Service,
Congress and the Nation 1945-1964, and Congress and the
Nation 1965-1968. For the Nixon Administration, see the
Congressional Quarterly Almanac, a volume published yearly;
Volume 25, for example, spans the year 1969, Volume 26,
1970, etc. These publications give breakdowns of the roll
calls on every foreign policy question before Congress, both
of major and of minor importance, as well as offering com-
mentary and analysis. Edward V. Schneier, Jr. also has
revised Julius Turner's Party and Constituency: Pressures on
Congress, with emphasis on the sessions of 1948, 1953, 1959,
and 1964. As for polls, the previously mentioned book by
Hadley Cantril, Public Opinion, unfortunately stops with the
year 1946. Thus for the post-World War II period one must
turn to the collections of polls published four times a year in
the Public Opinion Quarterly and, for the years since 1965,
the monthly Gallup Opinion Index. There also are a large
number of polls on file at the Roper Public Opinion Research
Center at Williams College, the Survey Research Archive at
the University of Michigan, and the Louis Harris Political
Data Center at the University of North Carolina, but the cost
of even sampling these is prohibitively expensive unless one
possesses a large research grant. Unfortunately, there is
no retrospective work discussing in a comprehensive manner
editorial reactions to foreign affairs over the last quarter-
century, and with the Literary Digest out of business since
the late 1930's one has no definitive contemporary source to
which to turn.

Shifting our attention to sectional studies, books dealing with the South include Alfred O. Hero, Jr. 's The Southerner and World Affairs (which relies heavily on public opinion polls); Charles O. Lerche, Jr. , The Uncertain South; and
Paul Seabury's pamphlet, The Waning of Southern Internationalism (an historical treatment). Among the key articles
are Malcolm E. Jewell, "Evaluating the Decline of Southern
Internationalism through Senatorial Roll Call Votes"; Charles
O. Lerche, Jr. , "Southern Congressmen and the 'New Isolationism'"; Frank E. Smith, "Valor's Second Prize: Southern
Racism and Internationalism"; and Marian D. Irish, "Foreign
Policy and the South. " The Middle West is dealt with more
sketchily in such publications as V. O. Key, Jr. , Public
Opinion and American Democracy, Russel B. Nye, Midwest-
ern Progressive Politics, and Maynard Kniskern, "Clues to

the Midwestern Mind. " A more extended treatment which
examines and modifies the midwestern isolationist hypothesis
is Ralph H. Smuckler, "The Region of Isolationism"; for the
most isolationist state (North Dakota), see the two articles
by Robert P. Wilkins, "Middle Western Isolationism: A Re-
examination" and "The Nonpartisan League and Upper Midwest
Isolationism, " as well as the article by Hanno R. E. Hardt,
"International News into North Dakota. " One may find information on the Far West and foreign policy in Earl Pomeroy's The Pacific Slope, and in Vincent Sheean's "From a
Lecturer's Notes. " An important study that examines in turn
the attitudes of the various sections to foreign affairs is
Alfred O. Hero, Jr., Americans in World Affairs; briefer is
Paul H. Douglas, "A New Isolationism--Ripples or Tide?"

We have previously discussed the validity, or lack
thereof, of various interpretations of isolationism in terms
of ethnic, rural, religious, educational, and other variables,
so that it is only necessary to cite the full title of certain
key bibliographical items here without going into a lengthy
evaluation of each.   Of prime importance are the two somewhat contradictory articles of Leroy N. Rieselbach, "The
Basis of Isolationist Behavior" and "The Demography of the
Congressional Vote on Foreign Aid, 1939-1958"; likewise
seminal are two publications by Samuel Lubell, "Who Votes
Isolationist and Why" and The Future of American Politics.
Also of value is the abovementioned book by Hero and his recently published American Religious Groups View Foreign
Policy, which analyzes the attitudes of Catholics and Protestants on a sectional basis.   Perhaps the most controversial
of these writings is Bruce M. Russett's article "Demography,
Salience, and Isolationist Behavior, " which in the space of a
few pages disposes of party, ethnic background, and ruralism
as variables significantly related to isolationism.

Fairly numerous are the treatments covering various
time-spans that measure sectional attitudes towards foreign
policy in general, or some specific issue such as tariff reduction or foreign aid, on the part of one or both houses of
Congress.   Aside from those previously mentioned studies of
a single section that touch upon Congressional voting patterns,
one might cite among the more broadly gauged works H.
Bradford Westerfield, Foreign Policy and Party Politics: Pearl
Harbor to Korea; Duncan MacRae, Jr., Dimensions of Congressional Voting: A Statistical Survey of the House of Representatives in the Eighty-First Congress; Gerald Marwell,
"Party, Region, and the Dimensions of Conflict in the House

of Representatives 1949-1954"; William T. Cozort, "House
Opposition to Foreign Aid Legislation"; Leroy N. Rieselbach,
The Roots of Isolationism; David Farnsworth, The Senate
Committee on Foreign Relations; Holbert N. Carroll, The
House of Representatives and Foreign Affairs; and W. Wayne
Shannon, Party, Constituency and Congressional Voting. In
addition, there is the doctoral dissertation by Robert B. De-
Janes, Southern Neo-Isolationism: Case Studies in Reciprocal
Trade and Foreign Aid, as well as the various Congressional
Quarterly Service publications cited at the beginning of this
bibliographical note, and the Congressional Record.

Next let us turn to specific topics. Many works touch
on American attitudes towards the United Nations, but particularly helpful are Alfred O. Hero, Jr., "The American Public and the U. N. "; Elmo Roper, "American Attitudes on
World Organization"; William A. Scott and Stephen B. Withey,
The United States and the United Nations: The Public View
1945-1955; and Carnegie Endowment for International Peace,
The United States Public and the United Nations. Of related
interest is an article published by Frederick W. Williams in
1945, "Regional Attitudes on International Cooperation. " For
the early years of the Cold War and the Berlin Blockade, see
George E. Simmons' "The 'Cold War' in Large-City Dailies
of the United States"; for the Marshall Plan, consult Harold
Hitchens' "Influences on the Congressional Decision to Pass
the Marshall Plan, " and Kimball Young's "Content Analysis
of the Treatment of the Marshall Plan in Certain Representative American Newspapers. " The previously mentioned book
and article by Samuel Lubell contain information on the Election of 1948, as does Louis L. Gerson, The Hyphenate in Recent American Politics and Diplomacy. Not as much is available on sectional attitudes towards the Korean War as one
would like, but there are polls on this conflict in the article
"The Polls: Is War a Mistake?, " while Richard K. Rovere
and Arthur M. Schlesinger, Jr. describe the triumphal return
of Douglas MacArthur after his firing by Harry Truman in
The General and the President and the Future of American
Foreign Policy. Also see Elmo Roper and Louis Harris,
"The Press and the Great Debate. " An extended treatment
of the events surrounding the Japanese Peace Treaty of 1952
is Bernard C. Cohen, The Political Process and Foreign
Policy: The Making of the Japanese Settlement. As for the
Presidential election of that year, Alfred de Grazia has set
forth a penetrating account in his The Western Public, 1952
and Beyond.

Interpretive studies of sectional attitudes toward the Eisenhower Administration and foreign affairs are regrettably few and far between, for which reason one is forced to piece together scraps of information on such vital topics as the Bricker Amendment, Formosa, and the Suez Crisis. In his The New Isolationism: A Study in Politics and Foreign Policy since 1950 Norman Graebner has produced a work that ranks among the best contemporary assessments of Ike's diplomacy; a much more specialized monograph is James N. Rosenau, National Leadership and Foreign Policy, a book that focuses on the 1958 National Conference on "The Foreign Aspects of U. S. National Security." As for Castro and Cuba, two articles that merit inspection, one scholarly and one contemporary, are Michael J. Francis, "The U. S. and Castro: A Study in Declining Relations," and the 1962 Newsweek account, "How U. S. Voters Feel about Cuba." Studies examining other aspects of John Kennedy's foreign policy include a series of polls on "The Berlin Situation" published in the Winter 1961 issue of the Public Opinion Quarterly. For American attitudes towards Africa in the recent past, see the December 1966 issue of Africa Today. "Africa in National Politics," and a 1968 pamphlet release of the African-American Institute, American Understanding of Africa. A contemporary treatment of American attitudes towards a quite different part of the globe is A. T. Steele, The American People and China.

A deluge of material, of course, has appeared on Vietnam, only a minute part of which is pertinent to our analysis. Among the books, Arthur M. Schlesinger, Jr.'s The Bitter Heritage: Vietnam and American Democracy 1941-1966 is representative. The above-mentioned article, "The Polls: Is War a Mistake?," also contains Gallup data on Vietnam for the years 1966-1969, as does the 1969 article by Louis Harris, "Americans on the War: Divided, Glum, Unwilling to Quit." The Nation also published a series of articles on local polls in 1967: "Choose Your Poll"; "The Zinn Position"; and "A Voice for the Voiceless." Political assessments include a Time article dealing with the 1966 Western Governors' Conference, "Support and Concern." For a contemporary examination of editorial reactions to the war, see the 1967 Newsweek article, "Doubts about Vietnam," and the 1968 one, "Shifting on the War"; for two retrospective treatments, consult David S. Myers' "Editorials and Foreign Affairs in the 1964 Presidential Campaign" and "Editorials and Foreign Affairs in the 1968 Presidential Campaign." The Congressional Quarterly Service publications and the Congressional Record are also a must.

CHAPTER 8

CONCLUSION: BEYOND POLITICS--
THE VARYING IMPACT OF OTHER FACTORS

As this work has demonstrated, once one passes beyond the political breakdown of votes in Congress on various
foreign policy issues to the vast universe of supplementary
data, it is clear that other factors in addition to political
considerations have influenced sectional attitudes towards diplomacy. Perhaps the most important of those have been
economics, race, ethnicity, and metropolitanism vs. ruralism, although others have been touched upon as well. While
in the case of politics it has been demonstrated that one-party
domination of a section frequently leads to sustained bloc
voting in Congress over a period of time, as with New England Federalism and Southern Democracy, in the case of
these other factors it is not as easy to summarize their impact on sectional attitudes towards foreign policy, especially
in the case of economics.

During every era of American history economic factors have been at the forefront when key diplomatic issues
have precipitated a vigorous reaction on the part of Congress,
the newspapers, and public opinion in general. This continuing prominence is one of the most convincing arguments that
one might advance in behalf of their overall significance. As
early as the American Revolution, for example, the Northeast was interested in the North Atlantic fisheries, the South
in the free navigation of the Mississippi River. Following
the end of this conflict the North expressed a willingness to
accede to the Jay-Gardoqui Treaty of 1786 with Spain--which
sacrificed the free navigation of the Mississippi--in return
for Spain opening itself and the Canaries to a number of
American products. In addition, New England merchants developed close ties with London exporters, importers, and
bankers, with the result that this section favored Jay's Treaty
of 1794 with Great Britain; the South, though, opposed it, the
planters being unhappy with the article that provided for the
settlement of the debt question. The fact that many planters

were personally in debt to England doubtless contributed to the widespread sympathy towards France, common throughout the South at this time. Southern planters and farmers both favored the Louisiana Purchase of 1803 from France, as they desired new land into which to expand. On the other hand, the Embargo of 1807 was especially distasteful to commercial New England, but this section managed to evade it to some extent through illicit trade and smuggling (and even manufacturing), while the South went along with it and suffered as a result.

By the time of the War of 1812 New England had begun to develop a substantial trade with the Spanish (and Portugese) colonial empire in the New World, as well as with the Iberian Peninsula, which unquestionably was a factor in its support of Spain and its ally England against France during the Napoleonic Wars. In contrast, the South, which feared Latin American economic competition, opposed the Panama Congress of 1826, but the desire for new land led the South to favor the annexation of Texas. Turning to the Pacific Coast, from approximately 1822 on, Boston merchants and Massachusetts whalers began taking an interest in Oregon. In 1846 New York City commercial interests abandoned "54°40' or fight" rather than jeopardize their trade with the Pacific Coast, while John C. Calhoun and the low tariff South sought a compromise on the Oregon issue so as to take advantage of Great Britain's repeal of the Corn Laws. During the Mexican War the manufacturing interests of New England opposed the enlargement of the low tariff South via expansion into what is now the American Southwest, but without success.

Thanks to the Gadsden Purchase of 1853, too, the South not only further satisfied its desire for additional land, but also obtained a railroad route to the Pacific. On the other hand, it failed in its drive to annex Cuba--a move which the New York City trading, shipping, and financial interests also favored--or to acquire Mexico and its considerable mineral wealth. Likewise unsuccessful was the attempt spearheaded by Minnesota and the North Central area to obtain Canada; these expansionists desired a lowering of freight rates and access to Canadian waterways. More ambiguous was the position of the South towards commercial reciprocity with Canada. In 1848 Southerners had opposed such a program out of fear that it would lead to annexation, but reversed their position in 1854 out of fear that Canada, irritated by the repeal of the British Corn Laws eight years earlier, might otherwise join the United States. On this occasion New Eng-

land fisherman and Maine lumbermen quarterbacked the movement on behalf of the Elgin-Marcy Treaty.

   With respect to the Pacific, by now such New England
towns as Salem, Boston, and Providence had come to dominate trade with the East Indies, and were also leading the
drive to open up China. New York City likewise played a
major role in the expansion of American commerce throughout this part of the world.   In 1855, however, the sugar-cane
Senators from Louisiana led a movement in the Senate to
block passage of a reciprocity treaty with Hawaii; both New
England whalers and traders were already active there, as
were various San Francisco and California interests.   Merchants from New England similarly were at the forefront of the
movement to open up Africa, with Salem dominating the trade
with Zanzibar.   During the Civil War the South, now an independent nation in competition with Egypt and India, prac-
ticed "King Cotton Diplomacy, " only to lose the war.

   Economic issues also arose frequently following this
conflict.   In 1878 the California wine industry and the San
Francisco Chamber of Commerce successfully blocked reciprocity with France, although in 1875 the sugar refiners
of the state had failed to defeat it with Hawaii.   During the
1880's middle western hog raisers and meat packers placed
pressure on Germany to drop its ban on the importation of
American pork, eventually succeeding, while in 1896 the Rocky
Mountain "Silver" Senators led the drive that climaxed in the
rejection of an arbitration treaty with Great Britain.   Earlier,
in 1867, California fur traders and Washington fishermen had
come out for the impending purchase of Alaska, as did New
England merchants and whalers; Westerners also desired
(but failed to obtain) British Columbia for its gold fields and
because of the Canadian threat to American trade with the
Far East.   After 1871 the eastern fishing states spearheaded
a movement culminating in the repeal of the fisheries article
of the Treaty of Washington in 1883, also blocking ratification
of the Bayard-Chamberlain Treaty in 1888.   Similarly, the
importing, sugar refining, banking, and sea transport interests of the East sabotaged implementary legislation for the
Mexican reciprocity treaty of 1884.   In 1882 the North unsuccessfully attempted to maintain Chinese immigration on
the grounds that its curtailment might have a negative impact
on American trade with China; certain groups on the Pacific
Coast, in fact, wished to exploit cheap Chinese labor, despite
the hostility towards the Orientals on the part of white workers and labor unions there.

Conclusion   277

As the United States began to assume the role of a
world power around the turn of the Twentieth Century, a
number of diplomatic crises arose.   In 1895 the moneyed interests of New York City and Boston generally favored a soft
stand towards Great Britain relative to the Venezuela boundary crisis; conversely, England's hostility towards the coinage of silver aroused the resentment of the South and the
West, Populists in these two sections regarding the former
mother country as an ally of the northeastern gold interests.
With the approach of the Spanish-American War many southern and western Populists also took up the cause of Cuban
independence, yet the 1898 amendment by Senator Henry Teller
of Colorado, pledging the United States not to annex Cuba, had
the objective of protecting the sugar beet interests of that
state.   Generally speaking, eastern business leaders, apart
from an imperialist minority, opposed the acquisition of a
colonial empire until the deteriorating situation in China at
the very end of the century forced them to change their minds.

Reciprocity with British North America again became
an issue in 1902, the fishing interests of Maine and Massachusetts successfully blocking the Hay-Bond Treaty with Newfoundland.   Yet in 1911 it was the agricultural interests of
Minnesota and North Dakota that opposed but failed to defeat
reciprocity with Canada itself, a treaty favored by the financial interests of the East; during the Presidential election of
1912 William Howard Taft, running for re-election, came in
third in these two states, and generally fared badly throughout the North Central area.   On the other hand, in the case
of the disputed Canadian-Alaskan boundary at the turn of the
century, it was the shipping and trading interests of the
Pacific Northwest that upheld the claims of Alaska.   The Far
West in particular was opposed to further Japanese immigration, and widespread resentment against Japanese landowners,
especially the small ones who were acquiring large acreage,
led the California legislature to pass the Webb Act of 1913
which forbade aliens to own land.   As for Wall Street, under
the auspices of William Howard Taft's Dollar Diplomacy it
invested in both Latin America and China during his Presidency.   At the time of World War I the Northeast was the
section most favorably disposed towards American loans to
the Allies; the economic and financial interests of the region
had forged innumerable ties with Great Britain by this time.
Early in World War I the South was disturbed by Britain's
placing of cotton on its absolute contraband list, but the English government then agreed to maintain the price of cotton
at a reasonable level, thus enabling the South to support the
Allied war effort more enthusiastically.

After unsuccessfully backing the League of Nations in 1919, in 1931 the South was the section most opposed to the Hoover Moratorium, southern fiscal generosity not matching earlier southern enthusiasm for world organization. On the other hand, there was almost unanimous southern backing for the Reciprocal Trade Agreements Act of 1934 after the prohibitively high Hawley-Smoot Tariff of 1930 had dealt a severe blow to southern commerce, as well as to American commerce in general. More futile was the support which the port of Duluth and the wheat-growing farm areas to the west of the Great Lakes gave around this time to an idea whose time had not yet come--the St. Lawrence Seaway. Then there was the silver bloc from the Rocky Mountain States, which emerged victorious in its campaign on behalf of another 1934 measure, the Silver Purchase Act, which undermined the already shaky Chinese currency. During this same decade the Pacific Northwest protested when the operations of the Japanese fishing canneries began to constitute a menace to Alaskan salmon, but with little success.

During the post-World War II era, in 1952, members of the West Coast fishing industry likewise favored placing restrictions on the Japanese when their nation finally signed a peace treaty with the United States. On the other hand, the South played a key role in sabotaging American financial aid in 1956 for the construction of the Aswan Dam in Egypt, Egyptian cotton long having competed with the southern variety. By this time, too, the South had begun to vote against foreign aid in general, especially when American financial assistance was extended to the underdeveloped areas of the so-called "Third World" rather than to Europe. The growing industrialization of the South since World War II has similarly undermined southern backing for reciprocal trade; southern internationalism has obviously undergone a noticeable metamorphosis since 1945.

Sometimes different economic groups within a section have disagreed on issues relating to foreign policy. Following the American Revolution New England sought to protect its fishing rights off the east coast of Canada, yet thanks in part to its economic ties with the former mother country, it proved to be the section most reluctant to go to war against England in 1812. As for the West, after 1850 there was a conflict between those employers in California who wished to hire inexpensive Chinese "coolie" labor and others, in particular labor unions, who attempted to block their immigration into this country. Around this time, too, there was dis-

agreement in the South between entrepreneurs desirous of annexing Mexico for its mineral riches, and anti-annexationist
slave-holders skeptical of the feasibility of introducing slavery
there. Turning to the present century, in 1911 Canadian reciprocity was opposed by middle western farmers, but favored by newspapers seeking cheap paper and by the millers
of the Twin Cities. These are only four of many examples.

As it requires a two-thirds favorable vote by the
Senate to ratify a treaty, the unanimous backing of a single
section is not sufficient to obtain Congressional approval of
it; nor is it for a foreign policy measure requiring a simple
majority in both houses. Sectional alliances, therefore, often
have been a sine qua non in effecting the passage of various
pieces of diplomatic legislation, and frequently these have
been economic in nature. At the Constitutional Convention
an alliance between the South and New England was responsible for the inclusion in that document of, the above-mentioned
two-thirds provision; the South wished to protect the free
navigation of the Mississippi River, New England its fishing
rights in the North Atlantic. In contrast, following the War
of 1812 various individuals in the mercantile Northeast and
the agrarian Northwest joined forces to promote "Manifest
Destiny. " More complex was the alliance of eastern sugar
refiners, southern sugar producers, and Pacific Coast sugar
consumers which fought unsuccessfully for the repeal of the
Hawaiian reciprocity treaty of 1875. Still another partnership
was that of the beet sugar states of the Northwest and the
cane sugar state of Louisiana, which was strongly in evidence
both at the time of the sabotaging of the Cuban reciprocity
bill in 1902 and the enacting of the Filipino independence one
in 1934.

Aside from the traditional allegiance to free trade, the
South long has been preoccupied with race. Thus at the time
that Jay's Treaty was drawn up the southern planters were
alienated by its failure to rectify the confiscation of a number
of their slaves by the British during the Revolutionary War.
When an uprising of slaves took place in Santo Domingo in
1791, the South not only welcomed numerous fleeing French
aristocrats, but several southern states also prohibited further
Negro immigration from the West Indies. Following the triumph of Toussaint L'Ouverture, moreover, the South blocked
the recognition of Haiti (as well as the black republic of Liberia) until it left the Union at the time of the Civil War.
As for the West, settlers from this section also were unhappy, because Jay's Treaty did not contain an article on the

Indian question; one interpretation of the War of 1812, in
fact, emphasizes the Indian threat in explaining western interest in Canada and southern interest in Florida.

Following the termination of the Latin American wars
for independence, there was widespread southern opposition
to the Panama Congress on the grounds that it represented a
threat to the institution of slavery. Many Northerners and
Easterners later opposed the annexation of Texas by the United
States, viewing it as a southern plot to spread slavery; conversely, the South backed this move, not only because it
feared the presence on its borders of an independent country
free from slavery, but also because it opposed anti-slavery
Great Britain dominating the "Lone Star Republic. " When
war broke out between America and Mexico in 1846, New
England abolitionists opposed this conflict as long as it seemed
likely to them that after the war Southerners would extend
their slave system into that country. It is not surprising,
therefore, that the North generally was friendly and the South
basically hostile to the Wilmot Proviso of 1846 excluding
slavery from any territory acquired from Mexico.

A decade later the South threw its support to the Ostend Manifesto calling for the annexation of Cuba by the United
States, that section fearing the establishment of a black republic there under British protection, and hoping to add another slave state to the Union. (Actually, slavery was not
abolished in Cuba until 1886, twenty-one years after it was
outlawed in America.) The South similarly tended to look
with disfavor upon the French Revolution of 1848, which led
to the permanent abolition of slavery throughout the French
Empire. At the time of the Crimean War the South did sympathize with Russia because of the parallels between Russian
serfdom and southern slavery; when Czar Alexander II freed
twenty million serfs in 1861, however, the South greeted the
news with decided coolness.

From the 1850's on, a growing number of Californians
supported placing restrictions of various sorts on the Chinese,
and the anti-Chinese protest movement later spread to the
remainder of the Pacific Coast and the Rocky Mountains. In
contrast the Northeast with its tradition of abolitionism, dis-
approved of the Chinese Exclusion Act of 1882, while the
West and the South were generally favorable. Despite Pacific
Coast hostility to the Chinese and by the turn of the century
to the Japanese, it was the South that most strongly opposed
the annexation of Hawaii and the Philippines in 1898 on the

grounds that their inhabitants were racially inferior. Back home, in 1906 the San Francisco Board of Education attempted to segregate Japanese school children; curiously, the Pacific Northwest tended to favor Japan over Russia during the Russo-Japanese War of 1904-5, as did the nation as a whole. In 1924, nevertheless, Southerners and Westerners joined forces in Congress to effect Japanese exclusion.

As World War II approached, in 1935 Representative Louis Ludlow of Indiana saw his resolution calling for a national referendum on a declaration of war go down to defeat after he had antagonized the South by unsuccessfully sponsoring an anti-lynching bill. When Chinese exclusion was repealed after sixty-one years in 1943, it was the South, not the West, which led the opposition, but during World War II it was the Pacific Coasters who were the most amenable to placing Japanese in relocation camps.

In more recent years Southerners hesitant to let Negroes vote or attend white schools have not viewed with much enthusiasm the activities of the United Nations, in whose General Assembly a small black republic (Liberia, for example) possesses voting strength equal to that of the much larger and populous United States. The South likewise tends to equate the independence movement throughout the former colonial world with the civil rights movement in this country. To cite an extremist reaction, the Mississippi legislature voted to congratulate the South African government on its handling of the affair when that country's police fired upon a group of Africans demonstrating at Sharpeville in March 1960. More typical has been the favoring by southern members of Congress during the late 1960's of an independent Southern Rhodesia. Today, as always, race remains an issue with numerous international ramifications, aside from its widespread domestic repercussions.

Unlike economics, politics, and race, the impact of ethnic attitudes on foreign policy formulation apparently did not reach major proportions until the period just before the Civil War, at which time the "Know-Nothing" American Party flourished with its anti-foreigner, anti-immigrant, and anti-Catholic program. Citing only two nationality groups, German immigrants tended to settle in such midwestern cities as Cincinnati, St. Louis, and Milwaukee, the Irish in such eastern ones as New York City and Boston, their presence quite naturally affecting the foreign policy stances of these sections on various issues. On the other hand, fewer immigrants established homes south of the Mason-Dixon Line, with the consequence that there were few, if any, ethnic rivalries to undermine emerging southern internationalism. (Racial antipathies, of course, were constantly present.)

During the Presidential election of 1860 the Republican nominee, Abraham Lincoln, rolled up a large vote among the Germans of the Middle West by running on a platform containing a pro-immigration plank. A quarter-century later, in 1884, the Reverend Burchard's "Rum, Romanism, and Rebellion" speech had the opposite effect of driving the Irish voters of New York City and Boston into the arms of the victorious Democratic Presidential candidate, Grover Cleveland. In 1888, however, Cleveland failed in his attempt to capitalize on anti-Chinese feeling along the Pacific Coast by signing an exclusion measure; the Republicans carried that section just as they had in the last several Presidential elections, Benjamin Harrison winning the Presidency.

At the time of World War I the Middle West was the section least favorably disposed to American aid to the Allies, thanks largely to the considerable number of German-Americans there. During the Presidential election of 1916 the Democratic Chief Executive, Woodrow Wilson, captured many heavily German counties in this section on his way to re-election by exploiting the ill-fated slogan: "He kept us out of war." (Wilson personally did not coin it.) Following World War I, in 1919, Senator Henry Cabot Lodge of Massachusetts emerged as the leader of the strong reservationists during the course of the Senatorial debate on the Treaty of Versailles and the League of Nations. Aside from his personal hatred of Wilson, Lodge dared not alienate the Irish of Boston and the Italians of Massachusetts by too strongly endorsing the treaty, and his obstructionist tactics eventually proved successful.

The presence of these and other foreign-born immigrant groups throughout the Northeast led that section to oppose the restrictive legislation that Congress passed during the early 1920's in an attempt to curtail the future entry of southeastern Europeans. On the other hand, the neutrality legislation of the middle and late 1930's was particularly favored by the Middle West, where, as noted before, many Germans resided; during the Presidential election of 1940 Democrat Franklin Roosevelt lost several Great Plains States in which this ethnic group was strong. Nevertheless, at the time that the Russians invaded Finland there was some midwestern support for aid to the latter, thanks to the presence of a large number of Scandinavians there.

Returning to the Northeast, there also is a heavy concentration of Jews in New York City, the hub of electoral vote-rich New York State. Prior to the Presidential election of 1948 both Democratic President Harry Truman and his Republican rival, Governor Thomas E. Dewey, adopted pro-Palestine stances. In this election, too, numerous German-Americans (as well as farmers) voted for H. S. T. in such midwestern states as Missouri, Ohio, Minnesota, Wisconsin, and Iowa, apparently having forgotten or forgiven F. D. R. for his internationalism. The political potency of the Jewish vote in the East manifested itself again in 1959, when 66 members of the House (nearly half of them from New York and New Jersey) sent telegrams to Eugene Black, President of the International Bank for Reconstruction and Development, attacking a proposed fifty-six million dollar loan to the United Arab Republic for the development of the Suez Canal.

As we have seen, some immigrant groups are concentrated in cities, others in rural areas. Urban attitudes in general often differ from rural ones on foreign policy, but it has been only during the last half-century that historians and political scientists have begun systematically to examine these differences. It must be remembered, too, that America was once heavily rural; Arthur Schlesinger, Sr. titled his book on the period 1878-98, The Rise of the City, and it was not until the present century that the urban population surpassed its rural counterpart. (By 1920 about 51 per cent of the American people lived in towns of more than 2, 500.) Between the two world wars isolationism tended to be more prevalent in rural areas and small towns than in the cities, those individuals representing metropolitan areas in Congress more frequently supporting the relaxation of neutrality legislation between 1935 and 1941. On the other hand, there was also a large number of Germans and Italians dwelling in the cities who exerted considerable political influence on behalf of both isolationism and neutrality. Since World War II this rural isolationist/urban internationalist interpretation remains popular with many historians and political scientists, foreign aid being a case in point, although a minority of commentators have raised their voices in protest.

Other factors, too, have influenced sectional attitudes toward foreign policy over the years, but rarely have they been the basic consideration; more frequently, they have man-

ifested themselves in a supporting role.   The southern military tradition doubtless has prejudiced that section in favor
of war on a number of occasions, while peace societies have
been active in New England since after the War of 1812.   In
addition, the presence of a number of pacifists throughout the
Middle West and Great Plains has similarly inclined those
sections twice to embrace isolationism during the present
century.   More sophisticated analyses have also been set
forth, such as those involving social mobility.   Since World
War II, for example, there appears to be a greater apathy
towards world affairs in the faster growing cities of the Far
West than anywhere else aside from Texas--in particular in
California, where only a quarter of the population is native-
born.   Alfred O. Hero, Jr., on the other hand, has just completed a study demonstrating the sectional variations in the
attitudes of Catholics and Protestants towards foreign policy.
Too complex for easy summary, his ideas are discussed in
Chapter Seven.   It will be recalled, too, that New York and
New England Democrats, mostly Catholics, opposed Philippine
independence in 1916.

Another factor of great consequence at times has been
the conflict of interests within a section on various foreign
policy issues.   Quite naturally, farmers often disagree with
manufacturers, Democrats with Republicans, whites with
blacks, English with Irish, urban residents with rural dwellers, and Protestants with Catholics.   It is surprising, therefore, that the representatives of the different sections in
Congress vote more or less as a unit on diplomatic questions
as often as they do.   To cite only one complex example, when
the Webb Act of 1913 restricting Japanese landowning in California was before the legislature, laborers, farmers, and
politicians generally were for it, merchants, educators, and
clergymen mostly against it.   This may be an atypical case,
but unanimity among interest groups on any given issue is
generally the exception rather than the rule.

In conclusion, it is apparent that the balance among
the interest groups within a section often changes from issue
to issue.   Why, then, are politics more important than
ethnicity on one issue, while on another metropolitanism is
more significant than race, and on a third economics are
more crucial than religion?   Fortunately, enough data is
available to make qualified guesses or even accurate judg-
ments in most cases, but it is doubtful that any magic formula could be devised to account for the relative impact of
each interest group on each occasion in American history that

there has been a sectional division on a diplomatic issue. This work, therefore, stops at charting prominent trends rather than attempting to formulate some universal law. Hopefully the material which has been presented here will prove of value in the unravelling of an at times highly complex series of relationships.

BIBLIOGRAPHY

Books, Doctoral Dissertations, and Pamphlets

Abbott, James Francis, Japanese Expansion and American
Policies (New York: Macmillan Company, 1916), pp.
268.

Abernethy, Thomas P. , The South in the New Nation 1789-
1819 (Baton Rouge: Louisiana State University Press,
1961), pp. 529.

Abernethy, Thomas Perkins, Western Lands and the American
Revolution (New York: Russell and Russell, 1959), pp.
410.

Adams, Ephraim Douglass, Great Britain and the American
Civil War, 2 volumes (Gloucester: Peter Smith, 1957).

Adams, James Truslow, New England in the Republic 1776-
1850 (Gloucester: Peter Smith, 1960), pp. 438.

Adler, Selig, The Isolationist Impulse: Its Twentieth Century
Reaction (London: Abelard-Schuman, 1957), pp. 538.

Adler, Selig, The Uncertain Giant: 1921-1941: American
Foreign Policy Between the Wars (New York: Macmillan Company, 1965), pp. 340.

Allen, H. C. , Great Britain and the United States (New York:
St. Martin's Press, 1955), pp. 1024.

Almond, Gabriel A. , The American People and Foreign
Policy (New York: Frederick A. Praeger, 1960), pp.
269.

Ambler, Charles Henry, Sectionalism in Virginia from 1776
to 1861 (New York: Russell and Russell, 1964), pp.
366.

American Understanding of Africa (New York: African-American Institute, 1968), pp. 9.

Bailey, Thomas A., America Faces Russia (Gloucester: Peter Smith, 1964), pp. 375.

Bailey, Thomas A., A Diplomatic History of the American People, 8th edition (New York: Appleton-Century-Crofts, 1969), pp. 1015.

Bailey, Thomas A., The Man in the Street (New York: Macmillan Company, 1948), pp. 334.

Bailey, Thomas A., The Policy of the United States Toward the Neutrals, 1917-1918 (Baltimore: Johns Hopkins Press, 1942), pp. 520.

Bailey, Thomas A., Theodore Roosevelt and the Japanese-American Crises (Stanford: Stanford University Press, 1934), pp. 353.

Bailey, Thomas A., Woodrow Wilson and the Great Betrayal (New York: Macmillan Company, 1945), pp. 429.

Bancroft, Frederic, Slave Trading in the Old South (New York: Frederick Ungar Publishing Company, 1959), pp. 415.

Battistini, Lawrence H., The Rise of American Influence in Asia and the Pacific (East Lansing: Michigan State University Press, 1960), pp. 241.

Beale, Howard K., Theodore Roosevelt and the Rise of America to World Power (Baltimore: Johns Hopkins Press, 1956), pp. 600.

Beard, Charles A., American Foreign Policy in the Making 1932-1940 (New Haven: Yale University Press, 1946), pp. 336.

Beard, Charles A., An Economic Interpretation of the Constitution of the United States (New York: Macmillan Company, 1913), pp. 330.

Beirne, Francis F., The War of 1812 (Hamden: Archon Books, 1965), pp. 410.

Beisner, Robert L., Twelve against Empire: The Anti-Imperialists 1898-1900 (New York: McGraw-Hill Book Company, 1968), pp. 310.

Bemis, Samuel Flagg, Jay's Treaty: A Study in Commerce and Diplomacy (New Haven: Yale University Press, 1962), pp. 526.

Bemis, Samuel Flagg, John Quincy Adams and the Foundations of American Foreign Policy (New York: Alfred A. Knopf, 1949), pp. 588.

Bemis, Samuel Flagg, Pinckney's Treaty (New Haven: Yale University Press, 1960), pp. 372.

Bennett, Norman R., and George E. Brooks, Jr., editors, New England Merchants in Africa: A History through Documents (Boston: Boston University Press, 1965), pp. 576.

Blumental, Henry, A Reappraisal of Franco-American Relations 1830-1871 (Chapel Hill: University of North Carolina Press, 1959), pp. 255.

Borchard, Edwin and William Lage, Neutrality for the United States (New Haven: Yale University Press, 1937), pp. 380.

Borg, Dorothy, American Policy and the Chinese Revolution 1925-1928 (New York: American Institute of Pacific Relations, 1947), pp. 440.

Borg, Dorothy, The United States and the Far Eastern Crisis of 1935-1938 (Cambridge: Harvard University Press, 1964), pp. 674.

Brebner, John Bartlett, North Atlantic Triangle: The Interplay of Canada, the United States, and Great Britain (New Haven: Yale University Press, 1945), pp. 385.

Bron, Saul G., Soviet Economic Development and American Business (New York: Horace Liveright, 1930), pp. 147.

Brown, Robert Craig: Canada's National Policy 1883-1900: A Study in Canadian-American Relations (Princeton: Princeton University Press, 1964), pp. 436.

Brown, Robert E., Charles Beard and the Constitution (Princeton: Princeton University Press, 1956), pp. 219.

Burt, A. L., The United States, Great Britain, and British North America (New York: Russell and Russell, 1961), pp. 447.

Bywater, Hector C., Sea-Power in the Pacific: A Study of the American-Japanese Naval Problem (Boston: Houghton Mifflin Company, 1934), pp. 319.

Callahan, James Morton, American Foreign Policy in Canadian Relations (New York: Macmillan Company, 1937), pp. 576.

Callahan, James Morton, American Foreign Policy in Mexican Relations (New York: Macmillan Company, 1932), pp. 644.

Campbell, Charles S., Jr., Anglo-American Understanding 1898-1903 (Baltimore: Johns Hopkins Press, 1957), pp. 385.

Campbell, Charles S., Jr., Special Business Interests and the Open Door Policy (Hamden: Archon Books, 1968), pp. 88.

Cantril, Hadley, Public Opinion 1935-1946 (Princeton: Princeton University Press, 1951), pp. 1191.

Capps, Finis Herbert, From Isolationism to Involvement: The Swedish Immigrant Press in America 1914-1945 (Chicago: Swedish Pioneer Historical Society, 1966), pp. 238.

Carroll, Holbert N., The House of Representatives and Foreign Affairs (Boston: Little, Brown and Company, 1966), pp. 386.

Casper, Henry W., American Attitudes towards the Rise of Napoleon III (Washington: Catholic University of America Press, 1947), pp. 242.

Chadwick, French Ensor, The Relations of the United States and Spain: Diplomacy (New York: Charles Scribner's Sons, 1909), pp. 610.

Chamberlain, Lawrence H. , and Richard C. Snyder, American
    Foreign Policy (New York: Rinehart and Company,
    1948), pp. 826.

Charles, Joseph, The Origins of the American Party System:
    Three Essays (Williamsburg: Institute of Early Amer-
    ican History and Culture, 1956), pp. 147.

Clark, Thomas D. , The Southern Country Editor (Indianap-
    olis: Bobbs-Merrill Company, 1948), pp. 365.

Clinard, Outten Jones, Japan's Influence on American Naval
    Power 1897-1917 (Berkeley: University of California
    Press, 1947), pp. 235.

Cohen, Bernard C. , The Political Process and Foreign
    Policy: The Making of the Japanese Peace Settlement
    (Princeton: Princeton University Press, 1957), pp.
    293.

Cohen, Warren I. , The American Revisionists: The Lessons
    of Intervention in World War I (Chicago: University of
    Chicago Press, 1967), pp. 252.

Cole, Wayne S. , An Interpretive History of American Foreign
    Relations (Homewood: Dorsey Press, 1968), pp. 598.

Cole, Wayne S. , Senator Gerald P. Nye and American
    Foreign Relations (Minneapolis: University of Minne-
    sota Press, 1962), pp. 293.

Colegrove, Kenneth, The American Senate and World Peace
    (New York: Vanguard Press, 1944), pp. 209.

Coleman, Arthur P. , The Polish Insurrection of 1863 in the
    Light of New York Editorial Opinion (Williamsport:
    Bayard Press, 1934), pp. 131. Slavonic Series.

Congressional Quarterly Service, Congress and the Nation
    1945-1964 (Washington: Congressional Quarterly
    Service, 1965), pp. 1784 plus pp. 231 appendix.

Congressional Quarterly Service, Congress and the Nation
    1965-1968 (Washington: Congressional Quarterly
    Service, 1969), pp. 974 plus pp. 146 appendix.

Congressional Quarterly Service, Congressional Quarterly

Almanac 1969 (Washington: Congressional Quarterly
Service, 1970), pp. 1248. Volume XXV in series.

Congressional Quarterly Service, Congressional Quarterly
    Almanac 1970 (Washington: Congressional Quarterly
    Service, 1971), pp. 1248. Volume XXVI in series.

Corey, Albert B., The Crisis of 1830-1842 in Canadian-
    American Relations (New Haven: Yale University Press,
    1941), pp. 203.

Costrell, Edwin, How Maine Viewed the War 1914-1917
    (Orono: University of Maine Press, 1940), pp. 101.
    University of Maine Studies/Second Series/Number 49.

Coulter, E. Merton, The Confederate States of America 1861-
    1865 (Baton Rouge: Louisiana State University Press,
    1950), pp. 644.

Council on Foreign Relations, The United States in World
    Affairs 1932 (New York: Harper and Brothers, 1933),
    pp. 355.

Coupland, Sir Reginald, The British Anti-Slavery Movement
    (New York: Barnes and Noble, 1964), pp. 256.

Cox, Isaac J., The West Florida Controversy, 1798-1813
    (Gloucester: Peter Smith, 1967), pp. 699.

Crabb, Cecil V., Jr., Bipartisan Foreign Policy: Myth or
    Reality? (Evanston: Row, Peterson and Company,
    1957), pp. 279.

Craven, Avery O., The Growth of Southern Sectionalism 1848-
    1861 (Baton Rouge: Louisiana State University Press,
    1953), pp. 433.

Crighton, John Clark, Missouri and the World War, 1914-
    1917: A Study in Public Opinion (Columbia: University
    of Missouri Press, 1947) pp. 190. University of
    Missouri Studies/Volume 21/Number 3.

Cummins, Cedric C., Indiana Public Opinion and the World
    War 1914-1917 (Indianapolis: Indiana Historical Bureau,
    1945), pp. 292. Indiana Historical Collections/Volume
    28.

Curry, Ray Watson, Woodrow Wilson and Far Eastern Policy
    1913-1921 (New York: Octagon Books, 1968), pp. 411.

Curli, Merle, The American Peace Crusade 1815-1860 (Dur-
    ham: Duke University Press, 1929), pp. 250.

Dangerfield, Royden J., In Defense of the Senate: A Study in
    Treaty Making (Norman: University of Oklahoma Press,
    1933), pp. 365.

Daniels, Roger, The Politics of Prejudice (New York: Athe-
    neum, 1968), pp. 165.

Davie, Maurice R., World Immigration (New York: Macmillan
    Company, 1947), pp. 588.

Davis, Calvin D., The United States and the First Hague
    Peace Conference (Ithaca: Cornell University Press,
    1962), pp. 236.

Dawson, Raymond H., The Decision to Aid Russia 1941
    (Chapel Hill: University of North Carolina Press,
    1959), pp. 315.

De Conde, Alexander, Entangling Alliance: Politics and Diplo-
    macy under George Washington (Durham: Duke Univer-
    sity Press, 1958), pp. 536.

De Conde, Alexander, A History of American Foreign Policy
    (New York: Charles Scribner's Sons, 1963), pp. 914;
    (New York: Charles Scribner's Sons, 1971), pp. 988.

De Conde, Alexander, and Armin Rappaport, editors, Essays
    Diplomatic and Undiplomatic of Thomas A. Bailey
    (New York: Appleton-Century-Crofts, 1969), pp. 256.

De Grazia, Alfred, The Western Public, 1952 and Beyond
    (Stanford: Stanford University Press, 1954), pp. 226.

De Janes, Robert D., Southern Neo-Isolationism: Case Studies
    in Reciprocal Trade and Foreign Aid, doctoral disser-
    tation, University of Virginia, 1965.

Dennett, Tyler, Americans in Eastern Asia (New York:
    Barnes and Noble, 1963), pp. 725.

Dennison, Eleanor E., The Senate Foreign Relations Committee (Stanford: Stanford University Press, 1942), pp. 201.

Divine, Robert A., The Illusion of Neutrality (Chicago: University of Chicago Press, 1962), pp. 370.

Divine, Robert A., Second Chance: The Triumph of Internationalism in America during World War II (New York: Atheneum, 1967), pp. 371.

Duignan, Peter, and Clarence Clendenen, The United States and the African Slave Trade 1619-1862 (Palo Alto: Hoover Institution, 1963), pp. 72.

Dulles, Foster Rhea, America in the Pacific: A Century of Expansion (Boston: Houghton Mifflin Company, 1938), pp. 299.

Dulles, Foster Rhea, China and America: The Story of Their Relations since 1784 (Port Washington: Kennikat Press, 1967), pp. 277.

Dulles, Foster Rhea, The Road to Teheran: The Story of Russia and America, 1781-1943 (Princeton: Princeton University Press, 1945), pp. 279.

Eaton, Clement, A History of the Old South (New York: Macmillan Company, 1949), pp. 636.

Ellis, L. Ethan, Reciprocity, 1911: A Study in Canadian-American Relations (New Haven: Yale University Press, 1939), pp. 207.

Esthus, Raymond A., Theodore Roosevelt and Japan (Seattle: University of Washington Press, 1966), pp. 329.

Ettinger, Amos, The Mission of Pierre Soule to Spain 1853-1855 (New Haven: Yale University Press, 1932), pp. 559.

Farnsworth, David N., The Senate Committee on Foreign Relations (Urbana: University of Illinois Press, 1961), pp. 189.

Fehrenbach, T. R., F. D. R. 's Undeclared War 1939 to 1941 (New York: David McKay Company, 1967), pp. 344.

Filene, Peter G., Americans and the Soviet Experiment, 1917-1933 (Cambridge: Harvard University Press, 1967), pp. 389.

Fleming, Denna F., The United States and the League of Nations 1918-1920 (New York: Russell and Russell, 1968), pp. 593.

Fleming, Denna Frank, The United States and World Organization 1920-1933 (New York: AMS Press, 1966), pp. 569.

Foner, Philip S., A History of Cuba and Its Relations with the United States, 2 volumes (New York: International Publishers, 1962-3).

Fox, Early Lee, The American Colonization Society 1817-1840 (Baltimore: Johns Hopkins Press, 1919), pp. 231.

Franklin, John Hope, The Militant South 1800-1861 (Cambridge: Belknap Press of Harvard University, 1956), pp. 317.

Fuller, Herbert Bruce, The Purchase of Florida: Its History and Diplomacy (Gainesville: University of Florida Press, 1964), pp. 399.

Gallup, George H., The Gallup Poll: Public Opinion 1935-1971 (New York: Random House, 1972). 3 volumes.

Garris, Roy L., Immigration Restriction (New York: Macmillan Company, 1927), pp. 376.

Genovese, Eugene, The Political Economy of Slavery (New York: Pantheon Books, 1965), pp. 304.

Gerson, Louis L., The Hyphenate in Recent American Politics and Diplomacy (Lawrence: University of Kansas Press, 1964), pp. 325.

Glueck, Alvin C., Jr., Minnesota and the Manifest Destiny of the Canadian Northwest (Toronto: University of Toronto Press, 1965), pp. 311.

Goetzmann, William H., When the Eagle Screamed: The Romantic Horizon in American Diplomacy 1800-1860 (New York: John Wiley and Sons, 1966), pp. 138.

Graber, Doris A., Public Opinion, the President, and Foreign
    Policy: Four Case Studies from the Formative Years
    (New York: Holt, Rinehart, and Winston, 1968), pp.
    374.

Graebner, Norman A., Empire on the Pacific (New York:
    Ronald Press, 1955), pp. 278.

Graebner, Norman A., The New Isolationism: A Study in
    Politics and Foreign Policy since 1950 (New York:
    Ronald Press, 1956), pp. 289.

Graham, Gerald S., Sea Power and British North America
    1783-1820 (New York: Greenwood Press, 1968), pp.302.

Graham, Malbone W., American Diplomacy in the Interna-
    tional Community (Freeport: Books for Libraries Press,
    1969), pp. 279.

Grassmuck, George L., Sectional Biases in Congress on
    Foreign Policy (Baltimore: Johns Hopkins Press, 1951),
    pp. 181. Johns Hopkins University Studies in His-
    torical and Political Science/Series 118/1950/Number 3.

Greene, Theodore P., American Imperialism in 1898 (Boston:
    D. C. Heath and Company, 1955), pp. 105.

Gregg, Robert D., The Influence of Border Troubles on Re-
    lations Between the United States and Mexico 1876-1910
    (Baltimore: Johns Hopkins University Press, 1937),
    pp. 200.

Grenville, John A. S., and George Berkeley Young, Politics,
    Strategy, and American Diplomacy: Studies in Foreign
    Policy, 1873-1917 (New Haven: Yale University Press,
    1966), pp. 352.

Griffin, Charles Carroll, The United States and the Disruption
    of the Spanish Empire 1810-1822 (New York: Columbia
    University Press, 1937), pp. 315.

Griswold, A. Whitney, The Far Eastern Policy of the United
    States (New York: Harcourt, Brace and Company, 1938),
    pp. 530.

Grunder, Garel A., and William E. Livezey, The Philippines
    and the United States (Norman: University of Oklahoma
    Press, 1951), pp. 315.

Hazen, Charles D., Contemporary American Opinion of the
    French Revolution (Gloucester: Peter Smith, 1964),
    pp. 315.

Hero, Alfred O., Jr., Americans in World Affairs (Boston:
    World Peace Foundation, 1959), pp. 165.

Hero, Alfred O., Jr., The Southerner and World Affairs
    (Baton Rouge: Louisiana State University Press, 1965),
    pp. 676.

Hesseltine, William B., and David L. Smiley, The South in
    American History (Englewood Cliffs: Prentice-Hall,
    1960), pp. 630.

Hoag, C. Leonard, Preface to Preparedness (Washington:
    American Council on Public Affairs, 1941), pp. 205.

Holt, W. Stull, Treaties Defeated by the Senate (Gloucester:
    Peter Smith, 1964), pp. 328.

Howard, Warren S., American Slavers and the Federal Law
    1837-1862 (Berkeley: University of California Press,
    1963), pp. 336.

Hubbart, Henry Clyde, The Older Middle West 1840-1880
    (New York: Russell and Russell, 1963), pp. 305.

Jenks, Leland H., Our Cuban Colony (New York: Vanguard
    Press, 1928), pp. 341.

Jensen, Merrill, The New Nation: A History of the United
    States during the Confederation (New York: Alfred A.
    Knopf, 1965), pp. 433.

Jessup, Philip C., International Security: The American Role
    in Collective Action for Peace (New York: Council on
    Foreign Relations, 1935), pp. 157.

Jonas, Manfred, Isolationism in America 1935-1941 (Ithaca:
    Cornell University Press, 1966), pp. 315.

Kaufman, Burton Ira, editor, Washington's Farewell Address:
    The View from the 20th Century (Chicago: Quadrangle
    Books, 1969), pp. 192.

Keenleyside, Hugh L., Canada and the United States (New

York: Alfred A. Knopf, 1952), pp. 406.

Keim, Jeannette, Forty Years of German-American Political
    Relations (Philadelphia: William J. Dorman, 1919),
    pp. 378.

Key, V. O., Jr., Public Opinion and American Democracy
    (New York: Alfred A. Knopf, 1964), pp. 566.

Key, V. O., Jr., Southern Politics: In State and Nation
    (New York: Vintage Books, 1949), pp. 675.

La Feber, Walter, The New Empire: An Interpretation of
    American Expansion 1860-1898 (Ithaca: Cornell Uni-
    versity Press, 1963), pp. 444.

Langer, William L., and S. Everett Gleason, The Challenge
    to Isolation 1937-1940 (New York: Harper and Broth-
    ers, 1952), pp. 794.

Langer, William L., and S. Everett Gleason, The Unde-
    clared War 1940-1941 (New York: Harper and Broth-
    ers, 1953), pp. 963.

Latourette, Kenneth Scott, The History of Early Relations
    Between the United States and China 1784-1844 (New
    Haven: Yale University Press, 1917), pp. 209.

Leopold, Richard W., The Growth of American Foreign
    Policy (New York: Alfred A. Knopf, 1962), pp. 848.

Lerche, Charles O., Jr., Foreign Policy of the American
    People (Englewood Cliffs: Prentice-Hall, 1958), pp.
    547.

Lerche, Charles O., Jr., The Uncertain South (Chicago:
    Quadrangle Books, 1964), pp. 324.

Li, Tien-yi, Woodrow Wilson's China Policy 1913-1917 (New
    York: University of Kansas City Press-Twayne Pub-
    lishers, 1952), pp. 268.

Lillehaugen, Nels Manuel, A Survey of North Dakota News-
    paper Opinion on Foreign Affairs, 1934-1939, Master's
    thesis, University of Wyoming, 1951.

Logan, Rayford, W., The Diplomatic Relations of the United

States with Haiti 1776-1891 (Chapel Hill: University of North Carolina Press, 1941), pp. 516.

Lovenstein, Meno, American Opinion of Soviet Russia (Washington: American Council on Public Affairs, 1941), pp. 210.

Lubell, Samuel, The Future of American Politics (New York: Harper and Brothers, 1965), pp. 270.

McInnis, Edgar W., The Unguarded Frontier: A History of American-Canadian Relations (New York: Russell and Russell, 1970), pp. 384.

McKay, Donald C., The United States and France (Cambridge: Harvard University Press, 1951), pp. 334.

MacRae, Duncan, Jr., Dimensions of Congressional Voting: A Statistical Survey of the House of Representatives in the Eighty-First Congress (Berkeley: University of California Press, 1958), pp. 390. University of California Publications in Sociology and Social Institutions /Volume 1/Number 3.

Mannix, Daniel P., Black Cargoes: A History of the Atlantic Slave Trade 1518-1865 (New York: Viking Press, 1962), pp. 306.

Markel, Lester, Public Opinion and Foreign Policy (New York: Harper and Brothers, 1949), pp. 227.

May, Arthur J., Contemporary American Opinion of the Mid-Century Revolutions in Central Europe, doctoral dissertation, University of Pennsylvania, 1927.

May, Ernest R., American Imperialism: A Speculative Essay (New York: Atheneum, 1968), pp. 239.

May, Ernest R., Imperial Democracy: The Emergence of America as a Great Power (New York: Harcourt, Brace and World, 1961), pp. 318.

May, Ernest R., The World War and American Isolation 1914-1917 (Cambridge: Harvard University Press, 1959), pp. 482.

Merk, Frederick, Manifest Destiny and Mission in American

History (New York: Alfred A. Knopf, 1963), pp. 266.

Merk, Frederick, The Monroe Doctrine and American Expansionism 1843-1849 (New York: Alfred A. Knopf, 1967), pp. 289.

Merk, Frederick, The Oregon Question: Essays in Anglo-American Diplomacy and Politics (Cambridge: Harvard University Press, 1967), pp. 427.

Merk, Frederick (with the collaboration of Lois Bannister Merk), Fruits of Propaganda in the Tyler Administration (Cambridge: Harvard University Press, 1971), pp. 259.

Millis, Walter, Road to War: America 1914-1917 (Boston: Houghton Mifflin Company, 1935), pp. 466.

Miner, Dwight Carroll, The Fight for the Panama Route (New York: Columbia University Press, 1940), pp. 469.

Montague, Ludwell Lee, Haiti and the United States 1714-1938 (Durham: Duke University Press, 1940), pp. 308.

Morison, Samuel Eliot, Frederick Merk, and Frank Freidel, Dissent in Three American Wars (Cambridge: Harvard University Press, 1970), pp. 104.

Morris, Richard B., Encyclopedia of American History (New York: Harper and Brothers, 1961), pp. 840.

Morris, Richard B., The Peacemakers: The Great Powers and American Independence (New York: Harper and Row, 1965), pp. 572.

Mowat, R. B., The Diplomatic Relations of Great Britain and the United States (New York: Longmans, Green and Company, 1925), pp. 350.

Neu, Charles E., An Uncertain Friendship: Theodore Roosevelt and Japan, 1906-1909 (Cambridge: Harvard University Press, 1967), pp. 347.

Notter, Harley, The Origins of the Foreign Policy of Woodrow Wilson (New York: Russell and Russell, 1965), pp. 695.

Nye, Russel B., Midwestern Progressive Politics (East Lan-
    sing: Michigan State University Press, 1959), pp. 398.

O'Connor, Richard, Pacific Destiny: An Informal History of
    the U. S. in the Far East, 1776-1968 (Boston: Little,
    Brown and Company, 1969), pp. 505.

Palmer, Thomas W., Jr., Search for a Latin American
    Policy (Gainesville: University of Florida Press, 1962),
    pp. 217.

Parry, Hugh Jones, The Spanish Civil War: A Study in
    American Public Opinion, Propaganda, and Pressure
    Groups, doctoral dissertation, University of Southern
    California, 1949.

Paul, Rodman W., The Abrogation of the Gentlemen's Agree-
    ment (Cambridge: Harvard Chapter of Phi Beta Kappa,
    1936), pp. 117. Harvard Phi Beta Kappa Prize Essay
    for 1936.

Perkins, Bradford, Castlereagh and Adams: England and the
    United States 1812-1823 (Berkeley: University of Cali-
    fornia Press, 1964), pp. 364.

Perkins, Bradford, The First Rapprochement: England and
    the United States 1795-1805 (Berkeley: University of
    California Press, 1967), pp. 257.

Perkins, Bradford, Prologue to War: England and the United
    States 1805-1812 (Berkeley: University of California
    Press, 1963), pp. 457.

Perkins, Dexter, A History of the Monroe Doctrine (Boston:
    Little, Brown and Company, 1963), pp. 462.

Perkins, Dexter, The Monroe Doctrine, 1823-1826 (Cam-
    bridge: Harvard University Press, 1927), pp. 280.

Perkins, Dexter, The Monroe Doctrine, 1826-1867 (Balti-
    more: Johns Hopkins Press, 1933), pp. 580.

Perkins, Dexter, The Monroe Doctrine, 1867-1907 (Balti-
    more: Johns Hopkins Press, 1937), pp. 480.

Philbrick, Francis S., The Rise of the West (New York:
    Harper and Row, 1965), pp. 398.

Phillips, Paul C., The West in the Diplomacy of the American
    Revolution (New York: Johnson Reprint Corporation,
    1967), pp. 247. University of Illinois Studies in the
    Social Sciences/Volume 11/Numbers 2 and 3/October
    1913/pp. 117-247.

Pletcher, David M., The Awkward Years: American Foreign
    Relations under Garfield and Arthur (Columbia: Uni-
    versity of Missouri Press, 1962), pp. 381.

Pomeroy, Earl, The Pacific Slope (New York: Alfred A.
    Knopf, 1965), pp. 404.

Pope Hennessy, James, Sins of the Fathers: A Study of the
    Atlantic Slave Traders 1441-1807 (New York: Alfred
    A. Knopf, 1968), pp. 286.

Pratt, Julius W., Expansionists of 1812 (Gloucester: Peter
    Smith, 1957), pp. 309.

Pratt, Julius W., Expansionists of 1898 (Gloucester: Peter
    Smith, 1959), pp. 393.

Radke, August Carl, Jr., John Tyler Morgan, An Expan-
    sionist Senator, 1877-1907, doctoral dissertation, Uni-
    versity of Washington, 1953.

Rappaport, Armin, Issues in American Diplomacy, 2 volumes
    (New York: Macmillan Company, 1965.

Rauch, Basil, American Interest in Cuba: 1848-1855 (New
    York: Columbia University Press, 1948), pp. 323.
    Studies in History, Economics, and Public Law/Num-
    ber 537.

Rauch, Basil, The History of the New Deal (New York: Cap-
    ricorn Books, 1963), pp. 368.

Rhodes, James Ford, History of the United States from the
    Compromise of 1850, 9 volumes (New York: Macmillan
    Company, 1893-1922).

Rieselbach, Leroy N., The Roots of Isolationism (Indianap-
    olis: Bobbs-Merrill Company, 1966), pp. 240.

Riggs, Fred W., Pressures on Congress: A Study of the Re-
    peal of Chinese Exclusion (New York: Columbia Uni-

versity-King's Crown Press, 1950), pp. 260.

Rives, George Lockhart, The United States and Mexico 1821-1848, 2 volumes (New York: Charles Scribner's Sons, 1913).

Rosenau, James N., National Leadership and Foreign Policy (Princeton: Princeton University Press, 1963), pp. 409.

Rossiter, Clinton, 1787: The Grand Convention (New York: Macmillan Company, 1966), pp. 443.

Rovere, Richard H., and Arthur M. Schlesinger, Jr., The General and the President and the Future of American Foreign Policy (New York: Farrar, Straus, and Young, 1951), pp. 336.

Russel, Robert Royal, Economic Aspects of Southern Sectionalism, 1840-1861 (New York: Russell and Russell, 1960), pp. 325.

Sanborn, Frederic R., Design for War: A Study of Secret Power Politics 1937-1941 (New York: Devin-Adair Company, 1951), pp. 607.

Sandmeyer, Elmer Clarence, The Anti-Chinese Movement in California (Urbana: University of Illinois Press, 1939), pp. 127.

Savelle, Max, The Origins of American Diplomacy: The International History of Angloamerica 1492-1763 (New York: Macmillan Company, 1967), pp. 624.

Schlesinger, Arthur M., Jr., The Bitter Heritage: Vietnam and American Democracy 1941-1966 (Boston: Houghton Mifflin Company, 1967), pp. 126.

Schultz, Harold S., Nationalism and Sectionalism in South Carolina 1852-1860 (New York: Da Capo Press, 1969), pp. 259.

Scott, William A., and Stephen B. Withey, The United States and the United Nations: The Public View 1945-1955 (New York: Manhattan Publishing Company, 1958, pp. 314.

Seabury, Paul, The Waning of Southern "Internationalism"

(Princeton: Princeton University Center of International Studies, 1957), pp. 30.

Sears, Louis Martin, Jefferson and the Embargo (Durham: Duke University Press, 1927), pp. 340.

Shannon, W. Wayne, Party, Constituency and Congressional Voting (Baton Rouge: Louisiana State University Press, 1968), pp. 202.

Shippee, Lester B., Canadian-American Relations 1849-1874 (New Haven: Yale University Press, 1939), pp. 514.

Simkins, Francis Butler, A History of the South (New York: Alfred A. Knopf, 1965), pp. 675.

Sitterson, J. Carlyle, Studies in Southern History (Chapel Hill: University of North Carolina, Press, 1957), pp. 168.

Smith, Daniel M., American Intervention, 1917: Sentiment, Self-Interest, or Ideals? (Boston: Houghton Mifflin Company, 1966), pp. 260.

Sobel, Robert, The Origins of Interventionism: The United States and the Russo-Finnish War (New York: Bookman Associates, 1960), pp. 204.

Spanier, John W., The Truman-MacArthur Controversy and the Korean War (Cambridge: Belknap Press of Harvard University, 1959), pp. 311.

Steele, A. T., The American People and China (New York: McGraw-Hill Book Company, 1966), pp. 321.

Stephenson, George, A History of American Immigration 1820-1914 (Boston: Ginn and Company, 1926), pp. 316.

Stone, I. F., The Hidden History of the Korean War (New York: Monthly Review Press, 1952), pp. 368.

Sydner, Charles S., The Development of Southern Sectionalism 1819-1848 (Baton Rouge: Louisiana State University Press, 1948), pp. 400.

Tansill, Charles Callan, America Goes to War (Gloucester: Peter Smith, 1963), pp. 731.

Tansill, Charles Callan, Back Door to War: The Roosevelt
    Foreign Policy 1933-1941 (Chicago: Henry Regnery
    Company, 1952), pp. 690.

Tansill, Charles Callan, The Foreign Policy of Thomas F.
    Bayard 1885-1897 (New York: Fordham University
    Press, 1940), pp. 800.

Tansill, Charles Callan, The United States and Santo Domingo,
    1798-1873 (Baltimore: Johns Hopkins Press, 1938),
    pp. 487.

Tarsaidze, Alexandre, Czars and Presidents (New York:
    McDowell, Obolensky, 1958), pp. 383.

Tate, Merze, The United States and the Hawaiian Kingdom:
    A Political History (New Haven: Yale University Press,
    1965), pp. 374.

Taylor, F. Jay, The United States and the Spanish Civil War
    (New York: Bookman Associates, 1956), pp. 288.

Thomas, Benjamin P., Russo-American Relations, 1815-1867
    (Baltimore: Johns Hopkins Press, 1930), pp. 185.

Thomas, Charles M., American Neutrality in 1793: A Study
    in Cabinet Government (New York: AMS Press, 1967),
    pp. 294.

Tindall, George Brown, The Emergence of the New South
    1913-1945 (Baton Rouge: Louisiana State University
    Press, 1967), pp. 807.

Tong, Te-kong, United States Diplomacy in China 1844-60
    (Seattle: University of Washington Press, 1964), pp.
    332.

Traina, Richard P., American Diplomacy and the Spanish
    Civil War (Bloomington: Indiana University Press,
    1968), pp. 301.

Treat, Payson J., Diplomatic Relations between the United
    States and Japan 1895-1905 (Gloucester: Peter Smith,
    1963), pp. 291.

Treat, Payson J., Japan and the United States 1853-1921
    (Boston: Houghton Mifflin Company, 1921), pp. 283.

Tupper, Eleanor, Japan in American Public Opinion (New York: Macmillan Company, 1937), pp. 465.

Turner, Frederick Jackson, The United States, 1830-1850; The Nation and Its Sections (Gloucester: Peter Smith, 1958), pp. 602.

Turner, Julius, Party and Constituency: Pressures on Congress (Baltimore: Johns Hopkins Press, 1951), pp. 190. Johns Hopkins University Studies in Historical and Political Science/Series 69/1951/Number 1.

Turner, Julius and Edward V. Schneier, Jr., reviser, Party and Constituency: Pressures on Congress (Baltimore: Johns Hopkins Press, 1970), pp. 312.

Tyler, Alice Felt, The Foreign Policy of James G. Blaine (Minneapolis: University of Minnesota Press, 1927), pp. 411.

U. S. Congress, 76th Congress, 1st Session, House of Representatives, Committee on Foreign Affairs, American Neutrality Policy: Editorials, revised edition (Washington: United States Government Printing Office, 1939), pp. 62.

The United States Public and the United Nations (New York: Carnegie Endowment for International Peace, 1958), pp. 52.

Updyke, Frank A., The Diplomacy of the War of 1812 (Baltimore: Johns Hopkins Press, 1915), pp. 494.

Varg, Paul A., Foreign Policies of the Founding Fathers (East Lansing: Michigan State University Press, 1963), pp. 316.

Warner, Donald F., The Idea of Continental Union: Agitation for the Annexation of Canada to the United States 1849-1893 (Lexington: University of Kentucky Press, 1960), pp. 276. Published for the Mississippi Valley Historical Association.

Welles, Sumner, Naboth's Vineyard: The Dominican Republic 1844-1924, 2 volumes (Mamaroneck: Paul Appel, Publisher, 1966).

Westerfield, H. Bradford, Foreign Policy and Party Politics:
    Pearl Harbor to Korea (New Haven: Yale University
    Press, 1955), pp. 448.

Weston, Rubin Francis, Racism in U.S. Imperialism (Colum-
    bia: University of South Carolina Press, 1972), pp. 291.

Whitaker, Arthur P., The United States and the Independence
    of Latin America 1800-1830 (Baltimore: Johns Hopkins
    Press, 1941), pp. 632.

White, Elizabeth Brett, American Opinion of France: From
    Lafayette to Poincaré (New York: Alfred A. Knopf,
    1927), pp. 346.

White, Patrick C. T., A Nation on Trial: America and the
    War of 1812 (New York: John Wiley and Sons, 1965),
    pp. 177.

Wilkerson, Marcus M., Public Opinion and the Spanish-
    American War (New York: Russell and Russell, 1932),
    pp. 141.

Williams, William A., American-Russian Relations 1781-1947
    (New York: Rinehart and Company, 1952), pp. 367.

Winks, Robin W., Canada and the United States: The Civil
    War Years (Baltimore: Johns Hopkins Press, 1960),
    pp. 430.

Wisan, Joseph, The Cuban Crisis as Reflected in the New
    York Press (1895-1898) (New York: Columbia Univer-
    sity Press, 1934), pp. 477. Studies in History, Eco-
    nomics, and Public Law/Number 403.

Woldman, Albert A., Lincoln and the Russians (Cleveland:
    World Publishing Company, 1952), pp. 311.

Wood, Bryce, The Making of the Good Neighbor Policy (New
    York: Columbia University Press, 1961), pp. 438.

Woodward, C. Vann, Origins of the New South 1877-1913
    (Baton Rouge: Louisiana State University Press, 1951),
    pp. 542.

Woodward, Julian L., Foreign News in American Morning
    Newspapers (New York: Columbia University Press,

1930), pp. 122.

Young, Marvin Blatt, The Rhetoric of Empire: American China Policy 1895-1901 (Cambridge: Harvard University Press, 1968), pp. 302.

Zu Stolbert-Wernigerode, Count Otto, Germany and the United States of America during the Era of Bismarck (Reading: Henry Janssen Foundation, 1937), pp. 358.

Magazine and Journal Articles

"Africa in American Politics, " in Africa Today (XIV, December 1966), passim.

"The American Scene, " in Living Age (CCCLV, January 1939), 467-8.

"Americans on the War: Divided, Glum, Unwilling to Quit" (Time-Louis Harris Poll), in Time (XCIV, October 31, 1969), 13-5.

Appel, John C., "The Unionization of Florida Cigarmakers and the Coming of the War with Spain, " in Hispanic American Historical Review (XXXVI, February 1956), 38-49.

Auxier, George W., "Middle Western Newspapers and the Spanish-American War, 1895-1898, " in Mississippi Valley Historical Review (XXVI, March 1940), 523-34.

Bacon, Corinne, "New England Sectionalism, " in New England Magazine (XII, April 1895), 241-54.

Bailey, Hugh C., "Alabama's Political Leaders and the Acquisition of Florida, " in Florida Historical Quarterly (XXXV, July 1956), 17-29.

Bailey, Thomas A., "The Russian Fleet Myth Re-Examined, " in Mississippi Valley Historical Review (XXXVIII, June 1951), 81-90.

Berg, Meredith W., and David M. Berg, "The Rhetoric of War Preparation: The New York Press in 1898, " in Journalism Quarterly (XLV, Winter 1968), 653-60.

Berthoff, Rowland T. , "Southern Attitudes toward Immigration, 1865-1914. " in Journal of Southern History (XVII, August 1951), 328-60.

Billington, Monroe, "Senator Thomas P. Gore: Southern Isolationist, " in Southwestern Social Science Quarterly (XLII, March 1962), 381-9.

Billington, Ray Allen, "The Origins of Middle Western Isolationism, " in Political Science Quarterly (LX, March 1945), 44-64.

Blakely, Robert J. , "The Midwest and the War, " in Foreign Affairs (XX, July 1942), 635-49.

Bradley, Harold Whitman, "Hawaii and the American Penetration of the Northeastern Pacific, 1800-1845, " in Pacific Historical Review (XII, September 1943), 277-86.

Bridges, Lamar W. , "Zimmermann Telegram: Reaction of Southern, Southwestern Newspapers, " in Journalism Quarterly (XLVI, Spring 1969), 81-6.

Brown, Maynard W. , "American Public Opinion and Events Leading to the World War, 1912-1914, " in Journalism Quarterly (XIV, March 1937), 23-34.

Buchanan, Russell, "American Editors Examine American War Aims and Plans in April, 1917, " in Pacific Historical Review (IX, September 1940), 253-65.

Burnette, O. Lawrence, Jr. , "John Tyler Morgan and Expansion Sentiment in the New South, " in Alabama Review (XVIII, July 1965), 163-82.

Campbell, Charles S. , Jr. , "American Tariff Interests and the Northeastern Fisheries, 1883-1888, " in Canadian Historical Review (XLV, September 1964), 212-28.

Cantril, Hadley, Donald Rugg, and Frederick Williams, "America Faces the War: Shifts in Opinion, " in Public Opinion Quarterly, (IV, December 1940), 651-3.

Cardon, A. F. , "Senator Reed Smoot and the Mexican Revolutions, " in Utah Historical Quarterly (XXXI, Spring 1963), 151-63.

Carleton, William G., "Isolationism and the Middle West, "
    in Mississippi Valley Historical Review (XXXIII, De-
    cember 1946), 377-90.

Carnathan, W. J., "The Proposal to Reopen the African Slave
    Trade in the South, 1854-1860, " in South Atlantic
    Quarterly (XXV, October 1926), 410-29.

"Choose Your Poll, " in Nation (CCV, July 31, 1967), 69-70.

Cogswell, Andrew C., "The Montana Press and War: 1914 to
    1917, " in Journalism Quarterly (XXI, Summer 1944),
    137-47.

Cole, Wayne S., "America First and the South, 1940-1941, "
    in Journal of Southern History (XXII, February 1956),
    36-47.

Congressional Record, passim.

"Contours, " in Time (XXXIII, April 24, 1939), 16-7.

Costrell, Edwin, "Newspaper Attitudes toward War in Maine,
    1914-17, " in Journalism Quarterly (XVI, December
    1939), 334-44.

Cozort, William T., "House Opposition to Foreign Aid Leg-
    islation, " in Southwestern Social Science Quarterly
    (XLII, September 1961), 159-61.

Curti, Merle E., "The Impact of the Revolutions of 1848 on
    American Thought, " in Proceedings of the American
    Philosophical Society (XCIII, June 1949), 209-15.

Curti, Merle E., "John C. Calhoun and the Unification of
    Germany, " in American Historical Review (XL, April
    1935), 476-8.

Curtis, Eugene N., "American Opinion of the French Nine-
    teenth-Century Revolutions, " in American Historical
    Review (XXIX, January 1924), 249-70.

Dawson, Jerry F., "Southern Baptist Efforts to Influence
    American Foreign Policy, 1878-1888, " in Rocky Moun-
    tain Social Science Journal (IV, April 1967), 78-87.

De Conde, Alexander, "The South and Isolationism, " in

Journal of Southern History (XXIV, August 1958), 332-46.

Detter, Raymond A., "The Cuban Junta and Michigan: 1895-1898, " in Michigan History (XLVIII, March 1964), 35-46.

Dodd, William E., "The West and the War with Mexico, " in Journal of the Illinois State Historical Society (V, July 1912), 159-72.

"Doubts about Vietnam, " in Newseek (LXX, October 23, 1967), 96.

Douglas, Paul H., "A New Isolationism--Ripples or Tide?" in New York Times Magazine, August 18, 1957, 18, 54-6.

Dozer, Donald Marquand, "The Opposition to Hawaiian Reciprocity, 1876-1888, " in Pacific Historical Review (XIV, June 1945), 157-83.

Dupre, Huntley, "The Kentucky Gazette Reports the French Revolution, " in Mississippi Valley Historical Review (XXVI, September 1939), 163-80.

Ellis, L. Ethan, "The Northwest and the Reciprocity Agreement of 1911, " in Mississippi Valley Historical Review (XXVI, June 1939), 55-66.

Erskine, Hazel Gaudet, "The Berlin Situation, " in Public Opinion Quarterly, (XXV, Winter 1961), 657-9.

Erskine, Hazel Gaudet, "Is War a Mistake?" in Public Opinion Quarterly (XXXIV, Spring 1970), 136-7, 141-2, 146-7.

Erskine, Hazel Gaudet, "Religious Prejudice, Part 2: Anti-Semitism, " in Public Opinion Quarterly (XXIX, Winter 1965-6), 662-3.

Erskine, Hazel Gaudet, "Western Partisanship in the Middle East, " in Public Opinion Quarterly (XXXIII, Winter 1970), 629.

Falk, Karen, "Public Opinion in Wisconsin during World War I, " in Wisconsin Magazine of History (XXV, June 1942), 389-407.

Falk, Stanley L. , "Some Contemporary Views of the Monroe Doctrine: The United States Press in 1823, " in Americas (XII, October 1955), 183-193.

"Fight for Berlin?--'If We Must...,'" in Newsweek (LVIII, July 17, 1961), 18-20.

Fornell, Earl W. , "Texans and Filibusters in the 1850's, " in Southwestern Historical Quarterly (LIX, April 1956), 411-28.

"47 States--Ike Was Right... In Facing Up to the Crisis With U. S. Forces, " in Newsweek (LII, August 4, 1958), 16-8.

Francis, Michael J. , "The U. S. Press and Castro: A Study in Declining Relations, " in Journalism Quarterly (XLIV, Summer 1967), 257-66.

Franklin, John Hope, "Southern Expansionists of 1846, " in Journal of Southern History (XXV, August 1959), 323-38.

French, J. Wymond, and Paul H. Wagner, "American Reporting of a Hitler Speech, " in Journalism Quarterly (XVII, September 1940), 201-6.

Gallup Opinion Index, 1965- , passim.

Gibson, George H. , "Attitudes in North Carolina Regarding the Independence of Cuba, 1868-1898, " in North Carolina Historical Review (XLIII, Winter 1966), 43-65.

Grantham, Dewey W. , Jr. , "The Southern Senators and the League of Nations, 1918-1920, " in North Carolina Historical Review (XXVI, April 1949), 187-205.

Hanna, Kathryn Abbey, "The Roles of the South in the French Intervention in Mexico, " in Journal of Southern History (XX, February 1954), 3-21.

Hardt, Hanno R. E. , "International News into North Dakota," in North Dakota Quarterly (XXXV, Autumn 1967), 114-8.

Harrington, Fred H. , "The Anti-Imperialist Movement in the United States, 1898-1900, " in Mississippi Valley Historical Review (XXII, September 1935), 211-30.

Haynes, Robert V., "The Southwest and the War of 1812, " in Louisiana History (V, Winter 1964), 41-51.

Henderson, Gavin B., "Southern Designs on Cuba, 1854-1857 and Some European Opinions, " in Journal of Southern History (V, August 1939), 371-85.

Hero, Alfred O., Jr., "The American Public and the U. N. ," in Journal of Conflict Resolution (X, December 1966), 464-5.

Hitchens, Harold L., "Influences on the Congressional Decision to Pass the Marshall Plan, " in Western Political Quarterly, (XXI, March 1968), 56-7.

Horsman, Reginald, "Western War Aims, 1811-1812, " in Indiana Magazine of History (LIII, March 1957), 1-18.

"How U. S. Voters Feel About Cuba, " in Newsweek (LX, October 22, 1962), 21-5.

Hundley, Norris, "The Politics of Water and Geography: California and the Mexican-American Treaty of 1944, " in Pacific Historical Review (XXXVI, May 1967), 209-26.

Hyslop, Beatrice F., "The American Press and the French Revolution of 1789, " in Proceedings of the American Philosophical Society (CIV, February 1960), 54-85.

Hyslop, Beatrice F., "American Press Reports of the French Revolution, 1789-1794, " in New York Historical Society Quarterly (XLII, October 1958), 329-48.

Irish, Marian D., "Foreign Policy and the South, " in Journal of Politics (X, May 1948), 306-26.

Jewell, Malcolm, "Evaluating the Decline of Southern Internationalism Through Senatorial Roll Call Votes, " in Journal of Politics (XXI, November 1959), 624-46.

Jones, Horace Perry, "Southern Opinion of the Crimean War, " in Journal of Mississippi History (XXIX, May 1967), 95-117.

Karlin, Jules Alexander, "The Anti-Chinese Outbreaks in

Seattle, 1885-1886, " in Pacific Northwest Quarterly (XXXIX, April 1948), 103-130.

Karlin, Jules Alexander, "The Anti-Chinese Outbreak in Tacoma, 1885, " in Pacific Historical Review (XXIII, August 1954), 271-83.

Karlin, Jules Alexander, "The Italo-American Incident of 1891 and the Road to Reunion, " in Journal of Southern History (VIII, May 1942), 242-6.

Kaufman, Martin, "1863: Poland, Russia and the United States, " in Polish-American Studies (XXI, January-June 1964), 10-5.

Kelley, Donald Brooks, "Mississippi and the 'Splendid Little War' of 1898, " in Journal of Mississippi History (XXVI, May 1964), 123-34.

Kennedy, Padraic Colum, "La Follette's Imperialist Flirta-tion, " in Pacific Historical Review (XXIX, May 1960), 131-44.

"King Saud's Visit, " in America (XCVI, February 16, 1957), 548.

Kniskern, Maynard, "Clues to the Midwestern Mind, " in New York Times Magazine, September 15, 1963, 33, 110, 2-3.

Larson, Bruce L. , "Kansas and the Panay Incident, 1937, " in Kansas Historical Quarterly (XXXI, Autumn 1965), 233-44.

Lasch, Christopher, "The Anti-Imperialists, the Philippines, and the Inequality of Man, " in Journal of Southern His-tory (XXIV, August 1958), 319-31.

Latimer, Margaret Kinard, "South Carolina - A Protagonist of the War of 1812, " in American Historical Review (LXI, July 1956), 914-29.

Lemons, J. Stanley, "The Cuban Crisis of 1895-1898: News-papers and Nativism, " in Missouri Historical Review (LX, October 1965), 63-74.

Leopold, Richard W. , "The Mississippi Valley and American

Foreign Policy, 1890-1941: An Assessment and an
Appeal, " in Mississippi Valley Historical Review
(XXXVII, March 1951), 625-42.

Lerche, Charles, "Southern Congressmen and the New Isolationism, " in Political Science Quarterly (LXXV, September 1960), 321-37.

Link, Arthur S., "The Middle West and the Coming of World
War I, " in Ohio State Archaeological and Historical
Quarterly (LXII, April 1953), 109-21.

Livermore, Seward W., "The Sectional Issue in the 1918
Congressional Elections, " in Mississippi Valley Historical Review (XXXV, June 1948), 29-36.

Long, Durwood, "Alabama Opinion and the Whig Cuban Policy,
1849-1851, " in Alabama Historical Quarterly (XXV,
Fall and Winter 1963), 262-79.

Lowenthal, David, "The Maine Press and the Aroostook War,"
in Canadian Historical Review (XXXII, December
1951), 315-36.

Lubell, Samuel, "Who Votes Isolationist and Why, " Harper's
Magazine (CCII, April 1951), 29-36.

Marraro, Howard R., "American Opinion on Sardinia's Participation in the Crimean War, " in South Atlantic
Quarterly (XLVI, October 1947), 496-510.

Marwell, Gerald, "Party, Region, and the Dimensions of Conflict in the House of Representatives 1949-1954, " in
American Political Science Review (LXI, June 1967),
395-9.

Maxwell, Anne, "After War--Peace?" in Woman's Home
Companion (LXX, April 1943), 18-19.

Mickelson, Peter, "Nationalism in Minnesota during the
Spanish-American War, " in Minnesota History (XLI,
Spring 1968), 1-12.

Moore, J. Preston, "Pierre Soule: Southern Expansionist and
Promoter, " in Journal of Southern History (XXI, May
1955), 203-23.

Myers, David S., "Editorials and Foreign Affairs in the 1964 Presidential Campaign, " in Journalism Quarterly (XLV, Summer 1968), 211-8.

Myers, David S., "Editorials and Foreign Affairs in the 1968 Presidential Campaign, " in Journalism Quarterly (XLVII, Spring 1970), 57-64.

Newby, I. A., "States' Rights and Southern Congressmen during World War I, " in Phylon (XXIV, Spring 1963), 34-50.

Oliva, L. Jay, "America Meets Russia: 1854, " in Journalism Quarterly (XL, Spring 1963), 65-9.

Oliver, John W., "Louis Kossuth's Appeal to the Middle West - 1852, " in Mississippi Valley Historical Review (XIV, March 1928), 481-95.

Paul, Rodman W., "The Origin of the Chinese Issue in California, " in Mississippi Valley Historical Review (XXV, September 1938), 181-96.

Ready, Milton L., "Georgia's Entry into World War I, " in Georgia Historical Quarterly (LII, September 1968), 256-64.

"A Restored Position: Popular Response to Korea Means the U. S. Has Mobility to Act, " in Life (XXIX, July 17, 1950), 40.

Rieselbach, Leroy N., "The Basis of Isolationist Behavior," in Public Opinion Quarterly (XXIV, Winter 1960), 645-57.

Rieselbach, Leroy N., "The Demography of the Congressional Vote on Foreign Aid, 1939-1958, " in American Political Science Review (LVIII, September 1964), 581-8.

Risjord, Norman K., "1812: Conservatives, War Hawks, and the Nation's Honor, " in William and Mary Quarterly (XVIII, April 1961), 196-210.

Rolle, Andrew F., "California Filibustering and the Hawaiian Kingdom, " in Pacific Historical Review (XIX, August 1950), 251-63.

Roper, Elmo, "American Attitudes on World Organization, " in Public Opinion Quarterly (XVII, Winter 1953), 410.

Roper, Elmo and Louis Harris, "The Press and the Great Debate, " in Saturday Review of Literature (XXXIV, July 14, 1951), 6-9, 29-31.

Rowell, Chester H. , "The Pacific Coast Looks Abroad, " in Foreign Affairs (XVIII, January 1940), 211-9.

Russell, James T. , and Quincy Wright, "National Attitudes on the Far Eastern Controversy, " in American Political Science Review (XXVII, August 1933).

Russett, Bruce M. , "Demography, Salience, and Isolationist Behavior, " in Public Opinion Quarterly (XXIV, Winter 1960), 658-64.

Sanders, Ralph, "Congressional Reaction in the United States to the Panama Congress of 1826, " in Americas (XI, October 1954), 141-54.

Scheips, Paul J. , "United States Commercial Pressures for a Nicaragua Canal in the 1890's, " in Americas (XX, April 1964), 333-58.

Schellings, William J. , "Florida and the Cuban Revolution, 1895-1898, " in Florida Historical Quarterly (XXXIX, October 1960), 175-86.

Sheean, Vincent, "From a Lecturer's Notes, " in Asia (XLVI, May 1946), 197-200.

"Shifting on the War, " in Newsweek (LXXI, March 25, 1968), 84-5.

Simmons, George E. , "The 'Cold War' in Large-City Dailies of the United States, " in Journalism Quarterly (XXV, Winter 1948), 354-9, 400.

"Sizing up the Public on the War, " in Business Week, February 24, 1968, 37.

Smith, Frank E. , "Valor's Second Prize: Southern Racism and Internationalism, " in South Atlantic Quarterly (LXIV, Summer 1965), 296-303.

Smuckler, Ralph H., "The Region of Isolationism, " in American Political Science Review (XLVII, June 1953), 386-401.

Startt, James D., "Early Press Reaction to Wilson's League Proposal, " in Journalism Quarterly (XXXIX, Summer 1962), 301-8.

Startt, James D., "Wilson's Trip to Paris: Profile of Press Response, " in Journalism Quarterly (XLVI, Winter 1969), 737-42.

"The States: Support & Concern, " in Time (LXXXVII, May 6, 1966), 21.

Talmadge, John E., "Georgia's Federalist Press and the War of 1812, " in Journal of Southern History (XIX, November 1953), 488-500.

Taylor, George R., "Agrarian Discontent in the Mississippi Valley Preceding the War of 1812, " in Journal of Political Economy (XXXIX, August 1931), 471-505.

Thorson, Winston B., "America Public Opinion and the Portsmouth Peace Conference, " in American Historical Review (LIII, April 1948), 439-64.

Thorson, Winston B., "Pacific Northwest Opinion on the Russo-Japanese War of 1904-1905, " in Pacific Northwest Quarterly (XXXV, October 1944), 305-22.

Tweton, D. Jerome, "The Border Farmer and the Canadian Reciprocity Issue, 1911-1912, " in Agricultural History (XXXVII, October 1963), 235-41.

Urban, C. Stanley, "The Ideology of Southern Imperialism; New Orleans and the Caribbean, 1845-1860, " in Louisiana Historical Quarterly (XXXIX, January 1956), 48-73.

"A Voice for the Voiceless, " in Nation (CCV, October 30, 1967), 421, 35.

Warner, Donald F., "Drang Nach Norden: The United States and the Riel Rebellion, " in Mississippi Valley Historical Review (XXXIX, March 1953), 693-712.

Waymack, W. W., "The Middle West Looks Abroad, " in

Foreign Affairs (XVIII, April 1940), 535-45.

Welch, Richard E., Jr., "American Public Opinion and the Purchase of Russian America, " in American Slavic and East European Review (XVII, December 1958), 481-94.

Wieczerzak, Joseph W., "American Opinion and the Warsaw Disturbances of 1861, " in Polish Review (VII, Summer 1962), 67-83.

Wieczerzak, Joseph W., "American Reactions to the Polish Insurrection of 1863, " in Polish American Studies (XXII, July-December 1965), 90-8.

Wiley, Alexander, "The Committee on Foreign Relations, " in Annals (CCLXXXIX, September 1953), 59.

Wilkerson, Marcus M., "The Press and the Spanish-American War, " in Journalism Quarterly (IX, June 1932), 129-48.

Wilkins, Robert P., "Middle Western Isolationism: A Re-examination, " in North Dakota Quarterly (XXV, Summer 1957), 69-76.

Wilkins, Robert P., "The Nonpartisan League and Upper Midwest Isolationism, " in Agricultural History (XXXIX, April 1965), 102-9.

Williams, Frederick W., "Regional Attitudes on International Cooperation, " in Public Opinion Quarterly (IX, Spring 1945), 38-50.

Wiltse, Charles M., "A Critical Southerner; John C. Calhoun on the Revolutions of 1848, " in Journal of Southern History (XV, August 1949), 299-310.

Wortman, Roy T., "Denver's Anti-Chinese Riot, 1880, " in Colorado Magazine (XLII, Fall 1965), 275-91.

Wright, James D., "Life, Time, and the Fortunes of War," in Trans-Action (IX, January 1972), 42-52.

Wright, Quincy, and Carl J. Nelson, "American Attitudes toward Japan and China, 1937-38, " in Public Opinion Quarterly (III, January 1939), 46-62.

Young, Kimball, "Content Analysis of the Treatment of the Marshall Plan in Certain Representative American Newspapers, " in Journal of Social Psychology (XXXIII, May 1951), 163-85.

"The Zinn Position, " in Nation (CCV, August 28, 1967), 131.

Executive Journal of the Proceedings of
the Senate of the United States of America

This the key source for Senatorial roll-call votes on treaties, which sometimes were debated and ratified in secret session, and the proceedings not made public until a much later date. Aside from the official continuing set that has been published over the years by the Government Printing Office in Washington, there is another set of 36 volumes covering the years 1789 through 1906 which the Johnson Reprint Corporation of New York City released in 1969. Invaluable for the roll-call votes, these two sets are not as valuable for the debates, although they do cover the amendments.

Congressional Record and Its Predecessors

Over the years the name has changed, but the contents have remained the same. Among the predecessors of the Congressional Record have been the Debates and Proceedings, sometimes called the Annals of Congress (1789-1824), the Register of Debates (1824-37), and the Congressional Globe (1833-1873). Unlike the Executive Proceedings, the Congressional Record includes the actual debates as well as the roll-call votes on treaties--except when the Senate met in executive session, in which case one must turn to the former. In addition, the Congressional Record sets forth the proceedings of the House of Representatives. While the House did not ratify treaties, it must pass on other legislation directly related to foreign policy, including all appropriation bills.

NAME INDEX

Note: Because of the frequency with which they occur throughout the text, the following items do not appear here: Democratic Party, Republican Party, Congress of the United States, House of Representatives, Senate.

A

Abolitionists 136
Acheson, Dean 250
Adams, Brooks 133
Adams, Charles Francis 70, 146
Adams, Ephraim D. 88
Adams, Henry 45
Adams, John 1-3, 6-7, 9, 18, 20, 32
Adams, John Quincy 21, 25-6, 31, 36, 41-4, 48-51, 56-7, 63, 65, 70, 79, 86, 93
Adams-Onis Transcontinental Treaty 36, 41-4, 46, 56
Addington 47
Adler, Selig 200
Africa Today 254, 260
African-American Institute 261
After Seven Years 202
"Agrarian Discontent in the Mississippi Valley" 26
Agriculture Department 234
Aguinaldo, Emilio 161
AIPO Polls 212, 218, 220, 223, 225-6, 257
Alabama 122
Alamo Siege 56-7
Alaskan annexation treaty 109
Albany Argus 61
Albuquerque Morning Journal 179
Alcott, Louisa M. 112
Aldrich, Nelson W. 132
Aldrich, Thomas Bailey 146
Alexander I 38-9, 48, 62, 103
Alexander II 104-5, 275
Alexis, Grand Duke 115-6

Algonquin 174
"All Mexico" 68-9, 71-2, 78, 102
"All Oregon" 37, 64-5, 68-9
Allen, H. C. 101
Allen, James 268
Allen, William 64-6, 68-70
Allen, William V. 140, 142
Alliance for Progress 257
Allison, William 145
Almond, Gabriel 220
Altgeld, John P. 130, 140
Alverstone, Lord 156
America First 221
"America to Germany" 112
American Federation of Teachers 261
American Foundation 203
American Party 76, 281
American Peace Society 38-9
American Revolution 3-10, 13, 15, 17, 51, 104, 130, 274, 278-9
American System 49
Ames, Fisher 14, 16
Anderson, Dice R. 27,
Anderson, Richard C. 49-50
Andrew, Governor 90
Anglo-Japanese Alliance 200
Annapolis Convention 11
Antarctic Treaty 255
Anti-Cominterm Pact 209
Anti-Federalists 1-2, 17, 21-2
"Appeal to the Citizens of the United States" 31
Appleton, Nathan 70

321

322   Sectionalism, Politics, Diplomacy

Arabs 261
Aranjuez Convention 3
Archer, William 63
Arizona Republican 179
Armed Ship Bill 153, 174-5
Arnold, Benedict 142
Arnold, Isaac 89
Aroostook War 51, 54
Arthur, Chester A. 110, 123, 137
Article 178, 231
Articles of Confederation 6, 8
Aryans 135, 145
Ashburton, Lord 55
Ashurst, Henry 160
Asiatics 134, 144
Astor, John Jacob 29
Aswan Dam 232, 253, 278
Atlanta Constitution 144, 163, 173, 263-4
Atlanta Journal 157
Atlas 61
Atoms for Peace Treaty 255
Attila the Hun 82
Austin, Moses 56
Austin, Stephen F. 56-7
Australia-New Zealand Security Treaty 249
Austrian Revolution of 1848 97
Austrian World War I peace treaty 193
Auxier, George W. 142

B

Babcock, O. O. 125
Bacon's Rebellion 3
Badger, George 72
Bailey, Cleveland 249
Bailey, Josiah 216
Bailey, Thomas A. 100, 105, 117, 133, 194, 208, 223, 246
Baldwin, Roger 72
Ball, Joseph 212
Baltimore Sun 62, 130, 144, 263-4
Bank of the United States (First) 9
Bank of the United States (Second) 36
Banks, Nathaniel P. 118, 120, 125
Barbour, William 206

Baring, Alexander 55
"The Basis of Isolationist Behavior" 236
Bastille 17
Bastille Day 16
Bath Board of Trade 123
Batista, Fulgencio 259
Battle of Fallen Timbers 15
Baxter, Portus 89
Bay of Pigs Invasion 259
Bayard, James 32
Bayard, Thomas F. 124, 133
Bayard-Chamberlain Treaty 111, 124, 276
Bayh, Birch 259
Baylor, Charles Goethe 112
Beard, Charles A. 3, 8
Becker, Carl 3
Bee newspapers 168
Beirne, Francis P. 23
Benjamin, Judah P. 92
Bennett, James Gordon 90
Benson, Ezra Taft 234
Benton, Thomas Hart 42, 49, 55-8, 63, 65, 72-3, 78
Berg, David M. 141
Berg, Meredith W. 141
Berger, Victor 170
Berlin airlift 246
Berlin blockade 257
Berlin Decree 21
Berrien, John 49
Beveridge, Albert J. 145-6, 195
"Big Stick" diplomacy 151, 158-60
Bigelow Papers 70
Bigler, John 135
Billington, Ray 142, 179, 183, 195, 213
Birney, James 59, 73
Bismarck, Otto von 112-3
The Bitter Heritage 261
Black, Eugene 254, 283
Black Warrior 81
Blaine, James G. 116
Blair, Francis 103
Blakely, Robert J. 221
Blease, Cole 195
Bliss, Tasker 178
Bloom Bill 211
Blumenthal, Henry 113
Bolívar, Simón 44, 49

GEOGRAPHICAL INDEX

340